VENICE

JP Garcin

Executive Editorial Director	David Brabis
Chief Editor	Cynthia Clayton Ochterbeck

THE GREEN GUIDE VENICE

Editor	Gwen Cannon
Contributing Writer	Gwen Cannon
Production Coordinator	Allison Michelle Simpson
Cartography	Michèle Cana
Photo Editor	Brigitta L. House, Lydia Strong
Proofreader	Gaven R. Watkins
Layout & Design	Tim Schulz
Cover Design	Ute Weber, Laurent Muller

Contact Us:

The Green Guide
Michelin Maps and Guides
One Parkway South
Greenville, SC 29615
USA
☎ 1-800-423-0485
www.michelintravel.com
michelin.guides@us.michelin.com

Michelin Maps and Guides
Hannay House
39 Clarendon Road
Watford, Herts WD17 1JA
UK
☎ (01923) 205 240
www.ViaMichelin.com
travelpubsales@uk.michelin.com

Special Sales:

For information regarding bulk sales,
customized editions and premium sales,
please contact our Customer Service
Departments:
USA   1-800-423-0485
UK   (01923) 205 240
Canada 1-800-361-8236

Note to the reader
While every effort is made to ensure that all information printed in this guide is correct and up-to-date, Michelin Maps and Guides (Michelin Tyre PLC; Michelin North America, Inc.) accepts no liability for any direct, indirect or consequential losses howsoever caused so far as such can be excluded by law.

One Team …
A Commitment to Quality

There's just one reason our team is dedicated to producing quality travel publications—you, our reader. We want you to get the maximum benefit from your trip—and from your money. In today's multiple-choice world of travel, the options are many, perhaps overwhelming.

In our guidebooks, we try to minimize the guesswork involved with travel. We scout out the attractions, prioritize them with star ratings, and describe what you'll discover when you visit them.

To help you orient yourself, we provide colorful and detailed, but easy-to-follow maps. Floor plans of some of the cathedrals and museums help you plan your tour.

Throughout the guides, we offer practical information, touring tips and suggestions for finding the best views, good places for a break and the most interesting shops.

Lodging and dining are always a big part of travel, so we compile a selection of hotels and restaurants that we think convey the feel of the destination, and organize them by geographic area and price. We also highlight shopping, recreational and entertainment venues, especially the popular spots.

If you're short on time, driving tours are included so you can hit the highlights and quickly absorb the best of the region.

For those who love to experience a destination on foot, we add walking tours, often with a map. And we list other companies who offer boat, bus or guided walking tours of the area, some with culinary, historical or other themes.

In short, we test and retest, check and recheck to make sure that our guidebooks are truly just that: a personalized guide to help you make the most of your visit. After all, we want you to enjoy traveling as much as we do.

The Michelin Green Guide Team

PLANNING YOUR TRIP

WELCOME TO THE CITY

SYMBOLS

🛈	**Tips to help improve your experience**
🛈	**Details to consider**
👓	**Entry Fees**
🚶	**Walking tours**
⚊o	**Closed to the public**
🕐	**Hours of operation**
🕐	**Periods of closure**

CONTENTS

EXPLORING THE CITY

YOUR STAY IN THE CITY

HOW TO USE THIS GUIDE

Orientation

To help you grasp the "lay of the land" quickly and easily, so you'll feel confident and comfortable finding your way around the city, we offer the following tools in this guide:

- Detailed table of contents for an overview of what you'll find in the guide, and how it is organized.
- Map of Principal Sights at the front to the guide, with the starred places highlighted for easy reference.
- Detailed maps for the city's six sestieri, or neighbourhoods.
- Walking tours with detailed directions.
- Index of street names in Venice.

Practicalities

At the front of the guide, you'll see a section called "Planning Your Trip" that contains information about planning your trip, the best time to go, getting to the city and getting around, sightseeing, kids' activities, basic facts and tips for making the most of your visit. You'll find suggestions for further reading. There's also a calendar of popular annual events and some useful words and phrases in Italian.

Information on shopping and entertainment can be found at the back in a section called "Your Stay in the City."

LODGINGS

We've made a selection of hotels and categorized them by price to fit all budgets (see the Legend on the cover flap for an explanation of the price categories). For the most part, we selected accommodations based on their unique regional quality, their Venetian feel, as it were. So, unless the individual hotel embodies local ambience, it's rare that we include chain properties, which typically have their own imprint. If you want a more comprehensive selection of accommodations in Venice, see the red-cover *Michelin Guide Italia*.

RESTAURANTS

We thought you'd like to know some of the popular eating spots in Venice. So we selected restaurants that capture regional flavors and local atmosphere. We're not rating the quality of the food per se. We selected restaurants for each of the neighbourhoods and as we did with the hotels, categorized them by price to appeal to all wallets. If you want a more comprehensive selection of dining recommendations in the region, see the red-cover *Michelin Guide Italia*.

Attractions

We've organized the city's attractions by neighbourhood, or by a Principal Sight itself, such as the Ca' d'Oro or La Fenice. They are arranged alphabetically, for easy reference (see the Contents page). Then come the outlying islands, arranged alphabetically, and finally the Brenta Valley. Contact information, admission charges and hours of operation are given for the majority of attractions. Unless otherwise noted, admission prices shown are for a single adult only. Discounts for children, seniors, students, teachers, etc. may be available; be sure to ask. If no admission charge is shown, entrance to the attraction is free.

If you're pressed for time, we recommend you visit the three- and two-star sights first: the stars are your guide.

STAR RATINGS

Michelin has used stars as a rating tool for more than 100 years:

★★★	Highly recommended
★★	Recommended
★	Interesting

SYMBOLS IN THE TEXT

Besides the stars, other symbols in the text indicate tourist information ⓘ; wheelchair access ♿; on-site eating facilities ✗; camping facilities ⚠; on-site parking 🅿; sights of interest to children Kids; and beaches ⚐.

See the box appearing on the Contents page for other symbols used in the text.

See the Maps explanation below for symbols appearing on the maps.

Throughout the guide you will find peach-coloured text boxes or sidebars containing anecdotal or background information. Green-coloured boxes contain information to help you save time or money.

Maps

All maps in this guide are oriented north, unless otherwise indicated by a directional arrow. See the map Legend at the back of the guide for an explanation of other map symbols. A complete list of the maps found in the guide appears at the back of this book.

Addresses, phone numbers, opening hours and prices published in this guide are accurate at press time. We welcome corrections and suggestions that may assist us in preparing the next edition. Please send your comments to:

Michelin Maps and Guides
Hannay House
39 Clarendon Road
Watford, Herts WD17 1JA
UK
travelpubsales@uk.michelin.com
www.michelin.co.uk

Michelin Maps and Guides
Editorial Department
P.O. Box 19001
Greenville, SC   29602-9001
USA
michelin.guides@us.michelin.com
www.michelintravel.com

WORLD HERITAGE SITES

In 1972, the United Nations Educational, Scientific and Cultural Organisation (UNESCO) adopted a Convention for the preservation of cultural and natural sites. To date, more than 150 States Parties have signed this international agreement, which has listed over 600 sites "of outstanding universal value" on the World Heritage List. Each year, a committee of representatives from 21 countries, assisted by technical organisations (ICOMOS – International Council on Monuments and Sites; IUCN – International Union for Conservation of Nature and Natural Resources; ICCROM – International Centre for the Study of the Preservation and Restoration of Cultural Property, the Rome Centre), evaluates the proposals for new sites to be included on the list, which grows longer as more countries sign the Convention. To be considered, a site must be nominated by the country in which it is located.

The protected **cultural heritage** may be monuments (buildings, sculptures, archaeological structures etc) with unique historical, artistic or scientific features; groups of buildings (such as religious communities, ancient cities); or sites (human settlements, examples of exceptional landscapes, cultural landscapes) which are the combined works of man and nature and of exceptional beauty. **Natural sites** may relate to the earth's geological history, the development of human cultures and significant ecological processes, or may contain superlative natural phenomena or provide a habitat for threatened species.

UNESCO World Heritage Sites in Italy

- Rock Drawings, Valcamonica
- Church and Dominican Convent of Santa Maria delle Grazie, with *The Last Supper* by Leonardo da Vinci, Milan
- Historic Centre of Florence
- Venice and its Lagoon
- Piazza del Duomo, Pisa
- Historic Centre of San Gimignano
- The Sassi (troglodyte dwellings) of Matera
- City of Vicenza and the Palladian Villas of the Veneto
- Historic Centre of Siena
- Historic Centre of Naples
- Crespi d'Adda
- The Renaissance City of Ferrara and the Po Delta
- Castel del Monte
- The Trulli of Alberobello
- Early Christian Monuments of Ravenna
- Historic Centre of Pienza
- 18C Royal Palace at Caserta with the Park, the Aqueduct of Vanvitelli and San Leucio Complex
- Residences of the Royal House of Savoy, Piedmont
- Botanical Garden, Padua
- Cathedral, Torre Civica and Piazza Grande, Modena
- The Archaeological Sites of Pompeii, Herculaneum and Torre Annunziata
- Villa Romana del Casale, Piazza Armerina
- Su Nuraxi, Barumini
- Portovenere, the Cinque Terre and the Islands (Palmaria, Tino and Tinetto)
- The Amalfi Coast
- The Archaeological Site of Agrigento
- Cilento and Vallo di Diano National Park with the Archaeological Sites of Paestum and Velia and the Certosa di Padula
- The Archaeological Site and Patriarchal Basilica of Aquileia
- Historic Centre of Urbino
- Villa Adriana and Villa d'Este, Tivoli
- Verona
- The Aeolian Islands
- Assisi, the Basilica di San Francesco and other Franciscan sites
- Late Baroque Towns of the Val di Noto (southeastern Sicily)
- Rome and the Holy See

2

3

S. GIULIANO 🅿

MESTRE

Ponte della Libertà

PADOVA

CANALE DELLA GIUDECCA

TRONCHETTO 🅿

P.te dei Tre Archi

Campo S. Giobbe

Fondam. di Cannaregio

Sinagoga Spagnola

Camp Ghetto

GHETT Rio T. S.

P.te d. Guglie

Campo S. Geremia

PALAZZ LABIA

Terà di

Lista Spagna

GR

P.te d. Scalzi

ℹ

S. LUCIA

CANAL

66   76

S. GIA DALL

S. CROCE

24

🅿

Piazzale Roma

6

7

Rio   Terà

dei   Pensieri

★★★ **I FRARI**

SCUOLA GRANDE DI S. ROCCO ★★★

S. Pantalon

d

B

★ **SCUOLA GRANDE DEI CARMINI**

Campo S. Margherita

Ca' Foscari

★★ **CA' REZZONICO**

C. del Traghetto

DORSODURO

Angelo Raffaele

★★ **S. SEBASTIANO**

C. Lunga S. Barnaba

T

Palazzo Lore dell'Ambascia

★★★ **GALLERIE ACCADEMI**

S. Trovaso

Rio Terà A. Foscar

ZATTERE ★

TRONCHETTO 🅿

PADOVA

🅿 FUSINA

ESTE

CANALE

Fondamenta S. Eufemia

ISOLA

0 ————— 300 m

★★ MURANO

ISOLA DI
S. MICHELE

★ S. ALVISE ★

MADONNA
DELL'ORTO ★

di
uovo

Campo
d. Mori

Fondamenta d. Misericordia

LAGUNA

Museo Ebraico
★★★

Fondamenta

Nove

onardo

CANNAREGIO

T

GESUITI ★

Calle del Fumo

★ PAL. VENDRAMIN
CALERGI (CASINO)
★

78

NDE

28

★★★ CA'
D'ORO

75

M

Campiello
Widman

★ CA'
PESARO

18

SCUOLA GRANDE
DI S. MARCO ★

COMO
ORIO

Ca'Corner
della Regina

28

S. MARIA
D. MIRACOLI ★

★★ S. ZANIPOLO ★★

34

Ruga d.
Orefici

A

43

Fondaco
d. Tedeschi

S. POLO

Campo
S. Maria
Formosa

10

Campo
S. Polo

Pte DI RIALTO ★★★

Salizz. S. Lio

45

Campo
S. Lorenzo

85

39

Campo
S. Silvestro

8

Pal.
Bernardo

★★★ CANAL GRANDE

61

MERCERIE

67

9

★★★ SCUOLA
DI S. GIORGIO
DEGLI SCHIAVONI

ampo
Frari

T

C. dei Fabbri

49

FOND.
QUERINI
STAMPALIA ★

H

E

Pal.
Fortuny

Campo
Manin

31

N

SAN
MARCO ★★★

S. ZACCARIA ★

★ S. GIOV.
IN BRAGORA

Pal.
Mocenigo

★ SCALA DEL
BOVOLO

21

M

PAL. GRASSI ★

70

82

Frezzeria

P ZA
S.MARCO
Q

52

Pte DEL
SOSPIRI ★

64

58

★ LA FENICE

MUSEO
CORRER

Riva d. Schiavo

★★ SANTO
STEFANO

55

22

Ci. Larga
Marzo

PAL. DUCALE ★★★

S. MARCO

79

★ BIBLIOTECA
MARCIANA

an
ore

3

P

Bacino di
S. Marco

CANAL

GRANDE ★★★

★ CA' DARIO

★★ COLL.
P. GUGGENHEIM

Dogana
da Mar

★ S. GIORGIO
MAGGIORE ★

★★ S. MARIA
DELLA SALUTE

ISOLA DI
S. GIORGIO

MAGGIORE ★★

ZATTERE ★

GIUDECCA

TEATRO
VERDE

DELLA

REDENTORE ★

DELLA

GIUDECCA

PRINCIPAL SIGHTS

 Highly recommended

 Recommended

★ **Interesting**

S. POLO   Name and boundaries of quarter (sestiere)

- - -   Vaporetto line and stop

[2]   Map number

MURANO ★★
TORCELLO ★★
BURANO ★★
S. FRANCESCO
D. DESERTO ★
Treporti
Punta Sabbioni

Accademia (Ponte dell')	3	S. Maurizio (Campo)	55
Bandiera e Moro (Campo)	6	San Moisé (Salizzada)	58
Capello (Ramo)	10	San Salvador (Merceria)	61
Gallina (Calle Larga G.)	18	San Samuele (Campo)	64
Leoncini (Piazzetta dei)	21	San Simeon Profeta (Campo)	66
Libertà (Ponte della)	24	San Zulian (Merceria)	67
Nuova (Strada)	28	Sant'Angelo (Campo)	70
Orologio (Merceria dell')	31	Santi Apostoli (Rio Terà dei)	75
Pescaria (Campo della)	34	Sauro Nazario (Campo)	76
San Bartolomeo (Campo)	39	Seriman (Salizzada)	78
San Giovanni Crisostomo (Salizzada)	43	Traghetto (Campo dei)	79
San Lorenzo (Calle Larga)	46	Verona (Calle della)	82
San Marco (Calle Larga)	49	2 Aprile (Via)	85
San Marco (Piazzetta)	52		

A	Palazzo dei Camerlenghi	**M⁵**	Fondaco dei Turchi (Museo di Storia Naturale)
B	Palazzo Balbi (Pal. della Regione)	**N**	Torre dell'Orologio
E	Palazzo Lando Corner Spinelli	**P**	Pal. Corner della Ca' Granda (Prefettura)
H	Palazzo Loredan (Municipio)	**Q**	Campanile
M	Museo diocesano di arte sacra	**T¹**	Teatro Goldoni

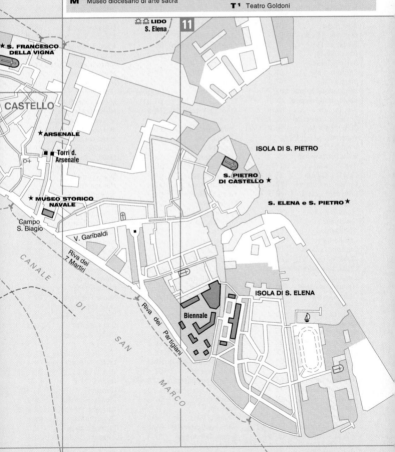

INDEX OF STREET NAMES

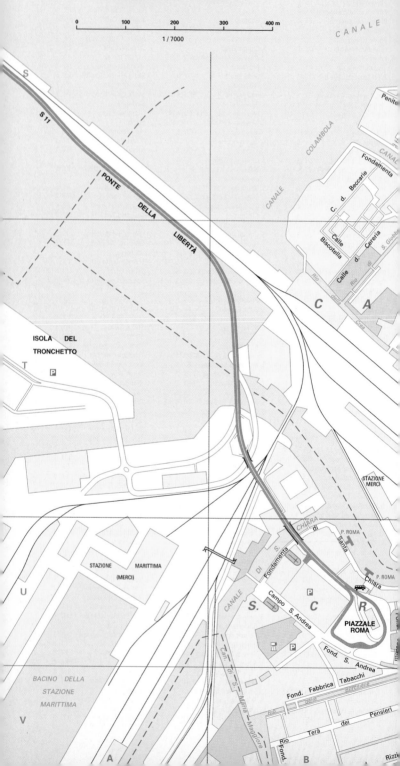

VENEZIA

0   100   200   300   400 m

1 / 7000

2

CANALE

S

S 11

PONTE

DELLA

LIBERTÀ

CANALE

CANALE

COLAMBOLA

CANAL

Penite

Fondamenta

C. d. Beccarie

Calle

Biscotella

Calle d. Cereria

S. Giob

Rio

Rio di

di

C

A

Canal

della

ISOLA   DEL
TRONCHETTO

T

P

STAZIONE
MERCI

CHIARA   di

S.

Santa

P. ROMA

STAZIONE   MARITTIMA

(MERCI)

DI

Fondamenta

S.

P. ROMA

Chiara

P

U

CANALE

Campo S. Andrea

S.

C

R

PIAZZALE
ROMA

Can. di S. Maria Maggiore

P

Fond. S. Andrea

Rizzi

BACINO   DELLA

STAZIONE

MARITTIMA

V

Fond. Fabbrica Tabacchi

Burchielle

Rio

della

Rio

Terà   dei   Pensieri

Fond.

A

B

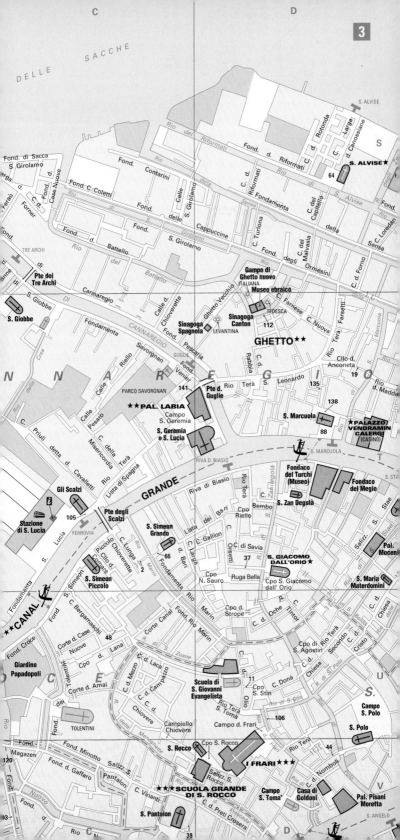

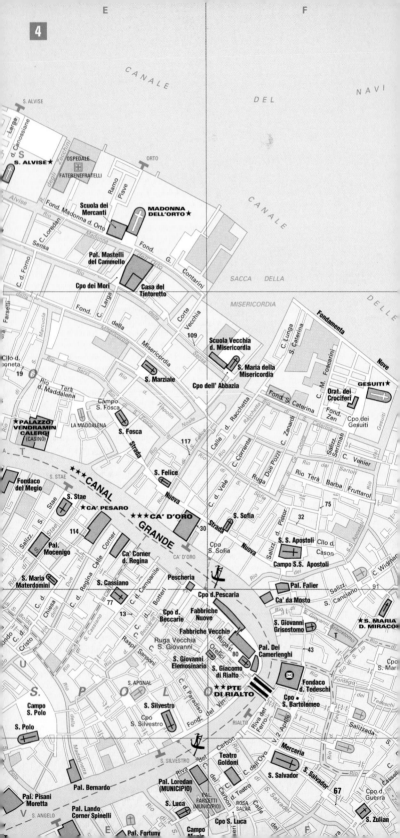

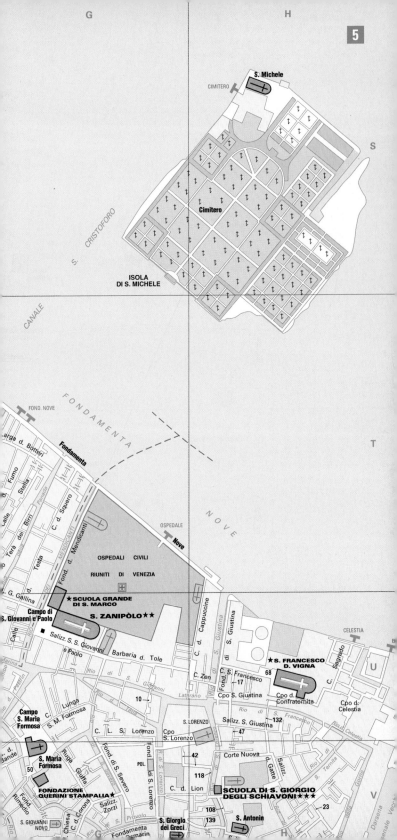

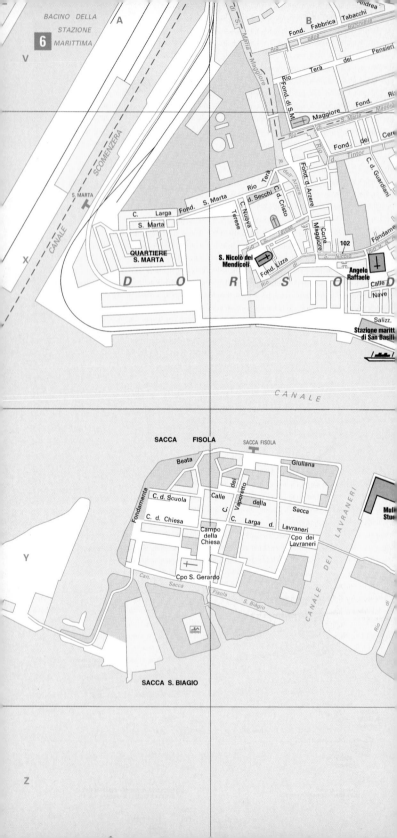

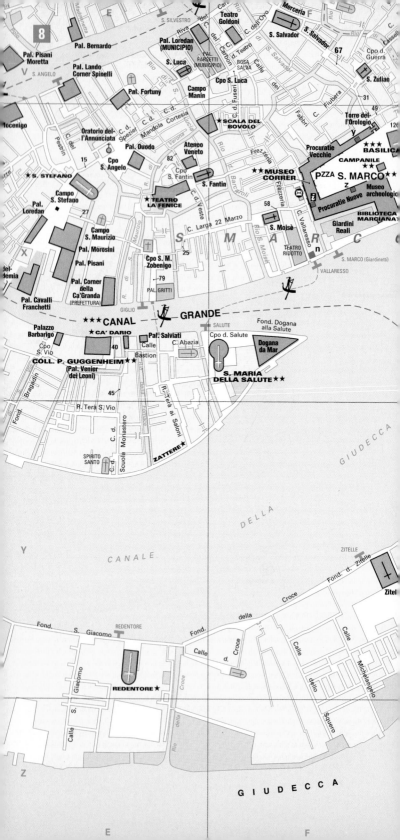

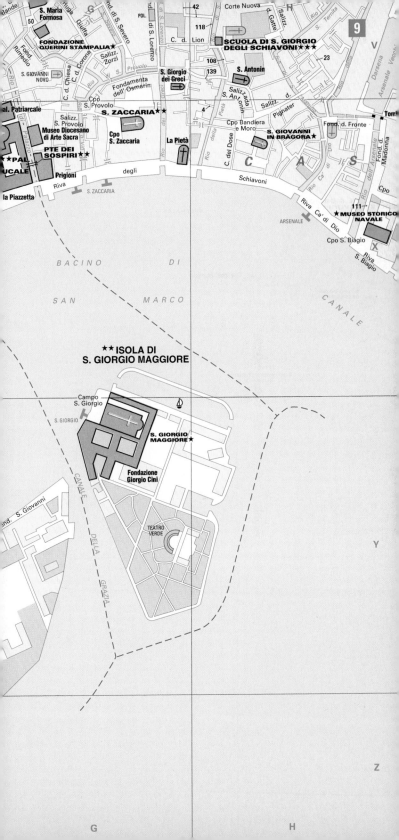

S. Maria
Formosa
50
FONDAZIONE
QUERINI STAMPALIA★

42
118
Corte Nuova

SCUOLA DI S. GIORGIO
DEGLI SCHIAVONI★★★

9
V

S. GIOVANNI
NOVO

108
139
S. Giorgio
dei Greci

S. Antonin

23

al. Patriarcale

S. ZACCARIA★★

Cpo
S. Zaccaria

4

Cpo Bandiera
e Moro

S. GIOVANNI
IN BRAGORA★

Fond. d. Fronte

Torr

★PAL
UCALE

PTE DEI
SOSPIRI★★

Museo Diocesano
di Arte Sacra

La Pietà

C   A   S

111
★MUSEO STORICO
NAVALE

la Piazzetta

Prigioni

Riva

S. ZACCARIA

degli

Schiavoni

ARSENALE

Riva Ca' di Dio

Cpo S. Biagio

Cpo

X

B A C I N O   D I

S A N   M A R C O

C A N A L E

**★★ ISOLA DI
S. GIORGIO MAGGIORE**

Campo
S. Giorgio

S. GIORGIO

**S. GIORGIO
MAGGIORE★**

Fondazione
Giorgio Cini

nd. S. Giovanni

TEATRO
VERDE

C A N A L E   D E L L A   G R A Z I A

Y

Z

G

H

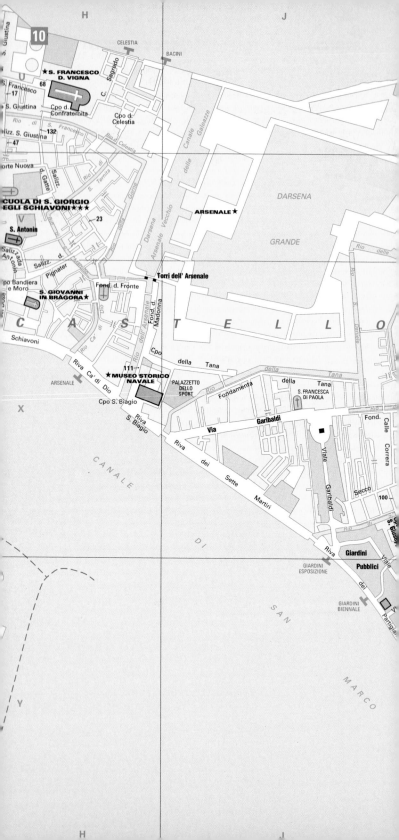

CELESTIA

BACINI

★ S. FRANCESCO
D. VIGNA

S. Francesco
17
68

S. Giustina

Cpo d.
Confraternita

Cpo d.
Celestia

aliz. S. Giustina 132

47

rte Nuova

CUOLA DI S. GIORGIO
EGLI SCHIAVONI ★★★

DARSENA

ARSENALE ★

23

GRANDE

S. Antonin

aliz ada
Antonin

Salizz. d.

Pignater

po Bandiera
e Moro

★ S. GIOVANNI
IN BRÀGORA ★

Fond. d. Fronte

■ Torri dell' Arsenale

C   A   S   T   E   L   L   O

Schiavoni

Cpo   della   Tana

della   Tana

ARSENALE

Riva Ca' di Dio

111

★ MUSEO STORICO
NAVALE

PALAZZETTO
DELLO
SPORT

Fondamenta

S. FRANCESCA
DI PAOLA

Fond.

Calle

Correra

Cpo S. Biagio

Riva
S. Biagio

Via   Garibaldi

Viale

Garibaldi

Secco

100

U. GIUSEPPE

X

C   A   N   A   L   E

Riva

dei

Sette

Martiri

Riva

dei

Giardini
Pubblici

Giardini

Viale

Partigiani

D   I

GIARDINI
ESPOSIZIONE

GIARDINI
BIENNALE

Y

S   A   N

M   A   R   C   O

H   J

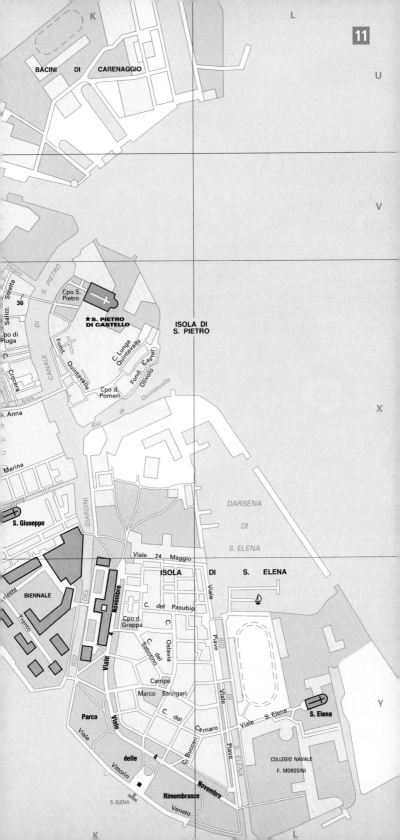

K
L
U
V
X
Y
L

BACINI DI CARENAGGIO

Vergini
S. PIETRO
Stretta
Salizz. 36
po di Ruga
C.
Crodera
S. Anna
CANALE
DI

Cpo S. Pietro

★ **S. PIETRO DI CASTELLO**

ISOLA DI S. PIETRO

Fond. Quintavalle
C. Lunga Quintavalle
Fond. Castel
Olivolo
Cpo d. Pomeri

Rio di Quintavalle

Marina
GIARDINI

S. Giuseppa

S. Giuseppe

DARSENA
DI
S. ELENA

Viale 24 Maggio

ISOLA DI S. ELENA

Trieste
BIENNALE
Trento
RIO DEL
Viale 4 Novembre

C. del Pasubio
Cpo d. Grappa
C.
C. del Oslavia
C. del Sabotino
Campo Marco Stringari
C. del

RIO DI PLAVE
Viale

Viale S. Elena
Viale DI S. ELENA

S. Elena

S. Elena

Parco
Viale
Viale
4
Vittorio
S. ELENA
delle
Novembre
Rimembranze
Veneto

Carnaro
C. Buccari

COLLEGIO NAVALE
F. MOROSINI

K

Costumed for Carnival

R. Mattes/MICHELIN

PLANNING YOUR TRIP

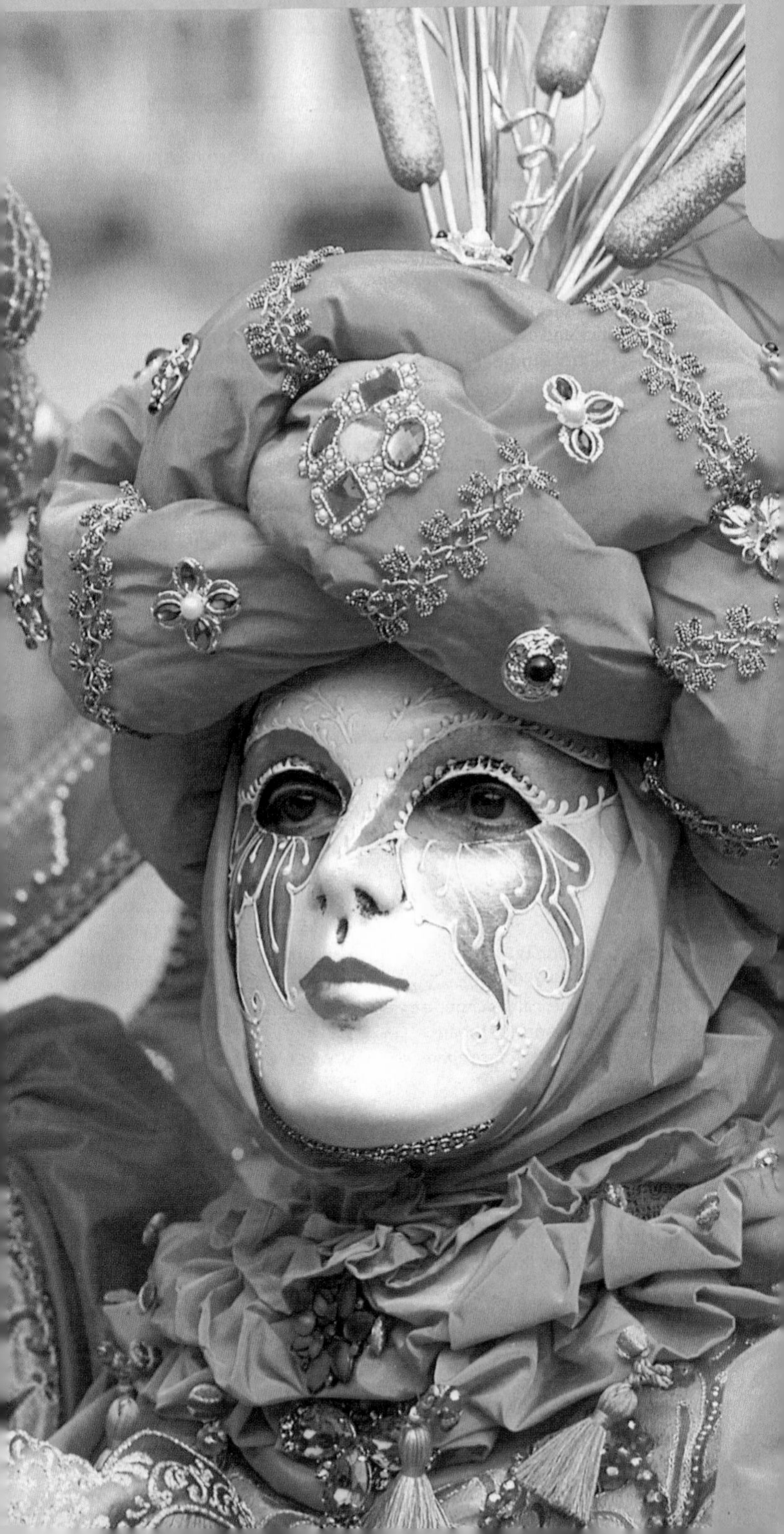

WHEN AND WHERE TO GO

When to Go

Spring (mid-Apr-Jun) and **autumn** (Sept-Oct) are ideal times to visit Venice. Mild temperatures (60°-70°F/15°-21°C) and absence of flooding (Mar and Nov) attract the greater part of the city's 10 million visitors per year. Make hotel reservations well in advance and expect long lines at the main sights. **Summer** brings hot, somewhat humid, weather with intense sunlight, but not as scorching as on the mainland; it's best to find a hotel with air-conditioned rooms. Yet the season's lengthy days and extended hours of operation are major draws. **Winter** temperatures usually range from 30°-40°F/-1°-4°C, with overcast skies; the crowds have thinned out, but hours of operation may be reduced.

Visitor Information

ITALIAN TOURIST BOARD

The **Ente Nazionale Italiano per il Turismo** (ENIT) has offices at home and abroad. *For local tourist information services, see above:*

UK

1 Princes St., London W1B 2AY; ☎ (020) 7408 1254; 09065 508 925 (24hr brochure line, calls charged at £1/min); italy@italiantouristboard. co.uk; www.enit.it (🕐 *office open year-round Mon-Fri 9am-5pm).*

USA

Suite 1565, 630 Fifth Ave., New York, NY 10111; ☎ (212) 245 5618; (212) 245 4822 (brochure line); enitny@italian-tourism.com. Los Angeles, ☎ (310) 820 1898; (310) 820 0098 (brochure line).

Canada

Italian Government Tourist Board, 175 Bloor St. East, Suite 907 – South Tower, Toronto, Ontario M4W 3R8; ☎ (416) 925 4882; enit.canada@on.aibn.com

LOCAL TOURIST OFFICES

The **Azienda Promozione Turismo (APT)** and its branches provide brochures, maps and lists of hotels, youth hostels and campsites free of charge. The main tourist office is the **Venice Pavilion** (☎ 041 529 87 11 or 041 522 51 50; www.turismovenezia. it; info@turismovenezia.it), situated near the Giardini Reali, between the Procuratie Nuove and St Mark's Basin. As well as providing tourist information, this office also sells novels, travel literature and other literary works on Venice in several languages. Other tourist offices are located at the west end of the Procuratie Nuove, off Piazza San Marco *(open daily 9am-3.30pm),* Piazzale Roma (Garage ASM), the Lido (Gran Viale, ☎ 041 526 5721; *open in summer only),* **Marco Polo airport** (☎ 041 54 5887) and **Santa Lucia Railway Station** (☎ 041 529 8727). For information on the **Brenta Valley**, contact Via don Minzoni 26, Mira Porte, Venice ☎ 041 42 49 73.

Useful Web Sites

www.italiantourism.com
Official Web site of the Italian Government Tourist Board. Trip planning and travel tips, regional overviews, museum highlights and more.

www.enit.it
Official Web site of the Italian Government Tourist Board for promotion of Italian tourism abroad. Events, lodgings, weather reports and more.

www.turismovenezia.it
Official Web site of the Agency of Tourism Promotion of the Venice Provincial. Events, attractions, etc.

www.veniceworld.com
Provides links to hotels, restaurants, transportation, events, entertainment.

Calendar of Events

Here is a selection of annual events:

6 JANUARY

Regata della Befana – Epiphany boat race.

10 DAYS BEFORE LENT

Carnival – *Feb-Mar*. Costumed revellers in masks throughout the city.

MARCH

Su e zo per i ponti – A race through Venice (👣 *see Unique to Venice*).

MAUNDY THURSDAY

Benediction – Candle-lighting procession outside Basilica di San Marco.

25 APRIL

Feast day of St Mark – Men give their sweethearts a *bòcolo* (a red rose).

MAY

The **Vogalonga** – Row boats race around the islands.

ASCENSION DAY

The **Sensa** commemorates Sposalizio del Mar (👣 *see Time Line 1177*).

WEEK OF 29 JUNE

For the feast days of St Peter and St Paul, 👣 see *SANT'ELENA e SAN PIETRO*.

THIRD SUNDAY IN JULY

Feast of the Redeemer (👣 see *GIUDECCA*).

16 AUGUST

St Roch's feast day – Procession from Scuola di San Rocco, and a Mass.

SEPTEMBER

Biennale – *Sept-Nov (Dance in Jun; Theatre end of Jul)*. International exhibitions of art and culture.

Campiello Prize – A literary prize from the business community.

Historic regatta – *First Sun in Sept*. C*aorline* (6-man boat originally from Caorle, a fishing village east of Jesolo) and the *dogeressa*.

Fish Festival – *Third Sun in Sept*. In Burano.

21 NOVEMBER

Feast of the Madonna della Salute (👣 see *La SALUTE*).

The Historic Regatta

SIGHTSEEING

General Information

VISITOR INFORMATION

From the APT ( see above), you can obtain the free events brochure *Eventi Manifestazioni*, which details exhibits and shows as well as museum and church visiting hours; a daily events calendar and useful numbers are included.

PRICES AND HOURS

Information on admission times and charges for museums and churches appears in the *Exploring the City* section of this guide. Admission times are subject to change, without prior notice. Admission prices shown are for a single adult only; reduced rates for students, senior citizens, military personnel, etc. may be available upon request. Discounts for young people are available (see *Basic Information*). The purchase of a **VENICEcard** offers general discounts on transportation and attractions, and a **CHORUS** pass offers entry to churches as a reduced rate (see *Basic Information*).

GUIDED TOURS

Information about and tickets for a number of daily guided tours of Venice or of specific attractions conducted in English or Italian may be obtained from the APT (see *Local Tourist Offices above*). Be sure to wear comfortable walking shoes.

Activities for Children

There are a number of places in Venice that are especially fun for children. In this guide, sights of particular interest to children are indicated with a symbol. Some attractions may offer discount fees for children.

Further Reading

ART

Venetian Painting: a Concise History – John Steer (Thames and Hudson 1970)
The Stones of Venice – John Ruskin (Da Capo Press 1985)
Palladio and Palladianism – Robert Tavernor (Thames and Hudson 1991)
Palladio – JS Ackerman, P Dearborn Massar (Illustrator) (Penguin Books 1991)
Palladio's Villas – Paul Holberton (John Murray 1991)
Five Centuries of Music in Venice – HC Robbins Landon, John Julius Norwich (Thames and Hudson 1991)
Ruskin's Venice: The Stones Revisited – Sarah Quill, Alan Windsor (Introduction) (Ashgate Publishing Limited 1999)

HISTORICAL REFERENCE

The Travels of Marco Polo – Marco Polo, R Latham (Trans) (Penguin Books 1965)

Tourist Office

Tourist Office

A History of Venice – John Julius Norwich (Penguin Books 1983)

The Venetian Empire – Jan Morris (Penguin Books 1990)

Venice Rediscovered – John Pemble (Oxford University Press 1996)

LITERATURE

Italian Journey – Goethe (Penguin Books 1970)

The Aspern Papers – Henry James, Anthony Curtis (Ed) (Penguin Books 1984)

The Wings of the Dove – Henry James, J Bayley (Ed), P Crick (Ed) (Penguin Books 1986)

Stone Virgin – Barry Unsworth (Penguin Books 1986)

The Desire and Pursuit of the Whole – Frederick Rolfe (Da Capo Press 1986)

Territorial Rights: Complete and Unabridged – Muriel Spark, Nigel Hawthorne (Narrator) (Chivers Audio Books 1990)

The Quest for Corvo – AJA Symons (Quartet Books 1993)

Across the River and into the Trees – Ernest Hemingway (Arrow 1994)

Thus was Adonis Murdered – Sarah Caudwell (Dell Publishing Company 1994)

A Literary Companion to Venice – Ian Littlewood (St Martin's Press 1995)

Dead Lagoon – Michael Dibdin (Faber and Faber 1995)

Death in Venice and Other Stories – Thomas Mann (Minerva 1996)

The Passion – Jeanette Winterson (Vintage 1996)

The Comfort of Strangers – Ian McEwan (Vintage 1997)

Volpone – Ben Jonson [can be found in *Volpone and Other Early Plays* – Ben Jonson, Lorna Hutson (Ed) (Penguin Books 1998)]

The Merchant of Venice – William Shakespeare, Jay L Halio (Ed) (Oxford Paperbacks 1998)

An Italian Journey – Jean Giono, J Cumming (Trans) (Northwestern University Press 1998)

Miss Garnet's Angel – Salley Vickers (HarperCollins 2001)

The City of Falling Angels – John Berendt (Companion Guides 1997)

OTHER GUIDES

Ghetto of Venice – Roberta Curiel, Bernard Dov Cooperman (Tauris Parke 1990)

Venice – Ian Littlewood (John Murray 1992)

Companion Guide to Venice – Hugh Honour (Companion Guides 1997)

Venice for Pleasure – JG Links (Pallas Athene 1999)

The Stones of Florence and Venice Observed – Mary McCarthy (Penguin Books 2000) Piazzale Roma

Gwen Cannon/ MICHELIN

Boy and pigeons

GETTING THERE

By Air

MARCO POLO AIRPORT

Venice is served by many international and domestic flights arriving directly at the **Marco Polo Airport** at Tessera (☎ (041 26 06 111), about 10km/6mi *(20min)* from the city by vehicle.

Getting to Venice from the airport

By Bus: The airport is linked to Venice by **ACTV bus** no 5 (€1.50; www.actv. it) or by **ATVO coach**, both to Piazzale Roma (€3; www.atvo.it). 🚌 From there you may have to walk with your luggage to the hotel. Vaporetto service is available, but boats are usually crowded and there's a fee for luggage. With a water taxi (expensive), luggage is less of a problem (🛥 *below*).

By Water: ALILAGUNA boats (*at least 90min*; €11) cross the lagoon to Piazza San Marco (other stops include Murano, Lido, Arsenale and Zattere). Private **water taxis** offer much faster service "door-to-door" *(35min)*, but are quite expensive (€100 and higher). The dock for Alilaguna and water taxis is a 5min walk from the airport, or a 1min-ride on the airport shuttle (€1).

By Taxi: Taxis are available from the airport to Piazzale Roma (about €30); from there, see By Bus (🛥 *above*).

International flights also arrive at the **Treviso** airport (30km/18mi from Venice), which is linked to the railway station by bus and then by train to Venice.

For information on **left luggage facilities**, call ☎ 041 52 31 107.

Many airline companies operate flights to Venice. The following is a brief selection:

Alitalia

🛫 4 Portman Square, Marble Arch, London W1H 9PS; ☎ (020) 7486 8432; Fax (020) 7486 8431; www. alitalia.co.uk Reservations can also be made (by telephone only) on ☎ 08705 448 259.

🛫 4-5 Dawson Street, Dublin 2; ☎ (01) 677 5171; Fax (01) 677 3373.

🛫 666 Fifth Avenue, New York, NY 10103; ☎ (212) 903 3300; 1 800 223 5730 (reservations from within the USA); Fax (212) 903 3350; www.alitaliausa.com

🛫 Viale Marchetti 111, 00148 Rome, ☎ 06 65 621; www.alitalia.com

Venice Simplon-Orient-Express

The Orient Express was the brainchild of the Belgian **Georges Nagelmackers**, who inaugurated service in 1883. In 1906 the Simplon tunnel was excavated through the mountains between Switzerland and Italy (19.8km/12mi). The route could extend from Milan to Venice and on to Constantinople (56hr from Paris). After World War II, the legendary luxury train's financial problems eventually forced its closure in 1977. Credited with its revival, American businessman **James B Sherwood** bought two sleeper cars from a Sotheby's auction. The Venice Simplon-Orient-Express, launched in 1982, leaves from London for Venice on Thursdays and Sundays, stopping in Paris, Innsbruck and Verona. Northbound trains leave Venice on Wednesdays and Saturdays. The full trip takes about 32hr, covering1 715km/1 065mi. The trains have been restored to their former splendour, and include wood panelling, Lalique glass and Art Deco-style lamps. For details, contact the office of **Venice Simplon-Orient-Express Ltd.** in the UK: ☎ 44 (0) 20 7960 0500, or in North America 1 401 351 7518; www.orient-express.com

British Airways

✈ 156 Regent Street,
London W1B 5LB;
☎ 0845 77 999 77 (enquiries);
0845 77 333 77 (reservations);
Fax (020) 7434 4640 (reservations);
www.british-airways.com

✈ USA – ☎ (1-800) AIRWAYS.

✈ Via Bissolati 54, 00187 Rome; ☎ 199
712 266 (from within Italy only).

Delta Airlines

✈ ☎ 800-241-4141; www.delta.com

Go

✈ ☎ 0845 605 4321; www.go-fly.com

Ryanair

✈ ☎ 0871 246 0000;
☎ 0818 30 30 30 (Ireland);
www.ryanair.com

By Train

The main line from Milan to Trieste
via Brescia, Verona, Vicenza and
Padua passes through Venice. A more
luxurious alternative is the **Venice
Simplon-Orient-Express Ltd**.
Travelling at a leisurely pace in original
1920s and 30s carriages, the VSOE
leaves from London and stops in Paris,
Innsbruck, Verona and Venice.
Special concessions (20% discount)
are available to rail-users in Italy under
the age of 26 and senior citizens over

the age of 65 (men) or 60 (women)
on presentation of an inter-rail card.
Children aged between 4 and 12 travel
half-price. Unlimited travel concessions are also available to visitors in
Italy: check for details.

A useful aid for travel by rail is the
**Thomas Cook European Rail Time-
table**, which gives all train schedules
and relevant information on touring
Europe by rail. Timetables are also
available from news-stands in Italy
and from the **Italian Tourist Office** in
London (C see When and Where to Go).
For tickets, prices and concessions
apply to:

♦ **Rail Europe**, 178 Piccadilly, London W1; ☎ 08705 848 848; www.
raileurope.co.uk

♦ **Ultima Travel**, 424 Chester Road,
Little Sutton, South Wirral CH66
3RB; ☎ (0151) 339 6171; Fax (0151)
339 9199.

♦ **Italian State Railways** (Ferrovie
dello Stato); ☎ 848-88088 (information from within Italy);
www.fs-on-line.com

By Coach

Coach services from Victoria Coach
Station, London, are organised by
Eurolines, 4 Cardiff Road, Luton,
Bedfordshire L41 1PP; ☎ 08705 143
219; Fax (01582) 400 694; welcome@
eurolinesuk.com; www.eurolines.co.uk
Alternatively, consult National Express,
75 Davies Street, London W1K 5HT;
☎ 0870 901 3190; 08705 80 80 80;
www.gobycoach.com, or the nearest
National Express office or agent.

By Car

FORMALITIES

Nationals of the European Union
require a valid **national driving
licence**. Nationals of non-EU countries
should get an **international driving
licence**, obtainable in the US from
the American Automobile Association (US$18 for members and US$20
for non-members). The AAA can be

Venice Simplon-Orient-Express

Highway Code

- In Italy vehicles drive on the **right-hand side** of the road.

- The **minimum driving age** is 18 years.

- **Seat belts** must be worn in the front and back of the vehicle. Drivers must wear **shoes**, carry **spare lights** and have a **red triangle** to be displayed in the event of a breakdown or accident.

- Emergency **road-rescue services** are offered by the **Automobile Club Italiano (ACI)**, ☎ 116.

- **Motorways** (*autostrade* – subject to tolls) and dual carriageways (*superstrade*) are indicated by green signs, ordinary roads by blue signs, and tourist sights by yellow signs.

- Italian **motorway tolls** can be paid for with cash or with the **Viacard**, a magnetic card that is sold in Italy at the entrances and exits of motorways, in Autogrill restaurants and in the offices of the ACI (Automobile Club Italiano).

- The following **speed restrictions** are enforced:
  - 50kph/31mph in built-up areas
  - 90-110kph/56-69mph on open country roads
  - 90kph/56mph (600cc) to 130kph/81mph (excess of 1 000cc) on motorways, depending on engine capacity.

- **Fuel** is sold as *super* (4 star), *senza piombo* (unleaded 95 octane), *super plus* or *Euro plus* (unleaded 98 octane) and *gasolio* (diesel). Petrol (US: Gas) stations are usually open from 7am to 7pm. Many close at lunch time (12.30–3pm), as well as on Sundays and public holidays; many refuse payment by credit card.

contacted at AAA National Headquarters, 1000 AAA Drive, Heathrow, FL 32746-5080, ☎ (407) 444 7000. Other documents required include the vehicle's current **registration document** and a **green card** for insurance.

MAIN ROADS

Venice is situated off the A 4 Torino-Trieste road, reached from the south by the A 13 Bologna to Padua road. Exit at Mestre onto the SS 11, then cross the Ponte della Libertà to Piazzale Roma.

MAPS

Michelin Tourist and Motoring Atlas Italy and Michelin Maps no. 705 Europe (1:3 000 000), no. 735 Italy (1:1 000 000) and no. 562 Northeast Italy (1:400 000) will make route planning easier.

PARKING

Piazzale Roma

The **ASM garage** (municipal car park) at Piazzale Roma charges a daily rate of €18.59. For more information, ☎ 041 27 27 211; www.asmvenezia.it. Another possibility at Piazzale Roma is the **Garage San Marco**, which charges €19 for 12hr and €26 for 24hr. For vehicles left overnight or on a public holiday, there will be an extra charge of €1.
🅿 For further information, ☎ 041 52 32 213; www.garagesanmarco.it.

Tronchetto

To the west of Piazzale Roma, the island of **Tronchetto** (*exit from the Liberty Bridge*) offers parking facilities for cars (€18 for 24hr), as well as for camper-vans and caravans (€2.50 for the first 30min; €21 for the first 12hr and €16 for additional 12hr periods).
🅿 For further information, ☎ 041 52 07 555; www.veniceparking.it. The island is serviced by vaporetto.

INTERNATIONAL VISITORS

Planning Your Trip

EMBASSIES AND CONSULATES

For further information, contact the nearest Italian embassy or consulate:

Embassies

* 14 Three Kings Yard, London
  W1Y 2EH, UK; ☎ (020) 7312 2200;
  Fax (020) 7499 2283;
  emblondon@embitaly.org.uk;
  www.embitaly.org.uk
* 3000 Whitehaven St, NW Washing-
  ton, DC 20008, USA; ☎ (202) 612
  4400; Fax (202) 518 2154;
  www.italyemb.org
* 275 Slater Street, 21st floor,
  Ottawa, Ontario K1P 5H9, Canada;
  ☎ (613) 232 2401/2/3;
  Fax (613) 233 1484;
  ambital@italyincanada.com;
  www.italyincanada.com

Consulates

* 38 Eaton Place, London SW1X 8AN,
  UK; ☎ (020) 7235 9371; 09065 508
  984 (visa information);
  Fax (020) 7823 1609.
* Rodwell Tower, 111 Piccadilly,
  Manchester M1 2HY, UK;
  ☎ (0161) 236 9024;
  Fax 0161 236 5574
* 32 Melville Street,
  Edinburgh EH3 7HA, UK;
  ☎ (0131) 226 3631;
  Fax 0131 226 6260; consedimb@
  consedimb.demon.co.uk
* 690 Park Avenue,
  New York, NY 10021, USA;
  ☎ (212) 737 9100;
  Fax (212) 249 4945;
  info@italconsulnyc.org;
  www.italconsulnyc.org
* 3489 Drummond Street,
  Montreal, Quebec H3G 1X6
  Canada;
  ☎ (514) 849 8351;
  Fax (514) 499 9471;
  cgi@italconsul.montreal.qc.ca
* 136 Beverley Street,
  Toronto, Ontario, M5T 1Y5,

Canada;
☎ (416) 977 1566 (from Canada
and USA); 00 1 (416) 977 2569
(from other countries);
(416) 977 1119;
www.toronto.italconsulate.org

FOREIGN EMBASSIES AND CONSULATES

Australia
Contact the consulate general in Milan
(☎ 02 777 04 217) or the Australian
embassy in Rome (Via Alessandria
215, 00198 Rome, Italy; ☎ 06 85 27 21;
www.australian-embassy.it).

Canada
Contact the Canadian consulate in
Padova (Riviera Ruvvante 25, 35129
Padova, Italy; ☎ 049 87 64 833;
Fax 049 878 1147) or the Canadian
embassy in Rome (Via GB de Rossi
27, 00161 Rome, Italy ☎ 06 44 59 81;
rome@dfait-maeci.gc.ca).

Ireland
Contact the Irish consulate in Milan
(Piazza San Pietro in Gessate 2, 20122
Milano, Italy; ☎ 02 55 18 75 69; Fax 02
55 18 75 70) or the Irish embassy in
Rome (Piazza di Campitelli 3, 00186
Rome, Italy; ☎ 06 69 79 121; Fax 06 67
92 354).

UK
Contact the honorary consulate in
Venice (Accademia Dorsoduro 1051,
30123 Venezia, Italy; ☎ 041 522 7207;
041 522 7408; Fax 041 522 2617) or out
of hours contact the British embassy
in Rome (Via XX Settembre 80a, Rome,
Italy; ☎ 06 42 20 00 01; Fax 06 48 73
324).

USA
Contact the consulate in Milan (Via
Principe Amedeo 2/10, 20121 Milano,
Italy; ☎ 02 290 351; Fax 02 2900 1165)
or the American embassy in Rome (Via
Veneto 119a, 00187 Rome, Italy; ☎ 06
46 741; Fax 06 48 82 672; www.usis.it).

ENTRY REQUIREMENTS

British visitors travelling to Italy must be in possession of a valid national passport. Citizens of other European Union countries need only a national identity card. In case of loss or theft report to the embassy or consulate and the local police.

Entry visas are required for Australian, New Zealand, Canadian and US citizens (if their intended stay exceeds three months). Apply to the Italian Consulate (visa issued same day; delay if submitted by mail). US citizens may find the booklet **Your Trip Abroad** useful for information on visa requirements, customs regulations, medical care, etc when travelling in Europe – available from the Superintendent of Documents, PO Box 371954, Pittsburgh, PA 15250-7954, USA; ☎ (202) 512 1800; Fax (202) 512 2250; www.access.gpo.gov.

CUSTOMS

As of 30 June 1999, those travelling between countries within the European Union can no longer purchase "duty-free" goods. For further information, a free leaflet entitled **Duty Paid** is available from HM Customs and Excise, Finchley Excise Advice Centre, Berkeley House, 304 Regents Park Road, London N3 2JY; ☎ 0845 010 9000; www.hmce.gov.uk. The US Customs Service offers a free publication, **Know Before You Go**, for US citizens, www.customs.gov

HEALTH

As the UK is a member of the European Union, British subjects should obtain an **E111 medical form** from the Ministry of Social Security, Newcastle-upon-Tyne, or from main post offices, before leaving home. Separate travel and medical insurance is highly recommended. Check with your local travel agent before departure.

Accessibility

Sights in this guide marked with the symbol ♿ have full or partial access for wheelchairs. *However, it is highly recommended that you call the sight in advance to determine the extent of their facilities.* Many Venetian historic monuments and attractions do not have modern lifts or wheelchair facilities, although ramps are being installed to facilitate movement over some of the bridges. Wheelchairs may easily be loaded onto the vaporettos but not onto the less stable gondolas. For detailed information contact **RADAR** (Royal Association for Disability and Rehabilitation), 12 City Forum, 250 City Road, London EC1V 8AF, UK; ☎ (020) 7250 3222; Fax (020) 7250 0212; www.radar.org.uk. Details can also be obtained from the **Associazione Italiana per l'Assistenza agli Spastici (AIAS)**, Via Cipro 4/H, 00136 Rome, Italy; ☎ 06 3973 1829. Information in English on hotels, restaurants, museums and monuments in Italy with facilities for disabled travellers is available from **Consorzio Cooperative Integrate** (CO.IN) at www.coinsociale.it/turismo/default.htm.

Other Information

ELECTRICITY

The voltage is 220ac, 50 cycles per second; the sockets are for two-pin plugs. It is therefore advisable to take an adaptor to Venice for hairdryers, shavers, computers etc.

EMERGENCIES

♿ *See Emergency Numbers under Telephones in Basic Information.*

MAIL

♿ *See Mail in Basic Information.*

MONEY

♿ *See Money in Basic Information.*

GETTING AROUND

Venice is served by a water-borne public transport system. When using this service visitors should note that the name of a vaporetto stop does not necessarily mean that the water-bus will stop outside the monument after which it is named. Traffic on the Grand Canal is often congested and services may sometimes be erratic.

On Foot

The least exasperating way of getting around is on foot, even if crossing the many bridges over the canals may prove tiring. 🅰 Always carry a map. Venice's system of house numbers can reach remarkable heights (up to almost 7 000), as these numbers refer to individually numbered addresses within the whole **sestiere** rather than to a particular street or square. Even numbers are not always on one side of the street or odd ones on the other! Watch for yellow signs with directional arrows to major sights like the Rialto.

Vaporetto

🅰 *See map of vaporetto routes on the inside back cover of the guide.*

The **water-buses** comprise two kinds of vehicle: the lumbering *vaporetto,* and the faster *motoscafo* (motor boat) for longer distances. A reduced service operates at night: it's best to check the timetables on display.

Tickets may be purchased individually or in tens *(un blochetto)* from kiosks at each landing stage and from shops displaying the ACTV sign: a single ticket costs €5; unlimited travel for 24hr is €12 *(biglietto turistico)*; €25 buys unlimited travel over 72hr from the start of your first journey. For further details contact **Azienda del Consorzio Trasporti Veneziano**, Casella Postale 688, Cannaregio 3935, 3031 Venice, ☎ 041 27 22 111; Fax 52 07 135; www.actv.it

Line 1 runs from Piazzale Roma and the railway station, the full length of the Grand Canal (14 stops) to Piazza San Marco and on to the Lido. It is known as the *accelerato,* although in some ways this is the slowest line.

Line 82 follows the same route as Line 1, but makes fewer stops and is therefore quicker. It runs from Tronchetto to Piazzale Roma, Giudecca, San Giorgio, San Marco and on to the Lido.

Vaporetto on the Grand Canal between the Salute and Accademia

Water Taxis

Beware of touts out to overcharge the unsuspecting visitor! 🕭 Look only for authorised motor launches bearing a yellow registration number plate inscribed with the symbol of Venice on the boarding side. It is also worth ensuring that the meter is clearly visible and that charge rates are displayed.

As a guideline, a journey through the city centre lasting up to seven minutes will cost approximately €14, with an additional €1.30 for every one minute thereafter.

Calling a water taxi by phone will incur an additional charge €6, as will journeys carried out between 10pm and 7am (standard night-rate supplement of €5.50) or on Sundays and public holidays (€5.90). Any luggage item in excess of 50cm/19in wide will be charged an extra €1.50. You will also have to pay an extra charge if the number of passengers exceeds four: €1.60 per person up to 20 passengers. In cases of suspected fraud, make a note of the taxi number, the time of the journey and request a receipt for the fare paid with details of the journey made. The matter should then be referred to the Tourist Information Service or to the local police for further action. However, there is little recourse if you use an unauthorised boat.

- **Radio Taxi** ☎ 041 52 22 303 or 041 72 31 12
- **Venezia Taxi** ☎ 041 72 30 09
- **Piazzale Roma (Santa Chiara)** ☎ 041 71 69 22
- **Rialto** ☎ 041 523 05 75; 041 72 31 12
- **San Marco (Molo)** ☎ 041 522 97 50
- **Lido** ☎ 041 526 00 59
- **Airport (Marco Polo)** ☎ 041 541 50 84
- **Coop Serenissima** ☎ 041 522 12 65
- **Coop San Marco** ☎ 041 522 23 03 or 041 523 57 75
- **Coop Veneziana** ☎ 041 71 61 24
- **Società Sotoriva** ☎ 041 520 95 86
- **Società Narduzzi Solemar** ☎ 041 520 08 38
- **Società Marco Polo** ☎ 041 96 61 70
- **Società Serenissima** ☎ 041 522 85 38

Traghetto

As there are only three bridges spanning the Grand Canal (Scalzi, Rialto and Accademia), the other practical means of crossing from one bank to another is by *traghetto* (€0.50; slightly higher from San Samuele during exhibitions at Palazzo Grassi), which ferries passengers Venetian-style, standing on two feet, at eight points along the canal (Ferrovia, San Marcuola, Santa Sofia, Riva del Carbon, San Tomà, San Samuele, Santa Maria del Giglio and Dogana).

Gondola

For a relaxing trip on a gondola, be prepared to spend a large sum: 40min along the canals will probably cost you €80 (official price excluding a musical serenade between 8am and 8pm), which can be shared among up to six passengers. Every additional 20min will be charged an extra €40. Travelling by gondola at night may seem romantic but it is costly: between 7pm and 8am, a 40-minute trip costs €100, with an extra fee of €50 for every further 20min. Charges are always subject to negotiation, however. Remember, too, that you can decide how to reach your destination and ask the gondoliere to follow the route you have chosen. For details, contact the **Istituzione per la Conservazione della Gondola e la Tutela del Gondoliere** ☎ 041 52 85 075.

For those who prefer gliding along canals at their own leisurely pace, **boats** may be hired privately from Brussa, Cannaregio 1293, ☎ 041 71 57 87 or 041 720 550.

USEFUL WORDS AND PHRASES

Basic Vocabulary

si/no – yes/no
per favore – please
grazie – thank you
buongiorno – good morning
buona sera – good afternoon/evening
buona notte – goodnight
arrivederci – goodbye
scusi – excuse me
piccolo/un po' – small/a little
grande – large/big
meno – less

molto – much/very
più – more
basta! – enough!
quando? – when?
perché? – why?
perché – because
con/senza – with/without
l'aeroporto – the airport
la stazione – the station
un biglietto – a ticket
una scheda per il telefono – a telephone card

Numbers and Numerals

1	uno	11	undici	30	trenta
2	due	12	dodici	40	quaranta
3	tre	13	tredici	50	cinquanta
4	quattro	14	quattordici	60	sessanta
5	cinque	15	quindici	70	settanta
6	sei	16	sedici	80	ottanta
7	sette	17	diciassette	90	novanta
8	otto	18	diciotto	100	cento
9	nove	19	diciannove	1 000	mille
10	dieci	20	venti	2 000	duemila

Time, Days of the Week, Seasons

1.00 – l'una
1.15 – una e un quarto – one fifteen
1.30 – un' ora e mezzo – one thirty
1.45 – l'una e quaranta cinque – one forty-five
mattina – morning
pomeriggio – afternoon
sera – evening
ieri – yesterday
oggi – today
domani – tomorrow
una settimana – a week

lunedì – Monday
martedì – Tuesday
mercoledì – Wednesday
giovedì – Thursday
venerdì – Friday
sabato – Saturday
domenica – Sunday
inverno – winter
primavera – spring
estate – summer
autunno – autumn/fall

Food and Drink

un piatto – a plate
un coltello – a knife
una forchetta – a fork
un cucchiaio – a spoon
il cibo – food
un piatto vegetariano – a vegetarian dish

un bicchiere – a glass
acqua minerale (gassata) – mineral water (fizzy)
vino rosso – red wine
vino bianco – white wine
una birra (alla spina) – a beer (draught)

carne – meat
manzo/vitello – beef/veal
maiale – pork
agnello – lamb
prosciutto cotto (crudo) – cooked ham (cured)
pollo – chicken
pesce – fish (**pesca** – peach)
uova – eggs (**uva** – grapes)
verdura – green vegetables

burro – butter
formaggio – cheese
un dolce – a dessert
frutta – fruit
zucchero – sugar
sale/pepe – salt/pepper
senape – mustard
olio/aceto – oil/vinegar
si puo visitare? – can one visit?

Shopping

un negozio – a shop
la posta – a post office
francobolli – stamps
macellaio – a butcher's
farmacia – a chemist's
sciroppo per la tosse – cough mixture
pastiglie per la gola – throat pastilles
cerotto – sticking plaster
scottato dal sole – sunburn

mal di pancia – stomach-ache
mal di testa – headache
punture di zanzara/ape/vespa – mosquito bite/bee-/wasp-sting
il panificio – a baker's
pane (integrale) – bread (wholemeal)
un supermercato – a supermarket
un giornale – a newspaper
pescivendolo – a fishmonger

Sightseeing

si puo visitare? – can one visit?
chiuso/aperto – closed/open
destra/sinistra – right/left
nord/sud – north/south
est/ovest – east/west
la strada per ...? – the road for ...?
una vista – a view
al primo piano – on the first floor
tirare – pull
spingere – push
bussare – ring (the bell)

le luci – lights
le scale – stairs
l'ascensore – lift
i bagni per uomo/per donna – WC facilities men's/ladies'
una camera singola/doppia/matrimoniale – a single room/with twin beds/double bed
con doccia/con bagno – with shower/bath
un giorno/una notte – one day/night

Urban Sites

la città – the town
una chiesa – a church
il duomo – the cathedral
una cappella – a chapel
il chiostro – the cloisters
la navata – the nave
il coro – the choir or chancel
il transetto – the transept
la cripta – the crypt
un palazzo – a town house or mansion
una casa – a house
un castello – a castle
un monastero/convento – an abbey/monastery
un cortile – a courtyard
un museo – a museum

una torre – a tower
un campanile – a belfry
una piazza – a square
un giardino – a garden
un parco – a park
una via/strada – a street/road
un ponte – a bridge
un molo – a pier or jetty
un cimitero – a cemetery
la barca – a boat
il motoscafo – motor boat
la spiaggia – the beach
il mare – the sea
pericolo – danger
vietato – prohibited or forbidden

Natural Sites

il fiume – the river
un lago – a lake

un belvedere – a viewpoint
un bosco – a wood

On the Road

l'autostrada – a motorway/highway
la patente – driving licence
un garage – a garage (for repairs)
nel parcheggio – in the car park
benzina – petrol/gas

una gomma – a tyre
le luci – headlights
il parabrezza – the windscreen
il motore – the engine

Useful Phrases

Parla inglese? – Do you speak English?
Non capisco – I do not understand
Parli piano per favore – Please speak slowly
Dove sono i bagni? – Where are the toilets?
A che ora parte il treno/l'autobus/l'aereo …? – At what time does the train/bus/plane leave?
A che ora arriva il treno …? – At what time does the train … arrive?
Quanto costa? – How much does it cost?
Dove posso comprare un giornale inglese? – Where can I buy an English newspaper?
Dove posso cambiare i miei soldi? – Where can I change my money?
Posso pagare con una carta di credito? – May I pay with a credit card?

Entri! – Come in!
Dov'è …? – Where's …?

BASIC INFORMATION

Fees and Hours

BEACHES

At the seaside there are supervised beaches where a fee is charged for umbrellas, chairs and sunbeds; beaches where no charge is levied may be less well-tended.

CHURCHES

The main churches are open 7am–noon and 4–6pm. Visitors should be dressed appropriately: long trousers for men; no bare shoulders or very short skirts for women; those who do not observe these conventions may be refused entry. Many churches charge an entry fee of €2 or €3, especially if works of art adorn the interior (🌎 *see CHORUS pass below)*. Small change is useful for activating light time-switches.

DISCOUNTS

Visitors can obtain discounts on a number of tourist sights and facilities, such as transport, public toilets, car parks and museums, by purchasing a **VENICEcard**, available in advance at the tourist office. One day is €29 (€22 ages 4-29), 3 days €54 (€45) and 7 days €76 (€67). 🛈 For further information, call ☎ 041 24 24 (from within Italy), or 39 041 24 24 (from abroad), or consult www.venicecard.it
If you plan on visiting the interiors of several churches, obtain a **CHORUS** pass in advance from the **Associazione Chiese di Venezia,** San Polo, 298, 30125 Venezia, Italy (☎ 041 27 50 462; www.chorusvenezia.org). Providing entry to 15 churches in Venice, a single pass, valid for one year, costs €8 (family pass €16).
If you are a museum buff, consider buying a **Museum Pass** (€18, valid

6 months) for entry to all Civic Museums. For details, ☎ 041 52 09 070; www.museicivicivenezi ani.it.

Youth Discounts

For €3, young people aged 14 to 29 can purchase a **Rolling Venice** card, which offers over 200 discounts at participating youth hostels, campsites, hotels, restaurants, university canteens, museums and shops, as well as reduced rates for public transport and the International Biennale of Art. The card is available from the following locations (official identification papers are required):

- **ACTV/Ve.La ticket offices** at Tronchetto, Piazzale Roma Santa Chiara, Santa Lucia Railway Station, Scalzi Railway Station, Rialto Diretti, Accademia, Vallaresso, San Zaccaria Danieli, Lido S.M. Elisabetta, Punta Sabbioni;
- **ACTV/Ve.La agents** at Calle Fuseri, Piazzale Roma, Mestre, Dolo, Mirano;
- **Assessorato alle politiche giovanili** in San Marco, Corte Contarina 1529; ☎ 041 27 47 616 *(open Mon-Fri, 9.30am-1pm; Tue and Thu, 3-5pm)*;
- **Centro Turistico Studentesco e Giovanile (CTS)** in Dorsoduro 3252; ☎ 041 520 56 60 *(open Mon–Fri, 9.30am–1.30pm and 3–7pm)*;
- **Agenzia Arte e Storia** in Santa Croce, Corte Canal 659; ☎ 041 52 40 232 *(open Mon-Thu, 9am-1pm and 3-6.15pm; Fri, 9am-1pm)*;
- **Associazione Italiana Alberghi per la Gioventù** in San Polo, Calle del Castelforte San Rocco 3101; ☎ 041 52 04 414 *(open Mon-Sat, 8am-2pm)*.

Mail

In Italy post offices are open 8.30am-2pm (noon Sat and last day of the month). The main post offices are to be found at the Fondaco dei Tedeschi and just off Piazza San Marco, behind the Napoleon Wing by the Correr museum. Letters sent **poste restante** *(fermo posta)* can be collected from

the main post office. Stamps are sold in post offices and tobacconists *(tabac- cheria)*. A stamp for an airmail letter to Europe costs €0.62, to North America €0.80 and to Australia €1. Airmail must be weighed at the post office.

Major Holidays

Public holidays *(giorni festivi)* include Saturdays and Sundays.
- January:
  1 (New Year) and 6 (Epiphany)
- Easter: Sunday and Monday *(lunedì dell'Angelo)*
- April: 25 (St Mark's Day and liberation in 1945)
- May: 1
- August: 15 (Assumption – *Ferragosto*)
- November: 1
- December:
  8 (Immaculate Conception), 25 and 26 (Christmas and St Stephen's day).

A working day is a *giorno feriale*.

Money

The unit of currency is the **euro** which is issued in notes (€5, €10, €20, €50, €100, €200 and €500) and in coins (1 cent, 2 cents, 5 cents, 10 cents, 20 cents, 50 cents, €1 and €2).

BANKS

ATMs are plentiful in Venice. Banks are usually open Monday to Friday, 8.30am-1.30pm and 2.30pm-4pm. Some branches open in the city centre and shopping centres on Saturday mornings, but most are closed on Saturdays, Sundays and public holidays. Most hotels will change travellers' cheques. Money can be changed in post offices (except travellers' cheques), exchange bureaus and at railway stations and airports. Commission is always charged. Money withdrawn from Bancomat machines with a PIN incurs a lower commission charge than from a withdrawal transacted over the counter at a bank.

CREDIT CARDS

Payment by credit card is widespread in shops, hotels and restaurants and at some petrol stations. The **MIchelin Guide Italia** and the **MIchelin Guide Main Cities of Europe** indicate which credit cards are accepted at hotels and restaurants. Money may also be withdrawn from a bank or ATM, but may incur interest pending repayment.

Pharmacies

A pharmacy *(farmacia)* is identified by a red and white cross. When it is closed, it will advertise the names of the nearest on-duty chemist and a list of doctors on call.

Telephones

The state telecommunication system is run by the **Compania Italiana Telecom (CIT)**. Telephone bureaux have banks of public telephones where customers pay for the line at the end of the trunk call *(Fondaco dei Tedeschi)*. Reduced rates for national calls apply after 6.30pm and between 10pm and 8am for international calls.

PUBLIC PHONES

Public telephone boxes are to be found along streets and in most bars. They may be operated by phone cards (☎ *see below)* and by telephone credit cards. To make a call, lift the receiver, insert payment, await dialling signal, punch in the required number and wait for a reply.

PHONE CARDS

These are sold in denominations of €1, €2.50, €5 and €8 and supplied by CIT offices and post offices as well as tobacconists *(tabaccaio* sign bearing a white T on a black background).

DIALING CODES

For calls **within Venice**, dial the correspondent's number, including the 041 prefix code for Venice.

Useful numbers
Assisted operator service (reverse charge calling): ☎ 15
Directory Enquiries: ☎ 12
Directory Enquiries (addresses): ☎ 14 12
International Enquiries: ☎ 176
OMNITEL Customer Care: ☎ 190
TIM Customer Service: ☎ 119
Urgent Calls: ☎ 197
Emergency numbers
ACI Emergency Breakdown Service: ☎ 116
Carabinieri (military police): ☎ 112
Fire Brigade: ☎ 115
General Emergency Services (equivalent of British 999, US 911): ☎ 113
Emergency Health Services: ☎ 118

For calls to **other towns in Italy**, dial the code for the town or district beginning with an 0, followed by the correspondent's number.
For **international calls** dial 00 followed by the country code:

- 61 for Australia
- 1 for Canada
- 64 for New Zealand
- 44 for the UK
- 1 for the USA

For calls from abroad to Italy, the international code for Italy is 39, the code for Venice is 041 – note that following changes to telephone codes in Italy, you should no longer drop the first 0 of the area code.

Time

The time in Italy is usually the same as in the rest of mainland Europe (one hour ahead of the United Kingdom) and changes during the last weekend in March and October between summer time *(ora legale)* and winter time *(ora solare)*.

*Antonio Canaletto's painting of the
Rialto Bridge*
J. G. BERITZ/RMN

NATURE

The mainland of Italy reaches out a finger towards Venice, and the gap is spanned by the Ponte della Libertà (Bridge of Liberty). Otherwise, the coast's ominous profile cast in reflection across the Venetian lagoon is that of industrial developments at Mestre and Porto Marghera. These have grown around the ageless waters of the Brenta Naviglio which flow peacefully into the lagoon at Malcontenta. The modern Tessera Airport and the prettified Jesolo beach huts betray the affluence of tourism.

The Venetian Lagoon

The Venetian Lagoon extends over an area of 550km²/213sq mi, making it the largest in Italy. It was formed at the end of the Ice Age by the convergence of flooded rivers, swollen by melted snow from the Alps and Apennines.

Today it provides a natural and complex habitat to wetland flora and fauna between the Cavallino coast to the northeast and the Lido and Chioggia to the southwest. Water levels are maintained by the sea: its tides constitute both an ever-present threat to the delicate make-up of the Venetian Lagoon while also providing its regular safeguard from stagnation. The sea merges with the canals' fresh water through three channels (**bocche di porto**) by the Lido, at Chioggia and Malamocco, where dikes were installed during the 19C and 20C.

AN AGE-OLD PROBLEM

In the 12C, Europe enjoyed a long period of mild weather followed by a noticeable rise in temperature; then came torrential rains that caused high tides and flooding. The **River Brenta** broke its banks and water flooded a large part of the lagoon, depositing silt, mud and detritus. Malaria broke out. The Republic of Venice tried to defend itself by placing palisades along the coast, diverting the course of the rivers and building great dikes, but the lagoon continued to pose a threat. Over the ensuing centuries (15C-17C), major drainage programmes were implemented that affected the River Brenta, River Piave, River Livenza and River Sile. In 1896 the operation aimed at diverting the waters of the Brenta was finally completed, channelling them into the mouth of the

Bacchiglione. Despite these measures, as water levels continue to rise and fall, the sand deposited in the lagoon by the rivers is buffeted back inland by the sea and the wind. Thus the sandbanks are formed and strengthened. All the while, caught between marine erosion and the rebuilding action of the rivers, the fate of Venice itself is at stake: after more than 1 000 years of existence, the city is slowly sinking.

The Venetian Lagoon can be likened to a sophisticated system that has achieved a subtle balance between excessive **sedimentation** (leading to the emergence of "new" land) and **erosion** (in which the deposits carried by the sea and rivers are so scarce that a stretch of lagoon can turn into a stretch of sea). This is pre-

A few lagoon terms

Bacino scolante: earth that carries rain- and river water into the lagoon.

Barene: sandbanks protruding from the water and immersed at high tide.

Bricole: groups of colourful wooden masts roped together which mark out canals fit for navigation.

Ghebi: tiny canals that meander their way across the sandbanks.

Punto zero: standard reference for measuring the water level in the lagoon, established by the Punta della Salute tide gauge. The levels are usually 23cm/9.3in higher than the average sea level.

Valli da pesca: diked stretches of the lagoon set aside for fishing.

Velme: small strips of land which, unlike the *barene*, can be seen only at low tide, when they appear on the surface.

cisely the risk currently threatening the lagoon. About one quarter of the lagoon surface is rendered unnavigable by the existence of sandbanks or **barene**. Their importance is huge: they encourage the proliferation of a great many animal and vegetal species while attracting sediments that might otherwise be scattered in the water, contributing to reducing the swell.

About 4 000ha/15sq mi are taken up by the large inhabited islands and smaller, deserted ones, leaving another 40 000ha/155sq mi occupied by water. Anyone surprised at seeing how shallow a Venetian canal may be when drained of its water (from an average of 1-2m/3-7ft to a maximum depth of 8-10m/26-33ft) will understand why the seabed of the open lagoon is often exposed at low tide. Despite this lack of depth, which gives the lagoon its millpond appearance, a complex network of crisscrossed channels maintains currents and easy movement. Navigable areas are marked by lone wooden posts or groups of poles roped together, known as **bricole**. The deepest channels are those nearest the mouths of the ports, and as the distance from the sea increases, these rivulets become shallower and narrower (**ghebi**), dwindling across the sandbanks before disappearing into *chiari*, basins where salt water and rainwater mingle.

TIDES

Tidal changes occur every six hours, fluctuating between two high points per day. Low atmospheric pressure and the sirocco and bora winds are known to accentuate high tide, whereas high atmospheric pressure and northwesterly winds tend to bring on a low tide. In this case, some of the rivers may dry up. Sea water is thereby drawn into the lagoon through the three ports, flushing "new" water in and "old" water out, assisted by a current from the rivers on the opposite side. Parts affected by these tides are therefore known as the "living" lagoon, whereas sections little affected by this lifeline are referred to as the "dead" lagoon. These outlying parts tend towards marsh, channelled with canals, *ghebi* between fishing banks and diked lakes built by and for the fishing industry.

The health of the lagoon is totally dependent upon the influx of "new" water brought by the tides. However, the inflow of fresh water provided by the rivers that once maintained saline levels has been greatly reduced as the rivers have progressively been diverted. This diversion has also reduced the strength of current across the lagoon and allowed vast quantities of polluting material to be deposited.

In the 20C the problem was exacerbated by the growth of industrial sites around Mestre and Porto Maghera and the accommodation of petrol tankers, with obvious implications on the environment of the lagoon. The reduction in oxygenated water flowing through the canals of Venice is gradually eroding the ability of plant and marine life to survive. Only those organisms with short life cycles have had time to adapt, and so quantities of macroalgae *(ulva rigida)* and insects (mosquitoes and the like) have increased at a fantastic rate.

The tide along the coasts can fluctuate wildly; for it to be classified as tidal flooding, its level has to reach or exceed 1.10m/3ft 6in. The last such occurrence happened on 4 November 1966 when consequences were felt way beyond the shores of Venice: the Arno overflowed in

Why do tides occur?

Gravitational forces caused by the earth's rotation around the sun and its relation to the moon are responsible for tides. Being nearer the earth, the moon exerts the greater force over changes in liquid levels and the movement of the oceans and seas. The strength of this force is affected by air pressure and winds. In the case of Venice, the greatest floods have always followed major sirocco storms. When the moon passes over the meridian of an area, it causes a high tide; when it is at 90° to that meridian, it produces a low tide. When the earth, moon and sun are aligned, the tide reaches its maximum levels.

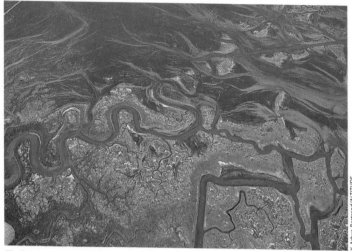

Y. Arhus-Bertrand/ALTITUDE

The lagoon, a network of waterways

Florence, with tragic results. That year an alarming prediction said that Venice might possibly disappear. Fortunately, radical action against further subsidence, including the closure of artesian wells on the mainland (1975), has proved the prophecy false. Plans for natural gas exploration 12 nautical miles off Chioggia are presently under review pending a feasibility study of environmental consequences (1995).

Similar crises of this kind are documented as far back as 589. Contemporary personal accounts are terrifying. **Paolo Diacono** (c 720-799) wrote of the first flood tide: *"non in terra neque in aqua sumus viventes"* (neither on earth nor in water were we alive). Records from 1410 state that "almost one thousand people coming from the fair at Mestre and other places drowned".

Since the 17C the water level of the Venetian Lagoon has dropped by 60cm/24in. In past centuries, once every five years, the tide would rise above the damp-proof foundations made of Istrian stone that were built to protect the houses against salt deposits. Nowadays, in the lower areas, these foundations are immersed in water more than 40 times in a single year and the buildings can do very little to stall the degradation process.

Venice, victim of the tides

On 4 November 1966 the mareograph at Punta della Salute registered an exceptionally high tide of 1.94m/6ft. Medium to high tides usually reach a level of around 70cm/28in, flooding the Piazza San Marco and, with a further 30cm/12in, even narrow alley streets would be inundated. Between December and February the city can be the scene of very low tides indeed, estimated at less than 90cm/36in.

At the end of the 18C, when the first part of the Riva degli Schiavoni promenade was completed, Venetian magistrates ordered that the letter "C" be engraved on the city houses and their foundations. The letter was to indicate the average level of the highest-known tides. However, today it is difficult to spot these inscriptions since most of them are located under the level of the sea.

LIFE FORMS

The lagoon comprises a vast and rich habitat for fauna and flora, part of which may even be glimpsed from the vaporetto between Venice and Burano or from a car driving through the section enclosed by the Cavallino coast. The best way, however, to appreciate the extent of vegetation and animal life thriving in this "watery plain" is to explore the sandbanks by boat.

Kingfisher

Cormorant

Coot

Black-winged stilt

Grey Heron

Little egret

Illustrations: M Dewynter (Kingfisher, Grey heron); R Corbel (Coot, Black-winged stilt, Little egret)

A marine haven

The external surface of a **bricola** seems literally corroded by crustaceans, whereas within, bivalvular molluscs called *teredini* have taken up residence. Closest to the surface and buffeted by the tides are live crustaceans *(balani)* and green algae. Below, in calmer currents, live mussels *(mitili)*. The submerged part is the kingdom of the sponges: the tube-shaped *ascidie* and the *hydrozoans*.

The waters of the lagoon vary in salt concentration depending on their proximity to the river outlets, where the water is almost fresh. In the middle they tend to be brackish; near the ports, where the tides inject sea water, they are far saltier. At the same time, areas around the river deltas tend to be muddy, whereas by the port mouths the lagoon bed is sandy.

Fauna

At the lower end of the food chain, different types of **molluscs** breed successfully on the wooden piles or *bricole*.
The principal category is undoubtedly that of the **fish kingdom**, which has defined the very character of the lagoon, with its distinctive collection in shoals around sandbanks, and the interaction of human beings with this environment as they seek to exploit such rich resources.
Crab and shrimp are central to the fishing industry and to Venetian cuisine. From a boat it soon becomes obvious where the fishing banks are situated as these attract various species of aquatic birds: wild duck (mallard and teal), tens of thousands of coots, herons and marsh harriers. Besides the common sparrows, swallows and blackbirds, the Venetian Lagoon is visited by special migratory birds, often with highly coloured plumage.

It is perhaps their beauty, strangeness and cleverness that is most fascinating: the black-whiskered bearded tit clings to the reeds; the reed warbler builds a floating nest between four reeds, which rises and falls with the tide; the kingfisher dives acrobatically and the moorhen nods her head in time to the rhythm of her strokes; little grebe pop out of the water only to dive quickly and silently below the surface again and emerge where least expected.

The very rich **bird life** of the lagoon also includes the cormorant, the inevitable sea-gull, the sea swallow, whose whirling wings and V-shaped tail allow it to swoop effortlessly time and again, and the little egret, recognisable by its elegant carriage and startlingly white feathers with which women adorned themselves at the beginning of the 20C. Even more beautiful is the black-winged stilt, whose somber wings contrast with its white body and the red of its long legs; its thin, distinguished beak adds a touch of refinement.

Elegance seems to be a trait shared by all the birds of the lagoon, among which the mute swan must reign supreme.
There are numerous marsh harriers and hen harriers among the birds of prey.
Among the mammals, the rodent provides a somewhat harmful presence. The rat, the so-called *pantagena*, is at home

Fishing Areas

Known as **valli da pesca**, these stretches of the lagoon are used for fishing, taking into consideration the migratory movements of the fish. Because they have been diked, they are not exposed to the ebbing of the water. During the spring season, the fish (mainly eel, sea bass and gilt-head bream) congregate in the lagoon, attracted by the organic vegetation brought along by rivers and mountain waters after the thaw. In winter, when weather conditions are especially harsh, the fish try to swim back towards the sea, but on reaching the **chiaveghe** (structures with bulkheads built to regulate the flow of the sea water) they are caught and sorted by traditional methods. Among the various nets used for fishing, two in particular stand out: the *bilancione*, a huge trawl net suspended from four tall piers, and the *cogolo*, a cylindrical net consisting of several parts, ending in a cone.

anywhere, on the city squares as well as in rubbish dumps and attics.

Flora

The **sandbanks** are abundantly cloaked in vegetation: glasswort, sea lavender and asters turn the mounds first green, then red, then blue, then grey. Rooted in the water are various reeds and rushes with long stalks and spiky flowers. On the beaches grow convolvulus with shiny dark-green leaves and pink flowers, and sea rocket with its violet blooms.

On the first dunes of shifting sands grows couch grass, a perennial member of the grass family. Farther back, tufts of coarse grass sprout among the spurges, with their long stalks of small lancet-like leaves and flowers with yellowish bracts. Tall bushy *gramineae (erianthus ravennae)* are also widely found.

Shrubs and trees grow beyond the dunes: along the Romea highway, south of Chioggia, between Santa Anna and Cavanella d'Adige, is the Bosco Nordio (Nordio Wood) of evergreen oaks. Even the market gardens form part of the vegetation of the lagoon, especially in the south at Chioggia, where red chicory *(radicchio)* is grown, highly prized but not as famous as the *radicchio* of Treviso.

Venice in Peril

Flooding

The Centro Previsioni e Segnalazioni Maree provides warnings of impending danger and information on forecasts and tide tables. Tidal flooding tends to occur between April and September, and forecast warnings are issued about 48 hours in advance. Details are published in the *Gazzettino* and posted up on the landing stages of the vaporettos. Should the level threaten to exceed 1.10m/3ft 7in, 16 sirens sound five times for 10 seconds each time, three or four hours in advance of the high point.

Should high tide not exceed 1.20m/3ft 11in, the **AMAV** (Azienda Multiservizio Ambientale Venezia) sees to the laying of footbridges along prescribed routes. However, if the water

level goes above this limit, then footbridges can become dangerous because they start to float. In the case of tidal flooding, the AMAV is unable to maintain its principal function which is rubbish collection, because its boats are no longer able to pass under the bridges. It is therefore made responsible for laying down emergency footbridges. Meanwhile, the Venetian Municipality requests the population to just hang on to their household waste! 😊 In case of a generalised flooding emergency, call the **Centro Maree** ☎ 041 27 48 787 or 041 52 06 344/52 07 722 *(answerphone)*, or send a fax to 041 52 10 378.

High tide, which is announced by the rather sinister sound of the sirens, floods the lowest-lying parts of the city not only by bursting the banks of St Mark's Basin and the canals and rivers of the city, but also by gushing out of the drains, cracks and manhole covers in Venice's streets and squares.

Today's concerns

In the past, land and water were clearly separated, with the lagoon acting as a link between the two, drawing on both to produce life and movement. However, the presence of factories, farms and areas inhabited by man have gradually changed the face of the *gronda*, the sloped land licking at the lagoon shores. Today, the lagoon has reached a sort of "standstill": it takes two weeks for waste material to leave the lagoon and end up in the open sea. Every year more than 1 million m^3/35.3 million cu ft of solid matter is lost. Erosion, the sediments lost in the water and the rising level of the sea all contribute to lowering the lagoon depths. This phenomenon is threatening the sandbanks known as

What is an insula?

In the lagoon city, an *insula* is a tiny piece of territory which is circumscribed by a river or a canal. These *insule* are therefore linked to each other by a network of bridges. A small cluster of them is said to form a *sestiere*, one of Venice's six administrative divisions.

Coping with flooding in the Piazzetta

De Soy/RAPHO

barene, which are doomed to disappear by the year 2050 if drastic action is not taken to remedy the situation.

Water fluctuations and land subsidence

Variations in the level of the water are referred to as *eustatismo*. In the course of the last century, this phenomenon caused the waters of Venice to rise by 8cm/3.2in. This rise has led to dire consequences, aggravated by the effects of local subsidence, causing the land to drop, representing around 15cm/6.2in for the same period. Therefore, the city of Venice has "sunk" by around 23cm/9.2in since the end of the 19C.

Erosion

Erosion is the result of a number of factors: higher water levels, subsidence, digging for artificial canals, and the swell, which slowly increases while the seabed slumps and the sandbanks dwindle.

Pollution

Finally, to crown this somewhat pessimistic picture, pollution is responsible for the destruction of phanerogamic flora, invaluable sea-water plants whose roots serve to prevent erosion and stabilise the seabed. Water pollution has also killed the algae and other marine varieties which once thrived on sandbanks

and mudflats and which are no longer able to attract sediments.

Tackling the problem

The risk of losing Venice through both tides and progressive depopulation is so great that the Italian State has declared the salvation of the city to be a question of "pre-eminent national interest". The residents of Venice appear to be particularly concerned about high-to-medium tides, which cause flooding of the city. Consequently, a number of projects currently being examined or implemented are aimed at making these inhabited areas far safer. It is a highly delicate and complex situation: the town of Venice and the myriad islands are home to many buildings, monuments and works of art which cohabit in perfect harmony but, technically speaking, require different forms of intervention.

Sluice-gates

These ambitious structures should be placed side by side to form a floating barrier linked to the seabed, rising and falling with the movement of the waves. Each gate, 20-30m/66-98ft long, 20m/66ft wide and 3-5m/10-16ft thick, contains compressed air controlled by valves, which enables the gate to be lowered.

On the San Marco and Tolentini islands, the stability of paved streets, bridges and houses was meticulously checked, as well as that of underground passages and sewage drains. In the lower sections, the paving has been raised (as is clearly visible on Campo San Zanipòlo) and the shores of the lagoon consolidated to cope more efficiently against tides below 100cm/40in (120cm/48in in Chioggia).

A project is under way to deal with exceptionally high tides by placing mobile barriers at the three entrances to the port. A prototype of this system, the MoSE (Experimental Electronic Module) comprises a huge mobile sluice-gate devised to regulate the movement of the tides. It was tested along the Canale di Treporti facing the Lido from 1988-1992. It is thought that the final project would need to provide 79 of these sluice-gates.

In the Experimental Centre for Hydraulic Models, at Voltabarozzo, near Padua, a simulated mock-up of the lagoon area allows studies to be carried out into projects for the harbour mouths, the safeguarding of the coastal region and of the jetties.

In the meantime, reconstruction of the coastal region of Cavallino and Pellestrina is being carried out. The coastal area has been consolidated with 2 million m^3/70.6 million cu ft of sand taken from the sea. These deposits were also used to reinforce sandbanks, which play a crucial role as they combat the swell and local winds while protecting the environment. In an attempt to increase their stability, these coastal dunes have been planted with *ammofila*, a special variety of grass that thrives on sandy soil.

The north pier at Chioggia has been strengthened, 50km/31mi of canals have been dredged and the sediment obtained through this operation used to rebuild 300ha/740 acres of sandbanks. The restoration of sandbanks is achieved by fencing off a stretch of the lagoon with wooden masts. A large canvas sheet is then fixed to the poles and laid down over the sea depths. Sediments are poured into this artificial basin as well as water, which is then filtered by the canvas.

Further operations currently under way involve cleaning up the lagoon waters, gathering the macroalgae and salvaging the smaller islands such as Lazzaretto Vecchio. The Magistrato alle Acque and the Consorzio Venezia Nuova are responsible for all this research and for the implementation of future developments.

The **Magistrato alle Acque** has its origins in an organisation established in 1501 for the protection of Venice and the Venetian Lagoon.

The **Consorzio Venezia \Nuova** is responsible for organising and carrying out any salvaging operations. *Further information on the work of this organisation is available on its Web site: www. salve.it*

The art world fights to save Venice

In 1966, the year in which record water levels were registered in Venice, UNESCO stressed the urgency of the fight to save this beautiful city and her lagoon. A number of organisations and committees, both public and private, were set up to salvage and restore Venice's cultural heritage, namely the **Ufficio per la Salvaguardia di Venezia**.

The Head of the Monuments and Fine Arts Department is involved in the technical aspects of this undertaking and UNESCO oversees the allocation of funds raised by several private committees. Every year millions of euros are spent on rescue operations aimed at preserving the architectural, historical and artistic treasures of the city, as well as on scholarships for artisans and research. Each of these committees is directly concerned with a specific project on a regular basis. Among the many organisations dedicated to saving Venice, the most important are **The Venice in Peril Fund** (Great Britain), **Save Venice** (United States), **Comité Français pour la Sauvegarde de Venise** (France) and **Venedig Lebt** (Austria).

HISTORY

Time Line

LEGENDARY BEGINNINGS

It seems reasonable to turn to Homer when tracing the very ancient and uncertain origins of the Venetians. In the *Iliad* they arrived from Paflagonia to aid Priam. They were called the **Enetii**. Having abandoned their native land, these people arrived in the territory occupied by the Eugeneans, whom they put to flight. They founded the future Altino, from where they left for Torcello.

1000-700 BC — The Venetian civilisation known as *atestino* is founded around the city of Este.

530 BC — Etruscan colony of Spina established.

181 BC — Colony of Aquileia is founded.

42 AD — First dated documentation regarding the port of Altino.

400 — From Padua, Altino, Concordia Sagittaria, Aquileia and Oderzo, the future inhabitants of Venice visit the lagoon solely for its provisions of salt and fish. In the 6C Cassiodoro (c 490-583) requests these watermen, fishermen and salt-workers to help supply Ravenna.

568 — The Lombards descend into Italy. The Roman-Byzantine province of Venetia is gradually conquered.

639 — Oderzo, the capital of Venetia, falls. The Byzantine governor moves to Cittanova, which takes the name **Heracleia**, from Emperor Heraclius. The Church of Santa Maria Assunta is built on the island of Torcello.

697 — **Paoluccio Anafesto** is named the first doge.

742 — Transfer of the ducal seat from Cittanova to Malamocco.

775 — Olivolo, the present-day San Pietro di Castello, becomes a bishop's see. It is accountable

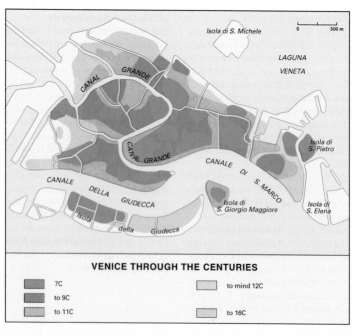

Isola di S. Michele

LAGUNA
VENETA

0   500 m

CANAL GRANDE

CANAL GRANDE

CANALE DI S. MARCO

CANALE DELLA GIUDECCA

Isola della Giudecca

Isola di S. Giorgio Maggiore

Isola di S. Pietro

Isola di S. Elena

VENICE THROUGH THE CENTURIES

- 7C
- to 9C
- to 11C
- to mind 12C
- to 16C

to the patriarchate of Gradi until 1451, when Lorenzo Giustinian is appointed First Patriarch of Venice.

810 — Pepin, son of Charlemagne, is defeated after an attempted invasion of Dalmatia and the lagoon. Many inhabitants of the lagoon move to the Realtine Islands, where the dogate is established. In 811 **Agnello Partecipazio** or "Particiaco" is elected doge. **Venice is born**.

During the 9C, when the dogeship was transferred, and for the three following centuries, Venice was made up of dozens of islands. The city was considerably smaller than it is today, however, because most of the land was below sea level.

THE INDEPENDENT CITY, RULER OF THE ADRIATIC

814 — With the **Pax Nicephori (Treaty of Nicephorus)**, Charlemagne cedes his claims to the lagoon, and Venice guarantees her neutrality throughout the political struggles that were to rage in Italy during the eras of feudalism and the inter-city state rivalry.

828 — The body of St Mark is stolen from Alexandria in Egypt and brought to Venice, where work begins on the construction of the first basilica the following year.

829 — In his will Doge Giustiniano Particiaco calls for the construction of **San Marco**, which was to become the ducal chapel.

840 — In the **Pactum Lotarii** (Peace of Lothar) the Byzantine ruler confirms the autonomy of Venice and assures her navy the control of the seas.

946 or 948 — Narentine Slav pirates carry out the legendary abduction of the maidens (👁 see SAN ZACCARIA).

976 — The Venetians rebel against the repressive **Doge Pietro Candiano IV**, who chooses to ignore the maritime power base of Venice and instead engages foreign troops to conquer territories on the mainland, which would enhance his own political standing and reputation. This provokes a fierce popular revolt: fire damages St Mark's, the Doges' Palace and San Teodoro, destroying more than 300 houses, at the time built almost exclusively in wood.

Pietro Orseolo I is elected doge at **San Pietro di Castello**.

1000 — After defeating the Croats and the Narentines, Venice assumes her role as ruler and protector of Dalmatia with the title *dux Dalmatinorum* (Duke of Dalmatia).

1032 — The Venetians' strong spirit of independence precipitated a dislike for any government that resembled a monarchy and so, to avoid such a danger, the power of the doge is "split" between two ducal councillors, each one responsible for half of the city, with

A Witness Recounts

Seized with panic, the doge, his wife and their young son sought safety by heading to the entrance of St Mark's. There they were stopped by noblemen. Pietro's promises to accept any compromise were of no avail. *"Affirming that he was...deserving of death, they shouted...that there could be no salvation for him. They immediately surrounded him and cruelly ran him through with the points of their swords so that his immortal spirit abandoned his bodily prison in search of the retreat of the blessed".* John Julius Norwich adds that *"for what we know of Pietro Candiano IV, this happy final destination is somewhat improbable".*

Musée du Louvre, Paris/SCALA

The Departure of the Bucintoro by Francesco Guardi (Louvre Museum)

the Grand Canal as the dividing line.

11C — In the second half of the century the new Basilica of St Mark is built, modelled upon the Basilica of the Apostles at Constantinople.

1081 — Venice defends Byzantium from attack by the Norman Robert Guiscard.
The following year, the **Crisobollo** issued by the Byzantine Emperor, Alessio I Comneno, allows Venetians to trade freely throughout the empire and to open shops in Constantinople without having to pay duty on their goods.

1099 — Venice defeats the Pisans near Rhodes, where the Venetian and Pisan fleets are taking part in the Crusades. The released Pisan prisoners undertake not to haunt the waters of Byzantium.

1104 — The first nucleus of the Arsenal is created.
The following year the city is ravaged by fire.

1122-24 — Under the dogeship of **Domenico Michiel**, Venice attacks and defeats the Egyptian fleet that was besieging Jaffa, taking possession of the merchant ships and their cargo of treasure trove and spices. She then goes on to participate in the victorious siege of Tyre, and the sacking of Byzantine ports in the Aegean and the Adriatic. These shows of force were crucial in restoring the reputation and political status enjoyed by the city before the King of Hungary had affirmed his power in Dalmatia, and in persuading the current Byzantine Emperor, **Giovanni Comneno**, to accept the fundamental independence of the city, recognised by his predecessors.

1143 — The **Council of the Wise Men**, or *Consilium Sapientium*, is already in existence by this date. Thought to have consisted of 35 members presided over by the doge, this organisation was to evolve into the Great Council.

1145-53 — Istria, already protected by Venice, now finds herself totally subjugated as the

Venetian Justice

Vitale Michiel's assassin found refuge among the houses around San Zaccaria. The complicity of the Venetians in that area was severely punished: their houses were destroyed and the construction of any building in stone was prohibited. This law was eventually abolished in 1948.

doge is proclaimed *totius Istriæ dominator*.

1171 — Emergency measures are implemented by the Eastern Empire angered by the plundering of their trade ships by Venetian, Genoese and Pisan navies. The disastrous expedition of **Doge Vitale Michiel II**, whose crew was decimated by the plague, is judged very harshly by the Venetians, and leads to his murder. His successor, **Sebastiano Ziani** (1172), is elected under a system similar to that which later (1268) was sanctioned by law and lasted into the following centuries.

During the dogeship of Vitale Michiel II, the six **sestieri** are created as subdivisions of the city, thereby facilitating the collection of taxes.

1175 — Construction of a wooden Rialto Bridge.

1177 — It is in Venice that **Pope Alexander III** and **Federico Barbarossa** end the conflict between the city states and their antagonists, the Church and the Swabian Empire.

According to legend, this is the occasion that saw Alexander III donate his ring in the "Sposalizio del Mare".

1178 — Eleven men are nominated to elect the 40 electors of the doge, including six ducal councillors – one for each *sestiere*.

1201-04 — **Fourth Crusade**. Doge **Enrico Dandolo**, a man of extraordinary energy despite being 90 and blind, attacks **Constantinople** (1203), which succumbs decisively to a second assault the following year. The Eastern Latin Empire is formed under an emperor nominated by six Venetians and six crusader barons. Spoils and lands are divided between the emperor, who took a quarter of the empire, the barons and the Venetians. Recognition is given to the doge's lordship over "a quarter and a half of the empire".

13C — Around 1220 the **Quarantia**, a bench of 40 magistrates with judicial powers, is formed as part of the Great Council.

1240 — Venice besieges Ferrara, thus securing commercial control of the Po Valley.

1255 — First dated documentation about the **Pregadi**, who are charged *(pregati)* with expressing opinions and fulfilling particular duties as members of the **Senate**. The Council of the Pregadi is appointed by the Great Council, to deal with questions of

The Marriage with the Sea

According to one version, a fisherman obtained the ring from St Mark on the night that Satan threatened to destroy Venice with a storm. Another legend relates that on Ascension Day, the doge solemnly proclaimed from the *Bucintoro* (state barge), in Latin *"We wed you, o sea, as a sign of true and perpetual dominion"*, casting a gold ring into the sea as he spoke. The ceremony began outside St Mark's, where the procession rallied before continuing on to the fort of San Andrea near the Lido. There the ring was cast into the sea. On his return, the doge stopped at San Nicolò on the Lido to attend Mass.

navigation and international politics, thus assuming both legislative and executive functions.

1257-70 —Venice enters into conflict with Genoa. The Venetians defeat the Genoese at Acre, from where they brought the **Acrean pillars** now in front and to the right of the basilica.

The Eastern Latin Empire falls when the Byzantine Emperor, **Michele Paleologo III**, an ally of the Genoese, takes possession of Constantinople. The Genoese are subsequently bound by treaty (1270) to Louis IX of France, who needs the Genoese fleet for the Crusades.

1268 — New rules are drafted for the election of the doge. The Great Council has first to nominate the **Council of Forty**, charged with electing the next doge, by means of a 10-stage process of elections and drawing lots. The first doge appointed in this way is **Lorenzo Tiepolo**.

1284 — The **gold ducat** is minted, equal in weight and gold content to the Florentine florin, which had been in circulation for 30 years (0.997g gold per 3.55g coin). The gold ducat was accepted currency until the fall of the Republic. When silver ducats were struck in 1561 the gold ducat became known as the *zecchino*.

1294-99 — Venice is once more at war with Genoa. At the **Battle of Curzola** (1298) the victorious Genoese sustain grievous losses. The treaty signed in 1299 sanctions the Genoese dominance over the Riviera and that of the Venetians over the Adriatic.

1297 — This is the year of the **Locking of the Great Council**, a reform that considerably increased the number of council members to more than 1 000, as well as tightening up the system for their selection. Current as well as former members have to conform to rigorous procedures. By 1323, nomination is standardised, membership is for life and passed down the generations. Later still, the Great Council degenerates into a corps for the Venetian nobility.

1308-13 — Venice, dissatisfied with the duty levied on all the goods travelling through the Po Valley and wishing to consolidate its power over the area, attacks Ferrara. **Pope Clement V**, keen to defend his right of sovereignty over the city, issues from Avignon an **interdict** on Venice, which lasts until 1313.

1310 — **Baiamonte Tiepolo**, a Venetian nobleman, tries to depose Doge Pietro Gradenigo. The revolt is suppressed with much bloodshed, and prompts the creation of a remarkable judicial body known as the **Council of Ten**, whose prime function is to protect constitutional institutions. Presided over by the doge, this body consisted of 10 members of the Senate and six wise men. It employed the service of secret police and informers to investigate sus-

El Paron de la Repubblica

The **Great Council** held a quintessential position at the heart of the Venetian Republic, since it carried out all the duties of state. Not only did it pass laws, it also had the power to select the most important people in Venice. When it met in the chamber of the Doges' Palace, the doge would preside from the centre of the Tribunale or Bench of St Mark, while nobles seated upon armchairs would line the walls or fill rows of parallel benches down the length of the room.

Lion's mouth (Palazzo Ducale)

E. Zane/MICHELIN

Bocca di Leone

The "lions' mouths" or "mouths of truth" *(see the example opposite)* were found along the streets or in the walls of public buildings. These lion-head masks were set with fierce expressions. The mouth was carved hollow to accommodate anonymous denunciations posted to the State. These denunciations were taken into account only if two witnesses were cited.

picious citizens and deal with denunciations and charges of libel against the State posted in the **lions' mouths**.

1321 — The poet **Dante Alighieri** stays in Venice in his capacity as ambassador to the Lords of Ravenna.

1347-48 — A Venetian galley introduces the **plague** from Crimea, which was to decimate the densely populated city (over 100 000 inhabitants) by three-fifths.

1350-55 — The conflict with Genoa continues.

In 1350, Venice is troubled by heavy traffic that often causes serious accidents; it is established that horses should be provided with "bell-collars to warn pedestrians of their passage".

THE DOGESHIP OF MARINO FALIER (1354-55)

Marino Falier was 80 when he was elected doge. Irascible and resentful, he began his dogeship under the worst of omens. The day he arrived in Venice, the **bucintoro**, the grandiose dogal barge, decorated with friezes and gold carvings, could not draw alongside its mooring because of fog; secondly, on arriving on the piazza, the doge entered the palace by passing between the two columns where outlaws were executed; thirdly, he was offended by insults about his wife scrawled on his chair by a young boy. Falier became even more viperish

when he found out how lightly the culprit had been punished.

He decided to mete out punishment and exact his revenge by plotting murder on those members of the nobility whom he thought had betrayed him. The conspiracy was exposed in time. The doge was accused of treason and sentence passed for his execution. A black-draped portrait in the chamber of the Great Council, recording his unhappy rule, bears a defamatory but accurate inscription. (see *PIAZZA SAN MARCO: Palazzo Ducale*). The story of Marino Falier inspired both Byron and Swinburne (who both wrote works bearing the same title: *Marino Falier*), Donizetti *(Marin Falier)* and Delacroix.

1358 — Dalmatia or *"Schiavonia"* is ceded to Hungary.

1378-81 — A fourth offence is mounted by the Venetians against Genoa to liberate Chioggia from Genoese and then Paduan hands.

1386 — Corfu comes under Venetian rule.

1389-1420 — Venice gradually gains dominion over a vast territory corresponding, more or less, to the present areas of Veneto and Friuli.

1409 — Venice regains possession of Dalmatia.

1410 — Venice is badly hit by a high tide.

1424 — Building begins on the Ca' d'Oro.

1425-54 — During the dogeship of **Francesco Foscari**, by now head of an oligarchic system (since 1423 the formula had been dropped which had once required the popular approval of the new doge: "If it is pleasing to you"), Venice is at war with the Lombards. **Carmagnola** takes part in the battles and, suspected of treason, is condemned by the Council of Ten to be beheaded between the columns of the Piazzetta. After three decades of battle, Venetian territory stretches as far as the River Adda.

In 1428 Venice is devastated by an exceptionally high tide.

1463-79 — The capture of the Venetian Argosy by the Turks is one of several humiliations to which Venice has to succumb, including the loss of Cumae and Scutari in Albania that prompts an annual levy of 10 000 ducats. This tribute is finally abolished at the death of Mehmet II.

1472 — **Caterina Cornaro** marries Giacomo Lusignano II, King of Cyprus, after whose death Queen Caterina is toppled by a coup d'état. (👉 see *RIALTO*).

1490 — The art of printing is introduced from Germany by **Aldo Manuzio**, who sets up his own printing press. It is famed for its refined italic characters and for the intellectual nature of his books, stamped with a dolphin and an anchor.

1494 — Charles VIII, King of France, arrives in Italy to conquer the Kingdom of Naples. The anti-French league, of which Venice was part, fails to defeat him in the **Battle of Fornovo** the following year.

1499 — The Turks attack Lepanto. Antonio Grimani is defeated off the coast of Sapienza: in Venice he earns the epithet *"Antonio Grimani, ruin of the Christians"*. The Turks sack Friuli. The peace treaty of 1503 sanctions the loss of Lepanto, Modone and Corone.

1500 — The **De' Barbari map** is published, providing a strangely evocative and realistic impression of the city.

1508 — In order to split up Venetian territory, Julius II, Louis XII and Emperor Maximilian I form the **League of Cambrai**, in alliance with Spain, Hungary, the Duke of Savoy, the Duke of Ferrara and the Marquis of Mantua. After an initial defeat, Venice takes seven years to recover her possessions as far as the Adda.

1514 — The Rialto market is destroyed by fire.

1516 — The Jews are segregated in the Ghetto district.

The De' Barbari map (Museo Correr)

Museo Correr/SCALA

DANGEROUS YEARS

1538 — Andrea Doria, admiral under Emperor Charles V and a Venetian ally, is defeated at Prevesa. The Turks now control the seas.

1539 — A secret service is set up by the **State Inquisitors**, the *Supreme Tribunale*, comprising three inquisitors: "the Red", a dogal councillor in a scarlet gown, and "the Blacks", two members of the Council of Ten. Working on information from informers, they take part in intrigue and counter-espionage.

1570 — The Turks land in Cyprus and conquer Nicosia.

1571 — After the siege and fall of Famagusta, **Marcantonio Bragadin**, the Venetian governor, is flayed alive by the Turks.

LEPANTO

Joined in the Holy League with the Pope and Spain, Venice confronted the Turks at Lepanto on 7 October 1571. The Christian fleet, commanded by **Sebastiano Venier**, comprised 202 galleys and six smaller ships, of which more than half were Venetian. The Turkish fleet comprised 208 galleys and a flotilla of 63 boats. The Turks were heavily defeated: 30 000 men were killed, 80 ships sunk and 140 captured. The League lost 7 600 men and 12 ships.

Among the wounded Christians was **Miguel de Cervantes**, author of *Don Quixote*, who always considered the Battle of Lepanto the most important event not only of his life, but of all history. Cervantes believed that the injury to his left hand, which was permanently crippled, was "to the greater glory of his right one".

1573 — Venice signs a treaty with the Turks that clinches control over Cyprus, which is abandoned and left to decline.

1577 — Fire damages much of the Doges' Palace. Refurbishment is undertaken by Antonio da Ponte.

1587 — The **Banco della Piazza**, the first public Venetian bank, is set up. The second, the **Banco Giro** (or Banco del Giro), is created in 1619 (🔗 *see RIALTO*).

1588 — The Rialto Bridge is rebuilt in stone.

1593 — The fortress of Palmanova is built, designed in the form of a nine-pointed star to defend

The Battle of Lepanto by Michieli (Palazzo Ducale)

Palazzo Ducale, Venezia /SCALA

Paradise Replaces the Coronation of the Virgin

In 1365 the Chamber of the Great Council was decorated with the fresco by Guariento (recorded 1338-70), representing *The Coronation of the Virgin*. After the fire, it was decided to "remake Paradise as it was before". After a first competition, won by Veronese and Bassano who, however, never executed the work, a second competition was held and the commission entrusted to Tintoretto, author of the immense *Paradise*.

the eastern borders against the Turks and Habsburgs. To commemorate the victory at the Battle of Lepanto, the foundation stone is laid down on 7 October.

1599-1604 — The **River Po**, which deposits huge quantities of sediments around Chioggia, is diverted towards Goro.

1600 — Once again, the city of Venice is flooded at high tide.

ANOTHER INTERDICT

In order to understand the relationship that existed between Venice and the Holy See, it is useful to note what the Venetians, who held themselves to be "first Venetian and then Christian", used boldly to claim: "We believe fully in St Mark, sufficiently in God and not at all in the Pope".

The Pope did not readily accept the right to religious freedom that Venice granted the Protestants. In 1605 the denunciation before the Council of Ten of two priests, accused of various crimes, proved to be the last straw. The Pope maintained that the two should have been handed over to the ecclesiastical authorities. On the Venetian side was a Servite priest, **Paolo Sarpi**, whose arguments appeared heretical to Rome. When the Pope threatened an interdict and excommunicated Venice, the city responded: "Your excommunication we regard as nothing and we care not a fig about it."

The interdict lasted for one year. Although the relationship between Venice and the Vatican normalised, Paolo Sarpi became the victim of an assassination attempt in 1607. Recovered from his wounds and surveying the dagger with which he had been stabbed, he is said

to have declared: "I recognise the style of the Roman Church."

1609 — **Galileo Galilei** presents the telescope to the doge.

1613-17 — After raids by the **Uskoks**, pirates from Bosnia and Turkish Dalmatia protected by the Habsburgs, Venice goes to war over Istria and Friuli, which results in the Uskoks being deported to central Croatia.

1618 — Spain instigates a complex conspiracy against Venice. The Council of Ten intervenes decisively as usual: one of the participants is sewn into a sack and thrown into the sea; another two are hung upside down on the gallows of the Piazzetta.

1622 — **Antonio Foscarini**, the illustrious senator and ambassador to France and England, is found guilty of spying. He is condemned to death and succumbs to the usual treatment of being hung by one foot in the Piazzetta. Some time later, it is revealed that the accusations against Foscarini were false. The man who had spread these accusations is tried by the Three (👉 *see above: 1539*) and condemned to death. Venice makes public admission of her grave error. A state declaration is sent to his family and to embassies, and copies are pasted around the city.

1628-30 — Following the death of Ferdinand of Gonzaga, Mantua is claimed both by the French, led by Charles of Gonzaga-Nevers, and the

Habsburgs. It is under siege from German troops when Venice intervenes: the city is nevertheless lost to the French. Mantua is savagely ransacked as the **plague** ravages the region, decimating the local population and Germans, before spreading to Venice. In little more than a year, the Serenessima loses 50 000 inhabitants. When at last the contagion subsides, construction is begun on the Church of Santa Maria della Salute in fulfilment of a vow.

THE SULTAN'S HAREM AND THE WAR OF CANDIA (CRETE)

The Knights of Malta habitually committed acts of piracy of which Venice disapproved because they were detrimental to her relationship with the East. In 1644 the Knights attacked a Turkish galleon in the Aegean and captured part of the Sultan's harem. The Sultan avenged himself not by attacking Malta, but Candia – Crete was then known by the name of its capital – convinced that the Venetians were behind this act.

The war dragged on for over 20 years, despite the Turkish fleet having suffered a naval defeat, second only to Lepanto, in 1656. Finally, Captain **Francesco Morosini**, backed by 3 600 men, signed the surrender in 1699, with which Venice lost the island.

1684-99 — Francesco Morosini, the ally of Austria and Russia, reconquers the Peloponnese peninsula, thereby acquiring the nickname "the Peloponnesian". Unfortunately, during this military operation, a Venetian mortar is fired at the Parthenon which, being used by the Turks to store their reserves of gunpowder, is severely damaged. He is elected doge in 1688. In 1699, although the former Venetian territories had not all been reclaimed, the Treaty of Carlowitz tempo-

rarily checks Turkish military campaigns.

18C AND DECLINE

Although in decline, when faced with a choice between alliance and independence, Venice once again opted for autonomy by refusing to side either with France or the Habsburgs in conflict for two centuries.

1714-18 — Venice loses the Peloponnese forever in a final battle against the Turks, sealed by the **Treaty of Passarowitz**, signed in 1718. She maintains possession of Istria, Dalmatia, the Ionian islands and a few territories in Albania.

1744-82 — The *Murazzi* (protective wall around the lagoon) is built at Pellestrina and Sottomarina, 14m/46ft wide and 4.5m/14ft 8in higher than the average level of the tide. It is made with Istrian stone and pozzolana, a type of volcanic dust which has remarkable binding qualities when mixed with water, sand and lime.

1784 — The Procurator **Andrea Tron**, nicknamed *el Paron* (the Leader) for his strong personality and political standing, which most citizens regarded as above the doge, laments that *"there are no shades of our old merchants among the citizens or subjects"* before the spread of *"weakness of character, overwhelming luxury, idle shows and presumptuous entertainment and vice"* in Venice.

1784-86 — These are the years of the final naval incursions. Admi-

The Libro d'Oro

The Golden Book, first drawn up in the 16C, was the register of the civil status of Venetian nobility. Specific conditions for entry had to be fulfilled. Whoever was not high-born, and thus not inscribed, could not hold a government office.

ral **Angelo Emo** wages battles against pirates along the North African coast.

A BREAK WITH TRADITION AND THE DEMISE OF THE REPUBLIC

1789 — The last doge to be elected, **Ludovico Manin**, ironically is the first not to be born of the old Venetian nobility, but of an émigré family from Friuli that had paid 100 000 ducats for inclusion in the **Golden Book** in 1651.

1792 — The opera house reopens as **La Fenice**.

Before the decline of Venice, the city still shows consideration for its fragile lagoon. It defines a series of boundaries referred to as the "lagoon perimeter", inside which it was forbidden to carry out any activity that might endanger the natural habitat of the lake.

1797 — **Napoleon** invades Venetian territory in 1796 while pursuing his Austrian enemy and successfully ejecting it from Italy – a possession he only maintains by posting troops in Verona and controlling access to the Brenner Pass. A temporary pact is made with the Austrians at Leoben (18 April 1797). This is ratified six months later on 18 October by the **Treaty of Campoformio** signed by Francis II, Emperor of Austria, and Napoleon Bonaparte. It confirms that Austria renounces her claim over Belgium and Lombardy to take possession of the Veneto as far as the Adige, Friuli, Istria, Dalmatia, the Po Valley and the islands in the Adriatic. France takes the Albanian coast and the Ionian islands. Venice is left with the former Papal States of Romagna, Ferrara and Bologna.

Venice's fate, in effect, is sealed by her resistance to ally

The dogal "corno" (Museo Correr)

Muso Correr, Venezia/SCALA

herself to Napoleon. Not only does she show no remorse when anti-French feeling is stoked by the clergy during Easter week to the point of vicious rioting in Verona (a Venetian dominion), but she positively congratulates her officers for firing at a French patrol in the Adriatic and killing the French crew. Napoleon's exasperation is documented: *"I will have no more Inquisition, no more Senate. I shall be an Attila to the State of Venice"*.

Without the reassurance of Venice's recapitulation, the government would have to be seized and war would be inevitable. The Senate meets for the last time on 29 April. By Friday 12 May, Napoleon's demands have to be conceded and the Great Council meets for a last, very tense sitting. A provisional government is approved by an "unconstitutional" Council falling short of its quorum of 600 by 63, many members having fled to their country estates on terra firma. Laying down the *cufieta*, the bonnet worn by the doge under his crown, Ludovico Manin turned with dignity to his servant: *"Take it away, I will have no further use for this"*.

AFTER THE FALL

1805 — With the Treaty of Presburg, Napoleon formally reclaims Venice as part of the Kingdom of Italy.

1815 — The Congress of Vienna establishes that Venice, the Veneto and Lombardy should belong to Austria.

1821 — The Italians show unrest caused by the failed attempts to achieve unification. Anti-Austrian movements break out.

1839-53 — Construction of the north and south dikes at Malamocco is completed.

1841 — The railway bridge linking Venice to Mestre is built.

1844 — The patriot founders of the secret organisation Esperia, Attilio and Emilio Bandiera, together with a sympathiser, Domenico Moro, are shot at Cosenza.

1847 — The lawyer **Daniele Manin** and the writer **Niccolò Tommaseo** are awarded prizes by the 11th Congresso degli Scienziati.

1848 — Daniele Manin is nominated President of the Republic of St Mark and begins reorganising a provisional government, before leading an insurrection against the Austrians supported by Niccolò Tommaseo. Both eminent men are subsequently exiled.

1854-58 — Identical iron bridges are built near the Accademia and the station.

1866 — After the Prussian defeat of the Austrians at Sadowa, Venice votes to be part of a unified Italy by a majority of 674 426 to 69.

1895 — The **International Biennale of Art** is founded. Exhibition facilities are expanded through the 19C with the erection of various modern pavilions.

1902 — The bell-tower of St Mark's collapses.

1915-18 — Venice suffers several bomb attacks but her misfortunes are not caused only by the war: once again the city is flooded by the rising waters.

1932 — First International Film Festival.

1933 — Inauguration of the Ponte Littorio, now called the Ponte della Libertà.

1953 — Giuseppe Roncalli is appointed Patriarch of Venice before being elected **Pope John XXIII** and instigating the Second Vatican Council.

1953-69 — Architect **Frank Lloyd Wright** (1869-1959) plans a student centre, the Masieri Memorial, to be built along the Grand Canal. In 1964 **Le Corbusier** (1887-1965) proposes designs for the Civil Hospital. **Louis Kahn** (1901-74) undertakes a project for a new Congress Hall. None of these undertakings sees the light of day.

1966 — During November the high tide rises to an alarming level. The waters flood the *Murazzi* at Pellestrina and reach many of the city houses.

1969 — Albino Luciani, Patriarch of Venice, is elected Pope in 1978, assuming the name **John Paul I**, which he bore for little more than a month.

THE LAGOON LIVES ON

If the glory of Venice belongs to a bygone era, its lagoon provides a continuous link with the past, preserving a quality and style of life unique to its shores, regardless of the threat of subsidence or flooding. In 1925 alone, the Piazza San Marco, the "salon of Venice", was flooded eight times. Since then it has succumbed to inundation on a further 50 occasions.

Pollution, today's worst enemy

The 20C was the era of industrialisation. Marghera was created in the 1920s and, after the Second World War, the areas taken up by industrial activity expanded quite considerably. Oil was known to seep into the canal, threatening the ecological balance of the lagoon, whose precarious state was further endangered by the draining of land to build industrial areas and Marco Polo Airport.

Between 1950 and 1970, the waste turned out by refineries and by chemical and metallurgical factories at **Porto Marghera** would often end up in the lagoon. During the 1980s a number of purification plants were set up nearby and they now recycle an estimated 80% of the area's industrial refuse. Pollution, caused by excessive amounts of nitrogen and phosphates, chemical fertilisers and insecticides, and organic substances generated by industrial complexes and urban communities, destroys part of the lagoon flora and fauna, encourages the proliferation of algae and stunts that of the phanerogamic species, whose roots are extremely useful, since they prevent the onslaught of erosion.

1973 — The Italian State declares that the preservation of Venice is of "pre-eminent national interest".

1988-92 — The MoSE prototype, a huge mobile sluice-gate devised to regulate the movement of the tides, is installed in the lagoon waters on an experimental basis.

1996 — The opera house **La Fenice** burns down on 29 January.

2001 — Approval is given for the completion of the mobile tide barriers designed to protect the city.

2003 — The reconstructed La Fenice opens to the public.

Unique to Venice

The inhospitable nature of the lagoon, from which Venice sprung up as if by magic, has demanded of the Vene-

Distinguishing Between Canals and Rivers

Although all Venetian waterways tend to be called canals, only three real canals exist in the city: Canal Grande, Canale della Giudecca and Canale di Cannaregio. Canals, which are wider, are tributaries of the lagoon, whereas the narrow rivers *(rii)* can be compared to streets: they are not linked to the sea and wend their way across the city along a sinuous, meandering course. The only exception is the Cannaregio *sestiere,* as any plan of Venice will show.

Whittling a new gondola

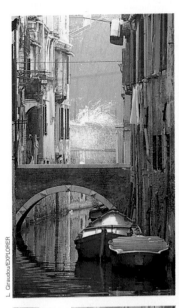

L. Giraudou/EXPLORER

B. Juge/MICHELIN

S. Fiore/EXPLORER

B. Morandi/MICHELIN

F. Alain/EXPLORER

E. Zane/MICHELIN

R. Mattes/MICHELIN

tians an extraordinary ability to adjust to a particular lifestyle implemented through a rare spirit of initiative. To combat the waters, either too high or too low, and to make their way around the myriad islands, the Venetians built the gondola and hundreds of bridges; they also planted thousands of poles.

THE GONDOLA

No one knows exactly when the gondola was invented: the word *gundula* appears as early as 1094 in a decree of Doge Vitale Falier, although the reference relates to a massive boat equipped with a large crew of rowers – a far cry from the gondola we know today.

In the 14C, small boats covered with a central canopy bore metal decorations on the prow and stern. At the end of the century the vessel began to be made longer and lighter, the prow and stern were raised and the **felze** or cabin was added, affording shelter in bad weather. Some had decorated prows. Others were painted in bright colours and decked with satin, silk and gleaming brass. On the prow and stern stood painted cherubs bearing the coat of arms of the family to which the gondola belonged.

From the 16C, boats were toned down by being painted black: a colour we might judge to be rather funereal, but in Venice red, not black, is the colour of mourning. Today the gondola is about 11m/36ft long, 1.42m/4ft wide and comprises 280 pieces of wood.

Building a gondola

The shipyards where gondolas are built and repaired are called **squeri**. At one time, each of these was allocated primarily to a family from Cadore, the wooden galleried constructions resem-

Draining the Rivers

Local authorities routinely undertake to dry out the city rivers to cleanse the water and restore bridges. It is only then that water depths and the hollowness of the river bed are apparent. Dark and malodorous, the waters tend to collect waste as well as objects that fall in by accident.

Documents relating to this practice can be traced back to the late 13C and the early 14C. It has been established that these dredging operations have been carried out regularly since the 15C to renew the water and facilitate navigation. The main bodies in charge of implementing this work are the Magistratura del Piovego and the Savi alle Acque.

bling alpine houses (👉 see ACCADEMIA: *Squero di San Trovaso*).

The **ferro**, a sabre-toothed projection made of iron placed at the prow and stern, is without doubt the most crucial element of the gondola: implemented initially as a fender to safeguard against knocks, today it serves as a counterweight to the gondoliere, and is used to align the boat around hazards in the narrowest passages. The curved fin is said to echo the dogal *corno* and to symbolise its power over the six **sestieri** or divisions of the city represented by the six serrations. The tooth that "guards" the gondola itself is the Giudecca.

The **forcola** or rowlock, is an intricate piece of carving hewn from walnut, designed as a pivot that allows the oar maximum mobility. The oar is made of well-seasoned beech. But perhaps only the most observant will notice the two

"... a Venetian gondola? That singular conveyance, came down unchanged from ballad times, black as nothing else on earth except a coffin – what pictures it calls up of lawless, silent adventures in the slashing night; or even more, what visions of death itself, the bier and solemn rites and last soundless voyage! And has anyone remarked that the seat in such a bark, the arm-chair lacquered in coffin-black, and dully black-upholstered, is the softest, most luxurious, most relaxing seat in the world?"

Thomas Mann – *Death in Venice*

The paline

bronze sea horses cleating the cords of the seats.

PALINE, DAME AND BRICOLE

Whether travelling by gondola, vaporetto or boat, there is always the risk of running aground. Navigable channels are identified by means of **bricole** – a series of large poles *(pali)* roped together – whereas the entrance to a canal or a junction is indicated by **dame**, which are smaller poles than the *bricole*.

The **paline** are those thin individual poles that project from the water at odd intervals, to which private craft are tethered. They are particularly evocative if painted with coloured swirling stripes, outside some fine building to mark the landing stage of a patrician family in days gone by.

THE BRIDGES

Among the hundreds of Venetian bridges crossed during the tussles of *su e zo per i ponti*, meaning "up and down the bridges" (👤 *see Calendar of Events in Planning Your Trip)*, there are several like the Ponte Chiodo (👤 *see CA'D'ORO*) without railings or parapet, where rival factions such as the Castellani and Nicolotti faced each other during "fist fights" (👤 *see I CARMINI*). Projects for bridges with three arches met with less success (👤 *see Il GHETTO*).

> "The bathing, on a calm day, must be the worst in Europe: water like hot saliva, cigar-ends floating into one's mouth, and shoals of jelly-fish."
>
> Robert Byron – *The Road to Oxiana*, 1937

ART AND CULTURE

The history of architecture, art and culture in general in Venice cannot be divorced from the physical and geographical constraints which, throughout the ages, the Venetians have had to overcome with mastery and ingenuity. The city still bears the stamp of the former Byzantine Empire, but over the years the streets have also succumbed to the influence of Renaissance, Classical and Baroque architecture.

Artists have played a role in forging the atmosphere of the city, while remaining faithful to the Venetian spirit.

Architecture

BUILDING IN VENICE

Houses on piles
The city is not built on water, but in the water. It was built either on sandbanks above the water level, which gave rise to real islands, or on small sandy mounds which had remained at the water's surface.

In either case, great larch or oak **pali** are driven deep through the sand, mud or silt, forming an unstable lagoon floor, to the bedrock of hard clay. These 2-4m/6ft 6in-13ft piles are organised in concentric circles or spirals starting from the outer perimeter of the building to be constructed, at intervals of 60-80cm/24-32in. In this way the piles provide a base onto which a raft-like platform (zattera) of horizontal beams (zatterone) may be secured. To reinforce this wooden floor, it is lined with boulders of **Istrian stone** that provide a solid course for the brick and mortar on which it is possible to build.

The number of piles used can sometimes be considerable: 1 106 657 for the Church of Santa Maria della Salute, and 10 000 for the Rialto Bridge!

Building materials
Unfortunately, since the lagoon offers very little in terms of building materials, it is necessary to import these from other areas.

Most of the **timber** is brought from the Cadore forests and the Balkans. It is used not only for the foundation piles, but also for the frames and ceilings of the houses. Occasionally it is incorporated into masonry walls, not so much as reinforcement but rather as "shock absorbers": this procedure lends greater flexibility to the structure, which resolves some of the problems raised by the instability of the subsoil. **Marble**, used to front façades, is principally sourced from the Euganei Hills (south of Padua) or from Greece. **Istria limestone**, hard, white and marble-like, has the added advantage of being resistant to salt erosion; it is therefore frequently used in Venice for bridge copings and to face palazzi, churches, bell-towers etc. Only **brick**, which in Gothic times lent its charming pink hues to I Frari and many other quaint buildings in Venice, is made on-site from local clay.

Originality
All the houses, palaces and churches that have been erected by the Serenissima through the ages survive on these reinforced, drained, dried and consolidated areas reclaimed from the lagoon. It is almost as if the early Venetians made a pact with the lagoon that they would live with it rather than view it as a problem to be reckoned with. And so from the water rise mists and fogs that swirl and fade again to confer a thousand different moods on the urban landscape: one moment the millpond mirrors a perfect reflection and in another the choppy, churlish surface dissolves the shimmering profile according to whim. The lagoon intensifies the ethereal sunlight to sparkle and glitter and lend a festive air to the city, but it may also invade the landscape with a spirit of melancholy. Water consorts with the changing light and density of the air to exaggerate or deform the delicate stone lacework, the crenellated roof ornaments, the many

recesses, loggias and arcades. However, poetic descriptions of atmosphere are an insubstantial preoccupation in comparison to the physical problems posed by the lagoon: it is rather the remoteness of mainland resources and the instability of the subsoil that preoccupy the Venetian authorities. Initially, it was the cost and transport of building materials that dictated a patron's choice and influenced an architect's design of a private palace or church. Up to the 16C, local brick had been the most obvious raw material available. However, when more sophisticated and reliable forms of transport were discovered, the economic factor became considerably less important. A second major element in the equation was the risk of subsidence. To reduce this threat, houses were erected no more than two or three storeys high, except in the Ghetto, where squat buildings had low ceilings so that the total weight was proportionally less. A constant reminder of instability was the angle at which certain palaces (Palazzo Dario) and bell-towers (Santo Stefano, San Barnaba) inclined, and the regularity with which the quays (Riva degli Schiavoni) and St Mark's Square flooded. Through determination, patience and perseverance in an unpredictable environment, strengthened by a spirit of enterprise and ambitious business acumen, the Venetians learned to construct and embellish their magnificent city. Yet despite everything that has been accomplished and all the expertise acquired, the unpropitious site for this wonderful city means that it will forever be at the mercy of natural forces: the corrosive action of salt and water, and the instability of the lagoon floor.

The Campo

A square provides a point at which all roads, streets and alleys converge. It is at the very heart of community life, where housewives chat and hang out their washing and where children play in the open. It is not to be confused with the **corte**, a closed public courtyard with a single entrance, or with the **cortile**, a private courtyard hidden within a patrician town house.

The *campo*, sometimes dotted with a few trees, is encircled by fine patrician houses, Gothic or Renaissance in style, and blessed with its own church. At its centre, a well might occupy a choice spot. Given that the city was built on salty water and therefore had no natural drinking-water supply, rainwater had to be collected, purified and stored in cisterns that were excavated to a depth of 5-6m/16-20ft. The brick-lined tank collected water through several apertures in the *campo* floor, filtering it through fine river sand. Often the well-head, the **vera da pozzo**, would have been paid for by a patron and would therefore have been sculpted as a work of art.

Domestic architecture

Throughout Venice, with the exception of the Grand Canal, palaces rub shoulders with modest houses. Simply built in pink brick or stone, most of these houses are low in height. A few retain their openwork external staircase, double façade and "double" front entrances: one on the street and one onto the canal with its "water porch". The inner courtyard is modelled on the Roman atrium: shaded in summer and protected from the wind in winter. On the first floor or **piano nobile**, a **portego** runs perpendicular to the main front, from the street, across the internal *cortile*, through the entire width of the house to open out onto a loggia on the canal side.

The **altana** is a veranda built on a tiled roof where typical Venetian high funnel-shaped chimneys, known as *fumaioli*, project; these distinctive features were immortalised by Carpaccio in his paintings. Forever short of space, the Venetians have made clever use of their rooftops by installing these charming terraces to increase their living area. The façades are enhanced with flower-decked balconies, small carved discs, ornamental reliefs and sculpted cornices. Down the side walls, houses with *barbacani* have corbelled projections to support the timber beams of upper floors (Calle del Paradiso).

The lack of space at ground level means that there are very few gardens in Venice, and those that do exist are small, sometimes consisting of a single tree or a few flower tubs, often jealously guarded from the public eye behind high walls.

CRAFTSMANSHIP VALUED

Veneto-Byzantine

The oldest monuments preserved by the Venetian Lagoon are to be found on the island of Torcello: the **Cattedrale di Santa Maria Assunta** and the complex of **Santa Fosca** bear witness to the close ties which once allied Venice with Ravenna, the Western heir to a Byzantine legacy.

For several centuries, Venice, through its conquests and trade links with the East, maintained a close relationship with Greece and Constantinople: the Basilica of St Mark, rebuilt in the 11C, was modelled on the 6C prototype of Byzantium churches, the Church of the Holy Apostles in Constantinople, destroyed in the 13C (the immense and sumptuous Hagia Sophia was built subsequently by the same architect along the same lines). St Mark's therefore directly transposes an expression of the Eastern Church in terms of form, structure, volume and style into the West.

This oriental Christianity was a major force in the fusion of an original "Veneto-Byzantine" style from the late Middle Ages onwards. The artistic iconography, strongly influenced by Byzantium, incorporates Islamic elements (decorative motifs, horseshoe arches), Palaeo-Christian features (*transennae*, capitals) and Roman details from sculpted fragments (marble blocks, column shafts, flat bricks) salvaged from villas along the Adriatic coast that had been destroyed during the barbarian invasions of the 5C and 6C.

Churches

The Byzantine-style churches like Santa Fosca, Torcello Cathedral, Santa Maria e Donato on Murano and St Mark's Basilica, best demonstrate the Eastern influence. This influence is clearly visible in the centrally planned Greek cross church or longitudinal hall church (nave and two aisles) prefixed by a narthex (covered porch which evolved into an arched portico) but independent of a free-standing baptistry (like that at Torcello). Structurally, Byzantium provided the expertise to erect domes over open spaces unencumbered by piers; it inspired the use of precious marble column shafts crowned with variously shaped capitals (basket-shaped, inverted pyramid) and carved ornament (organic decoration such as foliage, symmetrically arranged animals). The practice in Ravenna (12C-13C) of applying decoration in the form of shallow relief, open fretwork, or *niello* (deeply cut engraving) and mosaic with flat gold backgrounds to both internal and external walls, was quick to be emulated by Venetian mosaicists, who copied subjects from the Old and New Testaments. Other features to be accommodated include Palaeo-Christian *transennae* (open-work window screens), *plutei* (marble tablets) and *paterae* encircled within a twisted rope moulding, acanthus leaves and vine leaf tendrils, Palaeo-Christian figurative motifs (gryphons, eagles, peacocks and lions often quoted from embroideries or manuscript illuminations), marble ambos (pulpits before the chancel), and *iconostases* (screens in Greek churches separating the sanctuary from the nave).

The **Romanesque style**, which seems to appear in Venice during the 11C and 12C, is also in its own way modelled upon

The Foreign Merchants of Venice

Venetian trade also benefited from the different cultures brought over by foreign visitors to the city. In those days, a great many nationalities were living side by side, all engaged in commercial activities: Albanians, Armenians, Dalmatians, Jews, Greeks, Persians, Germans and Turks. In this context the storehouse *(fondaco)* played an essential role, as it was used for stocking goods and was seen as the heart of the business community. In Venice, the warehouses belonging to Persian, Turkish and German merchants were particularly active.

A traditional Venetian "altana" where girls used to sit and sunbleach their hair.

A "sottoportego"

An upstairs loggia and famous "fumaiolo" chimney

A carved well-head

The "porta d'acqua" or waterside entrance

Byzantine art. The main forces at play were revived by the Lombard invasion from the northwest and from Ravenna in the south through which the Crusader armies would have passed.

Typical of the Venetian Romanesque style is the external appearance of high, solid, austere walls, pierced with tiny windows, relieved only by simple decoration afforded by blind arcading. The interior featured a raised nave, a vestige of Palaeo-Christian civilisation, and two aisles. Churches were planned as basilicas with a tall nave flanked by side aisles. In simple terms it is a compromise of "Western" Romanesque and "Eastern" Byzantine styles, and it is precisely from this period that Venice's oldest churches survive: San Giacomo (Rialto), San Nicolò dei Mendicoli, San Zan Degolà, San Giacomo dall'Orio and Sant'Eufemia (Giudecca). Although these churches were heavily rebuilt in the following centuries, many have retained their original massive, square, brick **campanile** or bell-tower, articulated with pilasters and blind arcading, capped with a loggia that screens the bells (San Barnaba). Only the roof, added later, differs from the original by being hexagonal, pyramidal or conical in shape. In some cases, the original church has long gone, but the Romanesque tower remains, as at San Zaccaria (♿ *illustration: see SAN ZACCARIA)* and San Samuele. All that survives of the famous 12C Sant'Apollonia monastery is its superb cloisters, a rare vestige of Romanesque architecture.

Domestic buildings

The **Veneto-Byzantine palazzo** is no doubt the most original product of 11C-13C Venetian architecture. Known as the *casa-fondaco* (from the Arabic *funduk*, meaning depository or warehouse), this "storehouse" effectively combines the purpose of storage, commercial office and family home into one compact unit. The best preserved are the Fondaco dei Turchi, Ca' Farsetti, Palazzo Loredan and Ca' Da Mosto (*Ca'* being an abbreviation of *casa*, meaning house).

These houses further testify to the prodigiously rapid growth of the city's merchant aristocracy, empowered and enriched by maritime trade which, in turn, nurtured an interest and appreciation for Eastern Byzantine and Muslim craftsmanship.

As the need for defensive fortifications receded – on a scale seen at the first Doges' Palace – patrician town houses erected in the 11C began to conform to a set type that allowed for an easy and comfortable lifestyle. The structure would remain unchanged for several centuries to come, whereas its applied decoration would evolve according to contemporary taste. Split into three horizontal tiers, the main entrance into the storage or commercial area would have been on the canal side, through the *porta d'acqua*. On the first floor, the *piano nobile*, a continuous gallery or *loggia* would run the length of the façade between two solid walled towers, whereas at the top, a series of decorative crenellations would conceal the roofline. Only later would additional storeys sometimes be added.

Veneto-Byzantine arches have several forms: stilted round-headed arches (narrow arches with their springing line raised), horseshoe arches, Moorish ogee arches and high-pitched pointed "lancet" arches. These arches are often supported by highly prized marble shafts with decorated capitals, bearing Byzantine stylised and/or symmetrical foliage or animals. Further decoration might include Byzantine *paterae* (small carved discs) illustrating real or mythical animals (peacocks, griffins etc) or medallions of different coloured marble, crosses or historical emblems.

Venetian Gothic

The term "Gothic", a label attributed in the 17C to the style developed by the barbarian Goths, assumes a distinctive meaning when applied to Venetian building design from the 1400s. For it is this delicate, ornamental, elegant style that has given the city its most distinctive characteristics and its architectural unity. It graces nearly all the *campi* and houses giving onto the banks of canals, styling a pointed arch or a loggia's filigree stonework. Unlike the structural changes that facilitated a new form of civil engineering in France, England and

Cushion capital, Torcello (9-10C)

Pluteus with peacocks
Torcello Cathedral (11C)

Composite capital, Torcello

Campanile di San Barnaba

Fretwork stone screen
San Alipio door, St Mark's

Patera with Pascal lamb

Germany, Venice merely used the Gothic style to ornament, flatter and decorate her buildings until the late 16C.

Churches

Politically, Venice was reinforcing her strength and autonomy. This prosperity allowed institutions to flourish both in the secular and religious domains, as demonstrated by the large-scale building projects undertaken by the principal monastic communities (I Frari, San Zanipòlo). With time, these were endowed by aristocratic patrons who wished to celebrate and publicise their wealth and standing (Madonna dell'Orto, Santo Stefano), entrusting to the churches their refined funerary monuments.

These were days in which the plague was rapidly spreading and they were characterised by a strong sense of urgency: poverty and charity were preached by the **Mendicant Orders**, and measures were taken to build monasteries and scuole, the characteristic Venetian institutions that sustained their confraternities in exchange for charity. Thus around 1245, with the benediction of **Doge Giacomo Tiepolo**, the Dominicans and Franciscans began erecting the city's most beautiful churches.

Exterior – From the 14C, designers of religious buildings began combining curved and rectilinear features in drafting their façades (San Giovanni in Bragora, I Frari, Scuola Vecchia della Misericordia). Although the structures remained austerely simple, **porches** and **windows** suddenly became encrusted with Gothic features. The severe flat-brick west front was divided into three parts: the central, nave section soared high above the flanking aisles. Plain surfaces were relieved with decorative elements in white Istrian stone: portals were framed with engaged columns and pediments, hood mouldings articulated the gables, a cornice was supported by a frieze of niches that curved around the lateral walls. Only porches made in marble or white Istrian stone carry ornamentation: crowned by recessed arches with acanthus leaf motifs as well as elegant relief decoration such as cable fluting, knot-work and foliage, they are often

flanked by statuettes or engaged columns. At the east end, apses proliferated and extruded to form chevets (I Frari, San Zanipòlo), whereas the tall square pink-brick campanili point skyward with a white marble open loggia (St Mark's, I Frari, Madonna dell'Orto).

Interior – The Gothic church, based on the T-shaped Latin cross to accommodate the long processions required by the liturgy down the nave, was abutted by aisles; at the east end, a wide transept could accommodate a chancel and numerous transept chapels endowed by private patrons (I Frari, San Zanipòlo). Sometimes the internal space was enclosed by a fine open timbered roof built by local shipwrights in the form of an inverted hull (Santo Stefano, San Giacomo dall'Orio) and articulated by arches painted with string-courses of acanthus leaves, or by carved wooden tie-beams.

Domestic buildings

Gothic-fronted palazzi enclose all the campi and line the secondary canals, but the most magnificent examples are to be found along the Grand Canal, which began to resemble a wonderful "triumphal waterway".

Fanciful creativity – The Venetian-Gothic **palazzo** was derived from the Byzantine model, retaining its three main characteristics: portico, loggia and decorative merlons. However, it now assumed a more noble, confident and sophisticated canon of ornamentation, which continued to be implemented until the fall of the Republic. As the patrician families stabilised their social status, they affected changes to their houses, most notably on the piano nobile. The simplicity of the earlier Veneto-Byzantine façades (portico and continuous loggia) was replaced by a centralised, more important arcaded loggia with cusped arches and quatrefoil motifs. In the corner section, single isolated windows interrupt the solid wall area now enhanced by the use of brick and stucco in two-tone colour combinations.

San Giovanni in Brágora

Four-light window of Palazzo Sagredo

*Three-light window
with quatrefoil tracery*

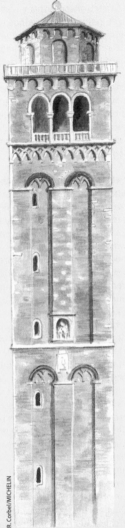

I Frari belltower

Four-light window on Murano

Interior layout – The *palazzo* is traditionally U-shaped in plan: a central block with perpendicular wings extended around a courtyard *(cortile)* with a wellhead. Access to the *piano nobile* would have been via an open external stairway supported on Gothic arches up to a colonnaded portico with wooden architrave (Palazzo Centani). On the first floor, a broad passageway or, if enclosed, a reception hall *(portego)* ran the entire width of the house to open out onto the loggia on the canalside.

Extrovert beauty – Unlike the Florentine *palazzo*, austere, plain and impersonal, the Venetian façade may be seen as an extrovert, openly flaunting its charms to those who walk by. The windows, the eyes that open onto the outside world, are therefore natural vehicles for additional decoration.

Venice is still laden with oriental references both Christian and Muslim, and the characteristic loggias are strongly reminiscent of Palaeo-Christian stone fretwork; windows borrow from their Moorish counterparts a profile that echoes a cusped lancet and the temptation of inserting sculpted Byzantine *paterae* is still too great to resist.

By looking at the windows and their arched profiles, the various phases of Venetian Gothic may be discerned. Curvilinear arches of Moorish influence from the 14C sometimes rest on colonnettes (Corte del Million); early-15C three-cusped, four-light centred arches are often topped with a finial (Palazzo Duodo); late-15C Gothic or High Gothic arches, the most original and varied phase which might be compared with the French Flamboyant, grace the Doges' Palace. Here, one or more rows of quatrefoil oculi surmount the three-cusped arches of the loggias. The Ca' d'Oro, where **Marco d'Amadio**, a member of the **Bon** family, worked from 1421-61, is also expressive of this joyful, endearing exuberance.

Gothic sculpture

As with building, the first notable works of sculpture by known craftsmen date from this period. With **Pier Paolo** and **Jacobello dalle Masegne** (d 1403 and

1409 respectively) a style, explored by the School of Pisa, was evolved out of the static Byzantine tradition towards greater movement and expression, and mixed with a taste for Gothic ornament. Their work combines the use of delicate and complicated architectural elements with figurative statuary (iconostatis at St Mark's).

The Venetian School of Sculpture seemed unable truly to inspire the artistic community. The Serenissima was therefore forced to continue soliciting foreign artists or awarding commissions to craftsmen passing through the city. Following in the footsteps of Pisa, Venice succumbed to the influence of Florentine art, to that of **Niccolò Lamberti** and to Sienese artists such as **Jacopo della Quercia**. **Marco Cozzi**, a remarkable woodcarver from Vicenza, created the splendid wooden chancel in the Church of the Frari, the only example of such work to survive in Venice.

Funerary monuments – The earliest 14C tombs consist of a simple sarcophagus with the recumbent figure of the deceased in front and the figures of the Madonna and Child and saints incorporated at the four corners; above, set into a recessed arch, is a lunette, painted or sometimes sculpted. Later a Gothic baldaquin of stone drapery was added, seemingly suspended in the middle from the ceiling, its drapes drawn aside by figures (angels or warriors). It is in this vein that the Dalle Masegne brothers worked from the 14C to the 15C.

Portals – Almost all the 15C portals that adorn the Venetian churches are attributed to the architect **Bartolomeo Bon** (Santo Stefano, San Zanipòlo, Madonna dell'Orto, I Frari). Each is made of stone or marble to contrast dramatically with the main fabric of the brick building, and each is decorated with a series of hood mouldings and courses of twisted rope with cusps of foliage around the pointed ogee archway; elements are further embellished with acanthus leaves, the gable is surmounted with a free-standing statue, and inside the portal shelter small niches or aedicules. Bartolomeo Bon's unquestionable masterpiece is the elegant Porta della Carta, the main entrance to the Doges' Palace, executed in Flamboyant Gothic.

Venetian Renaissance

The success and popularity of the International Gothic canon was such that it delayed the adoption of Renaissance principles in Venice. However, once introduced, the style quickly took hold and soon graced the traditional structures with a new refined magnificence. During the 1400s, under the patronage of **Doge Francesco Foscari**, the Serenissima's civilisation changed direction: artistic links with Tuscany and Lombardy were strengthened and, after the fall of Constantinople in 1453, ties with the Eastern Empire were severed. Humanism flourished: it drew its inspiration from Hellenistic culture and was enriched by the sagacity of Greek scholars who had fled from Constantinople.

In 1495 the printer **Aldo Manuzio** began publishing the Ancient Greek classics as the city witnessed the divide between **Scuole Grandi** and **Scuole Minori** (☞ see I CARMINI). By the second half of the 15C, Florentine supremacy had dwindled. The new style, which originated from Tuscany, spread throughout Italy thanks to the wandering lifestyle of her artists, and gradually began to display regional characteristics – elements which Venice, in her inimitable fashion, absorbed and interpreted in her own way.

In the beginning

The earliest traces of the **Early Renaissance** are to be found in archways.

The entrance to the Arsenale (1460) survives as the first full expression, complete with its Classical lions, mythological figures and Greek marble columns. Three other examples showing the same characteristics include the portal of San Giobbe, one at the Gesuiti in the Zattere quarter, and the Foscari doorway at the Doges' Palace.

In terms of sculpture, the Florentine masters Donatello and Verrocchio endowed the Serenissima with only two works, both of major importance: an evocative wooden polychrome figure of John the Baptist (1438) at I Frari, and an impressive equestrian monument in bronze of the Condottiere Bartolomeo Colleoni from Bergamo (1458) that now stands in the *campo* in front of San Zanipòlo.

Lombardo dynasty – At the turn of the 15C, the spirit of innovation that was to animate contemporary sculpture and architecture was largely due to the genius and expertise of the **Lombardo family** – from Lombardy as their name clearly implies – and in particular to **Pietro** (1435-1515) and his two sons, **Antonio** and **Tullio**. Seeking to promote a complete re-evaluation of contemporary design and the widespread implementation of the new canon, the Lombardo family fashioned the highly public façade of the Scuola San Marco dominating its prime site, the Church of Santa Maria dei Miracoli and the unusual yet noble Ca' Dario giving onto the Grand Canal. In each case structural and decorative elements (porphyry medallions, marble rosettes) interact to form a perfectly balanced ensemble governed by a harmonious system of proportions.

Stone and marble replace the brick used earlier by Gothic builders. Façades may be asymmetrical, articulated with cornices, sculpted busts, figurative statues, pilasters – fluted or with cartouches of delicate graffiti (Classical reliefs featuring masks, the attributes of the Liberal Arts and the Gods of War) – friezes of vines or festoons of foliage, animals and *putti*.

In the field of sculpture, Pietro Lombardo undertook for San Zanipòlo a series of important and distinguished funerary monuments in Istrian stone to commemorate doges (those of Pietro Mocenigo, Pasquale Malipiero and Nicolò Marcello). Tullio, meanwhile, who worked extensively with his father, is responsible for the fine reliefs set into the front of the Scuola San Marco, and for the monuments to Giovanni Mocenigo and Andrea Vendramin in San Zanipòlo.

The Lombard tradition is reflected in the formal design of such memorials, as shown in the use of the triumphal arch on several levels with superimposed niches housing allegorical statues of the Virtues, acting as a cornice over the sarcophagus. On the other hand, the fine workmanship of the figurines, along with the poise and elegance of their stance, undeniably testify to Tuscan influence.

Mauro Codussi (1440-1504) – This architect from Bergamo, a contemporary of the Lombardo brothers, seemed happier to celebrate the decorative rather than the structural function of architecture and to this end returned to the Tuscan vernacular for inspiration. Despite adhering to the guidelines pronounced by the Humanist Alberti in his treatises on architecture for a Canon of Beauty formulated according to mathematical proportion and harmony of component parts (spatial organisation, symmetrical elevations, correct application of the Classical orders – Doric, Ionic and Corinthian – the use of rustication and niches), Codussi's designs appeared to lack homogeneity. Instead, he forged a personal style distinguished by semicircular pediments for the fronts of churches and the Scuola San Marco, which he completed, rustication on the ground floor of his *palazzi*, engaged columns and cornices to differentiate superior storeys, and circular oculi inserted between the coupled arches of an arcade supported on coupled columns.

His early projects, which included the Clocktower and the Church of San Giovanni Grisostomo, all showed trace elements of Byzantine styling (portico decoration, Greek cross floorplan), whereas his more mature works, the sumptuous *palazzi* Corner Spinelli and Vendramin Calergi on the Grand Canal conformed to his distinctive style. This style developed into an even bolder statement at San Zaccaria and San Michele, his masterpiece, where marble or white Istrian stone were applied across all three carefully articulated sections of the elevation, both on the horizontal and vertical axes; the nave towers over the aisles linked with semicircular pediments, and friezes, shell niches and porphyry roundels provided ornamentation. Two additional designs by Codussi included Santa Maria Formosa and the beautiful Istrian stone campanile of San Pietro di Castello.

Antonio Rizzo – Antonio Rizzo (d 1499) was responsible for the internal (courtyard) façade of the Doges' Palace and the monumental Giant's Staircase faced in marble. Examples of his sculpture included the poised figures of Adam and Eve that once flanked the Foscari arch. He also varied the design of the archetypal funerary monument initiated at I Frari for Doge Nicolò Tron in 1473 by articulating it with five orders up to a semicircular pediment, and ornamenting it with several niches filled with freestanding figures.

Venetian High Renaissance

A heightened Classicism affirms itself only in the 16C, marking a distinctive, second phase of Renaissance design.
Rome, which had displaced Florence, the capital of the arts at the beginning of the previous century, as the seedbed for new ideas, was badly damaged by Charles V's Imperial army which sacked the Holy City in 1527. From 1530, Venice established herself as the model city of Italy. For a short period, she basked in the limelight, implementing a new Classicism that soon, alas, degenerated into Mannerism.
Arcaded porticoes proliferated at ground level with ever bigger openings, supporting ordered storeys above. Imposing *palazzi* with carefully articulated lines are rusticated the entire length of the ground floor, punctuated by large centrally planned openings and ornamented with masks. For the *piano nobile*, rectangular windows, framed with fluted or coupled columns, are pedimented with circular or triangular tympana in symmetrical formation; projecting balustraded balconies add to the sculptural effect. Below the entablature, the rhythm is maintained by a series of small oval apertures.

Sansovino, master of the Classical style – The Florentine-born Jacopo Tatti, known as Sansovino (1486-1570), an accomplished sculptor and architect, was responsible for introducing to Venice a Classical canon of design

Scuola di San Marco, front design
by the Lombardo family and Codussi

The funerary monument to
Doge Pietro Mocenigo
by Pietro Lombardo at San Zanipòlo

San Zaccaria façade
by Codussi

The Marciana Library by Sansovino

formulated from the Antique. Seeking refuge in Venice after the Sack of Rome (1527), where he had been apprenticed to Bramante and Raphael, Sansovino succeeded Bartolomeo Bon as *proto* or Chief Architect to St Mark's. He was thus entrusted with the Serenissima's ambitious plans for reconstruction and embellishment, beginning with the reorganisation of the Piazza San Marco. He drafted designs for the new Library, its portico based on an archaic model, the Fabbriche Nuove in the Rialto, Palazzo Corner della Ca' Granda on the Grand Canal, the elegant loggia at the foot of St Mark's campanile (for which he also produced the bronze statues and low-relief panels), the heavily rusticated, Tuscan-inspired Palazzo della Zecca, the imposing but incomplete Scuola Nuova della Misericordia and the Golden Staircase. Robust, but not overly austere, his initial projects (including Ca' Granda) show Sansovino completely at ease with the traditional Venetian vernacular style (buildings around the Piazza San Marco and the Piazzetta), enriching his Classical forms with original and majestic ornament; decorative detailing encrusts the portico arches and enhances the flat surfaces, whereas statuary, low-relief panels and festoons add a touch of fantasy and convey a vivid sense of movement.

To affirm Sansovino's brilliance as a sculptor, one need but cite the figures of Mars and Neptune that grace the Giant's Staircase and the highly expressive John the Baptist in I Frari – they speak for themselves.

Grandiose domestic buildings – At this time, the Grand Canal assumed its claim to be a true "triumphal way" fronted by ever more elegant and ennobled patrician houses.

Veronese Sanmicheli (1484-1559), having served his apprenticeship under Sansovino, earned recognition for his military projects (Fortress of Sant'Andrea on the Lido) and for his design of the Palazzo Corner Mocenigo in the San Polo *sestiere* and the Palazzo Grimani on the Grand Canal.

Andrea Palladio (1508-80) – Late in the 16C, the architect Andrea Palladio, a Paduan by birth, moved to Venice. He had established his reputation by designing villas in the Brenta Valley. His distinctive style, which is characterised by a balanced sense of proportion and formulated from a profound appreciation of Classical architecture, was applied to buildings that were designed to suit their purpose, their site and, most importantly, were practical to inhabit. Encouraged by the Humanist Trissino, Palladio visited Rome on several occasions to study Classical architecture in the context of theories outlined by Vitruvius (1C BC). In 1570, he published his theories based on observation in a treatise entitled *I Quattro Libri di Architettura (The Four Books on Architecture)*. This grand opus was to have far-reaching consequences in the spreading of Classicism to the rest of Europe.

The essential principle of this "modern" Classicism is structural simplicity, achieved with the use of basic geometrical volumes of space (cube, sphere and pyramid) and symmetry. Designs for building elevations conform to the same rules, with a façade having a central portico (San Giorgio Maggiore). Palladio received commissions, in particular from the Serenissima's important and wealthy patrician families with estates in the hinterland (La Malcontenta on the Brenta). These variations on the villa design provide a new canon for informal domestic buildings that reflects both their function as country retreats and their location: besides boasting pure Classical form and a sound knowledge of decoration as well as gardening, these houses blend in perfectly with the surrounding landscape. The scenery may therefore be enjoyed from the house and the house may be admired as a point of interest punctuating and enhancing the scenery. This consideration was later explored and developed in garden design by the 18C English exponents of Palladianism (Campbell, Burlington, Kent, Adam, Capability Brown and the like). Palladio based many of his villas on Antique pagan temples; only the domestic buildings have forsaken

La Malcontenta by Palladio

The façade of San Moisé designed by Tremignon

monumentality for utilitarian considerations.

In Venice itself, Palladio's sense of austerity and perfect harmony is reflected in his magnificent churches: San Giorgio Maggiore, Il Redentore, le Zitelle, San Francesco della Vigna. Recurring features in his architecture are long, slender engaged columns, Corinthian capitals, triangular pedimented porticoes borrowed from Roman temples, huge domes thrown into contrast by symmetrically arranged geometrical forms; whereas inside, the enclosed space is airy and light.

After Palladio's death, Vincenzo Scamozzi saw a number of his master's projects to completion, ensuring the final effect was true to Palladio's vision, and thereby consolidating his reputation.

Vincenzo Scamozzi (1552-1616), born in Vicenza, also inherited Sansovino's projects for the redevelopment of the Piazza San Marco and erected the Procuratie Nuove (1586) modelled on the Classical example proffered by the former Library nearby. What is new, however, is the interplay of decorative elements that pre-empt the advent of the Baroque. Also by Scamozzi is the Palazzo Contarini degli Scrigni on the Grand Canal.

Lo Scarpagnino completed the Fondacco dei Turchi and the Scuola di San Rocco initiated by Bartolomeo Bon. His style echoes that of Codussi (openings on the ground floor) although now there is a greater sense of movement and dramatic contrast, achieved in part by the use of free-standing columns that project from the façade. He was also involved in the rebuilding of the Palazzo dei Dieci Savi and the Fabbriche Vecchie in the Rialto district.

Spavento began the Classical façade onto the small Senators' courtyard of the Doges' Palace, while Guglielmo dei Grigi, better known by his epithet **il Bergamasco**, was working on the Palazzo Papadopoli and the Palazzo Camerlenghi on the Grand Canal.

High Renaissance Sculpture

Together with Palladio and Sansovino, the third important figure to import the artistic spirit of Michelangelo to Venice

was **Alessandro Vittoria** (1525-1608). Famous for his austere and dignified portraits, Vittoria sculpted two lively representations of St Jerome, now at San Zanipòlo and I Frari. He demonstrated further skills in the art of applied decoration by executing the stucco ceiling of the Libreria Vecchia and the fine gilded coffered vault of the Golden Staircase in the Doges' Palace.

Other artists of note working during the 1500s include **Lorenzo Bregno**, to whom several funerary monuments are attributed (including that of Benedetto Pesaro) and the high altar at I Frari; **Girolamo Campagna** (bronze figures – I Frari and Correr Museum); **Tiziano Aspetti** (bronzes in Correr Museum, statues of Hercules and Atlantes flanking the Golden Staircase) and **Andrea Riccio** (bronzes in Correr Museum).

Venetian Baroque

Throughout the 17C the predilection for the Classical style was underpinned by the continued popularity of Palladian design. As a result, Venetian Baroque is more tempered than it ever was in Rome or elsewhere.

Baldassare Longhena (1598-1682) – This architect and sculptor is both the instigator and leading representative of Baroque art in the City of the Doges. His lasting legacy was to inspire a taste for stone and a solemn architectural language which, some say, verges on the whimsical. It is essentially Classical in inspiration but with charged ornamentation, frequently copied from the Antique.

His undoubted masterpiece is the Church of the Salute. It is also the most eloquent embodiment of this peculiarly Venetian strain of Baroque: it exudes confidence and an air of triumph with its vast proportions, towering dome, sense of movement conveyed by modillions featuring curved scrolls, and crowds of angels and prophets.

Charged with designing the finest Baroque *palazzi* along the Grand Canal, Longhena turned to Sansovino for inspiration. He endowed both Ca' Rezzonico and Ca' Pesaro with grand entrances, heavily rusticated ground floors, superimposed orders of tall windows deeply recessed into archways, separated by large columns and richly ornamented with masks. Particular emphasis is given to the *piano nobile,* with sharply defined architectural elements such as cornices, balustraded balconies, and dramatically sculpted *putti* or coats of arms. A similar boldness marks his high altars and commemorative monuments, of which perhaps the most exuberant is the sepulchre of Doge Giovanni Pesaro at I Frari.

After Longhena – Following the death of Longhena, the completion of his main projects was supervised by **Antonio Gaspari** (Ca' Pesaro) and **Giorgio Massari** (Ca' Rezzonico) (1687-1766), possibly Venice's greatest architect in the first half of the 18C. The remarkably exuberant ornamentation (deeply cut garlands of fruit, niches, entablatures, pediments, fluted columns, crowning statuary) is evidenced in the Church dell'Ospedalletto with its great and ponderous atlantes. The three churches designed by **Sardi**, a collaborator of Longhena, are Santa Maria del Giglio, which houses depictions of naval battles and is planned like a military fortress, Gli Scalzi and San Salvador. Two other Baroque churches are San Moisé by Tremignon (1668) and San Stae. Among the bell-towers are those of Santa Maria Formosa and All Saints.

The architect responsible for the great Church of the Gesuati (18C) is **Domenico Rossi**, who also designed its splendid white and green marble decoration imitating huge draperies falling into heavy folds. In contrast, the interior ceilings painted by **Giambattista Tiepolo** attain an unchallenged brilliance and lightness more often associated with Rococo. In sculpture, however, perhaps the main representative of the Venetian Baroque is the Flemish artist **Juste Le Court**, whose works include altar fronts, allegorical figures and panels of low relief (Santa Maria del Giglio).

Neo-Classicism

During the 18C, Venice improved her image by erecting new buildings and remodelling a number of existing ones.

In counter-reaction to the Baroque, the city reverted to a pure form of Classicism that was to be labelled neo-Classicism – well before any revival had taken hold anywhere else in Europe. The emergence of rational thinking during the Age of Enlightenment had affected all disciplines, including architecture, and given birth to a novel trend dubbed neo-Classicism. One of the advocates of this new style was a Venetian Franciscan, **Carlo Lodoli**, who claimed *"only that which has a definite function or is born out of absolute necessity is worthy of existing in architecture"*; and so artists turned to Antiquity for inspiration. Simple arcading, domes and pronaoi (projecting vestibules fronted with columns and pediments) grace monumental *palazzi* and churches. The linearity of each structural element is clearly defined and elaborate schemes for interior decoration are replaced by plain, simple arrangements based on the Palladian or the Baroque model. The buildings that best illustrate this trend are the Palazzo Grassi by Massari and the Napoleon Wing enclosing the Piazza San Marco.

The architects **Andrea Tirali** (1660-1737), **Scalfarotto**, **Visentini** and **Temanza** all implemented a neo-Classical style founded on simple form and basic geometry derived from Palladio (including the use of the pronaos); a sense of grandeur was imparted from **Giovanni Battista Piranese** (1720-78), the Venetian-born architect and engraver who studied Roman civilisation and published the famous *Carceri d'Invenzione* (c 1745).

Tirali employed neo-Classical principles in designing the façade of the Church of the Tolentini, endowing it with a large pronaos and Corinthian columns, a design that was to be inspirational later for other buildings. Other neo-Classical monuments of note include the Church of San Simeone Piccolo, erected in 1720 by Scalfarotto on a circular plan, with a gigantic porch copied from that of the Tolentini, and reached up a massive staircase. Unfortunately it is somewhat overwhelmed by the gigantic green dome and **Temanza**'s Church of the Maddalena, also built on a circular plan that is crowned by a great dome, but with a foreshortened pronaos.

Perhaps the figure who dominates the artistic output of the period, however, is **Giorgio Massari** (1686-1766), from whom we have inherited such grandiose statements as the Gesuati Church on the Zattere with its Palladian façade, the Church of the Pietà, and the main door of the Accademia (1760).

Antonio Canova (1757-1822) – The last great personality in the Serenissima's illustrious history of art is Canova who, in many ways, embodies the very essence of neo-Classicism in sculpture. Highly esteemed by his patrons at home and by Napoleon, Canova left the Republic to work in Rome and Paris, where the spirit of the style was distilled into painting by Jacques-Louis David, another imperial protégé.

His work exudes great purity and sensitivity. The velvety polish imparted to the white marble – his favourite material – together with the fluid compositions and elegant forms, in which line rather than texture is emphasised, combine to suggest fragile sensuality. Venice still retains a series of low reliefs in the style of the Antique and the famous group of *Daedalus and Icarus* (Correr Museum). His grandiose memorial can be visited in I Frari: it was executed by pupils and lies opposite the monument he designed for Titian.

From eclectic to modern times

The second half of the 19C was dominated by an eclectic assortment of revivalist styles in architecture: neo-Byzantine (Hotel Excelsior on the Lido, 1898-1908), neo-Romanesque, and most especially neo-Gothic (Pescheria by Rupolo, 1907, Palazzo Cavalli-Franchetti by Camillo Boito, 1895); the curious Mulino Stucky on the Guidecca (1883), remodelled in the International Gothic canon, has high walls punctuated by a spired corner tower.

Since then, no particular trend has dominated Venice: only a few isolated personalities have had interesting projects built, now well integrated into the urban landscape. These include the residential districts around Sant' Elena from the 1920s, the railway station (1954) and the Savings Bank designed by Pier Luigi Nervi and Angelo Scattolin on Campo Manin (1968). Certain projects drafted by well-known personalities never got beyond the drawing board: a student hostel by the American Frank Lloyd Wright intended to stand on the Grand Canal (1953) and a public hospital by Le Corbusier (1964).

The area that accommodates the Biennale provides space for various contemporary experimental projects. Even if the gardens where the pavilions are built are dismissed as part of the urban environment, it is worth acknowledging the more original and obsolete: Hoffman's Austrian Pavilion (1933), the Venezuelan designed by Carlo Scarpa (1954) and the Finnish by Alvar Aalto (1956).

The most famous 20C Venetian sculptor is **Arturo Martini** (1889-1947).

Daedalus and Icarus by Canova (Museo Correr)

S Grandadam - Ag.: EXPLORER

Art

VENETIAN PAINTING

Venice's pictorial tradition has one constant: its profound sensuality achieved by a predilection for colour and for light, which lends a strong poetic touch to the landscape. It is an art that mirrors the personality of the lagoon city as a watery world where everything is suffused with light: the blur of the skyline, the shimmering volumes, the haze rising above the canals that adds a bluish tinge to the scene. It is this distinctive greyish light, opaque and iridescent at the same time, that inspired the artists of the 18C.

Mosaics

The art of mosaic, inherited from the Romans, came to the lagoon long before the art of painting. In the 12C and 13C, Venice, inspired by the art of Ravenna, proceeded to arrange the mosaic murals from Torcello *(Last Judgement),* Murano and St Mark's Basilica. After the fall of Constantinople in 1204, Greek decorators and mosaic artists came to Venice to work on the great Golden Altarpiece and the mosaics in St Mark's. Consequently, the biblical iconography of the Eastern Church became markedly oriental, with Christ featuring as the central character (central apse), opening and closing a story which unfolded along walls, arches and cupolas, thus observing established biblical chronology (*see PIAZZA SAN MARCO).*

The use of mosaic continued throughout the city's history. The very last ones to grace San Marco were executed over a rather long period running from the 16C to the 19C. The assumption that early mosaics were more impressive can be explained by the simple fact that artisans were unable to arrange the small pieces of glass in a regular fashion: the myriad uneven surfaces lent "flexibility" to the mural. This effect was enhanced by the light, which caught irregularities, acting as a kaleidoscope of twirling colours and reflections. If all the pieces were aligned on a perfect flat plain, the effect would be dull and lifeless.

Quattrocento Primitives

A few artists began to paint in fresco in the 13C, a process that involves applying pigment to small sections of wet lime-plaster. Paintings from this period, however, if they have survived, are all badly damaged. As regards the style of these first Venetian frescoes, they soon conformed both in design and subject matter to Byzantine iconography, drawn for the most part from portable devotional icons typical of the Eastern Church, where the Madonna and Child usually occupy pride of place.

Paolo Veneziano

This artist, also known as Paolo da Venezia (active 1333-58), emerged as the first distinctive personality in Venetian painting, his name appearing with that of his son Giovanni on a *Coronation of the Virgin* (now in the Frick Collection in New York). Working in the Byzantine tradition, his painting showed him moving away from archaic stylisation (gold backgrounds, flat and confrontational compositions, hieratic attitudes) towards greater decorative refinement and distinctive use of line. This freedom of expression and sensitive treatment of Western subject matter forestalled the evolution of the International Gothic style characterised by graceful movement and elegant form. The work of **Lorenzo Veneziano**, traced to the years 1356-72, is characterised by expressive faces, vigorous bodies and a subtle use of strong, bold colours. (Note: these painters were not actually related; the epithet *Veneziano* simply means Venetian.)

Venetian International Gothic

At the beginning of the 15C, the work of **Gentile da Fabriano** and **Pisanello** and that of the Paduan **Guariento**, who were engaged in painting a cycle of frescoes in the Doges' Palace (destroyed by fire in the 16C), marks the city's endorsement of the "International Gothic". This was a refined, bejewelled style that combined Tuscan elements already assimilated in Padua (derived from sculpted Antique decoration on the one hand and by Giotto's cycle of frescoes in the Scrovegni Chapel on the other) with a more courtly style practised in Ferrara (notably portraiture).

The stimulus provided by these two influences blended with the local, Venetian predilection for naturalism, elegant linearity, fluid movement and strong decorative appeal (even the gold-embroidered and brocade clothing is celebrated) led to a distinctive regional style akin to the International Gothic that flourished in Siena, Prague and Avignon.

Other painters worthy of note include **Nicolò di Pietro** (recorded 1394-1430), **Jacobello del Fiore** (recorded 1394-1439), a pupil of Gentile da Fabriano who practised a detailed and intricate style, and, most especially, **Michele Giambono** (recorded 1420-62) who produced highly refined works in which Eastern oriental influence can be felt (*St Crisogono* – San Trovaso, *St Michael* – Accademia).

A new pictorial tradition

By the mid-15C, attempts at perspective are reflected in the portrayal of floors and ceilings; depth of field is suggested in the background by landscape scenes or buildings.

The first hint of the Renaissance is to be found in the works of the **Vivarini** family from Murano. The shift in emphasis comes with the break of the generations: the earlier pictures have the same quality as Gothic goldsmithery and are markedly influenced by Byzantine iconography. These pictures are by the father, **Antonio** (active 1441-50), who worked with his brother-in-law, **Giovanni d'Alemagna** (*Triptych with Madonna and Child with Saints* – Accademia; polyptychs – San Zaccaria), and his brother **Bartolomeo** (*Triptych of St Mark* – I Frari). If these are compared with works by the son **Alvise**, however, the latter's awareness of the Renaissance becomes evident (*St Anthony of Padua* – Correr Museum; *Triumph of St Ambrose* – I Frari; *Christ Carrying the Cross* – San Zanipòlo). Strangely, in the following generation, **Marco Basaiti** (1470-1530), a pupil of Alvise Vivarini, is decidedly backward-looking in his delicate treatment of landscape and use of colour (*Vocation of the Sons of Zebedee* – Accademia).

Serenity in Early Renaissance Painting

Long after the flowering of the Renaissance in Florence in the early 1400s, during the latter half of the century, Venice's artists turned their attention to defining three-dimensional space and volume, and to an improved articulation of landscape and topographical views. They also gave up the abstract use of gold background and the Gothic taste for overly decorated and complicated pictures.

Bellini family

First Jacopo, the father (d 1470), followed by his two sons, Gentile and Giovanni, managed to emancipate Venetian painting from Byzantine and Gothic influences. The actual founder of the Venetian School is probably **Giovanni Bellini** (1430-1516), also known as Giambellino, who admired Florentine painting for its pure, idealised forms, and Flemish painting for its clarity in terms of light and observed realism. He was markedly influenced by his master and brother-in-law, the Paduan-born **Andrea Mantegna** (1431-1506), who settled and worked in Venice. Mantegna was fascinated by Roman Antiquities which were commonly traded in Padua at the time, an interest acquired from his adoptive father, the painter-archaeologist Squarcione. From his study of relief carving, Mantegna forged a bold style that is completely uncompromising to the point of coldness, where perspective is almost obsessively defined, and details are drawn with scientific precision (*St Sebastian* – Accademia).

His style was, however, in some ways tempered by the example of **Antonello da Messina** who worked in Venice c 1475-76 (*Pietà* – Correr Museum) after learning to use oil paints in Flanders. Giovanni adopted this medium and developed his own deeply sensitive style that is characterised by a playful suggestion of light, a delicate and harmonious use of colour, elegant rendering of form and a strong sense of realism derived from Mantegna. Landscape

St Michael
by Michele Giambono
(Accademia)

St Augustine
by Bartolomeo Vivarini
(San Zanipòlo)

St Sebastian
by Mantegna
(Ca' d'Oro)

The Madonna of the Orange Tree by Cima da Conegliano (Accademia)

The Barbarigo Alterpiece by Giovanni Bellini (San Pietro Martire, Murano)

assumes a dominant role and is used to convey the atmosphere of the picture: it provides a context in which the figures appear as pawns, set below an expanse of sky relieved by drifting clouds. These expressions of mood are worked over and over again in countless Madonnas looking tenderly down at a sleeping cherub or a Christ Child in benediction (*Madonna degli Alberetti* – Accademia), in portrayals of the Dead Christ and many *Sacre Conversazioni* (*St Vincent Ferrer Polyptych* – San Zanipòlo).

Giovanni's brother **Gentile** (1429-1507) was the first artist to be nominated Venice's official painter, a position which underpinned a brilliant career. He emerged as a talented portrait painter (Doge Giovanni Mocenigo) and applied his observational skills to portraying views of Venice, known as **vedute**, which became an influential genre in itself in the 18C. The overall objective was for painting to be true to life: *The Procession of the Relics of the True Cross in Piazza San Marco* (Accademia), for example, is a factual or documentary representation of 15C Venice, even if the painter, conscientious in every detail, was careful to align the façades and order the attendant crowds.

The advent of High Renaissance

Vittore Carpaccio (1455-1526), following in the wake of Bellini and Antonello, suffuses a lesson learned from Flemish painting with his own personal creativity to execute the cycles of paintings commissioned by the "Scuole" (👓 *see I CARMINI: The Venetian Scuole*): *Miracle of the Relic of the True Cross at Rialto* for Scuola di San Giovanni Evangelista; *Legend of St Ursula* (Accademia) in which Brittany is represented as a Venetian Renaissance city; and *Legends of St George and St Jerome* for Scuola di San Giorgio degli Schiavoni, which depicts an exotic Orient. Carpaccio surpassed Bellini in sensitivity and in his inimitable talent for story-telling. His pictures are imaginatively populated with well-observed and delightful details: he even manages to reconcile his penchant for miniaturist precision with a love of broad views. In his landscapes, a key element in his paintings, are representations of a luxuriant, flowery veg-

etation, peopled with a host of animals (dogs, birds, rabbits, peacocks, parrots and deer). Renaissance buildings stand out, embellished with marble inlays that might have been designed by the Lombardo family, surrounded by numerous oriental motifs (palm trees, Moorish turbans). All of Carpaccio's works display the same distinctive features: boldness of line, luminosity, vivid colours, perfect sense of proportion, attention to detail and crowd scenes.

Giambattista Cima (1459-1518), known as Cima da Conegliano, drew on Giovanni Bellini for his strong, radiant light and on Carpaccio for his love of detail. His are the glorious portrayals of dignified figures, pictured in beautiful landscapes under broad open skies (*Madonna of the Orange Tree* – Accademia; *Adoration of the Shepherds* – I Carmini). By the close of the 15C, Venetian painting had reached the height of its artistic expression.

Reform

His name was Giorgio di Castelfranco but he went by the name of **Giorgione** (1475-1510). It was he who revolutionised the course of painting in the early 16C despite his short life. Giorgione is considered the first "modern" artist in the history of painting. A Renaissance man in every sense, he drew inspiration for his work from Humanist ideology, making it intellectual and sometimes shrouded in mystery, as well as open to controversial interpretation. Few works have been attributed to him with any certainty, and these are poetic in feel, almost dreamlike, but always charged with allusions to literature, music and philosophy: ephemerality and vulnerability are the subject of *The Tempest*; *La Vecchia* depicts the passage of time (both in the Accademia). His style appears more sensual than Classical. The landscape now plays an essential role in the painting; man is no longer the main subject, it is Nature itself that becomes the true protagonist – human drama is reduced to just one element in the force of Nature (such as in *The Tempest*).

Palma il Vecchio (1480-1528) followed in the same vein, although in later life he betrays the influence of Titian's handling of light, his juxtaposition of contrasting colour and the asymmetry of his altarpiece compositions. Palma il Vecchio specialised in *Sacre Conversazioni* (🕭 *see SAN ZACCARIA*) and painted the portrait of Paola Priuli (Querini-Stampaglia Collection). His art does not match that of the most talented masters but its appeal is one of spontaneity and exuberant colour.

The Bergamo-born **Lorenzo Lotto** (1480-1556) is another major early-16C painter with a distinctively personal style. His pictures are disconcerting and strange, they betray the influence of Dürer's scientific treatment of detail (Dürer visited Venice in c 1495) and the painter's liking for bold contrasts (*Portrait of a Young Gentleman in his Study* – Accademia). He avoided the sensual, colourful appeal of Giorgione and Titian, preferring to employ a rather frigid, angular style modelled on the precise, slightly archaic style of Alvise Vivarini.

16C-masters and their pupils

In the 16C, Venetian painting affirmed its supremacy; this was the era of the great European masters and highly skilled painters who, thanks to their respective talents, succeeded in establishing a distinctive style which was to become the hallmark of Venice and which soon earned her European recognition.

Titian

Tiziano Vecellio, known as Titian (c 1485-1576), is unquestionably the most famous artist of his time. Born in Pieve di Cadore, he remained highly active until his death, aged 90. He served his apprenticeship under Giovanni Bellini and was subsequently influenced by Giorgione (some of whose works he completed) and then Raphael. The author of large altarpieces undertaken for churches (I Frari) and Scuole (La Carità) alike, he favoured colour over form and breathed life into his canvases with a dynamic handling of paint and bold composition (*The Assumption* – I Frari; *Martyrdom of St Lawrence* – Gesuiti). His reputation far outreached the realms of the lagoon city, and led to him being commissioned to paint portraits of all the leading lights of his time at the courts of Ferrara, Mantua, Florence and Urbino; he worked for the Pope, François I and Charles V, who knighted him in 1553.

During the early part of his career, Titian's painting was fundamentally Classical in inspiration. However, between 1535 and 1545, he was seduced by Mannerism before reverting to a more dignified and serene style. At the end of his life, the melodramatic tension inherent in some compositions (*The Pietà* – Accademia) betrays the artist's mysticism at the imminence of death.

In conclusion, Titian was largely responsible for reviving interest in the large altarpiece. He succeeded in taking painting to unimagined heights of monumentality by abandoning symmetry of composition (*Pesaro Altarpiece* – I Frari), opting for large contrasting blocks of colour, displaying a sure stroke and a perfect sense of harmony.

Il Tintoretto

Contemporary with Titian, Venice harboured the genius of Jacopo Robusti, known as *il Tintoretto* (1518-94), the most original and most prolific of the Venetian masters. He was born the son of a dyer (whence his name) and never left Venice (save once, maybe, to visit Rome), but he never really enjoyed success in his lifetime. Tireless and passionate about his work, an ardent admirer of Michelangelo, he preferred biblical subjects to those of Classical Antiquity (Scuola di San Rocco) and chose to portray common people instead of focusing on the excesses of the nobility. He developed a restless style: despite the interaction of rapid precise brush strokes and gentle soft touches, his work is always lyrical, a quality that apparently is projected from his dynamic handling of paint and from the arrangement of figures in groups or alone, brought together by strong lines of composition (*Crucifixion* – Scuola di San Rocco). The use of chiaroscuro (strong contrasts of light and shade), juxtaposed complementary colours, elongated figures, daring foreshortening and a filtering light that blurs the contours of figures and architectural settings, all contribute to reinforcing the charged atmosphere of his Mannerist work.

His best pictures include the *Miracles of St Mark* painted for the Scuola di San Marco (Accademia), the *Marriage of Cana* (Santa Maria della Salute), *Paradise* (Doges' Palace, Grand Council Chamber), *The Triumph of Venice* (Doges' Palace), and *The Presentation of the Virgin in the Temple* (Madonna dell'Orto), not forgetting the 50 paintings, the largest cycle of its kind in Venice, executed for the Scuola di San Rocco, on which he worked for 23 years in collaboration with his son **Domenico Tintoretto**.

Veronese

In direct contrast with Tintoretto, **Paolo Caliari** (1528-88), born in Verona, hence his nickname *Veronese*, specialised in portraying the wealthy, opulent and carefree aristocracy of the Renaissance, in luminous colour (including the famous "Veronese green") that set off to theatrical effect the most sumptuous fabrics used for their clothing. His works in the main are endowed with optimism, fantasy and spontaneity, they seem permeated with spring light; towards the end of his life, however, Veronese's paintings change to more sombre and melancholic mood, muddied by the influence of Tintoretto's chiaroscuro and Bassano's style. Mythological scenes proliferate on the walls and ceilings of the Doges' Palace *(Apotheosis of Venice)*. The subject of *The Last Supper* was reworked by Veronese several times for the refectories of Venetian monasteries, including the famous, huge canvas *Christ in the House of Levi* (Accademia), commissioned for the Dominican monastery of San Zanipòlo. This was contrived as a depiction of an entirely profane meal while providing an excellent pretext for a work of grandiose proportions. The magnificent decoration of San Sebastiano is another masterpiece, appropriate, perhaps, given that it was his chosen ultimate resting place.

Mannerism in Venice

Whereas Tintoretto forged his style from Titian and Michelangelo, and Veronese was heir to Bellini, Giorgione and Raphael, their legacy, like that of Titian, was both powerful and influential beyond the confines of Venice, for several gen-erations. It also naturally led to Venetian Mannerism.

Titian had many followers: **Palma il Vecchio** (1480-1528); **Pordenone** (c 1483-1539), who worked successfully in Venice from 1535-38; **Paris Bordone** (1500-71), who delighted in Venetian Renaissance architecture (*Handing the Ring to the Doge* – Accademia; *Martyrdom of St Theodore* – San Salvador) and charged his canvases with vivid colours; the prolific **Palma il Giovane** (1544-1628), the grandson of Palma il Vecchio, with an eclectic style, who provided nearly all the city's churches with large-scale paintings.

An exponent of the sensuality and silky colours explored by Giorgione and Titian, **Andrea Schiavone** (c 1510-63) moved away from realism in favour of elongated form and restless movement typical of Mannerism, in the style of Parmigianino.

Impressed by Tintoretto's painting, **Jacopo Bassano** (Jacopo da Ponte, 1512-92) paints in a provincial style marked by an exaggerated preoccupation with naturalism (*St Jerome Meditating* – Accademia), while using light effects to suggest the intensity of the scene (*Nativity* – San Giorgio Maggiore). His sons Leandro and Francesco shared this tradition of *maniera* painting, in which the pastoral and rustic element becomes the prime subject rather than the religious or profane content.

18C revival

Venetian painting, in decline during the 17C and overshadowed by the great personalities of the previous century and the Roman Baroque, enjoyed a new creative and glorious burst of energy during this period of lavish receptions in the Age of Enlightenment.

Decorative painting

Long after the taste for grandiose interior decoration had flourished in Rome and Florence during the 16C-17C, Venice revived her interest in the decorative art of Veronese found on the walls and ceilings of her churches and *palazzi* and in the Palladian villas along the Brenta. **Sebastiano Ricci** (1659-1734), the Baroque painter of rather sentimen-

Christ in the House of Lévi, by Véronese (Accademia)

The Fortune Teller by Giambattista Piazzetta (Accademia)

Pulchinella by Giandomenico Tiepolo (Ca' Rezzonico)

View over the Rio dei Mendicanti by Canaletto (Ca' Rezzonico)

tal religious pictures, reinforced his strong compositions with bright colour (*Madonna with Saints* – San Giorgio Maggiore). It was with **Giambattista Piazzetta** (1682-1754), who excelled in religious painting, that huge ceiling compositions became popular, and that figures began to be shown from below, aspiring to dizzy heights among the clouds, drawn awkwardly towards a mystical light (*Glorification of St Dominic* – San Zanipòlo). Influenced by Caravaggio, Piazzetta also painted genre pictures (featuring people from common, everyday life in mundane surroundings) with strong chiaroscuro (*The Fortune Teller* – Accademia).

Piazzetta influenced the greatest artist of the century: **Giambattista Tiepolo** (1696-1770), the pre-eminent genius of Venetian Baroque decoration and creator of huge compositions of great virtuosity full of delicate colour, golden light and infinite space. He painted vast altarpieces and covered entire ceilings with frescoes (Palazzo Labia, Scuola dei Carmini, Church of the Gesuiti, Ca' Rezzonico), turning his hand as easily to religious subjects (*Our Lady of Mount Carmel* – I Carmini) as to mythological ones, including huge Virtues set before grandiose architectural backdrops.

Portraiture and Genre

Long-established patrician families and those of an aspiring bourgeoisie altered their household arrangements to reflect changes in lifestyle. In keeping with fashions elsewhere, it became acceptable to have informal, intimate and private rooms, separate from grandiose function or occasion rooms, in which to conduct everyday business, and this trend was reflected in contemporary art. Painters were asked to provide portraits that were both flattering and informal, a genre favoured by **Rosalba Carriera** (1675-1758), who produced delicate, vibrant pastels that earned her international fame (Ca' Rezzonico, Accademia), and **Alessandro Longhi**.

Around the same time, Venetians appeared to appreciate the small-scale interior scenes painted by **Pietro Longhi** (1702-85), such as masquerades, dances and duck hunting scenes (Hemingway's future pastime in Torcello), all revealing his acute powers of observation (Ca' Rezzonico, Querini-Stampalla Collection).

Topographical painters

Besides the *maniera* and genre scenes devoid of religious, allegorical or mythological meaning, landscape for its own sake began to provide artists with a worthy subject for easel pictures. In Venice, studies of the environment focused on the city herself, and it is for these views, *vedute* in Italian, that Antonio Canal (1697-1768), known as **Canaletto**, became so famous. In his pictures, he delineates in minute detail his on-the-spot observations of the city. Although his vision is almost photographic, he exaggerates perspective and paints huge, monumental buildings. He was also known to portray festivals and regattas. Unfortunately, most of his works are now exhibited in museums outside Italy and few can be admired in Venice itself. Canaletto inspired a great many artists, namely **Bernardo Bellotto** (1720-80), one of his pupils who was also a relative.

Quite distinct from Canaletto, **Francesco Guardi** (1712-93) was bewitched by the atmosphere of the lagoon city. His vision is not photographic; instead his bold use of paint succeeds in freezing the ripples of the water and the flickering light – a preoccupation that was to fascinate the English Romantic painter Turner and the French Impressionists a century later. Besides views of the lagoon, he also painted scenes of everyday life in the manner of Pietro Longhi: *Nuns' Parlour, Interval Time in the Foyer* (Ca' Rezzonico), as did his brother **Giovanni Antonio**.

Freed from the influence of his father, after painting the Stations of the Cross in San Polo, **Giovanni Domenico (Giandomenico) Tiepolo** (1727-1804) painted 18C Venetian society on the Brenta Riviera with humour and irony, depicting the holidaymakers as buffoons (Ca' Rezzonico: Villa Zianigo frescoes).

Modern and contemporary age

Between the 19C and the 20C Venetian painting continued on academic lines, ever faithful to the traditions set in the 18C with landscapes or urban scenes by Caffi and Ciardi, and fine portraits by Alessandro Milesi.

Motivated by mainstream developments in Europe during the early 20C, several painters produced interesting work (International Museum of Modern Art in Ca' Pesaro): **Federico Zandomeneghi** (1841-1917) who was born in Venice, worked with the Macchiaioli group before moving to Paris where he befriended Degas; **Umberto Boccioni** (1882-1916) was a founding member of the Futurist movement and painted in a style reminiscent of Signal *(The Grand Canal)*; **Fragiacomo** was an Impressionist much inspired by Turner *(St Mark's Square)*; **Casorati** was a Symbolist painter and portraitist.

Members of the **Burano School (Scuola di Burano)**, such as Moggioli, Gino Rossi, Sibellato and Semeghini, painted the islands of the lagoon, experimenting with techniques inspired by Van Gogh, Gauguin and Cézanne, and of the Post-Impressionists Bonnard and Vuillard.

Literature

1200-1500

The history of Venetian literature begins in 1271 when "Master **Marco Polo**, a wise and noble citizen of Venice" embarked on a journey to the Orient. Despite his tender age, the 16 year-old decided to accompany his father Niccolò and uncle Matteo, both Levantine merchants, on a very long expedition to the court of "Kublai, the Great Khan of the Mongols". Never before had such an ambitious journey to those parts been undertaken by Westerners. Unfortunately the return journey was to prove Marco's undoing, for during one of the many naval battles between the Venetians and the Genoese, the explorer was taken prisoner by the enemy. As he languished in prison, he came to know a writer from Pisa, Rustichello, who undertook to set down on paper an account of the Venetian's experiences. So **The Book of the Wonders of the World** was born; it achieved success under the

> It would appear that the title of Marco Polo's book was in fact inspired by the word "Emilione", the nickname given to the family of the great navigator.

title *Il Milione*, an epithet given to Marco Polo when he described the quantities of gold he claimed to have seen. In the years that followed the death of the traveller, Venice appeared to dedicate itself less to literature than to commerce. Indeed, Venetian literary circles seem to have been affected by Humanism.

It was not until **Aldo Manuzio**, the *"ante litteram"* publisher, arrived in Venice that the situation changed. In 1499 he published the *Hypnerotomachia Poliphili*, an amusing, anonymous work written in an explosive style, using vernacular language bastardised from Venetian and Latin. Its success was modest but it seems to have heralded one of the most successful literary spells in Venice.

BEMBO TO GOLDONI: A PERIOD OF GREAT SPLENDOUR

A more conventional writer to be published by Aldo Manuzio was **Pietro Bembo**. Born into a very aristocratic

Museo Correr, Venezia

Marco Polo (Museo Correr Library)

Ca' Rezzonico, Venezia - Ag.: SCALA

In the Foyer during the Interval, genre by Pietro Longhi (Ca' Rezzonico)

family in Venice in 1470, Bembo remained the touchstone of literary developments for almost a century. His importance is largely due to *The Prose of Vulgar Language* which came out in 1528, and which contributed to the age-old debate over the use of vernacular language in literature. In it Bembo argued that he was violently opposed to the language adopted by Dante, and offered a convincing alternative that in part has influenced the evolution of Italian into the language of today.

The Paduan-born **Angelo Beolco** (1496), meanwhile, was moving in a different direction. His nickname, *il Ruzzante* (The Playful One), was derived from the peasant protagonist of his plays, whom the author often impersonated, and so the character and his creator became synonymous. The most famous play, *Il Parlamento del Ruzzante*, is a merciless portrait of peasant conditions at the time of a long and bloody war between the French and the Venetians.

Contemporary with Ruzzante was the unknown author of the **Veniexiana**, an entertaining comedy in dialect which depicted the vices and virtues (mainly the former) of the inhabitants of the lagoon city. Its significance, however, lies not so much in the amusing story it tells, full of melodramatic action, but in

its marking a turning point in the cultural milieu of Venice. For between 1530 and 1540, the popular trend suddenly passed from foreign imported theatrical productions to the blossoming of "original" domestic plays.

This radical change was no doubt precipitated by the presence of **Pietro Aretino** who, as his surname suggests, was born in Arezzo. After a stay in Rome, Aretino reached Venice in 1527, just in time to publish *Il Marescalco* and *La Cortegiana*, two of the most popular and well-crafted comedies of the 16C. Their success was immediate and very well exploited by Aretino, who was astute enough to engage the new resources proffered by the printing press to increase his fame. This collaboration was, in fact, to make both the Tuscan and his publisher Marcotini a fortune. Aretino, furthermore, showed himself capable of using popular, vernacular language for literature to nothing short of tumultuous effect. His plays mocked and lampooned the authorities, attracting audiences from all walks of life, but most notably from among those in power who were anxious to know what was indeed being said. It was no surprise therefore, that he soon earned the epithet "the scourge of the princes".

Thus during the 17C, the Republic's somewhat liberal attitude must have excused the considerable freedom of thought and action enjoyed in Venice: it is difficult otherwise to explain the success of Aretino and other such lax publications that would have been prohibited elsewhere. Venice became an important publishing centre, drawing all kinds of literary characters who wished to take particular care over typographical layouts and to oversee the output of their own book. Soon hundreds of printers mushroomed to service hundreds of authors, dependent one upon the other.

LARA PESSINA

Carlo Goldoni

Comedy

The theatre became a passion for citizens of all social classes. Plays proliferated, almost all written and produced on the spot. Comedies enacted in dialect enjoyed the greatest popularity; these were often based around sets of particular carnival characters identified by their traditional mask and costume, such as **Harlequin**. The needs of a growing number of theatre devotees, coupled with those of an important and thriving port, founded the beginnings of a modern news-spreading media.

Journalism

The advent of journalism in Italy could only have been feasible in a milieu like Venice. In 1760 Gasparo Gozzi launched the magazine *La Gazzetta Veneta*, which appeared twice a week for about a year. Conceived along the lines of an English periodical, features included articles on orders of the day and useful practical information on life in the city (financial announcements, public notices, advertisement listings, stock exchange reports etc). It was in *La Gazzetta* that Goldoni published his first reviews on Rusteghi.

Carlo Goldoni (1707-93)

Goldoni's father was a doctor who wished his son to follow in his footsteps but when Carlo was aged 13, he ran away from school to join a ship in Rimini that was carrying a troupe of actors to Chioggia. From there he went on to join his mother in Venice. Goldoni resumed his studies and qualified as a lawyer. Lacking the will to succeed, however, he soon turned his hand at challenging the tradition of the Commedia dell'Arte to improvise dialogue along the lines of a given plot.

In 1743 Goldoni wrote the script for *La donna di Garbo*. In 1750 the provocative comedy playwright impudently waged a bet with his rival Pietro Chiari that in less than a year he could write 16 new comedies: in fact he wrote 17, including the splendid *La Bottega del Caffè (The Coffee Shop)*, set in Venice and satirising the bourgeoisie. The ingredients were simple: he used colloquial language for immediacy and formulated rounded characters based on observation of real life. He avoided political incorrectness by importing his gentrified personalities from afar, able therefore to exaggerate their airs and graces. *Arlecchino, Servitore di due Padroni (Servant of Two Masters)*, *La Locandiera (The Innkeeper)* are all constructed according to the same format. Goldoni died in France.

An account of Goldoni's stay in Venice can be found in the author's memoirs *(Memorie)*.

HOW THE 18C AND 19C SAW VENICE

Venice as depicted by Goldoni, full of humour and moral integrity, was a vital place that attracted the talented, the eccentric and the curious. These included **Lorenzo da Ponte**, Mozart's celebrated librettist and author of the *Marriage of Figaro*, who lingered there for "a couple of years of adventurous libertinage", and that specialist master of licentiousness **Giacomo Casanova** (1725-98) who, between one amorous assignation and another, found time to write his interesting *Memoirs*.

Another reprobate of the same school, if the term is appropriate, the poet **Ugo Foscolo**, landed on the Riva degli Schiavoni in 1793. He stopped in the city for four years, during which he demonstrated the true colour of his personality on numerous occasions. Abandoning his regular studies, he embarked on teaching himself the Greek and Latin classics to engineer his infiltration of the very refined salon of Isabella Teorochi Albrizzi, with whom he initiated a passionate affair, he aged 16 and she 34. In the meantime, he wrote the famous *Ode to the Liberator Bonaparte*; only the "liberator", in his political intrigue, paid no heed to the revolutionary ideals of the young Foscolo, but ceded Venice to Austria to further his own hegemonic aims. The repercussions on the writer were enormous, forcing him to seek refuge in Milan, where he devoted himself to drafting *The Last Letters of Jacopo Ortis*, a prose account of the delusion he had suffered. During his sojourn in Venice, however, Foscolo also became involved with **Melchiorre Cesarotti**, an important forerunner of the early Romantic movement.

Cesarotti was a tutor in an aristocratic household whose salon Foscolo frequently attended. In 1760 Cesarotti came across a collection of poems by Ossian, a legendary bard, published by a certain MacPherson: in six months, Cesarotti had translated them into Italian verse, which he published in 1763. *Le Poesie di Ossian,* as they appeared in Italian, shot Cesarotti to fame, oblivious of the fact that these "Ossianic poems" were to be one of those most famous cases of literary fraud to be uncovered over the last 200 years. **James MacPherson** (1736-96) claimed they were a translation of a series of surviving fragments of some ancient Gaelic mythical poetry when in fact they had been fabricated,

for the most part, by the Scotsman himself. Poor Cesarotti was one of the many innocents to fall for the trick.

By the end of the century, the foundations of Italian Romanticism had been laid. The Piedmontese **Silvio Pellico**, the fervent patriot and anti-Austrian agitator, was soon to write his famous and doleful *Piombi*. In *Le mie Prigioni*, Pellico narrates his whole experience from the day of his arrest (13 October 1820) to that of his release (September 1830), thereby securing a place in the heart of the nation as a hero.

Throughout the Romantic period, Venice reigned supreme. This was not so much as a result of her literary output but rather because she continued to distract so many intellectuals, such as **Lord Byron**, on their travels through Italy, happy to meet up under the shaded porticoes of the Procuratie, a custom that was to extend well into the next century.

In 1886 the Russian author **Anton Chekhov** published a collection of short stories. *Story of a Stranger* recounts his overwhelming passion for Venice, to such an extent that he feels "intoxicated with life".

20C

The modern history of the lagoon city rests almost exclusively in the hands of foreigners, many of whom sought refuge there from persecution at home and soon enjoyed a protected social scene. Not only were there no Venetian-born writers of note to emerge, few Italians were attracted to the decadent beauty of the Serenissima. **Gabriele d'Annunzio** was a notable exception.

Marcel Proust arrived in 1900, inevitably accompanied by his mother, with whom he began translating the English writer **John Ruskin**, author of the famous *Stones of Venice*, while refining his own literary style. Proust's sojourn was a particularly happy one: reflecting in *A la recherche du temps perdu*, he writes *"However did the images of Venice give me such joy and confidence as to render me indifferent to death"*.

The reflections of **Thomas Mann** are of a very different order: in *Death in*

Venice, the city is portrayed as being in a state of decay. The protagonist of the novel is Gustav von Aschenbach, a German writer who, after a lifetime of rigorous discipline, feels attracted by a city described as crumbling and overrun with cholera.

In 1918 the Viennese author **Arthur Schnitzler** wrote *Casanova in Spa*, a book set in Venice and loosely based on his amorous adventures.

Among the most recent illustrious visitors to the city was **Ernest Hemingway** who set down his suitcases in the Hotel Gritti in 1948. He loved to be called "Papa" and while away the time with glasses of Montgomery, a strong Martini, at Harry's Bar. Far removed from the more rugged places associated with the writer, Hemingway once confessed to his translator Ferdinanda Pivano: *"Sitting by the Grand Canal and writing near where Mr Byron, Mr Browning and Mr D'Annunzio wrote makes Mr Papa feel he has arrived at where he is meant to be"*.

The same year saw the publication of *Cantos* by the American poet **Ezra Pound**, who died in Venice (see *SAN ZANIPÒLO: Cemetery*) and who wrote about the city in Canto LXXVI.

In the early sixties, the Italian author **Giorgio Bassani** used the Ghetto district as a backdrop to his novel *Il Giardino dei Finzi Contini*, which was made into a famous film by **Vittorio de Sica**.

The Russian writer **Josif Brodskij**, who received the Nobel Prize for Literature in 1987, was fascinated by Venetian water and canals, a passion he recounted in *Watermark*.

Hemingway Collection/John F Kennedy Library, Boston

"Papa" Hemingway and his wife Mary Welch, in front of the Salute

Another Slav author who evokes the lagoon city was Polish-born **Gustaw Herling** who, in *Portrait of Venice* (1994), evokes his "sentimental involvement with Venice".

Music

PRELUDE TO VIVALDI

Renaissance

Whereas in Rome a brilliant revival in music flourished under the auspices of **Giovanni Pierluigi da Palestrina** (1525-94), who headed a polyphonic school dedicated to sacred music, patronage in Venice was limited to more secular applications. Perhaps the turning point is marked by the Flemish

Literary Venice

Travellers with a keen eye and a writer's pen have provided many accounts of life in the lagoon city. In his notes about Italy (1729), **Charles Louis de Montesquieu** offers a sketchy description of Venice that nonetheless lists a great many figures (six *sestieri*, seven parishes, 25 houses for monks and 36 for nuns, 500 bridges, 20 000 residents etc). **Goethe's portrayal** is infused with sentiment: *"I suddenly felt that I too reigned supreme over the Adriatic, as do all Venetians as soon as they set foot on their gondola..."*. (*Italian Journey*, 1829). In his diary about Italy (1857), **Herman Melville** presents the reader with an interesting medley of thoughts, impressions and fleeting images: *"Shimmering silver thuribles swaying softly, scattering incense over the heads of the faithful ... The rich, deep complexion of the women painted by Titian is indeed close to nature ..."*.

Willaert (c 1490-1562), the choirmaster at St Mark's, who set a trend that was to be continued by his pupil Andrea Gabrieli.

Andrea Gabrieli (c 1510-86) – Organist at St Mark's, Gabrieli emerged as an important composer and influential teacher of organ and choral music in the Venetian tradition. His innovative use of the *concertato* (a small group of instruments or voices), contrasted with the *ripieno* (a larger body of musicians), forestalled the implementation of the *concerto* form developed and exploited later by Corelli. This allowed Gabrieli to experiment with harmony and dissonance by combining various "parts" for choir, or the human voice with instruments. His most lasting contribution is a large body of choral works for both sacred (motets for four to 12 voices, masses for six voices, the *Psalms of David* for six voices) and secular texts (madrigals for three to 12 voices).

Giovanni Gabrieli (c 1557-1612) – Andrea's nephew Giovanni inherited the position of organist at St Mark's and further propagated the fame of the Venetian School abroad (the Dutch master Sweelinck, Hans Leo Hassler, Heinrich Schutz, Bach's precursor and founder of German church music, were already pupils). Among his compositions, which comprised sacred, secular and instrumental pieces, the most notable are his motets, the **Sacred Symphonies**. His more avant-garde works include **sonatas** for violin, which he used to explore antiphonal effects: at the time the violin was the instrument that best sustained the popular taste for monophonic music (following a single line of notes). By adding a **basso continuo** or figured bass line, with long drawn notes, he was able to develop harmonies with the accompaniment, thereby providing sustained and textured melody. This Gabrieli applied not only to choral arrangements but to instrumental pieces for two violins and clavichord or cello.

Baroque

With the 17C began another rich and fruitful period for Venetian music. Melodrama became a formal genre; formulated from accounts of contemporary historical events or legends, exaggerated stories were re-enacted to audiences in elaborately contrived stage settings. Francesco Cavalli (1602-76), a chorister at St Mark's, Marc'Antonio Cesti (1623-69) and Giovanni Legrenzi (1626-90), choirmaster at St Mark's, all collaborated at an operatic school in Venice which, in 1637, opened the first commercial opera house, San Cassiano. Here Monteverdi's operas were later performed.

18C

By the mid-1700s, Venice was renowned for the more typically Neapolitan kind of comic operas by **Baldassarre Galuppi** (see BURANO), who, together with Giovanni Platti (1700-63), contributed to the development of the sonata (literally meaning "sounded", implying music that is instrumental rather than sung) for strings and keyboard. In response to works by the Bach dynasty in Germany, they composed pieces for one (harpsichord) or two instruments (harpsichord and violin) in homophonic (several lines of notes moving in chords) and polyphonic (several lines of notes each with its own distinctive pattern) arrangements in several movements (usually three).

The harpsichord enjoyed particular favour, despite the advent of the piano, developed by Bartolomeo Cristofori (1655-1732) by substituting hammers for quills. Among the most famous players of the harpsichord, besides Galuppi and Platti, were the two **Marcello** brothers, **Benedetto** (1686-1739), who also composed sacred music and concertos for

---

During the 17C, thanks to Claudio Monteverdi, who conducted the choir at San Marco, Venice became known as the world's leading centre for operatic art, placing herself ahead of Florence and Mantua. In those days, the lagoon city boasted a total of 17 theatres.

Famous organ-builders

Gaetano Callido (1727-1813) built about 400 organs throughout the Veneto, Dalmatia and even the Holy Land: all three organs at St Mark's were restored by him in 1766. Four years later, he was appointed the official, permanent organ-maker to the city. His sons Agostino and Antonio continued to practise their father's craft until 1821.

five instruments, and **Alessandro** (1684-1750), who wrote sonatas for violin and basso continuo and concertos for oboe and strings that hitherto have been attributed to Benedetto. Also active in Venice in this period was **Tomaso Albinoni** (1671-1750), who more closely followed in the German Baroque tradition and foreshadows Vivaldi in his instrumental compositions.

ANTONIO VIVALDI (1678-1741)

It is undoubtedly Vivaldi who best epitomises Venetian music: even JS Bach (1685-1750) drew openly on the compositions of the *"Prete Rosso"* (*see SAN GIORGIO degli SCHIAVONI)*, who was literally rediscovered in the mid-20C, after years of oblivion.

Vivaldi was a prolific composer, using a three-movement form of the concerto, *allegro-adagio-allegro*, and freeing up the *Sonata da Camera* as a series of contrasting descriptive passages as in the *Four Seasons*, the *Goldfinch* and *Night concerti*. Altogether, Vivaldi composed over 500 concertos for violin, viola d'amore, cello, mandolin, flute, oboe, bassoon, trumpet, cornet and string orchestra.

His parents

Giovanni Battista Vivaldi, father of Antonio, was a professional barber and musician: this would be surprising today, but many Venetians of the time combined both professions. Giovanni Battista, nicknamed *il Rosso* after the colour of his auburn hair, obviously a family trait, was a violin virtuoso in 17C Venice, more specifically in the area around **San Mar-**

tino where most of the city's musicians congregated at the Scuola, the *Sovvegno di Santa Cecilia*, whose patron naturally was St Cecilia.

Camilla Calicchio, mother of Antonio, came from the area around **San Giovanni in Bràgora** (*see ARSENALE)*, where Antonio was baptised a second time, having been subjected to the formalities of a blessing at home on 4 March 1678, shortly after his birth, when it appeared that he might not survive.

Il Prete Rosso

Antonio was ordained at **San Giovanni Novo**, even though he dedicated himself to the cause of music rather than to the priesthood, content to remain a secular priest or abbot. He took up residence in Fondamenta del Dose, near the Ponte del Paradiso, before abandoning the Castello *sestiere* in favour of St Mark's, where he lived on the Riva del Carbon. When he left these lodgings in 1740 it was to leave Venice completely, dying in poverty in Vienna the following year.

The Musician

Vivaldi's main musical activity is associated first and foremost with the Pietà and the Theatre of San Angelo.

The Pietà was one of the great **foundling hospitals** which, between the 17C and 18C, doubled as one of the musical conservatories of Venice, each having its own church where concerts were held. These "hospitals" functioned as chari-

Vivaldi – the "Prete Rosso"

101

table institutions and orphanages for girls *(ospitaliere)*, who received an education and, if gifted, musical instruction to enable them to take part in the choirs and orchestras of which the establishments were so proud.

Associated as it is with the fame of Vivaldi, the Pietà became the best known of the hospital-churches. Standing on the Riva degli Schiavoni it cannot be mistaken or missed, although the present church is not the original one where Vivaldi had been music teacher and composer. The former church stood where the Metropole Hotel now stands, slightly to the right of the present church.

The San Angelo Theatre no longer exists. It was there that the violin virtuoso acted as musical director, impresario, composer and performed more secular works.

AFTER VIVALDI

The musical splendour of Venice, which regaled contemporary ears for three centuries and continues to survive today in churches and concert halls, faded with the passing of its most illustrious representative. In more recent times, one interesting composer emerges from the Venetian and German traditions and that is **Ermanno Wolf-Ferrari** (1876-1948), who was particularly impressed by Mozart's operatic works and inspired by the theatre of Goldoni: both influences are evident in his own life's opus *Gioielli della Madonna, Le Donne Curiose, I Quattro rusteghi, Il Campiello,* etc.

Yet more recently still, the city has resumed its role as a lively and innovative artistic centre by playing host to such experimental musicians as **Bruno Maderna** (1920-73) and **Luigi Nono** (1924-90).

Venice was also the birthplace of the conductor Giuseppe Sinopoli (1946-

---

Venice in Music

From *The Four Seasons* by Vivaldi to traditional Venetian songs, music heard for the first time in Venice will evoke memories of its canals and piazzas. The works of classical and traditional music below embody a particularly Venetian flavour.

- Various artists, *Musiche veneziane per voce e strumenti,* Claves
- Various artists, *Music of the Tintoretto Age,* Edelweiss
- Various artists, *A Piano Recital for Venice,* Edelweiss
- Various artists, *Voice and Lute in Venice in the 16th Century,* Edelweiss
- Various artists, *Musiche veneziane per voce e strumenti (Teresa Berganza),* Claves
- Various artists, *Musiche veneziane per trombe e tromboni,* Claves
- Various artists, *Souvenirs de Venise: The Songmakers' Almanac,* Hyperion
- Tomaso Albinoni, *Musiche veneziane,* Claves
- Andrea and Giovanni Gabrieli, *Musica organistica,* Tactus
- Giovanni Gabrieli, *Sinfonie sacre,* Oiseau-lyre
- Baldassarre Galuppi, *Musiche veneziane: concerti e sinfonie,* Claves
- Baldassarre Galuppi, *Musiche veneziane: passatempo al cembalo,* Claves
- Baldassarre Galuppi; Antonio Vivaldi, *Musiche veneziane: Magnificat; Gloria,* Claves
- Alessandro Marcello, *Concerto in re minore per oboe, archi e organo,* Philips
- Monteverdi, Rigatti, Grandi, Cavalli, *Venetian Vespers,* Archiv
- Antonio Vivaldi, *The Four Seasons*
- Antonio Vivaldi, *Musiche veneziane: Six Concertos for Flute,* Claves
- Antonio Vivaldi, *Musiche veneziane: concerti,* Claves

Venetian music – The *Concerto in D minor for oboe, strings and organ* by Alessandro Marcello was long attributed to his brother Benedetto. This well-known piece of music accompanied the Italian film *The Anonymous Venetian*, which starred Tony Musante and Florinda Bolkan.

2001), who was to become an authority on Mahler's work.

VENETIAN BY ADOPTION

Tribute should also be paid to visiting composers who died in Venice.
Claudio Monteverdi (1567-1643) was one genius who breathed personality and characterisation into opera: he lies buried at I Frari *(see I FRARI).*
Domenico Cimarosa (1749-1801), often regarded as the Italian Mozart, died in Campo Sant' Angelo *(see La FENICE).*
The apparently aloof and detached **Igor Stravinsky** (1882-1971) is buried in the cemetery of San Michele.
However, it was **Richard Wagner** (1813-83), possibly the most controversial composer in musical history, who most desired to be adopted by his beloved Venice. The maestro died on 13 February in the Palazzo Vendramin Calergi *(see Il CANAL GRANDE)* in the company of his wife, Cosima, and the gondolier Gigio Trevisan, nicknamed Ganassete.
During Wagner's peaceful stay in Venice, he would go to St Mark's Square daily where, seated at Quadri's or Florian's, he was sometimes recognised by the leader of the municipal band who would ask him to conduct: Wagner would agree, happy to direct his own compositions for the Venetians. It was here that Wagner composed the second act of *Tristan* (the English horn part having been inspired by the evening song of the gondoliers), wrote part of *Parsifal* and initiated work on the *Maestri cantori* inspired by Titian's *Assumption* that he so admired at I Frari.

Cinema

Venice is a natural film set and has been used as a backdrop for many famous movies. In September, the Lido hosts the International Film Festival, when open-air cinemas are set up in squares throughout the city to show the films competing in the festival.

Cut!
The first rather primitive moving images of Venice are shot by Albert Promio in

1896, just one year after the birth of cinema. Since then, Venice has become one of the oldest, ageless, most sought-after *divas* ever!

1935
Mark Sandrich films *Top Hat* with Ginger Rogers and Fred Astaire.

1955
David Lean chooses Venice as the backdrop to the meeting between Rossano Brazzi and Katharine Hepburn in *Summertime*.

1963
In the second James Bond film, *From Russia with Love*, Sean Connery goes to Murano in search of a particular glassmaker. Special effects include an amphibious gondola scattering pigeons in St Mark's Square.

1971
Based on the novella *Death in Venice* by Thomas Mann, Luchino Visconti directs *Morte a Venezia* with Dirk Bogarde in the lead role; there are panoramic shots across the sultry waters of the lagoon – a classic!

1976
Fellini films *Casanova*, based on the life story of the notorious Venetian.

1979
Don Giovanni is a beautiful film adaptation of Mozart's opera, populated by masked figures stepping out of swirling mists from boats in the Brenta Valley.

1982
Giuliano Montaldo re-creates Malamocco in the 1200s for his film *Marco Polo*, starring Ken Marshall.

1988
Steven Spielberg gets archaeologist Harrison Ford to jump out of the library into Campo San Barnaba in *Indiana Jones*.

1992
In *Blame in on the Bellboy*, Dudley Moore and Bryan Brown are victims of mistaken identity in this farcical comedy of errors set in Venice.

CATS

Filming Carrington

1995
In *Carrington*, Christopher Hampton directs Emma Thompson (Dora Carrington) and Jonathan Pryce (Lytton Strachey) on a visit to Venice.

1996
Woody Allen directs and stars in the delightful musical, *Everyone Says I Love You*, set in New York, Venice and Paris. If you know the lagoon city, watch for the glorious Scuola di San Rocco.

2000
Silvio Soldini directs *Pane e tulipani* (Bread and Tulips), which portrays the real Venice, inhabited by mildly eccentric characters.

Carnival

During the 18C, the Venice Carnival opened at the beginning of October and ended on the Tuesday preceding Lent, with only one short interruption for Christmas festivities. In those days, masks were worn throughout the carnival but they were also used in other circumstances: during the Fiera della Sensa lasting for two weeks, on the occasion of doges' elections and their sons' weddings, and when famous personalities arrived in town.

Today, the Carnival starts 10 days before Lent (Feb-Mar) with the "volo dell'angelo" or "flight of the angel". In this ceremony, an acrobat descends the bell-tower of St Mark's and glides over the piazza to the Doges' Palace by means of two ropes. In the past, the acrobat was dressed as a Turk rather than an angel.

LEGEND HAS IT

Masks were introduced to Venice in 1204 when Doge Enrico Dandolo brought veiled Muslim women back to Venice after his conquest of Constantinople.

"BUONGIORNO, SIORA MASCARA"

As in Mozart's opera *Don Giovanni* (Act 2), masked people greeted each other with this saying during the 17C. To go about one's business dressed in the *baùta* – a mask complete with its hooded black shawl – was so normal that a formal request was lodged by the clergy for Venetians to remove their "disguise" at least in church.

RETURN OF THE CARNIVAL

The greater the decline of Venice, the sharper her sense of fun. Come 1797

N Bosques - Ag.: MICHELIN

Carnival attire

when the French assumed power, thus ending the glory of the Venetian Republic for all time, the city continued her revelries, thriving on her taste for jokes and riddles, laughter and carnival, which was eventually revived late in the 19C.

Even when this modern carnival was reinstated, with an open invitation to all to congregate in Piazza San Marco – the only time the space is truly filled by the crowds – it was a masked attendance. Whether it be with the *baùta*, the full-length cloak *(tabarro)*, the three-horned hat *(tricorno)* or the long-nosed mask *(maschera a becco)* that doctors used to wear during the plague epidemics, the rule of the game is always the same: never investigate the identity of the person wearing the mask.

The need to don a mask seems to come as second nature to a Venetian. Maybe because, in the words of Silvio Ceccat: *"The streets are narrow, the population is small. You meet someone at every corner. Everyone knows everyone else's business. Today there are no cars to protect anonymity as yesterday there were no coaches in which to hide … People used to and still do feel naked in Venice. So naked, indeed, that clothes are not enough and hence the need for the mask …".*

THE CITY TODAY

Even though the number of visitors in Venice far exceeds her resident population, it is the Venetians who, indifferent to the problems posed by the site, have created the city of their dreams from the mud of the lagoon and cultivated a historical and artistic heritage second to none.

The Venetians

To describe the countless faces of Venice and ignore the particular personality of the citizens who live here would present a misleading picture of the city: it would sustain the unfortunate, commonly held view of the place as a museum to which a cursory visit is made. To refute this, stroll down to Campo della Pescaria, linger in a bar in Campo San Luca over a glass of wine, or idle away on a bench in Campo San Giacomo dall'Orio to eavesdrop on a nearby conversation. Shopping around Sant'Elena will provide a glimpse of the living spirit of Venice. The best impressions of Venice are gleaned away from the obvious tourist areas.

Venetians can be unpredictable characters, both charming and astute (a quality sharpened by an age-old affinity for business), with a tendency to appear effusively genial in Italian and yet suspiciously distant in their native dialect.

THE CITY'S SPLIT PERSONALITY

If setting out to explore the tourist's Venice, the way is clearly signed at every step by shopkeepers standing in doorways, enticing menus at a competitive "fixed price", corn-sellers proffering grain to attract the pigeons for that classic but kitsch photo. This snapshot of Venice cannot do justice to the myriad impressions to be gained.

Every visitor must formulate his or her own opinion of Venice: it may be a highly personal response to the unique atmosphere of this enchanting city; it may be one tainted by bad weather. To stereotype the flavour of Venice would be detrimental to the magic of the place and offensive to her proud inhabitants.

Just outside the tourist mainstream, a local resident is often ready to regale the visitor with intriguing anecdotes; the long-serving employee at some magnificent *palazzo* will enjoy sharing its enthralling history with whoever gives him the chance; the parish priest, in his sacristy, is happy to unlock secret doors to hidden treasures in his custody. Theirs is "the" Venetian personality too complex to be defined but too colourful to be ignored.

VENETIAN IDIOSYNCRASY

The Venetian is born with a positive outlook on life that is maintained by an imperturbable nature in which emotional involvement is tempered by a certain indifference to anything that lies beyond the lagoon. This leads them to a noticeably predisposed state of tolerance, an innate quality acquired from a knowledge of different peoples distilled over the centuries. The blend of an almost Anglo-Saxon aplomb with boundless and all-embracing curiosity renders this personality even more fascinating.

Yet perhaps the attribute that most readily springs to mind is the pleasure the Venetian derives from gossiping, a pastime that delights all the more given the subtle sense of humour with which all Venetians are naturally and happily endowed, regardless of age, intellect or social class.

Jocular chatter is always conducted in dialect to allow quips and puns to sparkle and scintillate to full effect. It fills the bars and cafés, the shops and markets, but most of all the streets and squares, exchanged in passing or during a pause, which the Venetians take pleasure in granting themselves at every opportunity. Unlike citizens of other cities, Venetians are wholly sociable creatures, revelling in the advantages of sharing their environment with like-minded people who draw the calm and philosophical conclusion that only the truly essential priorities of life are worth worrying about, thus regarding the inconveniences of existence as relative. With a clear conscience and light heart, Venetians walk with a purposeful stride: it is clear when they are on their way somewhere, moving at a sustained speed, whether empty handed or earnestly pushing awkward carts up and over the bridges, heralded by a spritely *"Atansion!"* from behind.

It is rare to meet an ill-intentioned person in Venice, partly because the very structure of the city impedes criminal designs: where would you escape to? This underpins the genuinely happy atmosphere of the place, savoured in full by its contented residents, treasured by its temporary inhabitants and enjoyed by tourists who are able to roam the city at any time of the day or night.

Venetian Lexicon

The living breath of Venice is its dialect. Accents have been used to facilitate pronunciation.

COLLOQUIAL TERMS

Baùta: a carnival mask comprising a black hood and a lace shawl
Brìcola: wooden pole used for mooring boats or, if roped to others, to delineate navigable channels
Carèga: chair
Ciàcola: gossip or chatter
Fèlze: the gondola awning set up in winter to protect the main seat
Ocio!: Look out!
Ostreghèta!: Good heavens!
Pantegàna: a large rat
Putèo: a child
Tòco/tochetìn: a piece/little piece

EATING AND DRINKING

Armelìn: apricot
Bacalà mantecà: boiled salt-cod, mixed with oil, garlic and parsley
Bàcaro: a Venetian bistro, usually crowded from early morning
Bagìgi: peanuts
Baìcoli: typical dry, flat, cutlet-shaped sweet biscuits
Bìgoi: wholemeal spaghetti, generally served in *salsa* with a lightly fried mixture of anchovies and onions
Bìsi: peas
Bussolài buranèi: an S- or ring-shaped biscuit from Burano
Càpe sànte: scallops
Cichèto: Venetian tidbit (salt-cod, marinated sardine or a meatball) that accompanies a glass of wine.
Dìndio: turkey
Frìtole: carnival pancakes made with raisins and pinenuts.

Lugànega: a long thin sausage

Narà.nsa: orange

Ombra, ombrèta: the traditional and much respected glass of wine taken standing at a bar

Parsùto: ham

Peòci: mussels

Pòmi: apple

Prosecci: dry sparkling wine

Rìsi e bìsi: rice and peas traditionally eaten during the Feast of St Mark

Sàrde in saòr: fried sardines, with a sweet-and-sour sauce of onions, vinegar, pinenuts and raisins

Sgropìn: lemon sorbet of vodka and *prosecco*, served usually after fish.

Sprìz: famous Venetian aperitif: white wine with a dash of bitters and soda water

Stracaganàse: dried chestnuts, literally translated as "jaw-acher"

Sopprèssa: fresh salami

Tiramisù: famous dessert made of biscuits soaked in coffee, layered with full-fat *mascarpone* cream cheese blended with egg and sugar, powdered with bitter cocoa.

PLACE NAMES

Altàna: a wooden roof-terrace or veranda

Assassini: a canal or street name alluding to where a murderer might have sought refuge

Beccarìe: butchers who have lent their name to streets, squares, bridges

Calli: from the Latin *callis*, most streets in Venice bear this name (variations: *calli larghe*, *callette* and *calleselle*)

Campiello: a little *campo* or square

Campo: Venetian for a square; the only *piazza* in Venice is Piazza San Marco

Fiubèra: buckle sellers who have lent their name to streets or vaulted arcades where they once set up shop

Fondamenta: a road which runs parallel to a *rio* or canal

Fòntego: a warehouse where foreign merchants lodged

Fornèr: a common name identifying where the local bread ovens were

A somewhat confusing street sign

Frezzerìa: commercial zone around St Mark's that was once the site of an arrow factory

Lista: the stretch of street in front of an ambassador's residence; diplomatic immunity is indicated by its white stone

Luganeghèr: indicates a grocery store

Megio: millet; alludes to grain (millet or wheat) warehouses storing supplies for times of hardship.

Milìon: the nickname of Marco Polo's family, who lived over the Milion courtyard behind San Giovanni Grisostomo; also the title of the adventurer's travel experiences

Paradiso: this name given to a street or bridge refers to the lamps that were used on Good Friday to light the area of Santa Maria Formosa

Parrocchia: literally meaning "parish", this locality around a church serves as a subdivision of a *sestiere*

Pescarìa: a fish market

Piazzetta: little squares: the two in Venice are Piazzetta dei Leoncini and Piazzetta San Marco

Piovàn: common in Venetian topography; relating to a priest

Piscina: place where there used to be a pool or sheet of water

Pistòr: the baker who kneaded dough

Ponte: the 400 or so bridges in Venice are marked by this name

Ramo: a side street

Rialto: from the Latin *rivoaltus*, a word that indicates the islands from which the city originated

Rio terà: a street formed by a land-filled canal

Ruga: from the French *rue*, a synonym for street, usually one devoted to a commercial activity

Italian coffee

Espresso – very short, sharp, black and very strong

Caffè lungo/caffè americano – a short, strong espresso with added hot water

Caffè corretto – an espresso with added brandy or *grappa* (eau-de-vie)

Caffè macchiato – an espresso with a dash of cold milk

Cappuccino or **cappuccio** – an espresso topped with hot fluffy milk and pow-dered chocolate

Caffè latte – a glass of hot milk flavoured with an espresso coffee

Ice-cream flavours

Gelato is best bought from a *gelateria*.

Stracciatella – plain with chocolate chips. **Gianduia** – smooth chocolate and hazelnut. **Bacio** – milk chocolate. **Fior di latte** or **panna** – plain milk or cream. **Crema** – vanilla enriched with egg. **Cioccolato** – chocolate. **Nocciola** – hazelnut. **Frutta di bosco** – fruit from the forest (blueberries, blackberries). **Limone** – lemon sorbet. **Fragola** – strawberry. **Pistacchio** – bright green pistachio nut. **Pesca** – peach. **Albicocca** – apricot. **Lampone** – raspberry.

Salizzarda: from the word *salizo* or paving stone; denotes a paved street

San Stae: the Venetian contraction of San Eustachio – St Eustace

San Stin: another Venetian contraction of San Stefanino

San Zan Degolà: refers to San Giovanni Decollato – the beheaded John the Baptist

Scaletèr: a doughnut seller, from the word *scaleta*, a doughnut with marks like a flight of steps

Sestieri: the six divisions of Venice: **Cannaregio:** from the Latin *cannarecium* or *canaleclum*, a marshy area where cane grows; **Castello:** alluding, perhaps, to the Roman fortification at Olivolo; **Dorsoduro:** includes the Giudecca and is named after the type of hill on which it developed; **San Marco, San Polo** and **Santa Croce.**

Sottopòrtego: a vaulted passageway running perpendicular to the building's façade on the ground floor; at one time lined with shops

Squèro: a shipyard where gondolas are built and repaired

Tette: a bridge or street where bare-breasted women of easy virtue used to lean out of windows:

Zattere: the long *fondamenta* that extends to the Giudecca Canal, recalling the *zattere* or wood-laden rafts which used to stop there

Food and Wine

Venice has traded with Asia since the dawn of time; throughout its history the city has therefore been cosmopolitan in every sense of the word. A thousand different ethnic types have crowded the streets and squares as they have populated the pictures of Titian and Veronese. They have added colour to the Venetian scene, idiom and dialect to the vernacular language and, above all, exotic spice to the indigenous cultural and culinary traditions. The perfumes and fragrances exchanged in Venice have been blended and refined through time with more homely scents and flavours. Nothing has been lost. Only now the multicoloured multitude of merchants has been replaced with crowds of tourists, and so the alchemy continues.

Social history has also played its part: besides the gastronomic refinement inherited from an aristocratic past, solid peasant cooking still underpins many local dishes, even if the poorest have long since been enhanced by every sort of ingredient the mainland can provide before returning as a regional speciality.

Tourism has nurtured a demand for restaurants that alternate between luxurious and anonymous "tourist" catering, but the age-old rhythm of the city and the convivial habits of its citizens still survive and flourish: **un ombra di vin** (measure of wine) and a **cichèto**, (a bite of squid, salt-cod or such like) consumed in a **bàcaro** are luxuries that the Venetians would be loath to renounce.

SEAFOOD

Venetians are especially proud of their seafood. A traditional plate of *antipasto (hors d'oeuvre)* offers a chance to relish a wonderful selection of local shellfish including **peòci** (mussels), **bòvoli** (sea snails) and **canòce** (shrimps), as well as **granseole** and **gransipori** (crab).

As a *primo* or starter, **bigoi in salsa** (thick, coarse spaghetti served with lightly fried onions and anchovies) is one of the most popular first courses, but there are also many types of risotto made with meat and/or vegetables grown locally in market gardens, or more especially with fish or **'in tecia'** – with cuttlefish.

Polenta: a staple on Venetian menus

Fish from the Adriatic is often served grilled, accompanied, in spring, by **castraùre** (young fried artichokes); eels (**bisàto** in dialect), on the other hand, are either broiled or poached.

One common ingredient is vinegar. It is used in all kinds of ways, but notably for pickling and preparing **saòr**, a kind of carp.

Pasta

Cannelloni – stuffed tubes, topped with tomato and bechamel sauce, baked in the oven

Farfalle – butterfly or bows

Fettuccine – freshly made egg pasta – thin tagliatelle served with a creamy sauce

Fusilli – twists of pasta designed by aerodynamics engineers to hold sauces of particular consistencies

Gnocchi – made with potato and flour – an acquired taste

Lasagne – sheets of pasta layered with meat or fish, tomato and bechamel sauce and baked in the oven

Maccheroni – small tubes

Paglia e fieno – thin threads of freshly made egg and spinach pasta (literally meaning straw and hay)

Pappardelle – broad flat ribbons of freshly made pasta, very often served in a rich sauce (wild boar – *cinghiale*; hare – *lepre; porcini* mushrooms)

Polenta – a starchy semolina mixture served baked or with tomato sauce

Ravioli – cushions of freshly made egg pasta stuffed with meat, fish or spinach and cheese *(spinaci e ricotta)*; delicious with butter and sage *(burro e salvia)* or meat sauce *(al ragù)*

Spaghetti – long threads of pasta served with shellfish *(frutta di mare)* or clams *(vongole)*

Tatelle – freshly made egg pasta in long ribbons

Tortellini – little packets of freshly made egg pasta stuffed with meat or cheese, served either in a sauce or in clear broth *(in brodo)*

Pasta all'inchiostro di seppia – a dish prepared with squid ink

For a truly typical dish, try a bite of **bacalà mantecato**, salt-cod beaten to a smooth cream with oil, garlic and parsley and served with polenta.

MEAT DISHES

One of the most traditional *secondi* or main courses is **fegato alla veneziana**, (calf's liver and onions), a combination created in Venice but now popular everywhere. The defining factor for Venetians, however, is how thinly the meat is cut, and the long gentle cooking it undergoes.

During the Feast of the Madonna della Salute, **castrato** is eaten. This is succulent, sweet meat from a castrated lamb, slightly fatter than the norm but more delicate in flavour. At this time it is traditionally served with Savoy cabbage.

For flavoursome country cooking, try **panàda venexiana**, a wholesome soup made with bread, garlic, oil, bayleaf and Parmesan cheese, or **pastissàda**, an ingenious concoction of green vegetables, cheese, sausage, pasta or polenta bound together traditionally to use up leftovers!

DOLCI

For dessert, try the famous **baìcoli** biscuits which, according to local custom, are dunked in drinking chocolate or dessert wine; **bussolài**, biscuits moulded into ring or "S" shapes, called *essi buranèi*; or the **Veneziana**, a kind of brioche covered with chopped almonds and sugar. For Carnival, other seasonal goodies replace typical Shrove Tuesday pancakes: **frìtole** are made from a dough flavoured with raisins and pine nuts. **Pìnsa**, a biscuit flavoured with fennel seeds, raisins, dried figs and candied peel, is a speciality baked at Epiphany.

FOR A TOAST

The most commonly found wines are the **Soave** (white) and the **Cabernet del Friuli** (red). For dessert, there is the Verduzzo di Ramandolo DOC, Torcolato di Breganza or the Recioto.

As an apéritif, there is the famous **Bellini**, one-quarter measure of peach juice to three of *prosecco*, a dry Italian sparkling white wine; the **Tiziano**, made with a special strawberry-flavoured grape juice; the **Mimosa**, a blend of tangerine and orange juices; the **Rossini**, with strawberry juice added. Ernest Hemingway was a frequent visitor to **Harry's Bar**, where he would order his own special cocktail, the **Montgomery**, named after the famous general. It was made with one measure of vermouth to 15 measures of gin and is served only by that particular establishment.

For the best little places,
follow the leader.

Looking for the latest news on today's best hotels and restaurants?
Pick up the Michelin Guide and look for the Bib Gourmand and Bib
Hotel symbols. With 45,000 addresses in Europe, in every category and
price range, the perfect place to dine or stay is never far away.

Gondolas edging Piazza San Marco
G. Targat/MICHELIN

ACCADEMIA★★★

(**7**, DX)

VAPORETTO: ACCADEMIA OR ZATTERE

This area is permanently thronged by people on the move. Locals going about their everyday business, visitors drawn to the Academy of Fine Art, and students milling outside the nearby university lend a very artistic feel to the area. It is always worth stopping for a short break at one of the bars or trattorias.

▶ **Orient Yourself:** Because the **Accademia Bridge** is one of only three bridges that cross the Grand Canal, this area, sitting in the southern part of the city, is a busy one. Vaporetti continually disgorge and pick up passengers on the north side, dominated by the Academy of Fine Arts; the south side boasts the Zattere, the long promenade that overlooks the Guidecca canal and Guidecca island. Boats depart frequently from the Zattere for the airport.

⊛ **Don't Miss:** The academy, of course, but also the picturesque dockyard of Squero di San Trovaso.

⊕ **Organizing Your Time:** Allow 2hrs for the academy and 1hr for the area.

⊛ **Also See:** Neighbouring sights I CARMINI and La SALUTE.

Walking Tour

Ponte dell'Accademia (**7**, DX)

This wooden bridge replaces an old iron construction built by the Austrians in 1854 to allow their "peace-keeping" forces free access to both sides of the city. As then, it links the elegant and spacious Campo di San Stefano with the Accademia, eventually leading right up to the Zattere. The bridge is a popular spot for visitors to take their photograph with the lively Grand Canal as a backdrop.

Gallerie dell'Accademia★★★ (**7**, DX)

⊕*Open 8.15am-7.15pm (2pm Mon); last admission 30min before closing.* ⊕*Closed 1 Jan, 1 May and 25 Dec.* ⊛⊜€6.50. ☎ 041 52 00 345; www.gallerieaccademia.org.

The **Academy of Fine Art** exhibits an important collection of artworks encapsulating the development of Venetian painting from the 14C to the 18C, in a complex of buildings converted in the 19C. These structures include the Monastery of Lateran Canons, designed by Andrea Palladio (1508-80), the Church of La Carità, an atmospheric building that was redesigned by Bartolomeo Bon (recorded 1441-64), and the Scuola Santa Maria della Carità, the first Scuola Grande, which was erected in 1260 (⊛ *see I CARMINI: The Venetian Scuole).* The tour starts in the large Sala Capitolare at the top of the 18C staircase.

Room I

The Sala Capitolare (chapter house) is the place where, from the 15C, the Scuola Grande of the Santa Maria della Carità used to meet. This large room has a gilded panelled ceiling by Marco Cozzi (1484), divided into sections with a cherub in each. The figure of God in the central tondo, attributed to Alvise **Vivarini** (1445-1505), replaces that of the Madonna della Misericordia, the patron who would have occupied the section originally. The room is devoted to Venetian Gothic masters from the 14C and the first half of the 15C, including Paolo Veneziano (*Coronation of the Virgin* at the top of the stairs straight ahead) and Lorenzo Veneziano. The huge painting, *Coronation of the Virgin in Paradise,* at the end of the room, is by Jacobello del Fiore *(right).* Note Michele Giambino's works also on display here; Giambino, who worked between 1420 and 1462, is the most important artist to work in the International Gothic style in Venice.

Room II

This room displays eight important 15C altarpieces. On the entrance wall: the *Crucifixion and Apotheosis of the Ten Thousand Martyrs of Mount Ararat* by **Vittore Carpaccio** (c 1465-c 1526) depicts the legendary massacre of the Roman soldiers betrayed by their own captains after beating the Armenian rebels *(right)*. On the wall to the right hang the famous *Virgin and Child with Saints*, also known as the *Pala di San Giobbe*, by **Giovanni Bellini** (c 1470-1516) taken from the Church of San Giobbe; the *Agony in the Garden* by Marco Basaiti (c 1470-c 1530) *(right)* and the *Presentation of Christ in the Temple* by Vittorio Carpaccio *(left)*.

On the end wall: the *Madonna of the Orange Tree* by Cima da Conegliano (1459-1517) *(right)* hangs alongside his *Incredulity of St Thomas and the Great Bishop* in which the three figures are silhouetted against the sky with a village in the distance *(left)*. The *Calling of the Sons of Zebedee*, by Marco Basaiti, is a particularly beautiful and engaging treatment of the subject of Christ recruiting his Apostles, the variety of scenery with the focus on the water and the magical quality of the colour *(centre)*.

GALLERIE DELL'ACCADEMIA

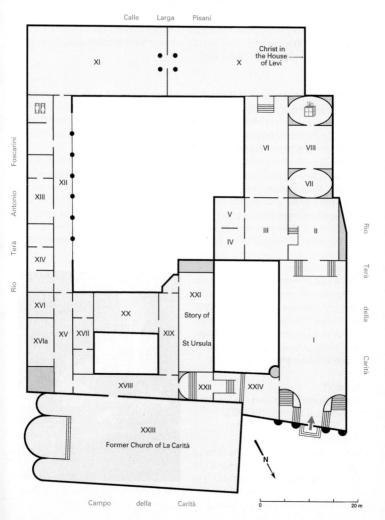

On the wall to the left: the *Mourning of the Dead Christ* by Giovanni Bellini and assistants *(right)* and the *Madonna with Child Enthroned* by Cima da Conegliano *(left)*.

Room III
This room contains works by Sebastiano del Piombo, Cima da Conegliano and Giovanni Bellini.

▸ *Cross to the far end for access to the small adjoining Rooms IV and V, among the most important rooms in the gallery.*

Room IV
St George by **Andrea Mantegna** (1431-1506) hangs on the wall to the left, one of only two paintings by the master who so influenced Bellini and consequently the evolution of Venetian painting. The painting has a Tuscan feel about it: the knight, a synthesis of Humanism, is reminiscent of Donatello.

On the wall to the right, Giovanni Bellini's *Madonna with Child between St Catherine and Mary Magdalene* depicts four figures thrown into relief by a strong transverse light that lifts them out of the darkness; note, however, the suggestion of serene beauty and tender spirituality so typical of Bellini. In contrast, on the right, is the *Portrait of a Young Man* by the Dutch artist Hans Memling (c 1435-94) with its sharp delineation of features and characterisation; lost in tranquil meditation, the young man's face is embued with inner calm.

Room V
The Tempest by **Giorgione** (c 1467-1510) is the crystallisation of a state of mind rather than the representation of a specific moment in time, an attempt at capturing the essence of a poetic narrative taken from literature. The protagonists of this "fantasy picture" are the three figures, the ruins, the water and the village dramatically caught in an iridescent green light by a flash of lightning.

Another famous work by Giorgione hangs on the left. *The Old Woman* is a compelling portrait, appealing yet uncompromising. Self-explanatory, it has been described as a "hymn to fleeing youth," touched with the inevitable sadness of realised awareness, highlighted by the inscription in the cartouche *col tempo* ("with time"). The picture is especially charged with meaning if one considers how Giorgione's untimely death in 1510 from the plague cut short a life full of promise. To the right of the door are the *Allegories* by Giovanni Bellini, particularly exquisite small paintings intended as decorative panels to set into a piece of furniture or mirror.

On the wall in front of the exit hang the *Madonna and the Seraphim* and the *Madonna under the Trees* by Giovanni Bellini. The title of the latter refers to the trees that serve as foreground to the landscape, channelling perspective across the countryside to distant snow-capped peaks.

Portrait of a Young Gentleman in his Study by Lotto (Accademia)

Accademia, Venezia /SCALA

Room VI
This long room houses works by Tintoretto (1518-94) and Veronese (1528-88).

Room VII
This little room is home to the famous 1524 *Portait of a Young Gentleman in his Study* by **Lorenzo Lotto** (c 1480-1577), in which the sitter's concentration seems to have been interrupted by a thought

or a memory; distracted from his reading, his long delicate fingers idly flick through the pages as he muses perhaps upon the passing of time, staring into the distance, his pale, chiselled face contrasting with his black coat.

Admire works by Vasari, Palma il Vecchio and Titian in **Room VIII**; then proceed to Room X.

Room X

The *Madonna with Child Enthroned* by Veronese *(left of the entrance)* recalls the Pesaro altarpiece in the Frari *(☙ see I FRARI)*. The *Pietà* by Titian (1490-1576) *(right of the entrance, in the middle)* was intended by the artist for his own tomb at the Frari but remained unfinished on his death. Note on the right, at the Sibyl's feet, the hand raised in supplication.

On the wall with the doorway into the next room hangs Veronese's *Betrothal of St Catherine (left)*.

Opposite the entrance hang Tintoretto's canvases depicting the life of St Mark. From left to right: *St Mark's Dream* (in fact the dream of St Mark's son, Dominic), *St Mark Saves a Saracen, St Mark Liberates a Slave* – the oblique lighting effects heighten the drama of the scene with St Mark falling head first; the *Theft of the Body of St Mark* (the final panel in the series, the *Finding of the Body of St Mark* is now in the Brera Collection in Milan). Note how the figures in the foreground appear thrown into relief by the use of chiaroscuro, where forms, picked out by strong light, are contrasted against another recessed into shadow; here phantom-like figures fade into the darkness, sloping off in search of safety in the palace.

The whole of the right wall is taken by Veronese's controversial *Christ in the House of Levi*, conceived as a *Last Supper* (1573) for the refectory of Santi Giovanni e Paolo *(☙ see SAN ZANIPÒLO)*. Shortly after the painting was unveiled, Veronese was summoned before a tribunal of the Inquisition on a charge of heresy for not adhering to the description of the event as related in the Gospels. Veronese defended himself on the grounds of artistic licence. He promptly changed the painting's title to suit a more secular subject that might also justify the painter's predilection for such opulent textures as brocade, glass, gold.

Rooms XI to XIX

This room accommodates works by **Giambattista Tiepolo** (1696-1770) including the frieze that depicts the *Castigation of the Serpents* and the fresco pendentives from the Scalzi Church (destroyed in 1915). *Dinner in the House of Simon* by **Bernardo Strozzi** (1581-1644) is particularly vibrant, notably animated by the expressive face of the figure filling the chalice. The *Crucifixion of St Peter* composed around its strong diagonal axes by Luca Giordano (1643-1705) is also here.

On the left wall hangs the masterpiece by Bonifacio de' Pitati (c 1487-1553). The *Rich Man Epulone* projects a tranquil scene, rich with incidental detail and contrasting personality, populated with musicians, a beggar, huntsmen and lovers converging in a wood, as a fire rages on the right. **Room XII** is dedicated to landscape painting from the late 17C and early 18C, including works by Marco Ricci, Giuseppe Zais and Francesco Zuccarelli. Access to the two side rooms, **Rooms XIII** (in which hang several works by Tintoretto, including his portrait of the Procurator Jacopo Soranzo) and **XIV**, which show works

Portrait of a Lady by Rosalba Carriera (Accademia)

from the 16C and 17C, is through Room XII. The corridor then becomes **Room XV** which leads to side rooms on the left **(Room XVII)** full of the most typical Venetian paintings: **Canaletto** (1697-1768) – although a prolific Venetian painter, all save a handful of his works hang in collections abroad, having been sold to foreign gentlemen on the Grand Tour or requisitioned by Napoleon; Bernardo Bellotto (1721-80); Francesco **Guardi** (1712-93); Giambattista Piazzetta (1683-1754); Rosalba Carriera (1675-1758), whose series of informal pastel portraits are provocative studies of personality; Pietro Longhi (1702-85) (the famous *Dancing Lesson*).

Room XVIa accommodates works from the 18C, including the *Fortune Teller* by Giambattista Piazzetta.

Room XVIII serves as a passageway into **Room XXIII**, the old Church of La Carità, which now contains works from the 15C/16C Venetian School.

The *Annunciation* by Antonello de Saliba (active 1497-1535), displayed in **Room XIX**, is, in fact, a copy of a work bearing the same title in the Galleria Nazionale di Palermo in Sicily, executed by Antonello da Messina, Da Saliba's uncle.

▶ *Access to Room XX is through Room XIX.*

Room XX

This room contains the famous collection of paintings illustrating the story of the *Miracles of the Relic of the True Cross*, executed by various artists between the 15C and 16C, for the Scuola di San Giovanni Evangelista.

The *Procession in St Mark's Square* by Gentile Bellini (1429-1507) covers the wall facing the entrance. The work is an important representation of the square in the mid-15C (&see PIAZZA SAN MARCO). Other paintings by Gentile Bellini on the right wall include *(from left to right)* the *Healing of Pietro de' Ludovici* and the *Miracle of the Cross on the Ponte di San Lorenzo* in which Andrea Vendramin is shown retrieving the Reliquary of the True Cross from the canal. Note that Caterina Cornaro (&see RIALTO: Ca' Corer della Regina) is just visible on the left-hand side of the latter work. On the same wall hangs a work by Giovanni Mansueti (active in Venice from 1485 to c 1526): the *Healing of Benvegnudo's Daughter of San Polo* sets the scene in a beautiful Renaissance interior *(right)*. Carpaccio's *Miracle of the Relic of the True Cross at Rialto* can be seen on the entrance wall. Interestingly, the subject of the painting – the miraculous healing of a madman taking place on the first-floor loggia on the left – seems secondary to the profusion of topographical detail showing Venice at the end of the 15C: the wooden Rialto Bridge, the Fondaco dei Tedeschi on the right as it was before the events of 1505 (&see La FENICE), the Ca' da Mosto (&see Il CANAL GRANDE) and the bell-towers of San Giovanni Grisostomo and the Church of All Saints (&see RIALTO).

Room XXI

This room contains the colourful and magical series of canvases by **Carpaccio** that retell the *Story of St Ursula* (1491-98).

▶ *Start with the wall facing the entrance (left) and proceed clockwise.*

The first panel, *Arrival of the English Ambassadors,* shows the ambassadors arriving at the (Catholic) court in Brittany bearing a proposal of marriage from their English (pagan) prince, Hereus. Ursula *(to the right)* is shown dictating her conditions of marriage (including his

The English Ambassadors Taking their Leave (detail) by Carpaccio (Accademia)

baptism and promise to undertake a pilgrimage accompanied by Ursula and a large number of virgins), in the presence of her wet nurse seated on the steps.

The next scene shows *The English Ambassadors Taking their Leave*, in which the king hands over the reply: it may well be that it is being written up by the scribe who is concentrating on his task.

In the *Return of the Ambassadors* the cortège bringing the reply to the king is followed by a crowd to the edge of the lagoon, the towers suggestive of the Arsenale. Certain details of the painting are particularly noteworthy: the central scene is almost theatrical, the eye caught by the handsome youth turning away as if affronted; the figure sitting on the bank is the "Steward," whose duty it is to herald the arrival of the ambassadors, invited by the doge, with music, while a monkey on the right watches a guinea fowl.

The *Meeting of Ursula and Hereus and the Departure of the Pilgrims* is a composite scene, divided by the pennant, showing the prince taking his leave; Hereus and Ursula bid farewell to the rulers of Brittany before departing for Rome. Note the sharp contrast between the harsh, darkened representation of the English capital on the left and the colourful Breton town on the right, represented according to Humanist ideals.

In *Ursula's Dream* the scene is more compact, set in Ursula's room where the light reveals more domestic details: reminiscent of *St Augustine in his Studio* (see SAN GIORGIO degli SCHIAVONI), the angel reaches out for the palm of martyrdom. The *Meeting of the Pilgrims with Pope Cyriac under the Walls of Rome* takes place against the background of the Castel Sant'Angelo, between two groups of virgin pilgrims (Ursula's companions) to the left and the prelates to the right. In the centre, the betrothed are waiting to be crowned. Note Carpaccio's delight in using strong and contrasting colours, notably red and white.

The *Arrival in Cologne* depicts how, on their arrival in the city, Ursula and her father, who has joined the pilgrims, learn that the city is in the hands of the Huns.

Ursula's eventful life on earth concludes with the *Martyrdom of the Pilgrims and Ursula's Funeral,* in which the two scenes are separated by the column. In the centre the warrior is removing blood from his sword. The final panel in the cycle, however, showing the *Apotheosis of St Ursula and her Companions*, is perhaps the saddest.

Room XXIV, on the way out, is the former Sala dell'Albergo. It houses one of the collection's highlights: Titian's *Presentation of the Virgin to the Temple* (1530s).

▶ *To reach San Trovaso, walk southwest of the Accademia, and cross the Rio di San Trovaso.*

San Trovaso (⁊, DX)

Entrance on the canal side. This church is dedicated to two saints (Gervasius and Protasius, the protomartyrs of Milan) whose names have been contracted to "Trovaso." Built in the 9C, the original church was totally remodelled by architects of the Palladian School between the 16C and 17C. Built in the plan of a Latin cross, it has a single nave with side chapels. In the presbytery, a chapel off to the right, hangs *Christ Crucified between the Two Marys,* by Jacopo Tintoretto's son Domenico (c 1560-1635) and *St Chrysogonus on Horseback* by Michele Giambono (active 1420-62). Other paintings by the Tintorettos as well as works by Palma il Giovane (1548-1628) and Andrea Vicentino (end 15C-early 16C) grace the church.

▶ *Farther along the Rio di San Trovaso between the church and the Zattere lies a quaint boatyard.*

Squero di San Trovaso (⁊, DX)

This is one of the few *squeri* still in operation in Venice; it is certainly the most famous, possibly because of its unusual character. In this city of elegantly refined Byzantine *palazzi*, this building seems idiosyncratic. Built of wood, with its geraniums tumbling

Squero di San Trovaso

from the balcony in summertime, it looks more like an alpine chalet. Elsewhere this little yard would be merely picturesque; here it continues to function as a dockyard where gondolas are built and repaired.

▶ *To reach the Church of the Gesuati, proceed eastward along the Zattere.*

Gesuati (**7**, DY)
◔*Open Mon-Sat, 10am-5pm.* ◔*Closed, 1 Jan, Easter, 15 Aug, 25 Dec.* ☞€2.50. ☎ 041 27 50 462; www.chorusvenezia.org
The Church of Santa Maria del Rosario ai Gesuati is dedicated to the Madonna of the Rosary, honoured by a 14C order of laymen, the Clerici apostolici S Hieronymi, not to be confused with the Jesuits. Shortly after the order was dissolved by Pope Clement IX in 1668, the incumbent order of Dominicans commissioned the architect Giorgio Massari (c 1686-1766) to remodel the building. For the new façade he borrowed elements from the Church of San Giorgio Maggiore. Highlights of the luminous interior include the *Crucifixion* by Tintoretto, *Three Saints* by Piazzetta (1683-1754) and a *Madonna* by **Giambattista Tiepolo**.

Chiesa della Visitazione (**7**, DXY)
Nearby, the Church of the Visitation was built in its present form between the 15C and the beginning of the 16C.

ARSENALE ★

(🔟, HX)

VAPORETTO: ARSENALE OR RIVA DEGLI SCHIAVONI

Renowned for its shipyards and famous towers, this area is steeped in the city's past naval prowess. It was thanks to her ships more than anything else that Venice flourished as a maritime power.

▶ **Orient Yourself:** An offshoot of the Castello neighbourhood, the Arsenale district lies in a more secluded part of Venice, east of the Piazza San Marco.

☺ **Don't Miss:** The sculpture-heavy entrance of the Arsenale *(which is closed to the public)*; note especially, the large ground-level lion sculptures.

🕓 **Organizing Your Time:** The suggested itinerary given here takes about 3hrs.

📷 **Especially for Kids:** The Naval Museum, with its dozens of watercraft.

🕯 **Also See:** Neighbouring sights SAN GIORGIO degli SCHIAVONI; SANT'ELENA e SAN PIETRO; and SAN ZACCARIA.

Walking Tour

Arsenale

○━▬*Closed to the public.* A naval base, depository for arms, and maintenance shop, the Arsenal served as the main shipyard, the heart of the Venetian State. Enclosed within medieval walls, it has two main entrances along the Rio dell'Arsenale: the **land entrance**, a grand Renaissance triumphal arch, constitutes the most important gateway, dating to c 1460, and presided over by the lions from Ancient Greece (Athens and Piraeus) brought over by Francesco Morosini after his victory over Morea in 1687. The **water entrance** (🔟, **HX**), through which the vaporetto passes, is marked by two towers rebuilt in 1686.

Gwen Cannon/ MICHELIN

Entrance to the Arsenale

A Bit of History

The first recorded dockyard in Venice, the **Arsenale Vecchio**, dates to about 1104 when the demands of the crusades stimulated shipbuilding. At one time, there were 24 active boatyards. In the 14C, the Arsenal was extended towards the southeast (**Arsenale Nuovo**). Altogether 16 000 *marangoni* were employed, men apprenticed as joiners and trained as shipwrights. The boat-building techniques were highly advanced, as the Venetians were already implementing production lines. During the second half of the 15C, the **Arsenale Nuovissimo** was extended to the north of the area – on the Galeazzi Canal (1564). Destroyed during the French occupation (1797), the Arsenal was rebuilt by the Austrians between 1814 and 1830. After the Venetians attacked it in 1848, the area was abandoned during the third Austrian occupation (1849-66). Restructuring work began in the late-19C, and continued to 1914.

The Buildings

The street names serve as a reminder of the various trades and activities of each street: Calle della Pegola (fish), Calle dei Bombardieri (cannon-ball foundries), Calle del Piombo (lead), and Calle delle Ancore (anchors). Mills churned out hemp rope; other structures included sail lofts, artillery warehouses and slipways.

Along the canal lies the **Scalo del Bucintoro** *(second on the right after the towers)*, designed by **Sanmicheli** (1484-1559). This dock is home to the famous ship built by the **arsenalotti**, artisans who worked in teams.

On entering the **Galeazzi Canal** the first building on the right is the **Complesso degli Squadratori**. Skeletons of the ships were squared here.

The final buildings sheltered the *galeazzi*, oar-propelled galleys, as they were being built. Alongside the Tana Canal to the south runs the **Tana**, a warehouse used to store hemp before being made into hawsers; its name is borrowed from the city formerly known as *Tanai*, situated on the River Don, from where the hemp was imported.

▶ *Walk south toward Campo San Biagio to reach the Museo Storico Navale.*

Museo Storico Navale★ (🔟, HX)

🔵 Open Mon-Sat, 8.45am-1.30pm (1pm Sat). 🕐Closed holidays. ☞€1.55, children ages 12-16 €0.77. ☎ 041 52 00 276.

This vast naval museum will delight any boat enthusiast and prove a veritable treasure trove to anyone intrigued by Venice's shipbuilding industry. The museum comprises five floors and houses a large collection of artifacts: a torpedo, taffrail lights, mortars, cannons, firearms and sabres and scale models of the city and her fortresses.

As you enter, the **ground floor** holds cannons, various weaponry and a room with models. Note the large lanterns from Venetian flagships.

On the **first floor** are examples of wooden sculptures that decorated the galleys, coats of arms, naval weaponry, nautical instruments (including compasses and octants), parchment *portolani* (pilots' charts and navigation material specifying details of coastal areas, harbours, anchorages and dangerous waters), engravings, models of ships, fine examples of galleys' broadsides, the supposed remains of Lazzarro Mocenigo's flagship which disappeared in the Dardanelles in 1657 and a model of the state barge, the *Bucintoro* (🔵 see PIAZZA SAN MARCO: Museo Correr).

The **second floor** is dedicated to naval history during the 19C and 20C and includes scale models and naval uniforms.

The **third floor** displays an extensive collection of ex-votos (offerings given by mariners to a church in thanks or commemoration of an event), a luxury vessel from the 18C, gondolas (including Peggy Guggenheim's) and a model of a working boatyard, the Squero di San Trovaso (🔵 see ACCADEMIA). One room is devoted to models of Asian giunca and sampans.

On the **fourth floor** there is a section dedicated to the Swedish navy and its relationship with Venice. The rescue expedition involving the airship *Italia* is remembered here.

▸ *On leaving the main building, rest on the benches outside to the left; then follow the Rio dell'Arsenale to the second section of the museum on the right.*

Even though the vessels are not displayed in their full glory in this setting, the pavilions house some interesting craft: a 1932 hydrofoil used for racing, a torpedo-launch (1942), an 1890 diving vessel and the remains of the steam ship **Elettra**.

▸ *Cross the Arsenale bridge, which leads into the Campo dell'Arsenale.*

Along the Fondamenta di Fronte, the visitor enters an almost traffic-free zone of quiet alleyways and peaceful squares. A short walk leads to the Church of San Francesco della Vigna.

▸ *Proceed along the Fondamenta di Fronte into Campo San Martino. Cross the bridge at the Fondamenta Penini and turn left into Calle delle Muneghette. In Campiello Due Pozzi, take Calle del Mandolin on the left. Turn right into Calle degli Scudi, which leads directly to Campo di San Francesco della Vigna.*

Coming from the south is particularly interesting as the route passes between the columns of an unusual 19C portico, of a delicate pinkish-brown colour, which links the naval headquarters with the Renaissance Palazzo Gritti, otherwise known as *La Nunziatura* (the Nunciature). Originally owned by **Doge Andrea Gritti** (1523-38), it was ceded by the Republic to Pope Pius IV (1559-65), who allowed it to be used by Apostolic delegates.

San Francesco della Vigna★ (🔟, HU)

There were vineyards here when the Franciscans first erected the church, begun in 1534. The main façade features a crowning pediment by **Palladio**. The *campanile* is one of the highest in Venice. Works of note include the *Four Evangelists* by **Giovanni Battista Tiepolo**, a *Virgin with Child* by **Veronese** and a *Madonna with Child and Saints* by **Giovanni Bellini**.

The church also accommodates the tomb of **Doge Marc'Antonio Trevisan** (1553-54). Its most famous masterpiece is **Madonna and Child Enthroned**★ painted in 1450 by the monk **Antonio da Negroponte**.

▸ *From Campo San Francesco della Vigna take Calle San Francesco and then, to the left, Calle de Te Deum. Continue south, crossing the canal for the first time to reach the Fondamenta San Giorgio degli Schiavoni. Take the next bridge and continue to the Scuola di San Giorgio degli Schiavoni (see SAN GIORGIO degli SCHIAVONI).*

The Fondamenta dei Furlani leads southwards to the **Church of San Antonin**, which was founded in the 7C and rebuilt by Baldassare Longhena (1598-1682). Salizzada San Antonin enters **Campo Bandiera e Moro** (🟫, HX). The square opens onto the back of Riva degli Schiavoni. The heroes of the Risorgimento, Attilio and Emilio Bandiera, were born here and remembered in the name of the square, together with Domenico Moro, another patriot who was shot down with them.

San Giovanni in Bràgora★ (🟫, HX)

The interior of this late 15C church comprises a nave with a trussed ceiling and two aisles. In the left aisle, near the font, a copy of deed confirming the baptism of Antonio Vivaldi is displayed. The highlight is the **Baptism of Christ**★★ by Cima da Conegliano (c 1459-c 1517). Also on view are works by **Alvise Vivarini**, Palma il Giovane (1544-1628) and Paris Bordone (1500-71). A stylised, truly Gothic *Madonna and Child with St John and St Andrew*★ (1478) by Alvise's uncle, Bartolomeo Vivarini (1432-c 1491) and *St Andrew with St Martin and St Jerome*, the work of Francesco Bissolo (c 1470-1554), are also featured.

CA' D'ORO★★★

(4, ET)

VAPORETTO: CA' D'ORO, SAN ALVISE OR MADONNA DELL'ORTO.

The tranquil *sestiere* of **Cannaregio** is a place of narrow alleyways and squares and includes the typically Venetian Ghetto quarter (*see Il GHETTO*), which is surprisingly unfrequented by tourists. The train station and the lively Strada Nuova are also found here. The area offers a wealth of boutiques and shops of every type and trade.

▶ **Orient Yourself:** One of Venice's six districts, Cannaregio dominates the north-west side of the Grand Canal and stretches eastward from the Santa Lucia train station, in the vicinity of the Ponta della Libertà, to include the Strada Nuova and the Ca' d'Oro.

🖧 **Don't Miss:** The magnificent Ca' d'Oro palace and its varied art collection.

🕐 **Organizing Your Time:** Allow half a day to explore this neighbourhood.

Kids **Especially for Kids:** A sweet treat from a bakery on the Strada Nuova.

🕯 **Also See:** Neighbouring sights Il GHETTO; SAN ZANIPOLO.

Visit

As the expression of the ultimate in Venetian Gothic domestic architecture, this *palazzo*, as it currently appears, does not justify its name "House of Gold." When Marino

Ca' d'Oro

Osvaldo Böhm

Contarini commissioned the construction of his *domus magna* at the beginning of the 15C, the French artist Jean Charlier, known as Zuane de Franza di Sant'Aponal, painted the façade in blue, black, white and gold, hence the name given to the *palazzo*.

A Bit of History

Several Lombard masters, followers of Matteo Raverti (active 1385-1436), were involved in the construction of the Ca' d'Oro and under the leadership of Giovanni (c 1360-1442) and Bartolomeo Bon (active 1441-64) the Venetian masters took over. The well-head at the centre of the courtyard is attributable to Bartolomeo Bon, the son of Giovanni. The figures represent the three theological virtues of Fortitude, Justice and Charity.

Nowadays it is the façade and its reflection in the Grand Canal which most captivates the visitor. After a long period of restoration, the subdued colours have regained their magical intensity and the delicate marble tracery and crenellation are complete. The façade is harmonious in its asymmetry, despite possible plans for a left wing.

The original structure commissioned by the Contarini was subject to various alterations requested by numerous owners who lived there over the course of the centuries. Restoration work started in the 19C, when Prince Troubetskoy bought the Ca' d'Oro as a present for the ballerina Maria Taglioni. The restoration was not faithful to the original construction. At the end of the 19C, more accurate restoration work was undertaken by **Baron Giorgio Franchetti**, who was responsible for the implementation of the gallery that now houses a varied collection of paintings, Renaissance bronze sculpture and medals spanning seven centuries from the 11C to the 18C.

Galleria Franchetti

&. ⏱Open 8.15am-7.15pm (2pm Mon); last admission 30min before closing. ⏱Closed 1 Jan, 1 May and 25 Dec. ☞€5. ☎ 041 52 00 345; www.cadoro.org

The first floor is devoted to Veneto-Byzantine art from the 11C to the 13C. Notable for its luminosity is the central panel of the polyptych dedicated to the *Passion* by **Antonio Vivarini** (c 1420-84), which depicts the Crucifixion. Another significant work is the English 15C *Scenes from the Passion of St Catherine*.

The highlight of the gallery is **Andrea Mantegna**'s uncompleted *Saint Sebastian*★★, in a niche at the end of the corridor on the right. Two similar treatments of the same subject by Mantegna exist, one in the Kunst-historisches Museum in Vienna and one in the Louvre in Paris, but this is the most dramatically tragic version. Note the *memento mori* attached to the candle stating *Nihil nisi divinum stabile est – Coetera fumus (Nothing if not divine is eternal – all the rest is smoke)* and the fact that the candle has just been blown out by the wind which ruffles St Sebastian's hair. The surge in popularity of St Sebastian during the early Renaissance is thought to be associated with his martyrdom by multiple arrow wounds, a fate involving the similar searing pain endured by those afflicted with the plague. The other was an opportunity for a painter to depict the nude torso of the young man modelled upon Classical sculpture. The other saint invoked by the plague-stricken is the pilgrim **San Rocco** (or Roch ☞see SAN ROCCO), who was believed to have protected Venice from the epidemic. The saint seems to indicate where the bubonic swellings have appeared by the position of his arms.

Among the bronzes, the work of **Pier Giacomo Bonaccolsi** (c 1460-1528) stands out. The official sculptor at the Gonzaga court at Mantua was better known for his emulation of sculptures in the Antique style and so nicknamed *l'Antico*; he embodies all the Classical ideals of Humanism (note the *Apollo* on display in one of the small showcases).

Note also the *Annunciation* which appears to be set in Venice itself and the *Death of the Virgin*, painted by **Vittorio Carpaccio** (c 1465-1526) and his studio for the Scuola degli Albanesi.

The *Flagellation* by **Luca Signorelli** (c 1445-1523) is to be found on the same floor, along with the vibrant sequence from the *Life of Lucretia* in two paintings by Biagio d'Antonio (active to 1508). The latter depicts the departure of Sextus Tarquin from the Roman camp at Ardea, and the rape of Lucretia, her suicide and funeral. The *Virgin with Child and St John*, a tondo by Jacopo del Sellaio (1442-93), is also on display here.

Exhibits on the floor above include the *Portrait of the Procurator Nicolò Priuli* by **Tintoretto**; Flemish tapestries from the second half of the 16C; *Venus with a Mirror* by **Titian** (1490-1576), which is incomplete on the right-hand side; *Portrait of a Gentleman* by **Sir Anthony van Dyck** (1599-1641) and *Venus Asleep with her Lover* executed by **Paris Bordone** (1500-71). Two more specifically Venetian scenes are by **Francesco Guardi** (1712-93): *St Mark's Square*, with the view of the Church of San Giorgio that was very dear to the artist, and the *View of the Wharf towards the Basilica of Santa Maria della Salute*.

Of great importance despite being very damaged are the frescoes painted by **Giorgione** (c 1476-1510) and Titian for the façades of the **Fondaco dei Tedeschi**. All that remains of Giorgione's work is the *Nude*. Titian's work is still discernible in the frieze with the *Justice* and the great coat of arms.

Other interesting works include: paintings by Flemish artists, notable for their domestic interiors and landscapes; The *Crucifixion* by a follower of Van Eyck, remarkable for topographical detail, particularly with regard to the fortified city that emerges from the background.

The Franchetti collection of ceramics is displayed in the adjoining Palazzo Duodo. Before exiting, rest on seating in the courtyard, with its exquisite marble flooring and statuary.

▶ *On leaving the Galleria Franchetti, turn left on Calle di Ca' d'Oro, then left onto Strada Nuova.*

Walking Tour

Strada Nuova (4, EFT)

This bustling thoroughfare runs almost parallel to the Grand Canal. It is part of the throbbing artery that starts at the Santa Lucia Station, snakes through the Cannaregio sestiere and eventually leads to the Rialto. Opened in 1871, the street is vibrant with the uninterrupted flow of people as visitors shuttle to and from the station and the Rialto, and locals do their shopping. It is lined with all sorts of shops, particularly the stretch of Rio Terrà San Leonardo near the station and around the lively market. Fish stalls run the length of the Fondamenta della Pescaria, alongside the Cannaregio Canal. Stop for a treat in a bakery, buy a souvenir or take a break at an outdoor cafe, while you watch the many passers-by.

▶ *Continue left to the Fondamenta San Felice off the campo of the same name.*

Once past the **Church of San Felice**, which houses *St Demetrius with his Follower* by Tintoretto (1518-94), the canal follows the *fondamenta* and emerges in a corner of the city that is rarely frequented by tourists. Time seems to stand still in this peaceful district, which is a world apart from the noise and crowds of the Strada Nuova.

▶ *Turn right at Campo San Fosca.*

Campo San Fosca is dominated by a church of the same name and a monument to **Paolo Sarpi** (1552-1623), a Venetian monk who defended the Republic while the Senate claimed the right of autonomy in the religious courts when pontifical claims were made.

▶ *Cross the first bridge, then the second to reach San Marziale church.*

The austere exterior of the **Chiesa di San Marziale** (▣, **ET**) contrasts sharply with its rich Baroque interior. The ceiling decoration is the work of Sebastiano Ricci (1659-1734).

▶ *Continue to Fond. della Misericordia. Turn right and follow it to the end.*

Here stands the **Scuola Nuova della Misericordia**, a building designed by Sansovino in 1534 as the "new" seat of the Order and built in brick, but never completed.

▶ *Turn left along the water and cross the bridge.*

Campo dell'Abbazia (▣, FT)

The centre of this square, paved in brick in a herringbone pattern, is marked by a fine well-head. Bordering on the Rio della Sensa and the Misericordia Canal, the *campo* is hemmed in by the **Church of Santa Maria della Misericordia** (▣, **FT**), otherwise known as Santa Maria Valverde after the island on which it was built in the 10C, and by the **Scuola Vecchia della Misericordia** (▣, **FT**). The Baroque façade of the church, the work of Clemente Moli (1651-59), contrasts sharply with the Gothic brick façade of the Scuola of 1451.

▶ *Head west along the Rio della Sensa. Turn right on Corte Vecchia.*

Corte Vecchia leads to a viewpoint overlooking the **Sacca della Misericordia** (▣, **FST**), a cove buffeted by the wind, from where the view stretches into the distance, punctuated only by the Island of San Michele, the tranquil cemetery on the water.

▶ *Retrace your steps, turn right and cross the bridge over Rio dei Muri. Pass **Casa del Tintoretto** at n° 3399, the house where the artist died in 1594 (a plaque marks the exterior). Turn right onto Campo dei Mori.*

Campo dei Mori (▣, ES)

The square's name alludes to the Moorish or Levantine Mastelli brothers (⟲*see below*). Intriguing 13C statues lean against the houses: the figure on the corner of the building is of Sior Antonio Rioba, the Paquino of Venice, whose nose is used as an object of satire when local politicians and visiting dignitaries are lampooned. Along the Rio della Madonna dell'Orto stands the **Palazzo Mastelli del Cammello** (▣, **ES**), notable for its Gothic detailing, corner column and low relief featuring a man pulling a camel. It belonged to a family of merchants from Morea in the Peloponnese who settled in Venice in 1112. The name Mastelli was coined after the thousands of *mastelli* (buckets) of gold *zecchini* or Venetian sequins they were meant to own.

▶ *Continue over the bridge to Fondamenta Gasparo Contarini.*

One of the "Moors"

Madonna dell'Orto★ (4, ES)

🕐Open Mon-Sat, 10am-5pm. 🕐Closed 1 Jan, Easter, 15 Aug, 25 Dec. ⊙€2.50. ☎ 041 27 50 462; www.chorusvenezia.org

Known as the Tintoretto Church, the parish church of the Tintoretto family overlooks a quiet square paved in a brick herringbone pattern. The richly ornamented façade, also in brick, betrays the various stages of construction from its foundation in the 14C, through early Gothic and Renaissance periods. Patronage was entrusted to the miracle-working Madonna dell'Orto (Our Lady of the Vegetable Patch!) when a statue of the Madonna and Child was found in a sculptor's garden.

The spacious interior accommodates important works of art: *John the Baptist* by Cima da Conegliano (1459-1517) *(right aisle, first bay)*; *St Vincent* by Jacopo Palma il Vecchio (c 1480-1528) *(second bay, altarpiece)*; *Martyrdom of St Lawrence* by Daniel van den Dyck (1614-63) *(last bay)*. Over the entrance to the Mauro Chapel is the *Presentation of the Virgin in the Temple* (1551) by **Tintoretto** (1518-94), whose burial place is marked by a slab in a chapel on the right. Other works by the master, as well as by his son Domenico and by Palma il Giovane, adorn the church.

Next to the church stands the **Scuola dei Mercanti** (4, **ES**), seat of the Guild of Merchants since 1570, when it transferred itself there from the Frari. Palladio participated in its renovation (1571-72) and is responsible for the portal which overlooks the *fondamenta*.

▶ *Return to Campo dei Mori and turn right onto Fondamenta della Sensa. To reach the Church of Sant' Alvise, turn right on Calle del Capitello.*

Sant'Alvise★ (3, DS)

🕐Open Mon-Sat,10am-5pm. 🕐Closed 1 Jan, Easter, 15 Aug, 25 Dec. ⊙€2.50. ☎ 041 27 50 462; www.chorusvenezia.org

The simple brick façade is pierced by a rose window and a portal under a delicate prothyrum. Originally Gothic in style, the façade was greatly modified during the 16C. The statue in the lunette is of St Louis of Anjou, who lived towards the end of the 13C and was named Alvise by the Venetians.

Madonna dell'Orto

The 17C frescoes by Antonio Torri and Pietro Ricchi lend an evocative three-dimensional effect to the flat ceiling. The entrance area is overlooked by the *barco*, the pensile choir stalls used by the nuns, supported by columns with 15C capitals and Gothic buttresses. Above the columns stand 15C statues of *Christ the Redeemer* and *John the Baptist*. As you enter, note the 15C **tempera panel paintings** on the left, which were executed by a pupil of Lazzaro Bastiani (active 1449-1512). On the right wall are Tiepolo's *Flagellation* and the *Crown of Thorns* (1740); his *Christ's Way to Calvary* (1749) is in the presbytery. The 16C wooden polychrome statue of Sant'Alvise shows the saint dressed in a Franciscan habit with a splendid crown.

▸ *Retrace your steps, heading toward the Grand Canal.*

IL CANAL GRANDE★★★

When he was living in Palazzo Mocenigo, Lord Byron was in the habit of swimming across the Grand Canal. Mark Twain described the appearance of the canal in moonlight as magical; Goethe felt himself to be "Lord of the Adriatic" here; and Dickens, convinced the ghost of Shylock roamed the bridges of the city, felt the spirit of Shakespeare strongly in Venice. To best experience the Grand Canal, take a vaporetto from the railway station to Piazza San Marco, the heart of the city. This short journey will undoubtedly leave as magical an impression on modern-day travellers as it did on its illustrious visitors of the past.

▸ **Orient Yourself:** The city's high street, the Grand Canal (3km/2mi long, 30m/98ft to 70m/229ft wide and, on average, 5.5m/18ft deep) bisects the island in the form of an inverted S, the bend marked by the Ca' Foscari.

🛆 **Don't Miss:** The famous Rialto Bridge, lined with shops.

🕐 **Organizing Your Time:** Allow two hours for a leisurely trip down the canal by gondola, vaporetto or water taxi; you may want to make a stop or two.

A Bit of History

The origins of the Grand Canal, which may once have been a branch of the River Medoacus (🕯*see VILLAS OF THE BRENTA*), are lost in time. The *traghetti* (gondolas which cross the river) have provided a ferry service between the banks of the canal since the year 1000: some of the existing landing stages have been in place since the 13C, many either serving mills that were operated by the tides or *squeri* where the gondolas were built; then there were the workshops for the Guild of Wool Weavers and Clothmakers, which employed the poor to card, finish, dye and press the textiles.

It is along the canal especially that the beauty of the city unfolds: façades of vibrant colours, resplendent with gilding, exude the festive spirit and optimism of the Venetians, who have never known the threat of oppression, not even in the Middle Ages, when the rest of the world had to build fortresses to defend themselves. The *palazzi* that flank the Grand Canal are the Venetian nobility's expression of pride and self-satisfaction: they were the only people who could vouchsafe a piece of this water garden (🕯*see Il GHETTO: Palazzo Labia*). Commercial, banking and state enterprises have been in operation along the canal since the Renaissance; churches and *palazzi* were being built right up until the Republic breathed its last breath.

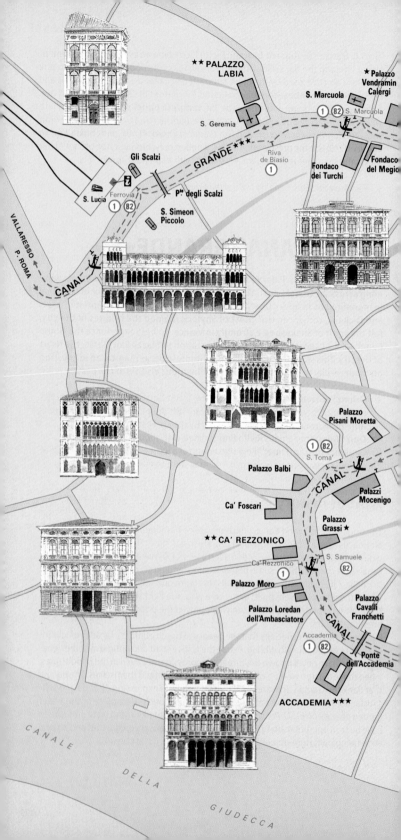

★★ PALAZZO LABIA

★ **Palazzo Vendramin Calergi**

S. Marcuola

① ⑧② S. Marcuola

S. Geremia

Gli Scalzi

GRANDE ★★★

Riva de Biasio
①

Fondaco dei Turchi

Fondaco del Megio

S. Lucia

Ferrovia
① ⑧②

P.te degli Scalzi

VALLARESSO

P. ROMA

S. Simeon Piccolo

CANAL

Palazzo Pisani Moretta

① ⑧②
S. Toma'

Palazzo Balbi

CANAL

Palazzi Mocenigo

Ca' Foscari

Palazzo Grassi ★

★★ CA' REZZONICO

Ca' Rezzonico
①

S. Samuele

⑧②

Palazzo Moro

Palazzo Loredan dell'Ambasciatore

Palazzo Cavalli Franchetti

CANAL

Accademia
① ⑧②

Ponte dell'Accademia

ACCADEMIA ★★★

C A N A L E

D E L L A

G I U D E C C A

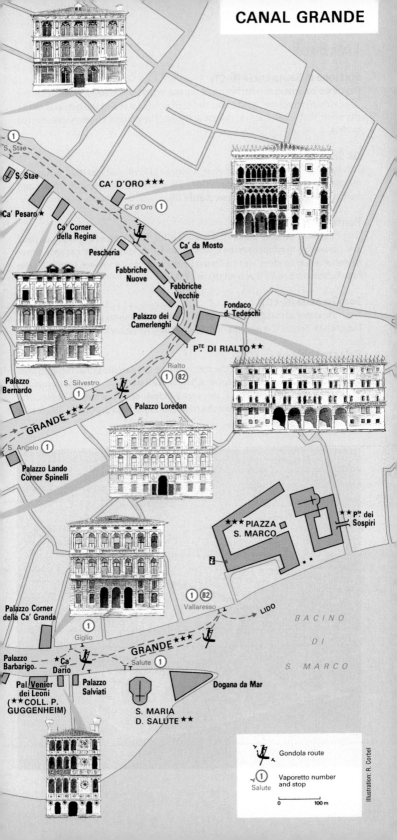

CANAL GRANDE

S. Stae

(1) S. Stae

CA' D'ORO ★★★

Ca' d'Oro (1)

Ca' Pesaro ★

Ca' Corner
della Regina

Pescheria

Ca' da Mosto

Fabbriche
Nuove

Fabbriche
Vecchie

Fondaco
d. Tedeschi

Palazzo dei
Camerlenghi

P.ᵀᴱ DI RIALTO ★★

Rialto

(1) (82)

**Palazzo
Bernardo**

S. Silvestro

(1)

Palazzo Loredan

GRANDE ★★★

S. Angelo (1)

**Palazzo Lando
Corner Spinelli**

★★★ PIAZZA
S. MARCO

★★ P.ᵗᵃ dei
Sospiri

**Palazzo Corner
della Ca' Granda**

(1) (82)

Vallaresso

LIDO

B A C I N O

(1)

Giglio

GRANDE ★★★

D I

**Palazzo
Barbarigo**

★ Ca'
Dario

Salute (1)

S. MARCO

**Pal. Venier
dei Leoni
(★★COLL. P.
GUGGENHEIM)**

Palazzo
Salviati

Dogana da Mar

**S. MARIA
D. SALUTE** ★★

Gondola route

(1)
Salute

Vaporetto number
and stop

0   100 m

Illustration: R. Corbel

Left Bank

Stazione di Santa Lucia (🗺, CT)

Described by Gustav von Aschenbach, the main character in *Death in Venice*, as the "tradesmen's entrance" to the city, the station has served as the gateway to the city since 1860 when the first station was built. The present building was erected in 1954.

Gli Scalzi (🗺, CT)

This Baroque church was designed by Longhena (1598-1682). Its most distinctive features are the niches in the façade (1672-78), which are adorned with statues and framed with paired columns (♿*see Il GHETTO*).

Ponte degli Scalzi (🗺, CT)

Originally built in 1858, the bridge, named after the discalced (meaning unshod and pertaining to religious orders, such as the Carmelites and Franciscans, whose members wear sandals), was designed by the same civil engineer, Neville, as the first Accademia Bridge. It was rebuilt in 1934.

San Geremia (🗺, CDT)

From the water all that can be seen of the Church of St Jerome is the Chapel of Saint Lucy, which houses the remains of the Sicilian martyr (♿*see Il GHETTO*).

Palazzo Labia★★ (🗺, CDT)

This elegant 18C residence on the corner of the Cannaregio Canal is slightly set back from the Grand Canal. The ground floor is rusticated, with Ionic and Corinthian pilasters on the two floors above: the large windows open out onto balconies. The eagles which protrude from under the roof refer to the heraldry of the Labia family (♿*see Il GHETTO*).

Bird's-eye view of the Grand Canal

Arthus-Bertrand/ALTITUDE

San Marcuola (🛐, DT)

This church is quite distinctive from others overlooking the Grand Canal: the roughly-bricked façade remains incomplete. Interestingly, this façade is actually the side of the church. Although its present appearance is Baroque in style, the church is altogether much older (🕭*see Il GHETTO*).

Palazzo Vendramin Calergi★ (🛂, ET)

This Renaissance palace, commissioned by the noble family of Loredan al Codussi, who worked in the city between 1502 and 1504, is a magnificent synthesis of Byzantine and Gothic architectural features. From 1844, it was home to the Duchesse de Berry, the daughter-in-law of Charles X of France. Here, too, **Richard Wagner** lived, composing the second act of *Tristan and Isolde* between 1858 and 1859. Although the composer died in the Palazzo Vendramin, where he had also worked on *Parsifal*, his memory is enshrined in the **Sala Richard Wagner** (🕭*Open by appointment only (telephone before noon the previous Fri.* 🕭*Closed in Aug and on national hols.* 🕭*Donations welcome. Apply to Associazione Richard Wagner di Venezia, near Associazione Culturale Italo Tedesca, 4118 Cannaregio, 30131 Venezia.* ☎ *041 52 32 544).* The *palazzo* currently serves as the winter headquarters of the municipal casino, although plans are afoot to use it for a different purpose.

Ca' d'Oro★★★ (🛂, ET)

The *palazzo*'s façade, in the ornate Gothic style, presents a colonnade lapped by the water's edge and, on the upper floors, two enclosed loggias with arched windows, interlaced with intersecting tracery and quatrefoils. Oddly, this decorative feature is not centred in the façade. The right section consists of a blank wall between single-arched windows. Cordons of marble accentuate the corners (🕭*see CA' D'ORO*).

Ca' da Mosto (🛂, FU)

Erected in the 13C, this Veneto-Byzantine *palazzo* was the birthplace of Alvise da Mosto (1432-88), the great navigator who explored the western coast of Africa. The portico betrays the building's dual function as house and warehouse. Note the first-floor ceiling decorated with circular coffering or patera. Between the 16C and 18C, the *palazzo* served as the city's finest hotel, the **Leon Bianco**.

Fondaco dei Tedeschi (🛂, FU)

This 13C *palazzo* served as the headquarters of German traders and as a warehouse for their goods. Devastated by fire (1505-08), it was rebuilt by Giorgio Spavento (in Venice between the 15C and 16C) and by Scarpagnino (in Venice between 1505 and 1549). The façade that overlooks the Grand Canal, and which was at one time frescoed by Giorgione (c 1476-1510) and Titian (1490-1576), has a portico on the ground floor, as befitted a *fondaco* (warehouse). Nowadays the building houses the main post office (🕭*see La FENICE*).

Ponte di Rialto★★ (🛂, FU)

The **Rialto Bridge** is the most important crossing point between the two banks of the Grand Canal. Although today's bridge is the sixth version – the original was built in 1175 – this is the first stone-built construction. The work of Antonio da Ponte, it was opened in 1591. The shops which are housed in the symmetrical arcades were originally used by money changers, bankers and moneylenders, in close proximity to the first Zecca (Mint – 🕭*see RIALTO*).

Palazzo Loredan (🛂, EFV)

Also a *fondaco* (warehouse), this Veneto-Byzantine *palazzo* retains some original features: part of the portico and windows opening out onto the loggia, interlaced with pateras, run the length of the *piano nobile* (first floor). Palazzo Loredan and the nearby Palazzo Farsetti now house municipal offices.

Palazzo Lando Corner Spinelli (⁴, EV)

Erected in 1490, this Renaissance *palazzo* was most probably designed by Mauro Codussi. The façade in Istrian stone is heavily rusticated. The upper storeys are punctuated with typical two-light windows, and a Renaissance frieze of festoons runs below the attic windows. It resembles the Palazzo Vendramin Calergi.

Right Bank

San Simeon Piccolo (³, CT)

This is the first eye-catching landmark after the station. Distinctive features include a Corinthian *pronaos* (front portico) up a flight of steps and a green dome. The church was designed by Scalfarotto (c 1700-64) in the tradition set by Palladio and Longhena.

Ponte degli Scalzi (³, CT) (🖐 *see Left Bank, above*).

Fondaco dei Turchi (³, DT)

Dating to the 13C, this Veneto-Byzantine *fondaco* was built as a private house and turned into commercial premises in 1621. Its current appearance is largely due to its restoration in the late-19C. With the side towers framing the façade, the portico and the floor above are laced with arches. Between 1621 and 1838 the warehouse was used by Turks, hence its name. The building houses the Natural History Museum (🖐 *see I FRARI*).

Fondaco del Megio (³, DT)

This distinctive building, with walls of roughly hewn brick and tiny windows, dates to the 15C. Note the lion below the ornate crenellation. The structure was used as a grain store, notably for millet (*miglio = megio* – hence the name).

San Stae (⁴, ET)

🕐*Open Mon-Sat, 10am-5pm.* 🕐*Closed 1 Jan, Easter, 15 Aug, 25 Dec.* 🎫€2.50. ☎ 041 27 50 462; www.chorusvenezia.org

Dedicated to St Eustace, this church was completely renovated during the 17C. The elaborate Baroque façade (1709), dominated by a pedimented bay set between two roughcast wings, is attributed to Domenico Rossi (1678-1742). Its broken tympanum, crowned with statues over the entrance, is original. Inside a single nave are works by Piazzetta (1683-1754), Ricci (1659-1734) and Tiepolo (1696-1770) that forestall a shift in style towards the Rococo. Doge Alvise Mocenigo is buried here.

Ca' Pesaro★ (⁴, ET)

At the death of Baldassare Longhena (1682), completion of the building was assigned to Antonio Gaspari (c 1670-c 1730). Unusual is its diamond-pointed rustication of the ground floor and row of lions' heads. On the second and third floors, great arched windows with single columns grace an open loggia. Today, the building is home to the Museum of Oriental Art and the International Gallery of Modern Art (🖐 *see RIALTO*).

Ca' Corner della Regina (⁴, ET)

Designed by Domenico Rossi (1678-1742), the heavily rusticated ground floor gives way to plainer upper storeys punctuated by balconies and windows framed with columns. Currently the home of the National Archives of Contemporary Art (🖐 *see RIALTO*).

Pescheria (⁴, ET)

The portico of this neo-Gothic building, which dates back to the beginning of the 20C, now accommodates the fish market, hence the name (🖐 *see RIALTO*).

Fabbriche Nuove (🜃, FU)

This rather plain building on the bend of the Grand Canal was designed by **Sansovino**. Its rusticated ground floor at one time would have consisted of *magazzini* (small shops) and warehousing. The first floor was occupied by magistrates' courts ruling on commercial matters (🕐 *see RIALTO*).

Fabbriche Vecchie (🜃, FU)

Destroyed by fire, the warehouses were rebuilt by Scarpagnino (active in Venice between 1505 and 1549). Even the "old workshops" boast their own columned portico (🕐 *see RIALTO*).

Palazzo dei Camerlenghi (🜃, FU)

Situated in the lee of the bridge, this Renaissance palace was designed by Guglielmo dei Grigi, known as Bergamasco (active in Venice between c 1515-30), for the Camerlenghi, who were government officials responsible for the State's financial affairs. The pentagonal building has large windows aligned below a frieze of festoons.

Ponte di Rialto★★ (🜃, FU) (🕐 *see Left Bank, above*).

Palazzo Bernardo (🜃, EV)

Gothic in style (1442), the building boasts splendid five-arched windows, pointed on the first floor, and quatrefoils on the second floor.

Palazzo Pisani Moretta (🜄, DV)

Also late Gothic, the Palazzo Pisani Moretta dates from the second half of the 15C. Like Palazzo Bernardo, the windows have five lights and intersecting tracery that enclose quatrefoils on the upper floors.

Palazzo Balbi (🜄, DX)

The façade of this *palazzo*, which is attributed to Alessandro Vittoria (1525-c 1600), is divided into three sections. Above a rusticated ground floor, the central bay is pierced by an arrangement of three arched windows. Note the two distinctive large coats of arms and the obelisks on the roof.

Left Bank

Palazzo Mocenigo (🜄, DX)

This building comprises four adjacent *palazzi*. The first dates back to 1579, when it was rebuilt according to the designs of Alessandro Vittoria. The second and third buildings, which are identical, are from the end of the 16C; the last, the so-called "Casa Vecchia," a Gothic construction, was remodelled by Francesco Contin during the first half of the 17C.

The Romantic poet **Lord Byron** (1788-1824) started work on his *Don Juan* while he lived here. This English "Don Giovanni" often swam home from a day at San Lazzaro (🕐 *see SAN LAZZARO degli ARMENI*) or an evening at the Lido, a habit that instituted a swimming race that was held until 1949 and rewarded by the Byron Cup.

Palazzo Grassi★ (🜄, DX)

Erected in 1749 by Giorgio Massari, this last Venetian palace to be built before the fall of the Republic is designed with all the majesty of neo-Classical domestic architecture. Outfront, the attention-grabbing, magenta-coloured sculpture, *Balloon Dog* (2000), is the creation of Jeff Koons; it is made of high-chromium stainless steel. Inside, the courtyard has a fine colonnade and a grand staircase frescoed by Alessandro Longhi populated with masked figures. Other rooms are frescoed by Jacopo Guarana (1720-1808) and Fabio Canal (1703-67). Today the building is used for prestigious temporary exhibitions.

Ponte dell'Accademia (**7**, DX)

Venice had to wait until 1854 for its second and third means of crossing the Grand Canal after the Rialto Bridge. The original iron construction, restricted in height, hindered the passage of the vaporettos; the bridge was therefore replaced in 1932, this time built of wood because of lack of funds. The present bridge is a copy of its wooden predecessor (*see ACCADEMIA*).

Palazzo Cavalli Franchetti (**7**, DX)

The splendid façade of this late-15C *palazzo*, complete with delicate tracery work, five-arched windows with intersecting tracery and quatrefoil motifs, casts its intricate reflection across the Grand Canal. It was rebuilt towards the end of the 19C by Camillo Boito, the brother of the musician.

Palazzo Corner della Ca' Granda (**8**, EX)

Nowadays this Renaissance palace is used as the police headquarters *(Prefettura)*. It was built for the nephew of Caterina Cornaro by Sansovino (1486-1570). The rusticated ground floor has a three-arch portico; elegantly aligned arched windows on the upper floors alternate with paired columns.

Next door, the little red house was used by **Canova** as his studio (1770s) and during the First World War by the novelist **Gabriele d'Annunzio**.

Right Bank

Ca' Foscari (**7**, DX)

The glorious façade of this *palazzo* rises above the Grand Canal at the junction with the Rio Foscari. Perfect symmetry aligns the three orders of arched windows that alternate with single light openings and stonework. The original 14C building was

View of the left bank from Ponte dell'Accademia (On the left, Palazzo Cavalli Franchetti)

rebuilt closer to the water's edge after 1550, resulting in an overall Gothic design with early Renaissance features (marble low relief above the ornate arcade of windows on the second floor). Nowadays it forms part of the university (👆see I CARMINI).

Ca' Rezzonico★★ (7, DX)

This house, commissioned by a wealthy Genoese banker, was the last palace designed by Longhena, who lived to see only the completion of the first floor, before Massari took over. Note the extensive embellishment of the *piano nobile* and the fine configuration of balconies. It presently contains the Museum of 18C Venice (👆see I CARMINI) and collections of Venetian finery that convey all the excitement of Carnival.

Palazzo Moro (7, DX)

Situated just beyond the Ca' Rezzonico vaporetto stop, beyond the gracious Palazzo Stern and its gardens overlooking the Grand Canal, this 16C *palazzo* is austere in its simplicity. It was here that the Moro family resided, one of whom suffered the tragic marriage that was to inspire **Shakespeare** (1564-1616) to write *Othello*, and portray the famous "Moor of Venice" as black.

Palazzo Loredan dell'Ambasciatore (7, DX)

Otherwise known as "The Ambassador's House," the late-Gothic Palazzo Loredan has splendid arched windows with a quatrefoil design. Between the single-arched windows at the sides are two shield-bearing pages.

Accademia★★★(7, DX)

The Academy of Fine Arts has been housed in this group of buildings since the beginning of the 19C. Whereas the former Scuola Grande della Carità is Gothic in style, its 18C façade is by Giorgio Massari and Bernardo Maccurzzi. The adjoining church, rebuilt between 1441 and 1452, most probably under the guidance of Bartolomeo Bon, has been subject to considerable restoration through the ages: one such instance involved Palladio (1508-80) (👆see ACCADEMIA).

Ponte dell'Accademia (7, DX) (👆see Left Bank, above).

Palazzo Barbarigo (8, EX)

The mosaics that decorate the façade depict Charles V in Titian's studio and Henry III of France on Murano. These were installed by the glass-blowers and mosaic-makers responsible for the reconstruction of the 16C palace in the late-19C. This building provided **Henry James** with inspiration for his novel *The Wings of the Dove*.

Palazzo Venier dei Leoni (8, EX)

It requires imagination to picture how the palace was intended to look by its designer Lorenzo Boschetti in 1749, despite the scale model of it in the Correr Museum. Financial problems forced the Venier family to stop work on the building. All that survives of the original is its rusticated ground floor.

The allusion to lions might stem from a story that the Venier family managed to tame a lion in the garden, or otherwise, more simply, from the lion masks along the base. The building currently houses the **Peggy Guggenheim Collection**.

Ca' Dario★ (8, EX)

This small, late-15C *palazzo* is most distinctively embellished with polychrome marble decoration. It was built by the Lombardo family for Giovanni Dario, the secretary to the Senate of the Republic at the Sultan's court. In recent times it has gained a sinister reputation as a result of mysterious circumstances surrounding the death of several of the building's owners.

Palazzo Salviati (⟨8⟩, EX)

Like Palazzo Barbarigo, the 19C Palazzo Salviati was owned by glass-makers who provided its fine mosaics.

Santa Maria della Salute★★ (⟨8⟩, FX)

The massive white structure with its distinctive spiral volutes (the so-called *orecchioni*, or big ears) is visible from afar. Designed by Longhena, it was erected upon the wishes of the doge as a gesture of supplication to end the plague of 1630, a story recounted in the Italian novel by Alessandro Manzoni, *I Promessi Sposi* (◖*see La SALUTE*).

Dogana da Mar (⟨8⟩, FX)

It was here on this extension of the Dorsoduro district that goods used to be unloaded and duty on them levied. The present construction, dominated by a tower on which two Atlantes support the weight of the World and the figure of Fortune, dates to the second half of the 17C (◖*see La SALUTE*).

I CARMINI★

(⟨7⟩, CX)

VAPORETTO: CA' REZZONICO, SAN TOMÀ OR SAN BASILIO

This stretch of the **Dorsoduro** district is a lively mix of the university life and the daily markets in the vast Campo Santa Margherita and along the Rio di San Barnaba: waterborne greengrocers sell the freshest produce, including delicate artichoke hearts whatever the season. It is not difficult to find an eatery catering to students and tourists, or indeed a quintessentially Italian bar. There are plenty of shops here, although the majority of outlets carry daily necessities. There is, however, the odd authentic *bottega*, particularly between San Barnaba and Campo di Santa Margherita, selling wood carvings and masks.

▶ **Orient Yourself:** South of the Grand Canal, the Dorsoduro neighbourhood sweeps west from La Salute to the Canale Scomenzera, encompassing the Zattere promenade along the Guidecca canal.

☺ **Don't Miss:** Ca'Rezzonico, an outstanding palazzo exquisitely furnished. If you have time to see only one palazzo, this must be it.

○ **Organizing Your Time:** About half a day, plus 2hrs for Ca'Rezzonico.

Kids **Especially for Kids:** Children will enjoy watching the constant parade of all manner of watercraft on the Guidecca canal, including massive cruise ships.

☙ **Also See:** Neighbouring sights ACCADEMIA; SAN ROCCO.

Walking Tour

Campo Santa Margherita (⟨7⟩, CX)

The distinctive features of this large square are the Scuola dei Varoteri or Confraternity of Tanners, situated in the "centre" (the *campo*'s oblong layout hardly justifies the description) and the stunted campanile of the former Church of Santa Margherita. The cafés, shops and market stalls also add to the animation. Its truly populist appeal derives largely from its position alongside the Rio della Scoazzera (meaning sewage channel), now running underground, which dissuaded the nobility from building patrician *palazzi* in its vicinity.

Scuola Grande dei Carmini★ (**7**, CX)

Open daily, 10am-5pm. Closed 1 Jan, 25 Dec. €5. ☎ 041 52 89 420.
The narrowest end of the Campo di Santa Margherita houses the Scuola dei Carmini (Guild of Dyers), devotees of the Virgin of Carmelo, borne out by the central picture on the ceiling of the Salone, *The Virgin in Glory Appearing to the Blessed Simon Stock, Consigning to him the Scapular* (a simple arrangement of two squares of white cloth tied together with strings over the shoulder, a standard part of the Order's costume). This panel and eight others were executed by **Giovanni Battista Tiepolo**. The **Sala dell'Archivio** is decorated with 18C wall hangings. On the wall next to the entrance to the **Sala dell'Albergo** is Piazzetta's (1683-1754) *Judith and Holofernes*.

I Carmini (**7**, CX)

The simple Renaissance façade of this church and its 14C porch, decorated with Veneto-Byzantine pateras framing the portal on the left side, are in stark contrast to the rich decoration of the interior. At first sight, the red columns dividing the three aisles, the dark 17C and 18C paintings and the heavy black and gold of the statues lend a lugubrious atmosphere; yet the brightness of the internal space, the woodwork decoration so typical of such 14C churches, and its many paintings soften the initial impression.

Dedicated to Santa Maria del Carmelo, the church contains some interesting works of art: among them are *(left aisle, near the entrance)* Padovanino's *San Liberale Saves Two Men Condemned to Death* and *St Nicholas between John the Baptist and Saint Lucy with Angels* by Lorenzo Lotto; *(right wall) Feeding of the Five Thousand* by Palma il Giovane; *(above the fourth altar, right aisle) Presentation of Christ in the Temple* by Tintoretto. Many of the paintings were restored by funds from the American Committee to Rescue Italian Art.

▶ *Cross the bridge, turn immediately left and proceed to the end of the fondamenta which runs alongside the canal. The Church of San Nicolò dei Mendicoli stands on the right.*

San Nicolò dei Mendicoli (**6**, BX)

The dedication of the church to the *Mendicoli* alludes to the beggars who used to live in the area, notably the *pinzochere* (impoverished religious women) who sheltered in the portico. Indications are that the church was founded in the 7C, although this building dates for the most part from the 12C, as does the massive bell-tower. The central bay of the façade and its portico echo those of the Church of San Giacomo di Rialto. Inside, the wooden statuary dates to the 16C, when the iconostasis was

---

The Venetian Scuole

Instituted during the Middle Ages, the Venetian Scuole (literally meaning "school") were lay confraternities or guilds drawn from the merchant classes active in all aspects of everyday life, until the fall of the Republic. Patricians subscribed to the most prestigious Scuole, which excluded the poor, those engaged in morally dubious activities, and women, unless they were part of a member's family.

Each Scuola had its own patron saint and **Mariegola**, a rule book and constitution of the guild. The Scuola di San Giorgio degli Schiavoni and the Scuola degli Albanesi were dedicated to assisting foreign workers financially and spiritually. Others were formed of artisans sharing a common trade. Those of a religious nature were known as the **Scuole di Battuti**, reflecting their penitential practices.

From the 15C, the Scuole were divided into *Scuole Grandi* and *Scuole Minori*, as resolved by the Council of Ten. At the time, some 400 Scuole were in existence: the buildings that housed the most important guilds were magnificent palaces, with their interiors decorated by famous artists.

The water-borne vegetable stalls, or verduriere

given its present appearance. The paintings by followers of Veronese (1528-88) depict *Episodes from the Life of Christ*.

▶ *Return along the fondamenta and cross the canal by the second bridge.*

Beyond the **Church of Angelo Raffaele (⑥, BX)**, which contains the *Stories of Tobias and the Angel* disputedly by Gian'Antonio Guardi (1699-1760) on the parapet of the organ, Calle Nave branches off to the left towards the Church of St Sebastian.

San Sebastiano★★ (⑦, CX)

🕐*Open Mon-Sat, 10am-5pm.* 🕐*Closed 1 Jan, Easter, 15 Aug, 25 Dec.* ⊛€2.50. ☎ 041 27 50 462; www.chorusvenezia.org

The true beauty of this church lies in its rich internal decoration: Vasari described Veronese's paintings as "joyous, beautiful and well-conceived". It is worth scanning the individual masterpieces before allowing time to absorb the overall effect.

Along the right side in the first side chapel hangs *St Nicholas* by **Titian** (c 1490-1576); in the third is a *Crucifixion* by Veronese (1528-88); the *Tomb of Livio Podacattaro*, Bishop of Candia (Cyprus), is by Sansovino (1486-1570); opposite, next to the organ, stands the **bust of Veronese** that marks the burial site of the master painter who so celebrated the beauty of the world with depictions of luxurious silk and velvet, buxom women in flesh and stone, surrounded by gold, glass and silver. It is the opulent quality of his art that renders the Church of St Sebastian unique; it was with this cycle of frescoes that the painter was preoccupied for the most significant part of his life.

St Sebastian recurs as the subject of many of the frescoes: above Podacattaro's tomb and behind the statue *(right),* St Sebastian is shown pierced by arrows from archers on the wall opposite. His martyrdom is also depicted.

▶ *Take the long calle that links the churches of San Sebastiano and San Barnaba.*

Calle Lunga S Barnaba boasts few monuments or important sights but remains a particularly genuine part of Venice, lined with friendly eating places, paint shops and a model-maker's shop selling intricate miniatures.

Campo San Barnaba (**7**, CX)

The buzz of this square is generated by a flow of tourists and determined Venetians alike. It is confined by the simple white façade of the titular church, small shops, cafes and the food stalls along the Rio di San Barnaba near the Ponte dei Pugni. Before visiting Ca'Rezzonico, stop for coffee or lunch at an outdoor cafe.

▸ *Cross the canal, either by the Ponte dei Pugni or another bridge immediately to the left of the façade of the church, and walk towards the Grand Canal.*

Ca' Rezzonico★★ (**7**, DX)

The last *palazzo* to be designed by **Baldassare Longhena** was, in fact, completed by **Giorgio Massari** (c 1686-1766). It is markedly the product of two very distinctive masters who, despite their differences of opinion, worked towards the same end. **Henry James** (1843-1916) considered the Ca' Rezzonico to be such a majestic piece of architecture as to be almost mythological; Ruskin (1819-1900), who detested the Baroque style, likened the pilasters to "piles of cheeses."

Originally commissioned for the Bon family, ownership was transferred incomplete to a family from Lake Como; one of its progeny was to become Pope Clement XIII (1758). Ca' Rezzonico was once owned by **Robert Browning** (1812-89) and his wife, the poet Elizabeth Barrett (1806-61), before passing to their son Pen (1849-1913), whose real name was Robert: the nickname Pen was coined as an abbreviation of *penini*, which in Venetian dialect means small feet. Robert Browning junior was forced to sell the *palazzo* in 1906 when his divorce obliged him to return a large dowry.

Ca' Rezzonico now houses the Museum of 18C Venice *(described below)*.

Museo del Settecento Veneziano

♿ ◷*Open daily except Tue, 10am-6pm (5pm Nov-Mar).* ◷*Closed 1 Jan, 1 May, 25 Dec.* ☞*€6.50.* ☎ *041 24 10 100; www.museicivicivenezia.it*

Climb an enormous staircase, designed, as with the other state rooms on the *piano nobile*, to impress guests and host elaborate Carnival fancy-dress parties. The **Salone da Ballo** (ballroom) is dominated by the great coat of arms of the Rezzonico family and frescoed by the master of *trompe l'oeil*, **Giambattista Crosato** (c 1685-1758). On the ceiling, *Apollo's Chariot* is flanked by the *Four Parts of the World*. Early-18C Venetian pieces include the ebony figurines and delicate chairs that once belonged to the Venier family.

The ceiling of the **Sala dell'Allegoria Nuziale** was frescoed by Tiepolo in 1757 for the society wedding of Ludovico, one of the members of the Rezzonico family, to Faustina Savorgan, the daughter of one of the oldest Venetian families.

Housed in the **Sala dei Pastelli** (Pastel Room) are portraits by **Rosalba Carriera** (1675-1757), including one of *Cecilia Guardi Tiepolo*, the wife of Giambattista Crosato and mother of the artist Lorenzo Tiepolo. The furniture is Rococo, delicate, ornamentally fanciful and over-decorative.

The **Sala degli Arazzi** (Tapestry Room) is hung with Flemish tapestries from the end of the late-17C that tell the story of Solomon and the Queen of Sheba. The furniture here is also Rococo. The frescoed ceiling from c 1756 is the work of Jacopo Guarana (1720-1808). Note the

Morning Hot Chocolate by Pietro Longhi (Ca' Rezzonico)

Ca' Rezzonico, Venezia/SCALA

yellow lacquer door with chinoiserie decoration, which was very fashionable at the time.

The **Sala del Trono** (Throne Room) derives its name from the majestic golden throne adorned with nymphs, sea horses and *putti* that was used by Pope Pius VI on his visit to Venice in 1782. It is worth noticing Bernardino Castelli's particularly impressive portrait of *Pietro Barbarigo* (c 1780) set in its grandiose frame decorated with allegorical figures. The ceiling panel depicting *Merit* (crowned with laurel and attended by Nobility and Virtue) *Ascending to the Temple of Glory* was painted by **Tiepolo**.

Continue into the **portego**, where a golden sedan chair covered in red silk is kept. The marble busts are 18C. The doorway onto the stairs, surmounted by the Rezzonico coat of arms, is ornamented with two sculptures by Alessandro Vittoria (1525-1608).

In the **Sala del Tiepolo** (Tiepolo Room) the ceiling depicts *Virtue and Nobility Bringing Down Perfidy*. The four *Heads* on either side of the chimney are attributed to Giandomenico (1727-1804) and Lorenzo Tiepolo. Other notable works hung here include the *Portrait of the Architect Bartolomeo Ferracina* by Alessandro Longhi (1733-1813) (*opposite wall*). The *bureau-trumeau* in walnut is 18C; the games table with carved legs dates back to the late 17C/early 18C; the 17C cabinet was used as a strongbox. The next room is the **library**, furnished with gilded leather chairs and a clock made in London.

Despite its name, the **Sala del Lazzarini** houses only one work by this artist, *Orpheus Massacred by the Bacchants* (1698), displayed on the left as you enter the room.

In the **Sala del Brustolon**, the flower-stand table is decorated with an *Allegory of Strength*, personified by Hector. The 18C Murano chandelier is the best example of its kind to have survived intact from this period.

▶ *Return to the portego for access to the second floor.*

Upstairs in the *portego* are topographical works by **Canaletto**: *View over the Rio dei Mendicanti* and *View of the Grand Canal from Ca' Balbi to the Rialto Bridge*. Other works include those by Gian Antonio Guardi, Giambattista Piazzetta, Gian Antonio Pellegrini and Bernardo Strozzi.

Giandomenico's frescoes from the Tiepolo Villa at Zianigo, near Mirano, are now housed in a room at the end of the *portego*, on the right. Pause to admire the frescoes that depict a crowd of peasants who are turned away from the viewer.

The **Sala del Clavicembalo** accommodates an early-18C harpsichord that gives the room its name. Works on display in the small corridor include *View of the Castel Cogolo* by Francesco Guardi (1712-39) in poor condition, *A Pastoral Scene* by Francesco Zuccarelli (1702-88) and *Teaching the Art of the Coroneri* (the *coroneri* being makers of crowns, rosaries and buttons) by Francesco Guardi.

The **Sala del Parlatorio** (Parlour Room) contains paintings by Pietro Longhi and two well-known pieces by Francesco Guardi: the *Parlour of the Nuns of San Zaccharia* and a miniature of *Palazzo Dandolo to San Moisé*.

▶ *Access to the Sala del Longhi (Longhi Room) is back through the portego.*

Among the 29 paintings by **Pietro Longhi**, note particularly his *Portrait of Francesco Guardi*. Longhi has been compared to the English-born William Hogarth as a social commentator of his times, although the depictions of quiet Venetian patrician domesticity are more benign, lacking the wit and satirical bite of paintings by the English counterpart. The ceiling panel of *Zephyr and Flora* is by Tiepolo.

Chinoiserie predominates in the **Sala delle Lacche Verdi** (Green Lacquer Room). The *Triumph of Diana* on the ceiling is by Gian Antonio Guardi. Note the particularly evocative painting of the *Frozen Lagoon* (1788) by a follower of Francesco Battaglia.

The three frescoes in the **Sala del Guardi** (Guardi Room) are by **Giovanni Antonio**: *Venus and Love, Apollo* and *Minerva*. Little biographical detail exists about the Guardi brothers, Francesco (1712-93) and Giovanni Antonio (1699-1760), other than the fact that they relied on the tourist market for most of their trade. Francesco, the "Veduta" painter, uses paint freely to capture sparkling light in his topographical landscapes (a quality to be later admired by the Impressionists), whereas the elder brother animated his scenes with figures in a way that was to affect 18C British watercolour painting (Sandby, Girtin, Turner, Prout, Varley).

The **Alcova** (Alcove) is a reconstruction of a bedroom and boudoir; the pastel *Madonna* is by **Rosalba Carriera**. The 17C silver toilette service is the work of Augsburg silversmiths. Giandomenico Tiepolo is responsible for the ceiling of the wardrobe; the stucco decoration and the frescoes in the boudoir are by Jacopo Guarana.

▶ *Access to the third floor is via the portego.*

The spacious **Pinacoteca Egidio Martini** houses a collection of paintings from the Venetian School dating from the 15C-20C. Your visit of 18C Venice concludes with a reconstruction of the **"Ai Do San Marchi"** pharmacy.

▶ *Retrace your steps along the Fondamenta Rezzonico and turn right into Calle delle Botteghe, take Calle della Malvasia on the right and then Calle del Cappeller on the left. Follow to Ca' Foscari.*

Ca' Foscari (**7**, DX)
A famous example of the Gothic style, Ca' Foscari was built in 1452 for the Doge Francesco Foscari. Today it accommodates the headquarters of the **University of Venice**. The approach from Calle Foscari is not ideal as the view of the *palazzo* is restricted by the crenellated wall that surrounds the courtyard. Bustling with student activity, the Ca' Foscari is best seen from the Grand Canal which, in turn, may be glimpsed from the salone on the ground floor (*see Il CANAL GRANDE).*

LA FENICE★

(**8**, EX)

VAPORETTO: S. MARCO, S. MARIA DEL GIGLIO, S. SAMUELE, S. ANGELO OR RIALTO.

On 29 January 1996, La Fenice burned down, succumbing to the same fate that befell it in 1836. The theatre is well-named, though (*Fenice* is Italian for phoenix) for on 13 December 2003, it reopened, true to its name as it was in the 18C. Walking through the area in the loop of the Grand Canal takes in a very lively part of Venice. There are also plenty of shops in this district: bookshops in the Campo San Luca and mask shops between Campo Manin and Campo Sant'Angelo. The route between St Mark's and Campo Santo Stefano boasts many elegant shops and hotels around the Church of San Moisé that gradually give way to art, glass and bookbinding workshops.

▶ **Orient Yourself:** The area in the vicinity of the theatre is known as the "seven campi between the bridges," a reference to the Campi di San Bartolomeo, San Salvador, San Luca, Manin, Sant'Angelo, Santo Stefano and San Vidal, situated between the Rialto Bridge and Accademia Bridge. Although the theatre occupies a fairly quiet setting, it is edged by a bustling commercial hub of restaurants and stores.

▶ **Don't Miss:** The designer boutiques and street entertainers along the Calle Larga 22 Marzo.

▶ **Organizing Your Time:** Allow 2hrs for itinerary and another 1hr for a guided tour of the theatre.

The foyer of Teatro La Fenice

Kids Especially for Kids: The interactive exhibits at Telecom Italia Future Centre.
Also See: Neighbouring sights PIAZZA SAN MARCO and RIALTO.

Walking Tour

Gran Teatro La Fenice★ (8, EX)

Guided tours (1hr) in several languages daily, times vary. Closed 1 Jan, 1 May, 25 Dec. €7. 041 78 65 11; www.theatrolafenice.it
Situated in a secluded and picturesque little square of Campo San Fantin, the opera house and music-theatre was inaugurated in 1792 after its predecessor (1673) burned down in 1774. Construction was initiated by **Giannantonio Selva** (1751-1819), a friend of Canova, who was awarded the commission by winning a competition. Almost completely destroyed by fire in 1836, it was rebuilt and renamed La Fenice (The Phoenix) in honour of its emergence from the ashes. Neo-Classical in style, La Fenice had two façades and two entrances, including one overlooking the canal. It is not difficult to imagine the difficulties posed by the spatial requirements of the auditorium, which was much bigger than the apparently narrow façade, a problem overcome by means of an ingenious series of stairways.

This "jewel box of a theatre" (Isaac Sterne) burned down again on 29 January 1996 when it was closed for restoration. Damage was exacerbated by the fact that fire services were unable to reach the scene along normal routes as neighbouring canals had been drained for cleaning. John Berendt gives a fascinating account of the event in his book *The City of Falling Angels* (see Further Reading in Planning Your Trip). Special

Famous Premieres

Celebrated works that have been performed for the first time in the Fenice include *Tancredi* (1813), *Sigismondo* (1814) and *Semiramide* (1823) by **Gioachino Rossini**, and *Ernani* (1844), *Attila* (1846), *Rigoletto* (1851), *La Traviata* (1853) and *Simon Boccanegra* (1857) by **Giuseppe Verdi**.

funds were set up by the Italian government, the Venice in Peril Fund and the American Save Venice Committee. Reconstructed to architect **Aldo Rossi**'s plan, the theatre reopened on 14 December 2003.

Campo San Fantin (8, EX)

Also situated in Campo San Fantin are the **Chiesa** and **Scuola di San Fantin** (8, **EX**) (*Open Mon-Fri, 10am-12.30pm. Closed holidays, Aug, 21 Nov, 23 Dec to 6 Jan. No charge.* 041 52 24 459). The Renaissance church was begun by Scarpagnino (active in Venice between 1505 and 1549) and completed by Sansovino. Inside are two works by Palma il Giovane (1544-1628).

The Scuola belonged to the Guild of San Girolamo for *picai* (hangmen), who escorted the condemned to the site of their execution and oversaw their burial. The front (c 1580) was designed by Alessandro Vittoria. Today, the building accommodates the **Ateneo Veneto** (8, **EX**). The Aula Magna on the ground floor has a fine wooden panelled ceiling decorated by Palma il Giovane; the Aula Tommaseo houses works by Antonio Zanchi (1631-1722) *(ceiling and, on entering, the right wall)* and Francesco Fontebasso (1709-69) *(opposite)*. The Sala di Lettura (Reading Room) is decorated by Veronese (1528-88).

▶ *Follow Calle delle Veste off Campo San Fantin to Calle Larga XXII Marzo, which is closed off on the left by the sumptuous façade of the Church of San Moisè.*

(⟳ In the other direction, Calle del Fruttarol leads to a bridge with a view of the *palazzo* on the canal where **Mozart** stayed during the Carnival in 1771, marked by a commemorative wall plaque.)

San Moisè (8, FX)

Undoubtedly, the most striking feature of the church is its façade: built by Longhena's pupil **Alessandro Tremignon** in the 17C with the help of the Flemish artist Meyring, a disciple of Bernini, it is the epitome of excess. Divided into three sections both horizontally and vertically, the edifice features every sort of adornment on the front. The lower tier is designed as a triumphal arch, dominated by memorials to members of the Fini family. The interior is also Baroque. Its sense of dramatic gesture is conveyed in Tintoretto's *Christ Washing his Disciples' Feet (in the chapel)*.

At the other end of Calle Larga XXII Marzo is **Campo Santa Maria Zobenigo**, situated in front of the **church** of the same name (*Open Mon-Sat, 10am-5pm. Closed 1 Jan, Easter, 15 Aug, 25 Dec.* €2.50. 041 27 50 462; www.chorusvenezia.org). The magnificent façade by Giuseppe Sardi is reminiscent of that of the Church of San Moisè in style and eulogy: in this case, the dedication is to a naval captain. Its incompleted 18C bell-tower remains a box covered with a small roof. On the inside wall of the façade, note the small 15C Lombard-style relief of St Jerome. Inside hangs Tintoretto's *Four Evangelists (behind the high altar, under the organ)*.

▶ *Continue straight on (west) for Campo San Maurizio and Campo Santo Stefano.*

Campo San Maurizio (8, EX)

The peace of this square is sometimes broken by a busy antiques market. To the right of the church is a view of the campanile of Santo Stefano. The former **Scuola degli Albanesi**, with its Renaissance reliefs, sits on the left. Previous residents of the *palazzo* opposite include the novelist Alessandro Manzoni (1785-1873) and Giorgio Baffo (1694-1768), who wrote salacious poetry in Venetian dialect.

Campo Santo Stefano (8, EX)

This *campo* is one of the most elegant squares in the city. Dominated by a church in which concerts are regularly given, this lively meeting place is animated by busy outdoor cafes and people making their way to and from the Accademia Bridge. It's a perfect venue for an early evening stroll or *passeggiata*. Towering over the square is a monument (1882) to **Niccolò Tommaseo**.

Overlooking the square is the **Palazzo Loredan** (⑧, **EV**), now home to the Venetian Institute of Science, Arts and Letters and its prestigious library. In 1536 the Loredan family commissioned Scarpagnino (active in Venice between 1505 and 1549) to rebuild the palace recently acquired from the Mocenigo family. Note its Palladian northern façade.

Straight ahead is the **Palazzo Pisani** (⑧, **EX**), one of the largest private palaces in the city, on the square of the same name. Having been acquired by a noble family between the 17C and 18C, Girolamo Frigimelica (1653-1732) was commissioned to remodel the building. The *palazzo* is now the home of the **Benedetto Marcello Music Conservatory**.

Palazzo Morosini (⑧, **EX**), which dates to the 14C, was restored at the end of the 17C by Antonio Gaspari. Former residents include Francesco Morosini, Doge between 1688 and 1694. The *palazzo* is now the home of the New Consortium of Venice.

Santo Stefano★ (⑧, EX)

🕐*Open Mon-Sat, 10am-5pm.* 🕐*Closed 1 Jan, Easter, 15 Aug, 25 Dec.* €2.50. ☎ 041 27 50 462; www.chorusvenezia.org

Gothic in style, the church comprises a central vaulted nave flanked by lower side bays. Construction of St Stephen's and the adjacent convent was begun in the latter half of the 13C; the church, however, was modified in the 15C. The campanile (60m/196ft 10in high) is one of the most famous in Venice. Building on the lower section was resumed in 1544; when it collapsed in 1585, it was the new masonry that crumbled, hit by lightning so violent that the bells melted. Further damage incurred by subsidence between the 17C and 18C has left the tower leaning at an angle, as do all the other bell-towers in Venice.

Like other churches in Venice, St Stephen's is a pantheon to the glory of the city: it contains the tombs of **Giovanni Gabrieli** and of **Francesco Morosini**, the Peloponnesian, as well as Baldassare Longhena's monument to Capt. Bartolomeo d'Alviano. In the sacristy hang works by Tintoretto: in the *Last Supper*, the dog and cat allude to the dispute raging between the Catholic and Protestant Churches over belief in the mystery of the Eucharist.

Campo Sant'Angelo (⑧, EX)

By day, one might pass through this rather austere square en route between St Mark's and the Accademia, without giving it a second glance: at night, however, the *palazzi* overlooking the canal turn the square into a veritable stage set.

The **Oratorio dell'Annunciata** (Oratory of the Annunziata) has replaced the church that gave the square its name, formerly associated with the Scuola dei Zoti, the guild for disabled sailors. Note the plaque on the wall of **Palazzo Duodo** commemorating the composer Domenico Cimarosa (1749-1801) who died there.

The Gothic portal on the bridge leads into the cloisters of St Stephen (now the headquarters of the Regional Accountancy Board).

▶ *Rio Terrà della Mandola branches left off Calle dello Spezièr and leads to the Palazzo Fortuny.*

Palazzo Fortuny (⑧, EV)

Dating to the 15C, the building boasts two mullioned windows with five arches. The Palazzo Pesaro degli Orfei was acquired by the painter, photographer and textile designer, **Mariano Fortuny y Madrazo** (1871-1949), in 1899. The former music school is now a **museum** of the artist's work. &. 🕐*Open Tue-Sun, 10am-6pm (ticket office closes at 5.30pm).* 🕐*Closed 1 Jan, 1 May and 25 Dec.* €4. ☎ 041 52 00 995.

The Renaissance Palazzo

Based on Roman originals, the Italian *palazzo* was designed to fulfil commercial and residential demands. Arranged around a central courtyard, it most often comprises three storeys. The ground floor was used for storage or shops *(magazzini)* that opened out onto the street; this level tends to be heavily rusticated. The first floor, or *piano nobile*, was used by the occupying family as living quarters: externally lighter in texture, the interior had high ceilings and large windows providing ample light and ventilation. The top storey, below the roof and much lower in proportion, served as quarters for servants and children.

The *calle* that leads from Campo Sant'Angelo to Campo Manin is always busy with people coming and going, distracted by the many shops along the way.

▶ *The bridge over the Rio di San Luca leads into the modern Campo Manin.*

Campo Manin (⑧, EV)
Few features distinguish this square other than the monument to **Daniele Manin** (1875), the shops down along one side and the **Cassa di Risparmio di Venezia**, designed by **Pierluigi Nervi** (1891-1979) and Angelo Scattolin, which provides an idea of modern Venetian architecture.

▶ *Take the calle on the right.*

Scala del Bovolo★ (⑧, EFX)
🕐*Open Apr-Oct, daily 10am-6pm (last admission 5.30pm); Nov-Mar, Sat-Sun only, 10am-4pm; mid-Dec-mid-Jan, daily 10am-5pm.* 🕐*Closed 1 Jan and 25 Dec.* 💶€3.50. ☎ *041 53 22 920; www.scalabovolo.org*
The **Bovolo Staircase** is all the more impressive, situated as it is off a tiny, peaceful courtyard overlooked by private houses. The delicate spiral staircase (*bovolo* in Venetian dialect), which seems to harmonise with a composite style drawn from both Gothic and Renaissance styles, is attrib-

uted to Giovanni Candi, who died in 1506. Encased in a tower, the staircase provides access to the *palazzo's* loggias. From the top extends a lovely, yet disorientating, **view**★★ over the Venetian rooftops.

▶ *To get to Campo San Luca pass either to the left or the right of the Cassa di Risparmio; to reach the church of the same name, continue along the Salizzada.*

Campo San Luca (⑧, FV)
This lively *campo* is one of the most popular meeting places in Venice. There is everything here: cafés, well-known stores, bookshops, travel agencies, fast-food outlets and a host of shops in the immediate vicinity. The **Church of St Luke** (San Luca) contains the *Virgin in Glory Appearing to St Luke While Writing the Gospel* by Veronese (1528-88). When the floor was

The Bovolo Staircase

Laea Pessina/MICHELIN

repaved at the beginning of the 20C, the gravestones of those buried there, including the writer Aretino, were not relaid.

Farther along Calle del Teatro is the **Goldoni Theatre** (8, **FV**), named in honour of Italy's famed playwright, Carlo Goldoni. At one time, there were many theatres in Venice: today, only La Fenice, the Goldoni and the Teatro Màlibran are active theaters.

San Salvador (8, FV)

The 7C Church of San Salvador would have been consecrated by Pope Alexander III during his visit to Venice to meet Barbarossa in 1177. Despite having been subjected to various phases of rebuilding, the 17C façade, designed by Giuseppe Sardi (1621/30-99), survives with its cannon ball embedded in the masonry since 1849. The main layout was designed by Spavento, who combines an assured use of Classical structural elements with refined sculptural ornament, a style that foreshadows Mannerism and the bold Classicism of Palladio.

Inside, three square bays are aligned to form a nave, each cubic space rising to a semicircular dome. A number of significant paintings include the main altarpiece, *The Transfiguration* by **Titian** (c 1490-1576) and, in the last bay on the right before the transept, his *Annunciation*. To the right of the main chapel hangs *The Martyrdom of St Theodoric* by Paris Bordone (1500-71). In the Santissimo Chapel on the left of the main altar is *The Disciples at Emmaus* by **Giovanni Bellini** (c 1432-1516); the organ doors *(by the side door)* are painted by Titian's brother, Francesco Vecellio (1475-1560).

Telecom Italia Future Centre★

Kids ○*Open Tue-Sun, 10am to 6pm (Sat 7pm). No charge.* ☎ *041 521 3200/3211; www. telecomfuturecentre.it.*

Housed in the restored San Salvador convent adjacent to the San Salvador church, this research lab of Telecom Italia, Italy's unified telephone company, offers a glimpse of future technology through interactive exhibits and games. Visitors move from station to station within the cloisters, listening to computer-based historical figures, drawing without the aid of a pen, conversing with a talking well, and viewing water art, for starters. A game room, a coffeehouse with communications devices on the tables, and a refectory filled with high-tech exhibits round out this futuristic funhouse of learning.

Campo San Bartolomeo (4, FU)

This *campo* is a busy crossroads between St Mark's, the Rialto, the Accademia and the Strada Nuova. Bars and tourist shops surround the square, which is dominated by a spirited **statue of Goldoni** (1883).

Fondaco dei Tedeschi (4, FU)

What once served an association of German traders (13C onwards) now houses the main post office headquarters. Destroyed in a fire in 1505, the Fondaco was rebuilt by Giorgio Spavento and Scarpagnino, who conceived the idea of a square courtyard. The frescoes that adorn the façade facing the Grand Canal are the work of **Giorgione** and the earliest-known works by Titian.

I FRARI ★★★

(🆑, DV)

VAPORETTO: S. TOMÀ, STAZIONE, RIVA DI BIASIO, S. STAE

After visiting the Frari Church, it is well worth strolling in the vicinity of the nearby railway station. Being some distance, relatively speaking, from any major monument of great artistic merit or tourist interest, there are few enticing craft shop window displays to distract the eye. This is a residential quarter that provides insight into the sort of daily life that goes on in many other cities.

▸ **Orient Yourself:** Located on the west side of the Grand Canal in the San Polo *sestiere*, the environs of this church also include the adjacent Scuola Grande di San Rocco (👆 *see SAN ROCCO*).

👀 **Don't Miss:** Titian's masterpiece, *Assumption of the Virgin,* in the Maggiore Chapel within the Frari Church.

🕐 **Organizing Your Time:** The suggested itinerary takes about half a day.

Kids Especially for Kids: The natural history museum.

👆 **Also See:** Neighbouring sights: I CARMINI; SAN ROCCO.

Visit

🕐*Open daily, 9am (1pm Sun) to 6pm (last admission at 4.45pm).* 🕐*Closed 1 Jan, Easter, 15 Aug, 25 Dec.* 👆*€2.50.* ☎ *041 27 50 462; www.chorusvenezia.org*

This great church, whose name is derived from the abbreviation of Fra*(ti Mino)*ri, has been compared with the Church of Santi Giovanni e Paolo because of its sheer scale and style. Monumental in stature, flanked by the second tallest campanile (70m/229ft 6in) after St Mark's, this building is strikingly magnificent, massive yet articulated with fine architectural detail, conforming to Franciscan archetypes yet quite original. It impresses from every angle. The best view of the apses, the oldest part, is to be had from the Scuola di San Rocco; if contemplated from the bridge built by the monks in 1428, it appears just as breathtaking, its late-Gothic tripartite façade a masterpiece of design.

Exterior

The doorway is surmounted by a *Risen Christ* by Alessandro Vittoria (1581), flanked slightly below by the *Virgin with Child* and *St Francis* by Bartolomeo Bon (active 1441-64), supported on two finely crafted engaged columns. High above, inserted into the plain brickwork, are four circular window openings edged in white Istrian stone.

Over the side door into St Mark's or the Corner Chapel *(at the end on the left)* the Madonna is shown restraining the Christ child from struggling to break free.

Gwen Cannon/ MICHELIN

I Frari

Interior

Santa Maria Gloriosa dei Frari (the church's full title) is in the form of a Latin cross. The nave is divided from the aisles by 12 huge cylindrical piers that soar up to the crisscross of transverse and longitudinal timber beams underpinning the quadripartite vaults. The red and white floor tiles are from Verona.

The first noteworthy monument *(left aisle)* is neo-Classical and dedicated to **Canova** (1757-1822) (**1**). It was designed by the sculptor to commemorate Titian but was never completed. The allegorical figures before the pyramid represent Sorrow (portrait of Canova) with Venice *(left)*, in the company of Sculpture, heavily veiled, Painting and Architecture.

Beyond the Baroque monument to **Doge Giovanni Pesaro** is the famous **Madonna di Ca'Pesaro Chapel**, dominated by Titian's altarpiece.

Serving as a glorious harbinger to the Maggiore Chapel and Titian's *Assumption* are the 15C **choir stalls**, comprising 124 decorated stalls. The two organs on the right are signed Gaetano Callido (1794) and Giovanni Piaggia (1732) respectively. Beyond, early-17C paintings by Andrea Micheli, known as Vicentino, illustrate the Works of Corporeal Mercy *(left)* alongside his *Creation of the World*, the *Brazen Serpent*, a *Last Judgement* and the *Glory of Paradise (right)*.

In the left transept, the first chapel on the left is the St Mark's or Corner Chapel, which houses the *Triptych of St Mark* by Bartolomeo Vivarini (c 1432-91). High up on the wall opposite is *Christ's Descent into Limbo* by Jacopo Palma il Giovane. The marble baptismal font with John the Baptist is by Sansovino.

Next comes the Milanese Chapel with its *Sant'Ambrogio* altarpiece by Alvise Vivarini and Marco Basaiti.

The Maggiore Chapel is the focal point of the magnificent perspective of the Frari Church. All points converge on **Titian's** *Assumption of the Virgin*, which was commissioned by the Franciscans in 1516. This major work, the first religious subject undertaken by the painter, caused the friars some consternation because of its unorthodox iconography. Instead of Mary's restful contemplation, the crowded painting shows the Apostles disturbed by the mystery of this supernatural event; *putti* and winged angels, singing and playing music, emphasise the upward movement of the composition, as the (nervous) Virgin looking ever upwards towards God the Father is received in the Kingdom of Heaven in a triumph of light and colour. The brilliance of heaven is exaggerated by the careful portrayal of light from the realms of shadow and darkness on earth, via the more shaded zone occupied by angels, up to the explosion of bright light pushing the figure of the Virgin into bold perspective.

Against the presbytery walls are two important monuments, one commemorating **Doge Nicolò Tron** by Antonio Rizzo – probably the most important Renaissance sculptural group in Venice *(left)* – and the other, from the 15C, to **Doge Francesco Foscari**, attributed to Nicolò di Giovanni Fiorentino.

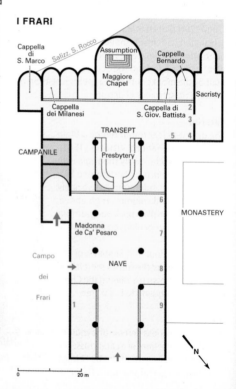

I FRARI

Cappella di S. Marco · Salizz. S. Rocco

Assumption · Maggiore Chapel

Cappella Bernardo

Sacristy

Cappella dei Milanesi

Cappella di S. Giov. Battista · 2 · 3 · 5 · 4

TRANSEPT

CAMPANILE

Presbytery

6

MONASTERY

Madonna de Ca' Pesaro · 7

Campo · NAVE · 8

dei

Frari · 1 · 9

N

0 — 20 m

In the right arm of the transept, the jewel of the Chapel of John the Baptist is the only Venetian work by **Donatello**, his *John the Baptist* depicted with the index finger of his right hand raised against Herod as a sign of admonition (unfortunately the finger is missing). Beyond the former Santissimo Chapel, now dedicated to Maximilian Kolbe, comes the Bernardo Chapel containing the *Polyptych* by Bartolomeo Vivarini (1482).

The Assumption of the Virgin by Titian

Before going into the sacristy watch for:

♦ the equestrian monument to **Paolo Savelli** (d 1405) (**2**) who fought for Venice against the Carraresi.

♦ on the door to the sacristy, the 16C monument to **Benedetto Pesaro** (**3**), the captain who died in 1503, by Giovambattista Bregno. Between the columns that frame the doorway, note the Lion of St Mark's holding the closed Gospel: during periods of political conflict, Venice, unable to listen to the biblical teachings of peace, would "close" the Gospel and leave it under the lion's paw;

♦ the terra-cotta monument to the **Blessed Peacemaker of the Frari** (**4**) with the 15C portrayal of the Baptism of Christ in the lunette;

♦ to the right of the transept, the monument to **Jacopo Marcello** (**5**), the captain of the Venetian fleet who died in 1488 during the conquest of the city of Gallipoli. The work is by Pietro Lombardo.

The **sacristy** houses the splendid **Triptych** by **Giovanni Bellini**. Opposite is a lunette (1339) by Paolo Veneziano that was designed to be set above the Byzantine sarcophagus of **Doge Francesco Dandolo** (1329-39) in the adjacent Sala del Capitolo (⊙ *closed to the public)*, the Capitolo being the periodic assembly of religious orders.

The **Chapel of St Catherine of Alexandria** (**6**) is decorated with an altarpiece by Palma il Giovane, illustrating the saint's salvation from the torture of the wheel. In the next bay is the unusual statue of *St Jerome* (1504) (**7**) by Alessandro Vittoria, which recalls the style of Michelangelo. The **altar of Purification** (**8**) is ornamented with a painting by Salviati.

Titian's Mausoleum (**9**), hewn in marble from Carrara, was executed during the decade 1842-52. Titian, who died of the plague in 1576, was buried in the Frari in accord with his wishes, but by the end of the 16C all traces of his body had disappeared.

Walking Tour

▶ *Cross the canal in front of the church and turn left to Campo San Stin. Then take Calle del Tabacco and Calle dell'Olio as far as Campiello della Scuola.*

Scuola di San Giovanni Evangelista (⊞, DU)

⊙*Open late Jun-mid-Jul, daily 10.30am-7pm; rest of the year by appointment only.* ⊜ *Suggested donation €5 .* ☎ *041 71 82 34.*

The courtyard outside the Scuola of St John the Evangelist has been described by Sir Hugh Honour as *"a little masterpiece of Venetian Renaissance architecture."*

The Scuola was the second of the **Scuole Grandi** (ⓒ*see I CARMINI: The Venetian Scuole)* to be founded in 1201 and honoured by a confraternity of flagellants who attended religious processions stripped to the waist and whipping themselves with scourges. They are represented in the relief carvings dated 1349 at the front, which itself dates from 1454, when the large ogee windows were inserted.

The double stairway inside, lit with large arched windows, was built by Codussi. On the first floor, the oval windows were added by Giorgio Massari (1727), who raised the height of the **salone**. Various craftsmen are responsible for the decoration on the ceiling and the walls, including Domenico Tintoretto and Pietro Longhi.

The salone adjoins the Oratory of the Cross built to house Carpaccio's cycle of the *Miracles of the Relic of the True Cross,* now on display in the Accademia.

▶ *Continue straight on as far as the Grand Canal, to come out opposite Santa Lucia Station. Turn right along the water's edge.*

San Simeon Piccolo – &See Il CANAL GRANDE.

▶ *At Ponte degli Scalzi, turn right and then left into Calle Bergami.*

San Simeon Grando (🖪, CT)

So-called to distinguish it from the Church of San Simeon Piccolo, the church is also known as San Simeon Profeta. Although its origins go back as far as 967, the building has undergone considerable remodelling, particularly in the 18C. The neo-Classical white façade dates from 1861.

The internal space is divided into nave and aisles by a series of columns crowned with Byzantine capitals and shrouded in heavy red damask drapes, as is fairly common in Venice. Although the ornamentation is generally heavy, there is an exquisite *Last Supper* by Tintoretto on the left of the entrance.

▶ *Calle Larga dei Barbi, behind the church, leads into Campo Nazario Sauro. From here continue on to Campo San Giacomo dall'Orio and down Ruga Bella or the parallel Ruga Vecchia, which comes out directly in front of another church.*

San Giacomo dall'Orio★ (🖪, DT)

🕐*Open Mon-Sat, 10am-5pm.* 🕐*Closed Sun, 1 Jan, Easter, 15 Aug, 25 Dec.* ⊗€2.50. ☎ *041 27 50 462; www.chorusvenezia.org*

The church was founded in 976 but most of its present fabric dates from 1225. The centre of the main façade features a Veneto-Byzantine patera with a statue in Istrian stone of the Apostle St James the Great standing above the portal. The bell-tower, erected in the 12C or 13C, is reminiscent of that on the island of Torcello. The three apses date back to different periods. The transept frontage dates from the 14C.

The Gothic lacunar **ceiling**, shaped like an inverted ship's hull, is striking. The nave is divided from its aisles by five baseless columns. Beside the entrance, David is depicted with excerpts from Psalm 150. The unusual stoop for the holy water is made of cipolin (onion) marble from Anatolia. Of the paintings in the choir stalls attributed to Schiavone *The Apostles in the Boat* is the most likely to be by him.The organ was built by Gaetano Callido. It is likely that the Ionic column of ancient green marble, which was brought to Venice from Byzantium has been in the church since the 13C.

In the **New Sacristy** are Palma il Giovane's *Crucifixion with the Virgin and St John* and a version of *The Marriage at Cana* also thought to be by him. The **Santissimo Chapel**, is dedicated to faith in the Eucharist.

The **Old Sacristy** *(apply to the custodian)*, besides its fine wood panelling, is decorated with a cycle of paintings by Palma il Giovane.

▶ *To get to Campo San Giovanni Decollato and the church of the same name (Zan Degolà in Venetian), take Calle Larga and branch left down Calle dello Spezier.*

The Council of Trent

Established in 1545 and dissolved in 1563, the Council of Trent aimed to encapsulate Catholic ideals in dogma and to structure its ministry by disciplinary reform. This ecclesiastical body confirmed the Church's sole right to interpret the Bible and underlined the role of the clergy as the only intercessors between man and God. The value of the seven sacraments was reaffirmed, and the practices of baptism and confirmation were ratified. The acknowledged existence of Purgatory, the invocation of saints, the veneration of relics, and the granting of indulgences were also endorsed and rationalised. Those opposed to the rationalisation of the Roman Church went on to precipitate the Counter-Reformation and found the Protestant faction.

San Zan Degolà (⁸, DT)

Dedicated to the beheaded John the Baptist, this church can trace its origins back to 1007, when the first parish church was built on the site. The terra-cotta façade is early 18C. A rose window is the main feature of the central section of the three-tier façade, framed by pilasters supporting a triangular tympanum. The relief on the right wall retells the story of John's decapitation.

As with the façade, a harmonious simplicity pervades the interior. The ceiling takes the form of an inverted ship's hull. The intense silence enhances the air of contemplation inspired by the frescoed chapels at the end of the side aisles.

▷ *Follow the calle behind the church as far as the Grand Canal. At the end, directly opposite the plain façade of the Church of San Marcuola sits the elegant palazzo that was the residence of the Turkish merchants (⌚ see Il CANAL GRANDE).*

Fondaco dei Turchi (⁸, DT)

This building now accommodates the **Museo di Storia Naturale** (Natural History Museum).

Museo di Storia Naturale (⁸, DT)

Kids ♿ 🕐*Open Tues-Fri, 9am-1pm; Sat-Sun 10am-4pm; last admission 30min before closing.* 🕐*Closed 1 Jan, 1 May, 25 Dec.* ⊜*No charge.* ☎ *041 27 50 206*

Displays are arranged by theme using dioramas to complement the clear explanations given on the showcases: from cells to protozoa, porifera, worms, molluscs, arthropods, crustaceans and echinoderms. Fossils from Bolca, in the vicinity of Verona and noted for its wealth of palaeontological finds, illustrate the evolution of vertebrates. One room is dedicated to animal species from the lagoon; another focuses on the insect world's defence facilities. The dinosaur room is worth visiting to see the enormous skeleton, brought to Italy from the Ligabue expedition to the Sahara in 1973. Molluscs and minerals follow the Bolca fossils, among which the most spectacular are those that show their progression before petrifaction sets in.

IL GHETTO★★

(🗺, DT)

VAPORETTO: FERROVIA, PONTE DELLE GUGLIE, SAN MARCUOLA

The Ghetto of Venice is the ghetto par excellence, being the first Jewish quarter to be differentiated as such in Western Europe. The term, which seems to testify to the periods of persecution endured by the Jewish community rather than a history enjoyed, was originally coined from the word *geto* in Venetian dialect. This referred to a local bombard or mortar foundry: the g, normally pronounced soft (as in George), was hardened by the first Jews who came from Germany.

▶ **Orient Yourself:** Northeast of the train station, the Ghetto occupies a corner of the Cannaregio sestiere near the Cannaregio Canal. Incessant activity in the shops and market around Fondamenta della Pescaria and Rio Terrà San Leonardo *(right bank of the canal)* contrasts with the tranquillity of the squares and the *calli* – with their yellow signs and elegant Hebrew characters – that lead to the heart of the Ghetto, clustered around Campo di Ghetto Nuovo.

😊 **Don't Miss:** The monumental Palazzo Labia and its attractive square.

🕐 **Organizing Your Time:** Allow 3 to 4hrs to visit the area leisurely.

Kids **Especially for Kids:** The playground at Parco Savorgnan.

♿ **Also See:** Neighbouring sights: CA' D'ORO.

A Bit of History

The distinction of *Vecchio* (old) and *Nuovo* (new) should not be interpreted in any chronological sense: they are references to the old and new foundries. In fact, the Jews were first confined to the Ghetto Nuovo – then a fortified island – which was practically impenetrable. At the time, the houses were still rather squat and low-lying; the area was subjected to a form of curfew at nightfall, after which time the drawbridge was raised and the area sealed off. It was only in 1866 that access to the Ghetto was freed up and Jews were granted the same rights as other Venetian citizens. As long as the Jews were obliged to stay there, however, they were at least protected.

Indeed, it was precisely because their community was confined to this small area that their houses climbed ever taller. It seems odd, now, to acknowledge that Jews were prohibited from undertaking any kind of building work, be it on their houses or any of the five synagogues, or *scuole*. Instead, they became *strazzaroli* (dealers in secondhand clothes and goods), doctors and bankers involved in moneylending activities: the colours of their stalls were red *(n° 2912)*, green and black.

Visit

The approach to Campo di Ghetto Nuovo from Calle Farnese might suggest that the area is fortified. From the bridge before the *sottoportego* the view is particularly evocative: unusually tall houses seem to tower out of the canal, tenuously strung together by a crisscross of washing lines that seem permanently weighted with laundry.

Above Eye Level

An 18C notice in the Old Ghetto warns Jews converted to Christianity to frequent the ghetto, and the houses of other Jews, on pain of "hanging, prison, hard labour, flogging, pillory." The means by which the Serenissima authorities were to be informed were secret denunciation via the infamous holes in the wall known as **bocca di leone**. These tablets also advertise the dues to be expected by the accuser, paid in recompense from the property of the accused.

Museo Ebraico (🅑, DT)

👤Guided tours only of the synagogues, daily except Sat, in various languages; Jun-Sept, 10am-7pm, Oct-May, 10am-5.30pm; last admission 30min before closing. 🕐Closed 1 Jan, 1 May, 25 Dec and Jewish festivals. Full tour ⊛€8.50; entrance to museum only ⊛€3. ☎ 041 71 53 59; www.museoebraico.it

The **Jewish Museum** has assembled together many precious artifacts relating to Judaism: decorative objects and ornaments or paraphernalia connected with the sacred scrolls (rotoli della Legge). Of all the Toràh covers in the collection, the one featuring the Jews encamped, the manna and the hand of Moses issuing forth water from the rock is particularly famous.

The Sacred Scrolls

For the Jews, the Law (Toràh, literally "teaching") comes in the form of the Pentateuch: the five Books of Moses, comprising Genesis, Exodus, Leviticus, Numbers and Deuteronomy. Transcribed onto parchment, the scrolls are wound around two batons that are unfurled during readings. The scrolls are stored in a rigid container or rolled up in a mantle.

The rolls are stored in the Holy Ark. Given their sacredness, they can be neither exposed nor touched: a silver holder is used during readings.

Synagogues★★

Occupying the upper floors of various buildings, the five windows and the lanterns peeping out from under the roofs indicate the presence of a place of prayer.

All five synagogues in Venice (the Italiana, Levantina, Spagnola, Canton and the oldest, Tedesca) share the same bifocal layout in which the pulpit (bimà) and the cupboard that contains the scrolls (aròn) are placed, one in front of the other, along the smaller side of the room, with the women's gallery above.

The Spagnola and Levantina Synagogues are situated in the Ghetto Vecchio, which was assigned to the Jews in 1541. Their names indicate the different rites practised. The **Spagnola Synagogue** (🅑, **DT**), the largest, was rebuilt by Longhena in the 17C. Longhena and his followers were probably responsible also for the restoration of the Levantina Synagogue, which is used during the summer months. The Tedesca (Ashkenazi), Canton and Italiana Synagogues are situated in Campo di Ghetto Nuovo.

The **Canton Synagogue** (🅑, **DT**), named either after the banker who commissioned its construction in the 16C or the Venetian term canton which refers to its corner position, is particularly renowned for its series of rare illustrations along the upper section of the walls. Strict observation of the second commandment prohibits the representation of any creature in the sky, on land or in water, of God or of man; even a suggestion of landscape inside a synagogue could be considered a distraction from prayer. However, the most important moments of Jewish history are recounted here.

Rio di San Girolamo in the Ghetto

B. Juge/MICHELIN

These include: *the Sending of Manna from Heaven, the Parting of the Red Sea* (interestingly, a hand can be seen protruding from the water, a detail that might indicate that the artist was Egyptian), *Moses Bringing Forth Water from the Rock, the Ark of the Covenant, the Symbol of the Jewish People who Crossed the River Jordan.*

Campo di Ghetto Nuovo (🟦, DS)

A walk in this square will inevitably recall the most tragic moments in the history of the Jews in Venice: reminders include a relief (1979) by the Lithuanian artist Blatas and a *Monument to the Deportees* (1993), which commemorates the Venetian Jews who died. At the same time, the square projects a picture of mundane tranquillity where ancient Jewish traditions live on: workshops manufacture objects relating to the Jewish faith, and glass ornaments and cards bear images of rabbis for those who seek inspiration to devotion or who just want to buy a memento of a very special corner of Venice.

Walking Tour

Approaching the Ghetto from Santa Lucia Station, there are several distractions: window shopping in **Rio Terrà Lista di Spagna**; observing the fish stalls along the Fondamenta della Pescheria or the market in Rio Terrà San Leonardo; exploring the Scalzi and San Geremia, and Palazzo Labia churches. Of particular interest for visitors to the area is the Church of Gli Scalzi.

Gli Scalzi (🟦, CT)

Literally the Church of "the Discalced," its name refers to the Carmelite Order, whose members, like the Franciscans, were obliged to go about their duties barefoot (today they wear sandals). Designed by Longhena, the church features a Baroque façade faced with Carrara marble. The rather sombre interior shelters the tomb of the last doge, **Ludovico Manin**. Prior to its destruction during World War I, the ceiling was decorated with a fresco by Tiepolo: the current painting dates from 1934. Fortunately, Tiepolo's frescoes in the vaults of the first chapel off the left aisle and second chapel of the right aisle survive (🔵*see Il CANAL GRANDE*).

▶ *Follow Rio Terrà Lista di Spagna, lined with numerous workshops, which eventually leads to Campo San Geremia.*

San Geremia e Santa Lucia (🟦, CDT)

Bathed in light, the interior of this 18C church is similar in plan to the Church of La Salute. It is here that the body of **St Lucy** lies. A Sicilian martyred under the persecution of Diocletian, she is the patron saint of the blind whose feast day is celebrated in Sweden and Finland. Also of note is a painting by Palma il Giovane, *The Virgin Attending the Coronation in Venice.* The brick campanile, alongside, dates from the 13C (🔵*see Il CANAL GRANDE*).

Palazzo Labia★★ (🟦, CDT)

⊶*May be temporarily closed for restoration.* ☎ 041 78 11 11.

The Ostentations of the Labia Family

Perhaps a little maliciously, legend has it that at the end of a banquet the Labia family would hurl their gold dinner plates and cutlery out of the window and into the canal to cries proclaiming their indifference to their wealth. The infamous family was more astute, however, than they might have appeared, for by placing fishing nets at the bottom of the canal, they were later able to retrieve their precious treasure for use another day.

The construction of this *palazzo*, built of Istrian stone, was commissioned in the late-17C by a wealthy family of Spanish merchants, to whom the building owes its name. The three façades, adorned with eagles – the family emblem – overlook Campo San Geremia, the Cannaregio Canal and a small square next to the Grand Canal. It was the exclusive prerogative of the Venetian nobility to have a residence overlooking the canal. The Labia family, who had paid to be listed in the **Libro d'Oro** (*see History: 1789*) had to settle for a residence with a view of the Grand Canal, without actually overlooking it.

In honour of Maria Labia's marriage in the 18C, **Giambattista Tiepolo** was commissioned to fresco the Salone delle Festa (Banqueting Hall); it would appear that the depiction of Cleopatra was inspired by her beauty. After the fall of the Republic, the family abandoned the *palazzo*, and when Napoleon handed it over to the Austrians, a long period of neglect began. In 1948 the palace was acquired by a wealthy Mexican oil magnate who organised a sumptuous ball in 18C costume to which the international jet set were invited. Abandoned again, restoration was postponed until the 1960s when it accommodated the Veneto arm of RAI, Italy's national television network. It belongs to the Labia Services Company, which holds seminars and conventions there.

Apartments arranged around the *salone*, or main room, and the courtyard, include the Stanza degli Specchi (Hall of Mirrors), with *trompe l'oeil* walls; the Stanza del Mappamondo (Map of the World) and chapel adjacent; a corridor decorated with Cordoba leather; the Stanza dei Stucchi, hung with portraits of the Labia family; and a room with a lively 18C representation of the *Signs of the Zodiac*.

▶ *Take the narrow alley leading to Parco Savorgnan.*

Parco Savorgnan (⑧, CT)

Kids This large, tree-shaded expanse off Campo San Geremia offers rest and relaxation to the district. Its playground is popular with children, especially little ones who are drawn to the swing set and the slide. A pathway is the perfect place for kids to ride their bikes, and the grassy field provides plenty of space simply to run around.

▶ *Exit the park on its east side and turn left at the Cannaregio Canal.*

Parco Savorgnan

Gwen Cannon/ MICHELIN

Bridge with Three Arches

Much appreciated by pedestrians who do not have to cope with a single steep ramp, the three-arched structure is less popular with the canal traffic, which is forced to slow down and proceed with caution. All the three-arched bridges in Venice have disappeared except the **Ponte dei Tre Archi** on the Cannaregio Canal, which was constructed at the end of the 17C by Andrea Tirali (c 1657-1737).

The Cannaregio Canal is crossed by two bridges *(ponti):* the Ponte delle Guglie and the Ponte dei Tre Archi (*see sidebar above),* farther along the canal.

▶ *Follow Fondamenta Venier, which runs along the canal, to the Ponte dei Tre Archi. Turn left onto the calle which leads to the Church of San Giobbe.*

San Giobbe (⧆, CT)

This church is dedicated to Job, the figure in the Old Testament who rejected the view that suffering is the result of sin. Antonio Gambello began construction in the late-15C; it was completed by Pietro Lombardo. The plain façade is broken by a Renaissance portal. St Francis and Job appear in the low relief enclosed in the lunette.
Interior features include the coat of arms of **Doge Cristoforo Moro** (1462-71), who is buried in the presbytery alongside his wife.

▶ *Retrace your steps, following Fondamenta Venier to the Ponte delle Guglie.*

Ponte delle Guglie (⧆, DT)

Passing over the Ponte delle Guglie (1580) is practically obligatory, given that it is the bridge linking the railway station to the Strada Nuova. It takes its name from the architectural features that adorn the balustrade.

▶ *Cross the bridge and walk along Rio Terrà San Leonardo as far as Rio Terrà del Cristo on the right, which leads to the Church of San Marcuola.*

San Marcuola (⧆, DT)

Like Zanipòlo (*see ACCADEMIA: San Trovaso),* this name is a contraction of the two saints' names: Ermagora and Fortunato.
The original construction dates back to around the 10C, but the church was subsequently restructured during the course of the 18C, although the *campo's* façade, which overlooks the Grand Canal, was never completed.
Inside, the altars are the work of Giovanni Morlaiter (1699-1781), who sculpted the high altar in the Church of La Salute. (*see Il CANAL GRANDE).*

LA GIUDECCA

(◻️7️⃣, ◻️8️⃣, ◻️9️⃣, BGYZ)

VAPORETTO: ZITELLE, REDENTORE, GIUDECCA, S. EUFEMIA

At one time this island was dotted with the villas of wealthy Venetian nobles; today the prestigious Cipriani hotel is the only one left to perpetuate the luxurious living of the past. Nowadays Guidecca is a haven for visitors wishing to take in the island's relaxed and peaceful atmosphere, if only for an hour or so, and the contrasting views of Venice extending beyond the canal.

▶ **Orient Yourself:** Laid out in the shape of a fishbone, the eight islands that make up the Giudecca justify its original name: **spinalonga** (long spine). The origins of the current name may be twofold: one a reference to the Jews *(giudei)* who lived there; the second an allusion to the 11C *zudegà* (judgement) that guaranteed land to noble families who had been exiled from elsewhere.

👀 **Don't Miss:** A long meander along the *fondamenta* following the canals that divide it up, from Mulino Stucky east toward the Church of San Giorgio Maggiore.

🕐 **Organizing Your Time:** Allow 30-45min for the walk and visit of Redentore. Then stop in the Hotel Cipriani for lunch or afternoon tea; it's advisable to make advance reservations (👜 *see Where to Stay in Your Stay in the City).*

♿ **Also See:** Neighbouring sight: SAN GIORGIO MAGGIORE.

Il Redentore

SCALA

The Feast of the Redeemer

The Feast of the Redeemer is still held on the third Sunday in July, perpetuating the tradition started by Doge Alvise Mocenigo. A bridge of boats across the Giudecca Canal used to be assembled to enable the procession to reach the island and allow free access to the faithful. In the evening of the preceding Saturday, a fireworks display would – as it still does today – illuminate the sky and the lagoon with sparkling lights, bewitching the vast and animated audience of Venetians and tourists gathered on the Riva degli Schiavoni.

Walking Tour

Mulino Stucky (**7**, BY)
This prepossessing but rather awkward construction, which would perhaps be more at home in Dickens' London, is the work of late-19C German architects. It earns its name from the Swiss entrepreneur who commissioned it.

▶ *Follow Fondamenta S. Biagio eastward.*

Sant'Eufemia (**7**, CY)
This is the oldest church on the island, its origins dating back to the 9C. The late 16C *portico* on the left side, facing onto the Giudecca Canal, is from another church, now destroyed. Still graced with the 11C Veneto-Byzantine capitals, the interior houses the colourful *San Rocco and the Angel* by **Bartolomeo Vivarini** (c 1432-91) *(first altar, right aisle)*; the frescoed ceiling is by Giambattista Canal (1745-1825) and exalts the life of the saint to which the church is dedicated.

Il Redentore★ (**8**, EY)
◷*Open Mon-Sat, 10am-5pm.* ◷*Closed 1 Jan, Easter, 15 Aug, 25 Dec.* ✍€2.50. ☎ *041 27 50 462; www.chorusvenezia.org*
With Venice decimated by the plague, which had been raging for more than a year, **Doge Alvise Mocenigo** proposed (1576) that a new church be dedicated to the Redeemer, and every year thereafter honoured by a solemn procession.
In designing the church, **Palladio** sought to make it fulfil its votive function above all. Its longitudinal axis was necessary for the long procession of clergy and dignitaries. The flat, rigorously Classical façade, set back from a flight of steps inspired by biblical descriptions of the Temple in Jerusalem, embodies an idealised view of the Catholic Church accommodating a modern, Classically ordered building.
Flooded with light, the unified interior is contained in a single nave lined with side chapels. As with the architecture, the paintings (by Bassano, Tintoretto, and others) are arranged in such a way as to reveal their significance and unfurl the mystery of life as the procession progresses. In the **sacristy** hang a *Baptism of Christ* by Veronese and a *Madonna with Child and Angels* by Alvise Vivarini.

Le Zitelle (**8**, FY)
The **Church of Santa Maria della Presentazione** was designed by **Palladio**. The name *Zitelle* was coined from a reference to the girls accommodated in the adjoining hospice that forms part of the façade. Characteristic features of the main front include the dominant triangular tympanum, flanked by bell-turrets, over a semicircular window.

PIAZZA SAN MARCO ★★★

(⬛,FGX)

VAPORETTO: S. MARCO

"The finest drawing room in Europe" according to Napoleon, **St Mark's Square** is the daily destination for thousands of visitors. Beyond the columns of St Mark and St Theodore, the gondolas and vaporettos come and go while noisy crowds gather around the souvenir stalls. Tourists follow their tour guide's raised umbrella into the basilica or loiter under the porticoes, bewitched by windows of *passementerie* and sparkling jewellery and glass. Musicians play to the habitués of the legendary cafes, while vendors of bird feed cater to the pigeon-feeders. Since time immemorial, the passing of the hours is still ceremoniously sounded by the Moors on the clock tower and the mighty bells of the campanile.

▶ **Orient Yourself:** The square, the heart of the city, houses Basilica di San Marco and the Palazzo Ducale on its east side; the Marciana Library, Procuratie Nuove, Museo Correr and the Procuratie Vecchie form a U-shaped border to the west

⊘ **Don't Miss:** The piazza when an orchestra is playing outdoors near Caffè Florian: a thoroughly romantic, magical experience.

🕓 **Organizing Your Time:** For a tour of the basilica, the Doges' Palace and the museums allow at least a half a day. Avoid the square in summer and on special occasions such as the Carnival: the early hours of the morning and evening and spring and autumn, when the colours and the sounds are crisp and clear, are infinitely preferable.

Kids Especially for Kids: Feeding the famous flocks of pigeons.

👣 **Also See:** Neighbouring sights: La FENICE; RIALTO; SAN ZACCARIA.

The domes of St Mark's Basilica

A Bit of History

A canal once ran in front of the basilica. By covering it over in 1160, the length of the only piazza in Venice was tripled. The columns of St Mark and St Theodore (℃ *see below*) were erected in the piazzetta, and the entire architectural complex, as adapted, became the setting before which Pope Alexander III met with Barbarossa (1177).

Florentine sculptor and architect Jacopo Sansovino (1486-1570) redesigned the piazza, linking it to the piazzetta. He is also responsible for the **Library**. Towards the close of the 16C, attention was turned to the redevelopment of the south side of the piazza; old buildings were remoed to make way for the Procuratie Nuove.

The present trachyte paving was designed by Andrea Tirali (c 1657-1737), who also resurfaced the area known as the **Piazzetta dei Leoncini**, called after the two lions by Giovanni Bonazza (1654-1736). Tirali then conceived the idea of accenting lines of perspective in the piazza by inlaying four "fasciae" in Carrara marble in concentric geometrical formation. Two such bands converge on the Basilica; the other two running oblique to the first pair are aligned with the columns of St Mark and St Theodore. At their speculative point of intersection stands the square base of the campanile (best appreciated from above).

Little changed, then, until the collapse of the campanile on 14 July 1902. Miraculously, the only damage incurred was to Sansovino's Loggetta and to a small part of the Biblioteca Marciana. By 1911, the new campanile, which is an exact reproduction of the old one, restored the square's traditional appearance.

The vast trapezoidal space (176m/577ft in length, 82m/269ft maximum width) is enclosed on the north side by the Procuratie Vecchie and by the later 16C Procuratie Nuove opposite. In between, the neo-Classical Napoleon Wing or **Ala nuovissimo** was built in accordance with the wishes of Emperor Bonaparte after the demolition in the early 1800s of the 16C Sansovino Church of San Geminiano.

Basilica di San Marco★★★ (Saint Mark's Basilica) (🕭, FGX)

"Peace unto you, Mark, my Evangelist. Here rests your body," the angel said to St Mark near the Rialto, as the Evangelist was journeying from Aquileia to Rome. Almost another 800 years were to elapse before the legendary prophecy was fulfilled: the symbol of St Mark has been synonymous with the Venetian flag.

According to legend

In Egypt around the year 800 two merchants set out for Alexandria with the intention of stealing the saint's body as it was felt that the relics would bestow upon Venice the prestige needed to "compete" with Rome or, at least, would affirm its politico-religious independence from the capital. The body was taken in a chest aboard a Venetian vessel. On arrival in Venice, the precious relic was placed in the chapel of a castle belonging to Doge Giustiniano Partecipazio, subsequently consecrated in 832 as the first church dedicated to St Mark.

History of the church

In this way the first patron saint of Venice, San Teodoro, *Todaro* in dialect, was demoted even if not forgotten.

After the fire of 976, which seriously damaged the church, St. Mark's body was lost. On the occasion of the consecration of the third church to be erected on this site (25 June 1094), a part of a pilaster in the right transept crumbled to reveal a human arm. The sacred relic was removed to the crypt and later (19C) to below the high altar.

The 11C basilica is modelled upon the Church of the Holy Apostles in Constantinople. It came to be the pride of the Venetians: **Doge Domenico Selvo** (1071-84) would ask merchants travelling to the East to bring back marble and other stone pieces (alabaster, jasper, porphyry, serpentine) for its embellishment. Indeed this was how the mosaics in the domes and the vaults came about.

Exterior

Silhouetted against the sky are the Basilica's five 13C Byzantine domes which culminate in a cross over the lantern. The lateral façades face onto Piazzetta dei Leoncini and Piazzetta San Marco.

West front

The façade is articulated horizontally by a terrace and balustrade that extends down the lateral walls; vertically, the width is divided into five bays, pierced at both levels by arches, opening at ground level into porches.

The iconography of the 17C mosaics from the left arch is as follows:

1st arch: *Transportation of the Body of St Mark into the Church* (1260-70), the only complete mosaic to survive from the façade's original decoration;

2nd arch: *St Mark Venerated by Venetian Magistrates*, based on a cartoon by Sebastiano Ricci (1659-1734);

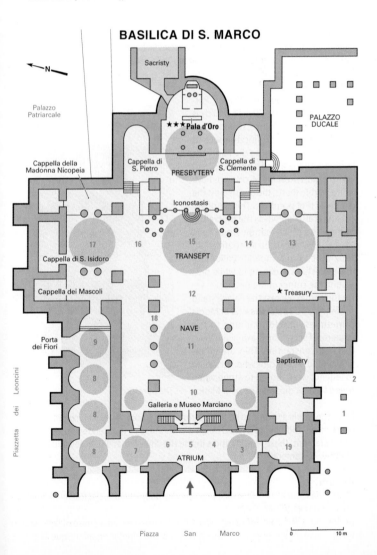

BASILICA DI S. MARCO

N

Sacristy

Palazzo Patriarcale

PALAZZO DUCALE

★★★ Pala d'Oro

Cappella della Madonna Nicopeia

Cappella di S. Pietro

PRESBYTERY

Cappella di S. Clemente

Iconostasis

17   16   15   14   13

TRANSEPT

Cappella di S. Isidoro

Cappella dei Mascoli

★ Treasury

12

18

Porta dei Fiori

9   NAVE

11

8   Baptistery

8   10

Galleria e Museo Marciano

Piazzetta   dei   Leoncini

8   7   6   5   4   3   19

ATRIUM

Piazza   San   Marco

0   10 m

3rd arch: (main, central archway) the 19C replacement mosaics, *Christ in Glory* and *The Last Judgement*, are enclosed in an arch populated with figures among foliage; below the mosaics, the three archivolts (inner arches) are illustrated with Romanesque-Byzantine carvings representing *the Three Kingdoms: Land, Ocean and Animal, the Labours of the Months* and the *Signs of the Zodiac, the Virtues and Beatitudes*. Running along the intrados of the main arch (underside) are depictions of the typical Venetian trades: note the man on the left with the crutches, thought to allude to the architect of St Mark's, gnawing his hand, preoccupied by the imperfection of his work.

4th arch: *The Body of St Mark Welcomed by the Venetians;*
5th arch: *The Theft of the Relic of St Mark.*

Modern copies now replace the four bronze horses on the balcony; the originals are conserved in the museum. On the upper level, the arches terminate in Gothic cusps. The 17C mosaics (see below) depict (from left to right): *The Deposition, The Descent into Limbo, The Resurrection* and *The Ascension*.

Left side
Walk down the left flank, overlooking Piazzetta dei Leoncini, to admire the Porta dei Fiori (4th arch, on the corner) with its Romanesque relief of *The Nativity*.

Right side
The south side abuts the Doges' Palace on the piazzetta. The first arch is framed by two columns surmounted with Romanesque griffins; the second arch contains the door to the Baptistry, framed with the **Acrean pillars (1)**. Syrian in origin, two of the 6C columns have white marble shafts; the one nearest the piazzetta is of porphyry. This porphyry column is also known as the **pietra del bando**, the proclamation stone from where laws would be announced. In 1902, when the campanile collapsed, this pedestal was damaged while protecting the corner of the Basilica.

On the corner nearest the Palace stand the famous 4C **Tetrarchs★ (2)** or Moors sometimes upheld to allude to the Emperors Diocletian, Maximilian, Valerian and Constantine. They are otherwise said to be Saracens who, according to legend, were turned to stone when trying to steal the treasure of St Mark.

P. de Franqueville/MICHELIN

The Tetrarchs

Enter the basilica through the large atrium that would have been reserved for the unbaptised and new converts. Decked with mosaics that relate stories from the Old Testament, these herald others inside the church that illustrate incidents from the New Testament.

Atrium
Guided tours (1hr) of the mosaics, Apr-Oct, daily at 11am. Closed holidays. For reservations ☎ 041 27 02 421.

At the end of the Fourth Crusade (1201-04), Venice entered a phase of self-esteem on the wave of victory after the conquest of Constantinople. Romanesque and early

Christian iconography in these early mosaics are borrowed from 5C-6C illuminated manuscripts that appear to have reached Venice with the Fourth Crusade.

▶ *Start with the right dome, and follow towards the left:*

The Creation according to Genesis (3)

These are the oldest mosaics in the atrium: in three concentric circles, in an anti-clockwise direction, they tell the story of Genesis, beginning with the dove, the smallest mosaic, to the east. In synthesis with the tradition of the Eastern Church, based upon the Gospel of St John *(The word was God …)*, the figure of the Creator is that of Christ, beardless, to signify the period before the Incarnation. Each stage of the Creation is attended by the angels which gradually increase in numbers as the days go by.

Note, on the day of the creation of the animals, the lions before God that symbolise Venice's atmosphere of pride and self-congratulation; on the day on which the Creator blesses the seventh angel – the day of rest and the day that Adam and Eve were chased from the Garden of Paradise – how they are depicted dressed in clothes. On the eighth day, Christ is born, heralding the beginning of a new Creation.

The *Arch of Noah* (**4**) depicts the story of Noah and the Flood: notice the ark's little window during the deluge.

Continuing with the iconographic theme initiated in the entrance, the mosaics of the *Arch of Paradise* (**5**), designed in part by Tintoretto (1518-94) and Aliense (1556-1629), exalt the mission of the Church as the Salvation of Man by means of the Cross, Paradise and Hell; represented as symbols that break with the narrative of the Old Testament stories illustrated previously. Before passing through the doorway, it is worth looking up at the vault, where St Mark in Ecstasy is based on a cartoon by **Titian** (1490-1576).

In the niches on either side of the doorway stand the Madonna, Apostles and Evangelists; the ornamentation is Byzantine.

The story of Noah continues in the next arch with a particularly beautiful depiction of the *Tower of Babel* (**6**), marking a prelude to the division of the human race.

Story of Abraham (7)

The mosaics in the second dome comprise one cycle, dedicated to the life of Abraham. Between the various scenes are lunettes which illustrate God's promises to Abraham. In the next arch, Abraham is depicted with the confirmation in writing, as the prefiguration of Christ.

Story of Joseph (8)

The last dome on the left and the next two in the left arm illustrate the story of Joseph. In order to portray a person who is dreaming – in this case the Pharaoh – the mosaic artists resorted to a sort of bubble that unfurls. The second and third dome of this series postdate the first by about 20 years, which explains why the images and landscapes appear richer and more vibrant.

Story of Moses (9)

In the last dome of the atrium, this part of the biblical cycle concludes with the life of Moses.

Above the door, the Madonna presents her Son, flanked by St John and St Mark. This concludes the Old Testament cycle and serves as a link to the New Testament by encouraging the visitor to carry on "reading" inside the Basilica.

▶ *A steep flight of stairs leads to the Galleria and the Museo di San Marco.*

Museo di San Marco

 ♿🕐*Open daily, 9.45am-5.30pm (4.30pm Nov-Mar); Sun and public hols 2-4pm.* ⊗€3. ☎ *041 52 25 205; www.museosanmarco.it*

Access to the Marciano Museum is via the Gallery, from where there is a marvellous view of the mosaics and an opportunity to look out over the piazza from the balcony. The museum houses tapestries, mosaics and some interesting documents relating to the history of the Basilica. The greatest draw for visitors must be the **gilded bronze horses**★★. They arrived in Venice as part of the booty from the Fourth Crusade but undoubtedly date back to a much earlier period, although opinion on their origin is divided as to whether they are 4C-3C BC Greek or 4C Roman works.

Given pride of place on the balcony, these wonderful equestrian statues were taken to Paris by Napoleon after his crushing Italian campaign, but returned in 1815. In 1974 they were removed from their original position for restoration and replaced with copies.

St Mark's Interior

In the form of a Greek cross, St Mark's has a raised presbytery separated from the central nave by an iconostasis.

Mosaics★★★

 👁*Visitors are advised to view the mosaics inside St Mark's when the basilica is illumi-nated: Mon-Fri, 11.30am-12.30pm; Sat-Sun and holidays, all day.*

As a general orientation, the lower part of the walls depict the saints, the middle section is reserved for the Apostles and the domes are dedicated to the Creator. The key to each story is held in the dome of the apse from where the story unfolds chronologically. Christ as Pantocrator towers over the four patrons of Venice: St Nicholas, St Peter, St Mark and St Ermagora, with the area above the atrium given over to the Last Judgement. These last mosaics are also the most recent, dating as they do from the 16C.

The entrance door depicts the *Deesis*, the Saviour in benediction between the Virgin and St Mark.

The **Arch of the Apocalypse (10)** illustrates the visions described in the Gospel of St John; the seven candelabra symbolise the seven churches.

The dome nearest the doorway is dedicated to the *Pentecost* **(11)**. Between the win-dows, the populace listens to the preaching of St Peter in Jerusalem; to correspond with the angels, the Four Evangelists are illustrated in the pendentives.

Approaching the central dome, the **West Arch (12)** presents a synthesis of the *Passion* and *Death of Christ*. Worthy of note are the cartouches in the hand of the Judeans, bearing Pilate and Christ.

In the right transept, illuminated by a Gothic rose window, the **Dome of St Leonard (13)** or the Saints of the Sacrament, is decorated with 13C mosaics representing St Nicholas, St Clement, St Blaise and St Leonard. The **South Arch (14)** has Byzantine mosaics which depict the *Temptations of Christ* and *His Entry into Jerusalem,* the *Last Supper* and the *Washing of the Feet.*

In the centre is the **Dome of the Ascension (15)**. This encapsulates the most impor-tant moments in the story of the Salvation. Witnesses to the *Ascension* include the Apostles, the Madonna and, between the windows, the Virtues and some of the Beatitudes. Christ in benediction dominates the scene. Beneath the pendentives which depict the Four Evangelists are the Four Rivers of the Earth.

The **Presbytery Dome** is dedicated to the Season of Advent, dominated by Emmanuel in the company of Prophets, with the Virgin in the middle. The decoration of this dome dates back to the beginning of 1100. Symbols of the Evangelists adorn the pendentives.

The mosaics on the **North Arch (16)** designed by Tintoretto show *St Michael with Sword Drawn* with the *Last Supper* on the left and the *Marriage at Cana* on the right. In the centre, the *Healing of the Leper* is taken from a cartoon by Veronese (1528-88), the *Healing of the Bleeding Woman* and the *Resurrection of Naim's Widow's Son* are based on cartoons by Salviati (1520/25-75). The *Christ in Glory* is a 19C reconstruction.

The **Dome of St John the Evangelist** (**17**) is in the left arm of the transept. The 13C mosaics reproduce a Greek cross with biblical verses on the *Sermon on the Mount* and episodes from the Life of St John the Evangelist.

▶ *Continue along the left aisle.*

In the north aisle is the **Capital of the Crucifixion** (**18**), a white and black marble structure with a pyramidal roof surmounted by an agate. The crucifix contained therein, coming from Constantinople, would have been the cause of much bloodshed.

The mosaic panels (c 1230) opposite the side aisles depict *Christ Blessing the Prophets* – Hosea, Joel, Micah and Jeremiah *(in the left aisle)* and Ezekiel, Solomon, the Madonna in prayer, David and Isaiah *(in the right aisle)*.

St Mark's golden interior

Pala d'Oro★★★

♿ 🕐 *Open May–Sept, daily 9.45am (2pm Sun and public hols) to 5.30pm; Oct–Apr 9.45am to 4.30pm, public holidays 2–4pm; last admission 30min before closing.* 🎫*€1.50.* ☎ *041 52 25 205; www.basilicasanmarco.it*

The **Golden Altarpiece** is preceded by a ciborium on **columns of alabaster**★★ inscribed with reliefs inspired by the Gospels and the Apocrypha. The exact date and provenance of these reliefs remain uncertain, but are usually classified as 5C–6C Greek (from Ravenna), Syrian, Egyptian or Coptic. Contained within the high altar rest the remains of St Mark and, beyond, towers the great altarpiece.

Commissioned and made in Constantinople in the 10C, the Golden Altarpiece is a masterpiece of the goldsmith's craft. Gleaming with precious stones set among enamelled panels, it continued to be embellished with new and valuable sections until the 14C.

The top section is dominated by the figure of the Archangel Michael in the centre, framed between scenes (starting

The Golden Altarpiece – detail (San Marco)

from the left) of the *Entry into Jerusalem*, the *Resurrection*, the *Crucifixion*, the *Ascension*, the *Pentecost* and the *Death of the Virgin*. The focal point of the lower section is Christ Pantocrator (the Ruler of the Universe) flanked by the figures of the Evangelists. Below, the Virgin appears between the Empress Irene and the Emperor Giovanni Commeno, Prophets, Apostles and Angels. On either side, the iconographic cycle continues with episodes from the lives of Christ and St Mark.

In the apse, the doors to the tabernacle and to the sacristy are by Sansovino.

Chapels

Grouped around the presbytery it is worth stopping to look at the **iconostasis** (openwork screen) in polychrome marble. Eight columns support an architrave bearing figures of the **Apostles**, the **Madonna** and **John the Baptist** by Dalle Masegne (14C–15C). This great line is broken in the middle by a bronze and silver **Crucifix**. At either end, the iconostasis terminates with a pulpit, each reconstructed in the 14C. The **Double Pulpit** on the left comprises two sections from which lessons are read from the Gospels *(upper tier)* and the Epistles *(lower tier)*. To honour the Word of God, it is crowned with a fine golden cupola which is decidedly oriental in style. The pulpit on the right, the **Pulpit of the Reliquary**, was where the relics would be displayed and where the newly elected doge would make his first appearance.

Both chapels dedicated to **St Clement** *(right apse)* and **St Peter** *(left apse)* are screened off by their own iconostasis; the one for St Clement, complete with statues, is by Dalle Masegne. Outside each chapel, the wall is covered with mosaics (12C) illustrating episodes from the lives of St Mark and St Peter respectively; inside the domed vault of each are representations of the saints to whom each chapel is dedicated (St Peter is 13C).

The window on the right wall of the Chapel of St Clement enabled the doge to follow functions and services being held in church without leaving the comfortable confines of his palace apartments.

In the **Chapel of the Madonna Nicopeia** is a particularly venerated image of the Madonna and Child, called *Nicopeia* (meaning the Bringer of Victory or Leader), because she served as the standard of the Byzantine army. Coming from Constantinople, the figure may have been brought to Venice as booty from the Fourth Crusade.

The **Chapel of St Isidore** is off the transept, whose end wall bears *Mary's Genealogical Tree*, which dates back to the end of the 12C.

The next chapel, the **Mascoli Chapel**, is dedicated to the members of the confraternity of male worshippers. The mosaics are the work of Giambono (active 1420-62), Andrea del Castagno (c 1421-57), Jacopo Bellini (c 1396-c 1470) and **Andrea Mantegna** (1431-1506).

Treasury★

⌖⏲*Same hours as Pala d'Oro.* 👓€2. ☎ *041 52 25 205; www.basilicasanmarco.it*
This very valuable collection of religious objects, reliquaries and ornaments, which came into Venice's possession after the conquest of Constantinople in 1204, includes one notable exhibit, the *Artophoron,* an 11C container for the Bread of the Eucharist in the shape of a church, crowned with oriental-style domes.

Baptistery

⏲*Open for prayer only.*
The baptistery is divided into three interconnecting areas; 14C mosaics recount the life of John the Baptist and the Infant Jesus. The most famous panel shows *Salome Dancing before Herod.* The baptismal font is by Sansovino (1486-1570), who is buried here, before the altar. The mosaics in the **Cappella Zen (19)**, the funeral chapel of Cardinal Zen who died in 1501, date from the 13C.

Il Campanile★★ (⑧, FX)

⌖⏲*Open Jul-Aug, 9am-9pm; Apr-Jun and Sept-Oct, 9am-7pm; rest of the year 9.30am-4.15pm. Last admission 30min before closing.* ⏲*Closed 2 weeks in Jan.* 👓€6. ☎ *041 52 24 064; www.basilicasanmarco.it.*
Although the present bell-tower was erected at the beginning of the 20C, it was rebuilt according to its predecessor's early-16C designs by Bartolomeo Bon in brick. The campanile stands 96m/315ft high, culminating in a golden angel weathervane that turns in the wind.

The square tower is articulated as if by a gigantic order of pilasters up to an arched white marble section pierced by a four-light loggia where the bells hang. Above a balustraded section, the four sides rise cleanly to a pyramid.

At the top, from where **Galileo Galilei** once extended his telescope (1609), a magnificent **view**★★ stretches from the Giudecca Canal to the Grand Canal across roofs, chimneys and *altane* to the islands in the lagoon.

Loggetta Sansoviniana

At the base of the tower, and facing St Mark's, the richly decorated Sansovino Loggetta comprises three arches supported on columns reminiscent of a triumphal arch; columns also frame the niches that accommodate the figures of Minerva, Apollo, Mercury and Peace. The reliefs above depict *(from left to right),* the Island of Candia, Venice as an allegory of Justice, and the island of Cyprus. The terrace at the front is enclosed by a balustrade, broken in the middle by a bronze gate designed by Antonio Gai (1686-1769).

The present *loggetta* was first built during the early part of the 16C by **Jacopo Tatti Sansovino** and rebuilt after the collapse of the campanile.

On the right side of the basilica, near the Porta della Carta, stand the remains of a tower decorated with low-relief sculptures; as they are not directly at eye level, they tend to elude the attention of visitors. However, ⌖if you bend down a little, you will notice one in particular that is located under the Tetrarchs, just on the right. It represents two putti escaping from the jaws of two dragons. They are pictured framing a 13C inscription, believed to be one of the very first texts written in Venetian dialect.

Palazzo Ducale★★★ (Doges' Palace) (🅖, GX)

&. ⏱Open daily 9am-7pm (5pm Nov-Mar); last admission 1hr before closing. ⏱Closed 1 Jan and 25 Dec. 🎫€12 (MUSEUM CARD with Musei di Piazza S.Marco). ☎ 041 27 15 911; www.museiciviciveneziani.it

The origins of this Byzantine, Gothic and Renaissance palace go back almost as far as those of Venice itself. It was **Doge Agnello Partecipazio** who decided, in 810, that the seat of his public offices should be located on the site of the present Doges' Palace. At the time, the buildings, which included the Church of St Mark, were more of a citadel than a government office. The need for a fortified residence gradually gave way towards one with an institutional role, with loggias and porticoes on the outside and a host of offices inside where various affairs of State could be conducted by the doge's staff.

Exterior

The harmony of the structural whole is striking: the "hollow" spaces of the portico and the loggia contrast with blocks of "solid" masonry in the upper section of the

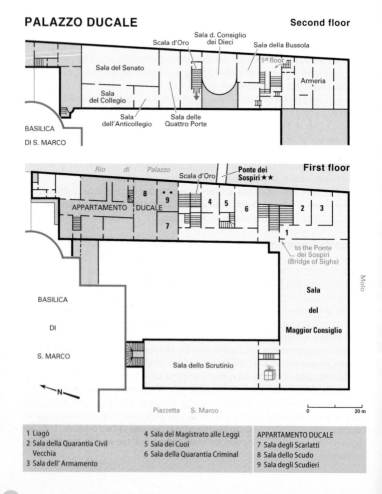

PALAZZO DUCALE

Second floor

Sala d. Consiglio dei Dieci
Scala d'Oro
Sala della Bussola
Sala del Senato
Sala del Collegio
Sala dell'Anticollegio
Sala delle Quattro Porte
1st floor
Armeria
BASILICA DI S. MARCO

First floor

Rio di Palazzo
Scala d'Oro
Ponte dei Sospiri ★★
APPARTAMENTO DUCALE
8
9
4
5
6
2
3
7
1
to the Ponte dei Sospiri (Bridge of Sighs)
BASILICA DI S. MARCO
Sala del Maggior Consiglio
Molo
N
Sala dello Scrutinio
Piazzetta S. Marco
0 20 m

1 Liagò	4 Sala del Magistrato alle Leggi	APPARTAMENTO DUCALE
2 Sala della Quarantia Civil Vecchia	5 Sala dei Cuoi	7 Sala degli Scarlatti
3 Sala dell'Armamento	6 Sala della Quarantia Criminal	8 Sala dello Scudo
		9 Sala degli Scudieri

building. The effect is mitigated, however, by the rose-coloured tint of the upper floor and the darkness of the multi-arched lower floors.

The narrative function of the mosaics inside the basilica is transposed here onto the sculptural iconography that adorns the capitals, the corners of the *palazzo* and its pillars. Decorating the palace are allegorical figures representing the Vices and Virtues, the Ages of Man and Signs of the Zodiac, all charged with moral example. The façade onto the piazzetta rises from an arcade of 18 pointed arches along the ground floor, supported on baseless columns. The first-floor loggia also runs continuously along the façade, the horizontal emphasis accentuated by the balustrade and sequence of 34 roundels between the ogive, cusped arches, punctured with quatrefoil cut-outs. From between the two red marble columns, public announcements of capital sentences were made, later to be carried out between the columns of St Mark and St Theodore in the square below.

The two upper storeys, which together are as tall as the two lower floors, seem lost in solid wall. From a distance, the building appears a distinctively soft shade of pinky-rose, with surface relief at closer proximity, provided by the interplay of terra-cotta and white bricks disposed in diamond patterns. Its massiveness is further offset by the delicate line of gables along the top.

On the first floor, the central balcony overlooking the piazzetta is 16C (artists unknown). The portrait above it is of **Doge Andrea Gritti** (1523-38) and at each corner is a sculptural group: that projecting into the square shows the *Judgement of Solomon,* an allegory of Wisdom, thought to be by Bartolomeo Bon (active 1441-64), beyond which stands the Porta della Carta.

Porta della Carta★★

The **"Paper Doorway"** is the entrance to the palace per se. Flamboyant Gothic in style, it was constructed by Giovanni and Bartolomeo Bon between 1438 and 1442. Explanations for the name have been attributed to the many scribes who used the entrance, which also served the archives *(cartarum).* The superimposed niches are occupied by the four Cardinal Virtues sculpted by Antonio Bregno (c 1418-c 1503). Above the doorway, kneeling before the winged lion, is the Doge Francesco Foscari, who was in power when the portal was constructed. Above the window, in the roundel, is St Mark, overlooked by Justice on the pinnacle.

▸ *To reach the canal quayside from the Piazzetta San Marco, walk round the full length of both sides of the palace.*

The façade overlooking the Basin stretches between the corner sculpture groups of *(left) Adam, Eve and the Serpent* (late 14C) – an allegory of Sin – surmounted by the figures of Tobias and the Angel Raphael (late 14C) and *The Drunkenness of Noah* (14C-15C), a symbol of the virtue of compassion *(near the Paglia Bridge).*

The second capital from the left, known as the Capital of the Sages *(dei Sapienti),* is inscribed with the date 1344, the year in which this wing was constructed. The central balcony on the second floor was inserted in the early 15C, designed by Dalle Masegne.

The last two, more decorative, windows appear out of alignment with the others because of the internal room arrangement.

Gwen Cannon/ MICHELIN

The Drunkenness of Noah

To the right, the Ponte della Paglia (literally translated as the Bridge of Straw) precedes that second and much more famous bridge across the canal.

Ponte dei Sospiri★★ (⑨, GX)

Universally known, the Bridge of Sighs owes its name to Romantic literary notions: overwhelmed by the enchanting view from the windows of this bridge, this was where the prisoners would suffer their final torment.

The bridge, constructed in Istrian stone, links the palace with the Prigioni Nuove (New Prisons). It was built during the dogeship of **Marino Grimani** (1595-1605) and bears his coat of arms. Inside, the bridge is divided into two passages through which visitors pass on their tour of the Doges' Palace. Given the number of rooms and the length of the tour, ⓟ it is easy to lose one's bearings and to cross the bridge without realising it, so beware!

The Bridge of Sighs

Palace Entrance

The entrance to the Palazzo is to the right of the Porta della Carta (through which visitors pass on their way out). The courtyard is graced with a fine mid-16C well-head, the mid-15C **Porticato Foscari** leading through to the **Foscari Arch**, and the **Scala dei Giganti** directly opposite. The Giants' Staircase, constructed at the end of the 15C, was designed by Antonio Rizzo (c 1440-99) and is dominated by two magnificent statues of Mars and Neptune (the gods of War and Sea) by Sansovino (1486-1570). It was at the top of these stairs that the doges used to be crowned. The well-heads in the courtyard date to the mid-16C; the east end façade, designed by Rizzo, is early Renaissance in style.

Interior

From the portico, take the **Scala d'Oro** or Golden Staircase up to the second floor. Sansovino initiated work on the staircase during the reign of **Doge Andrea Gritti** (1523-38), although work was not to be completed by Scarpagnino (recorded in Venice 1505-49) until after the appointment of Lorenzo Priuli (1556-59): note the coats of arms of the two

Palazzo Ducale

doges on the large arch. Its Baroque-sounding name comes from reference to the rich stucco decoration in white and gold around Giovan Battista Franco's (1498-1561) frescoes depicting *The Glorification of the Defence of Cyprus and Crete* and *The Virtues Necessary for Good Government*. The portrait in the atrium of Doge Gerolamo Priuli was painted by Tintoretto.

L'Appartamento Ducale
Follow the signs through to the Ducal Appartment, where a *Pietà* by Giovanni Bellini and the famous *Lion* by Vittore Carpaccio are displayed.

Sala delle Quattro Porte
Ambassadors would wait for their audience with the doge in this first room, the Chamber of the Four Doors. The decoration postdates 1574, following one of the many fires caused by the use of wood and candles. Propped up on the easel is *Venice Receiving the Homage of Neptune*, a famous canvas by Tiepolo. The frescoed ceiling is by Tintoretto and the four doorways by Palladio. The paintings on the walls depict allegorical scenes or historical subjects. Among these, *Doge Antonio Grimani in Adoration before the Faith and St Mark in Glory* was started by Titian and finished by his nephew. The painting, commemorating a visit made by Henry III, King of France, in 1574, depicts the Triumphal Arch designed by Palladio that would have been made of papier mâché, a material commonly used to create temporary stage sets for special occasions.

Sala dell'Anticollegio
An antechamber for diplomatic delegations, the room houses the *Return of Jacob with Family* by Jacopo Bassano (c 1517-92) and the *Rape of Europa* by Veronese *(facing*

SCALA

the windows). The paintings on either side of the doors are by Tintoretto. The fresco on the ceiling is by Veronese.

Sala del Collegio

Here in the College Chamber the doge, his throne raised on the wooden platform, presided over meetings. The "Full College" dealt with legal matters that were subsequently presented to the Senate, and political relationships between Venice and foreign courts on diplomatic missions. The stalls date to 1575. The paintings decorating the gilded wooden ceiling exalt the city; above the throne, the great panel depicting Doge Sebastiano Venier is also by Veronese. The paintings on the wall with the clock set in black Belgian marble are by Tintoretto: left of the clock, *Alvise Mocenigo Thanking the Redeemer* commemorates the votive plea for an end to the plague of 1576. Tintoretto's painting on the door continues in the same spirit of celebration.

Sala del Senato

Here in the Senate Chamber, or "Pregadi Chamber," members of the Senate were asked *(pregati)* to submit written request to participate in the meetings. The assembly presided here over all matters of State. The decor, refurbished after the fire of 1574, is peopled with doges and patron saints, in audience before the Redeemer or the Virgin. In the central panel of the ceiling Tintoretto depicted *The Triumph of Venice*. Behind the throne hangs a work of Palma il Giovane. In the painter's *Allegory of Victory over the League of Cambrai*, Venice appears as a young warrior on the attack, preceded by the lion. The pulpit was used by those taking part in the debates.

Sala del Consiglio dei Dieci

The powerful and notorious council, whose origins go back as far as 1310, used to meet in this Chamber of the Council of Ten. On the ceiling preside allegories of good government and the power of the Republic: most notable is Veronese's *Juno Offering the Doge's Corno*; the central painting of Jove is a copy after Veronese: the original, "stolen" by Napoleon, is now in the Louvre in Paris. On the walls two important historical events are depicted: *The Peace of Bologna between Pope Clement VII and Emperor Charles V* by Marco Vecellio (1545-1611), a cousin of Titian *(left)*, and *Pope Alexander III Blesses Doge Sebastiano Ziani after the Battle of Salvore* by Francesco da Ponte, also known as Bassano (1549-92), and his brother Leandro (1557-1622) *(right)*.

Sala della Bussola

The Ballot Chamber was also the waiting room for those who were to be interrogated by the heads *(capi)* of the Council of Ten. To the left of the ballot box is a painting by Marco Vecellio. Beside the exit door is the wooden hatch that allowed the secret denunciations to be removed from the **bocca di leone** or lion's mouth outside. Ceiling paintings are largely by followers of Veronese, although the central painting of St Mark is a copy; the original is in the Louvre.

Armeria

The various rooms making up the Armoury house a objects such as trophies, relics of war, and the suit of armour of the infamous *condottiere* Gattamelata identified by the badge with a cat on the knee, and instruments of torture. The room dedicated to Francesco Morosini is marked with the sign CX, the Council of Ten's monogram.

Sala del Maggior Consiglio

The enormous Grand Council Chamber is perhaps the highlight of the tour. Here and in the nearby Sala dello Scrutinio, the new doge was elected. Except for the undamaged 14C Guariente fresco the *Coronation of the Virgin*, now in the Sala del Armamento, the paintings destroyed by the fire of 1577 were swiftly replaced with more magnificent decoration. The subject of the long wall overlooking the Basin is

Sala del Maggior Consiglio

the Fourth Crusade. Other notable paintings are those by Carlo Saraceni and Jean Le Clerc, Palma il Giovane, Domenico Tintoretto, Andrea Micheli (also known as Vicentino) and Federico Zuccari. The vast painting behind the throne was executed by Tintoretto, his son and followers.

Below the ceiling are portraits of the 76 doges who governed Venice between 804 and 1554, almost all by Domenico Tintoretto. **Marino Falier** who, in the 14C, conspired against the State and was beheaded, is remembered rather unfavourably. Portraits of the last 39 doges, spanning the years 1556-1797, are in the Scrutinio. The trussed wooden ceiling is dominated by Veronese's *Apotheosis of Venice* (1582). Other paintings on the ceiling celebrate Venice's victory in battle.

Sala dello Scrutinio

Here the *scrutinio* (counting) of the votes took place. The series of portraits of the governors of Venice concludes with the last doge, **Ludovico Manin** (1789-97), who ceded to Napoleon, which marked the subjugation of the Serenissima. The first works are by Tintoretto and assistants.

The decoration of this room celebrates grandiose events in Venice's history. The ceiling comprises five large paintings, the most noteworthy being *The Naval Victory of the Venetians over the Pisans at Rodi* by Vicentino and *The Venetian Victory over the Genoese at Trapani* by Giovanni Bellini. The partition wall dividing this room from the **Sala della Quarantia Civil Nuova** bears Palma il Giovane's *Last Judgement*, which replaced Tintoretto's painting destroyed during the fire..

Just before the prisons, the **Sala del Magistrato alle Leggi** preserves *The Mocking of Christ* by the Flemish master Quentin Metsys (1466-1530) and the only works by Hieronymus Bosch (c 1450-1516) in Italy.

Prigioni Nuove

Steps lead up to the Bridge of Sighs and beyond to the New Prisons on the other side of the canal. These prisons also served as the seat of the magistrature of the **Signori di Notte al Criminal**, a sort of vice squad. Note the graffiti inscribed on the stone walls.

▸ *Cross the bridge to the palace.*

Sala dei Censori

Lined with wooden seats, this chamber, known as the Censors' Chamber, accommodated a judiciary body. The paintings, mostly by Domenico Tintoretto, consist of formal portraits of magistrating censors.

Sala dell'Avogaria

The last room of the tour, the Avagoria Chamber, was the seat of another part of the former magistrature, whose members, the *avogadori*, consisted of lawyers appointed by the State. Their duty was to ensure that the law was obeyed. It is unusual for such portraits to have been presented in this way, a practice that hitherto was reserved for religious subjects.

The tour concludes with the **Sala dello Scrigno** and the **Sala della Milizia da Mar**.

The Palace Corridors

Guided tours daily. Reservations strongly encouraged. €16. ☎ 041 52 09 070.
The various magistratures that had seats in the palace operated in an environment that was anything but ostentatious. Many of the activities, most of which were secret, took place in very restricted surroundings just off the grand chambers. Linked by a maze of hidden stairs and passageways, these still exude an air of mystery.

The **Cancelleria segreta** (Secret Chancellery), which resembles a ship's deck, is ornamented with the chancellor's coats of arms.

The impressive **Sala delle Torture** (Torture Room) betrays the more intolerant, if not more characteristic face of the Republic (see sidebar). The prison cells located in the Palace were referred to as the **Pozzi e Piombi** (Wells and Leads): the *pozzi* were the deep, damp dungeons for hardened criminals; the *piombi*, so-called because

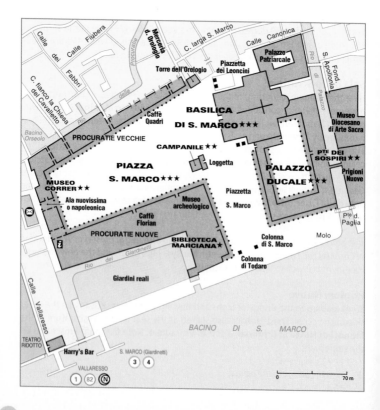

After Florence, Venice was the second State in the world to abolish torture and the first to abolish slavery. Ttreatment of prisoners was guided more by diplomatic and political acumen than piety. Should their contribution lead to victory, galley slaves condemned to row ships in battle were rewarded with liberty. The "law of the repentent" *ante litteram* applied to informers, whereby anyone with a relation accused of a minor crime could ensure their release from prison if they revealed valuable information that led to the capture and conviction of an assassin. In cases of murder, religious theft, crimes against children, criminal offences against the State, return from exile or causing pollution, however, the sentence resulted in capital punishment.

they were roofed in lead, were for those imprisoned for a couple of months. Life in the cells was not necessarily that severe: prisoners were allowed to bring some furniture and a little money with them. Punishment was intended to induce remorse by exerted psychological pressure rather than by inflicting physical suffering.

It was from the *piombi* that **Giacomo Casanova** (1725-98) made his daring escape, emerging onto the roof above the Grand Council Chamber. From here one can picture the view over Venice in former times when it was almost entirely built of wood.

After the fire of 1577, Antonio da Ponte was given only 16 months to complete the Palace's reconstruction. He drew upon the skills of the *arsenalotti* who were capable of assembling a ship in one day.

In the **Sala dei Tre Capi del Consiglio dei Dieci**, the magistrates *(capi)* who had been elected from the Council of Ten to preside over court cases would meet. Of particular interest on the ceiling are *Virtue Driving Away Vice (centre)* by Zelotti, and two paintings in the corner panels by Veronese.

In the **Sala dei Tre Inquisitori** (Inquisitors' Chamber) officials would pass judgement on crimes against the State. The ceiling features paintings by Tintoretto.

The Procuratie (🔢, FX)

Procuratie Nuove
Replacing the Orseolo hospice, the second seat of the Procurators was planned by Scamozzi and completed by Longhena (during the first half of the 17C. Under Napoleon, the Procuratie Nuove became the **Palazzo Reale**.

▸ *To get to the Museo Correr, go through the Ala Napoleonica.*

Museo Correr★★
♿ *Same admission times and charges as Palazzo Ducale.* ☎ *041 52 25 625; www. museicivicineveneziani.it*
This Museum of the City and Civilisation of Venice takes its name from **Teodoro Correr** (1750-1830), a Venetian gentleman who wanted to leave his rich collection of artifacts relating to the history and art of the Serenissima to the city. Up the magnificent 19C staircase, the tour proceeds through the neo-Classical **Sale Canoviane** (Canova Rooms) and on to the **History, Arts, Crafts** and **Games** Departments *(first floor)*. Among its historical maps, the Museo Correr boasts one of the **De' Barbari** maps (c 1445-1515) and the vivid, typically Venetian topographical works of the German artist Joseph Heintz the Younger (c 1600-78), including *Bull Baiting in Campo San Polo*. Among the sculptures by **Antonio Canova** (1757-1822) are his *Orpheus and Eurydice* and the celebrated *Daedalus and Icarus*. Other works, by Francesco Hayez (1791-1882) betray Canova's influence.

Beyond the dining room, with its particularly neo-Classical decoration, objects testify to the nobility and rich symbolism of the city's history: exhibits include doges' *corni* (caps), staffs of command, and *manine* (modelled hands used, along with the ballot urn, for counting votes in the lengthy procedure in electing a doge.

Paintings include those by Vicentino, Vassilacchi, and Longhi. The *Lion of St Mark's* attributed to Michele Giambono represents Venice in one of its most typical allegories.

The **Libreria dei Teatini**, complete with 17C furnishings, accommodates books from the Teatini Convent. The **Sale dei Costumi** (Costume Rooms) contain official 17C and 18C garments worn by senators and procurators.

The **Collezione Numismatica** (Numismatic Collection) comprises coinage minted by the Republic, including the famous *zecchino* and a painting by Tintoretto.

One room is dedicated to the **Bucintoro**, the doge's ship aboard which the Marriage with the Sea took place. Measuring 35m/115ft long and 7m/23ft wide and propelled by 168 rowers, the ship could sail only in the calmest conditions, because, being as tall as it was, it would easily have tipped over.

Exhibits relevant to the Arsenal include a map, engravings and banners. .

The section "Venice and the Sea" is followed by one dedicated to war, which includes the weaponry and armour from the Correr and Morosini Armouries.

From here, ascend to the second floor, and on to the **Quadreria** (Paintings Section), which presents a synthesis of the Venetian School of painting up to the early 16C.

Among Veneto-Byzantine examples is perhaps the earliest Venetian painting on wood, the lid of a wooden chest.

The following rooms are dedicated to **Paolo Veneziano** (c 1290-1362) and **Lorenzo Veneziano** (1356-72) and **Jacobello dalle Masegne**. Among the other Gothic artists represented here is **Stefano Veneziano**. In Venice **International Gothic** arrived at the beginning of the 15C. Examples include the paintings of Michele Giambono (active 1420-62) and Jacobello del Fiore (c 1370-1439).

The suggestive *Pietà*, marked by brittle form and metallic colour, is the work of **Cosmè Tura** (c 1430-1495), who came from Ferrara. *Portrait of a Young Man*, characterised by strong contrasting colours, is attributed to another 15C artist from Ferrara, Antonio da Crevalcore.

The next room is dedicated to **Bartolomeo Vivarini** from Murano. His works betray the strong influence of Mantegna. His use of gold-leaf background, however, is more archaic and Byzantine in style.

Particularly worthy of note from the 15C Flemish School is an *Adoration of the Magi* by **Brueghel the Younger** (1564-1638), a Holy scene set in a Northern landscape blanketed with snow. The influence of Northern oil paintings on Italian art is suggested in a *Pietà*★★, the only work here by **Antonello da Messina** (c 1430-79), who visited Venice in 1475/6. The two other Flemish works in the room are by Hugo van der Goes and Dieric Bouts. One painting from the later 15C and 16C **Flemish School** is the *Temptations of St Anthony* by a follower of Hieronymus Bosch; its complex symbolism adds a disquieting, nightmarish dimension to the subject.

The **Bellini** are gathered together in one room: they include the *Crucifixion* by **Jacopo** (1400-c 70), the *Portrait of Doge Giovanni Mocenigo* by Gentile (1429-1507) and four works by **Giovanni** (1430-1516).

Alvise Vivarini and Venetian painters from the late 15C forestall the works of **Vittore Carpaccio**, one of Venice's most acclaimed artists. His enigmatic *Two Venetian Ladies* are apparently animated by a private joke, their slightly dismissive expressions giving rise to various explanations.

The *Gentleman in the Red Cap*★★ is presently attributed to a painter from Ferrara/Bologna, although in the past it was thought to have been executed by Lotto (c 1480-1556), Giovanni Bellini or Carpaccio.

The evolution of art through the **High Renaissance** continues with **Lorenzo Lotto** (*Madonna with the Christ Child at her Breast*), before being interrupted by displays of works by 16C and 17C Greek *Madonneri* (painters depicting the Madonna in the traditional manner) and 15C and 16C majolica extending to the room beyond the Manin Library.

Museo del Risorgimento

Housed on the same floor, this museum documents the years that do not strictly belong to the story of Venice whose end came in 1797 when, after 1 000 years of glory, the Republic surrendered. Themes explored tend toward social history touching upon freemasonry, the temporary Municipality (the Government which, on the arrival of the French, pursued the abdication of Ludovico Manin), the rule of Napoleon and the Austrians.

This period is divided into three eras. The first extends from the end of 1797 to 1805 when Venice became part of Napoleon's Italian Kingdom; the second lasts from the Vienna Congress (1815), through the Manin and Tommaseo period to 1848, and from 1849 to 1866, when Italy was unified.

Returning to the first floor of the Museo Corer, one room displays Renaissance bronzes and a section dedicated to **Arts and Crafts** (*Arti e Mestieri*) exhibits the insignia of the various guilds. Other exhibits include a collection of textiles made by the weavers' guild, shoes produced by the *calegheri* (cobblers) guild and the workmanship of painters and *tagiapiera* (stonemasons).

The **Giochi** (Games) collection includes examples of the Strength of Hercules or human pyramids that were "built" on wooden platforms on the Thursday before Lent and other feast days; fist fights that developed between the rival Castellani, who were mostly sailors, and Nicolotti, who were mostly fishermen; and bull-baiting (*Caccia ai Tori*), during which dogs that had been excited to a frenzy would be unleashed.

Procuratie Vecchie (🗗, FX)

The original residence of the Procurators in the 12C, these ancient loggias were initially Veneto-Byzantine in style before being rebuilt up to the first floor probably by Scarpagnino or possibly by **Mauro Codussi**. Still incomplete, they were damaged by fire in 1512, after which first Bartolomeo Bon (active c 1463-1529) then Guglielmo Grigi (active c 1515-30) added their mark, before Sansovino (1486-1570) completed work in 1532.

Famous Bars

In the arcaded portico of the Procuratie Vecchie is the **Caffè Quadri** (🗗, FX Y), which was founded by Giorgio Quadri in 1775 to serve Turkish coffee.

Opposite, on the other side of the piazza, is the older **Caffè Florian** (🗗 FX Z), also named after its first proprietor, Floriano Francesconi, which was opened in 1720. Its most renowned previous habitués have included the playwright **Carlo Goldoni** (1707-93) and the neo-Classical sculptor **Antonio Canova** (1757-1822).

West of the Procuratie Nuove, on Calle Vallaresso, sits famed **Harry's Bar**, haunt of Ernest Hemingway.

La Piazzetta (🗗, FGX)

This extension of St Mark's Square, between the Doges' Palace and the Biblioteca Nazionale Marciana, overlooks the sea through a magnificent portal framed by the two **Colonne di Marco e Todaro**. These two column shafts used as pedestals for St Mark and St Theodore were brought back from the East in 1172, although their specific provenance remains uncertain. The second one is a copy, the original being in the courtyard in the Doges' Palace. The lion, which the Venetians identify with their Evangelist-Saint, could be a chimera.

Biblioteca Nazionale Marciana★ (🗗, FX)

The library premises are included in the ticket valid for the museums in Piazza San Marco, along with the Palazzo Ducale, Museo Correr and Museo Archeologico Nazionale. ⏱Open

Apr-Oct, daily 9am-7pm; Nov-Mar, daily 9am-5pm. Library reading rooms ◐Open Mon-Sat, 8.10am-7pm (1.30pm Sat). ◐Closed 1 Jan, 25 Dec and 2 weeks in Aug. For a reader's pass, apply to the Ufficio Orientamento with personal identification.

As the first example of Classical architecture in Venice, this prestigious seat of Venetian culture is almost as glorious as its neighbour, the Doges' Palace. Over the Doric portico runs the loggia, its windows framed by Ionic columns, true to the Classical architectural canon of orders. **Sansovino** worked on the library from 1537. On his death, the project was completed by Scamozzi.

The Biblioteca's sculptural decoration draws on Classical mythology: the keystones of the arches are marked by leonine protomes and mythological heads, and statues in various expressive poses overlook the piazzetta from the balustrade.

Inside, the Reading Room is located off the **Zecca** courtyard (the Mint).

With its two flights, the **staircase** is reminiscent of the Scala d'Oro (*see Palazzo Ducale*). The vaulted ceiling and cupola stucco decoration are by **Alessandro Vittoria**, the frescoes are by **Battista Franco** *(first flight)* and Battista del Moro *(second flight)*. The thematic iconography is defined by a neo-Platonic concept of Man, who, influenced by cosmic forces *(first flight)* and fashioned by the Virtues *(second flight)* finally arrives at Universal Knowledge, symbolised by the book and the circle.

First floor

One important exhibit is the famous map of Venice by **Jacopo De' Barbari**, executed in 1500, the other version being in the Museo Correr. Nearby is the *Mappamondo* (1457-59) by Fra Mauro, the Camaldolite monk from San Michele in Isola. The planisphere is painted, in colour and gold, on parchment stuck down on wood.

Vestibule

Sansovino intended the Vestibule as a salon for Humanist lectures. Instead, it was turned into the Republic's Sculpture Museum when the Patriarch of Aquileia, Giovanni Grimani, donated his collection of sculpture and statuary to Venice; some pieces have overflowed into the Archaeological Museum (*see below*).

On the ceiling, *Wisdom*, painted by Titian, has been inserted into a *trompe l'oeil* perspective by Cristoforo and Stefano Rosa, executed around 1559.

Salone Sansoviniano

At the heart of the original Library, the Sansovino Room houses the codices and manuscripts bequeathed to the Republic by **Cardinale Bessarione** (1403-72), the famous Greek Humanist. The grotesque ceiling decoration, the work of Battista Franco, is completed with 21 tondos illustrating mythological subjects, virtues and disciplines against a gold background.

The artists responsible for this ultimate "manifestation of Mannerism in Venice" are Giovanni De Mio, author of the first trio (*best viewed walking backwards away from the entrance);* Giuseppe Porta, known as Salviati (second trio); Battista Franco, (third trio); Giulio Licinio, whose third tondo, in poor condition, was replaced with one by Bernardo Strozzi depicting Sculpture; Giambattista Zelotti, whose third painting was also replaced, this time by a panel representing the *Nile, Atlas, Geometry* and *Astrology* by Padovanino, Veronese and Andrea Schiavone. Portraits of philosophers line the walls, including two by Veronese *(door side);* four by Tintoretto *(left),* then two by Schiavone, and another two by Tintoretto, although the attribution of the one on the right is uncertain *(end wall).* One by Salviati, one by Franco and one by Lambert Sustris adorn the right wall.

Museo Archeologico (🎱, FX)

◐*Open daily 8.15am-7.15pm (5pm Nov-Mar); last admission 30min before closing.* ◐*Closed 1 Jan, 25 Dec.* ◍€4. ☏ 041 52 25 978.

The Archaeological Museum is housed in the Procuratie Nuove, two doors away from the Biblioteca Marciana. It holds Greek sculpture, Egyptian and Roman fragments and a collection of coins and medals.

Start in the loggia containing the Greek inscriptions and pass through the coins and medals section before reaching the most ancient Archaic pieces, such as the famous **Grimani** Greek statues (5C-4C BC); sculpture from the 5C-4C BC including the Classical and Hellenistic phases; small sculptures from the times of Alexander the Great to the 1C BC; Assyrian-Babylonian and Egyptian antiquities; Cypriot and Mycenaen vases; early Venetian ceramics and Etruscan *buccheri* (clay drinking vessels).

▶ *From the quayside, the view of the piazzetta is punctuated by the clock tower.*

Torre dell'Orologio (🗗, FX)
Reopened in 2006 after 10 years of restoration. For information, call ☎ 041 52 24 951; www.museiciviciveneziani.it
Designed by Codussi, the clock tower was erected between 1496 and 1499, and constitutes the main entrance to the **Mercerie**, Venice's principal shopping street (👌*see RIALTO*).
The striking astronomical quadrant probably attracts less attention than the two Moors who sound the hour on a big bell at the top of the tower. Below it stands the lion passant of St Mark set against a starry background. Below this tier comes a Virgin and Child before whom, on Ascension Day, appear mechanical figurines of the Three Kings. To the left, the Roman numerals tell the hour and the minutes are marked out at intervals of five to the right.

Additional Sights

Piazzetta dei Leoncini (🗗, FX 126)
This small area tucked between the Basilica, the Palazzo Patriarcale and the side of the former Church of San Basso was designed by Longhena. Its name is derived from the red marble lions from Verona, sculpted by Giovanni Bonazza (1722).

One of the Moorish bellstrikers in action

Lara Pessina

▶ *Follow Calle della Canonica and cross the canal: the Diocesan Museum of Religious Art is on Fondamenta Sant'Apollonia on the right.*

Museo Diocesano di Arte Sacra (🔟, GX)

Call for hours and charges. ☎ *041 27 02 464; www.museodiocesanovenezia.it*
Romanesque in style, the building was once part of the Benedictine Convent of Sant'Apollonia (12C-13C); its cloisters so inspired D'Annunzio that he described it in his work *Il Fuoco* (The Fire). Its arches have double-arched lintels supported along the longer sides by paired columns. The well-head in the centre is 13C. Fragments of Roman, Byzantine and Veneto-Byzantine (9C-11C) stonework line the walls.
Originally conceived by the Patriarch of Venice, **Albino Luciani** (1912-78), and Pope Giovanni Paolo, whose reign lasted just one month, the museum houses paintings and sculptures, sacred objects and congregational banners from deconsecrated churches. Its collection boasts works by artists such as Antonio Zanchi, Palma il Giovane and Jacopo Guarana.

RIALTO★★

(🔟, FU)

VAPORETTO: RIALTO, SAN MARCO

Situated in the heart of the commercial area, the Rialto Bridge crosses the Grand Canal and continues the long line of shops that snakes its way from St Mark's Square, along the Mercerie, as far as the side stalls and market in the **San Polo** district. Given the overwhelming hustle and bustle of the small workshops and local bars, it is easy to forget the significance and long history of the Rialto, which was so fundamental to the development of Venice.

- 😺 **Don't Miss:** Walking over the famous Rialto Bridge, with its colourful shops.
- 🕐 **Organizing Your Time:** To follow the prescribed routes, allow about 3hrs, and more time if you wish to do some shopping along the Mercerie.
- 🖐 **Also See:** Neighbouring sights: La FENICE; PIAZZA SAN MARCO; SAN ZACCARIA; SAN ZANIPÒLO.

A Bit of History

Out of this very group of islands, referred to in Latin as the *Rivoaltus*, evolved Venice. The "birth" of the city occurred during the reign of Charlemagne, who, after his coronation on Christmas Eve in the year 800, ruled the Eastern Empire. Meanwhile dissidents from both Empires disrupted the lives of the Venetians.
When Charlemagne's son and King of Italy, Pepin, failed to capture the lagoon (the Venetians had resisted with dogged force), **Agnello Partecipazio** (811-27), Venice's first doge, transferred the seat of government from Malamocco to the Rialto.

Not Just Pedestrian Traffic

In the Middle Ages, the main means of transport in Venice was on horseback; movement through the streets became impossible given the number of horses. In 1291, it was decreed that horsemen should dismount their charges in Campo San Salvador before continuing on foot and that, in any event, horses should not be allowed into the Piazza. Instead, they had to be left by the clock tower, where (as hard as it might be to imagine) stood a copse of elder.

Rialto Bridge and the Mercerie

Ponte di Rialto★★ (▣, FU)

Built c 1175, the first bridge over the Grand Canal was to be a significant factor in the commercial development of the area. The wooden bridge had to be replaced several times following its deliberate destruction during the uprisings led by Baiamonte Tiepolo, and two subsequent occasions when it collapsed. Its design proved to be ever complicated by the requirements of established shopkeepers and boatmen.

At one time Palladio proposed a cumbersome Roman-style design with three arches, which was dismissed on the grounds that it might hinder canal traffic. Some 80 years later, one of these considerations became less of an issue as restrictions were imposed upon larger ships using the Grand Canal.

The new construction, designed by **Antonio da Ponte** (1512-97), was simplified to a single span, thereby ensuring ease of use by boats and barges as well as safeguarding a flow of water that prevented stagnation and maintained the delicate equilibrium of the lagoon.

The present bridge consists of a single stone archway, 28m/92ft long and 7.5m/25ft high, which supports a central graduated alley lined with commercial units, flanked on either side by a narrower parallel passageway. Access from one aisle of shops to another is from either end of the bridge or via transverse arches in the middle. The whole complex is sheltered by a sloping roof.

The Rialto was to remain the only means of crossing from one bank of the Grand Canal to the other until the mid-19C, when the Accademia Bridge and the Scalzi Bridge were built.

Mercerie★

The countless number of shops selling a variety of goods gives rise to the name of this historic commercial street in Venice. The *mercerie* (traditionally these were haberdashers selling cloth, ribbons and other merchandise) provide access between St Mark's and the Rialto. In the past, this was the route chosen by nobles intending to make some triumphal entry into the Piazza San Marco.

The Mercerie, which are as busy today as they were in the Middle Ages, fall into three main sections, starting from the clock tower: **Merceria dell'Orologio** (▣, **FV** 121), **Merceria di San Zulin** (▣, **FV** 124) and **Merceria di San Salvador** (▣, **FV**). At Merceria dell'Orologio 149 there is a relief recording the event that spread panic among the rebels led by Baiamonte Tiepolo, who disbanded when a stone mortar was dropped on a standard-bearer.

Ponte di Rialto

San Zulian (◢, FV)

This is the first church encountered along Merceria di San Marco. Cramped by adjacent buildings, the façade is richly ornamented. Above the portal, Tommaso Rangone, the benefactor of the church, is portrayed by Sansovino. Note also the columns that frame the cartouches and the windows below the pediments. Under the main tympanum is a typically Venetian feature, a *serliana* consisting of a window with three openings named after **Sebastiano Serlio**.

Founded in the 9C, the church was remodelled during the late Renaissance by Sansovino and Alessandro Vittoria. The square internal space extends to a presbytery with two side chapels. Paintings by Palma il Giovane and Veronese grace the interior.

San Salvador (◢, FV) – ⟳ *See La FENICE.*

Walking Tours

Three different walks are possible from Campo San Bartolomeo (⟳ *see La FENICE*): southwest towards the Accademia (⟳ *see ACCADEMIA*), north towards the Strada Nuova or across the Rialto Bridge.

Towards Strada Nuova

This route makes its way past all kinds of shops; it is nonetheless attractive for being a busy urban area between the Accademia and the Mercerie.

Fondaco dei Tedeschi (◢, FU) – ⟳ *See La FENICE.*

San Giovanni Grisostomo (◢, FU)

Shoehorned between the houses into a rather narrow passageway is the simple yet remarkable reddish façade of the **Church of St John Chrysostom**. Founded in 1080 the church was given its current appearance by **Mauro Codussi** and his son Domenico, who completed the project at his father's death. The compact and well-proportioned interior, dominated by a dome resting on four piers, is in the form of a Greek cross. In the first chapel on the right is a painting on canvas by **Giovanni Bellini**; the second chapel is dedicated to St Joseph, with an altarpiece by Johann Karl Loth. The presbytery is literally plastered with 17C scenes from the life of the church's patron saint, coupled with episodes from the life of Christ. The central section by Sebastiano del Piombo depicts Saints John Chrysostom, Paul, John the Baptist, Liberale, Mary Magdelene, Cecilia and Catherine. In the left transept, the marble *Coronation of the Virgin* is by Tullio Lombardo.

▸ *Continue straight on to the large but crowded Campo Santi Apostoli.*

Campo Santi Apostoli (◢, FT)

This square is in some ways the start of the Strada Nuova, and as such it serves as a busy thoroughfare, with shops and bars in almost all the nearby *calli*.

Only one side of the rectangular **Church of All Saints** (dei Santi Apostoli), rebuilt in the 16C and restored in the 18C, opens onto the square. The tall campanile is here detached from the church.

Inside, the 15C **Corner Chapel**, attributed to Codussi, contains the *Communion of St Lucy* by Tiepolo. On the left wall of the presbytery is a depiction drafted by Veronese (1528–88) and executed by "Heredes Pauli;" in the chapel on the right are a series of early-14C Byzantine-style frescoes.

On the far side of the canal stands the 13C **Palazzo Falier** (◢, FTU), named after its most eminent resident, **Doge Marino Falier**. At ground level, the portico shelters shops and restaurants; the two superior levels are decorated with pateras and arcaded windows.

Beyond the Rialto Bridge

San Giacomo di Rialto (4, FU)

Partially hidden by the stalls and the market in Campo San Giacomo di Rialto, the church is best viewed when approaching the Rialto from the San Polo *sestiere*. This church is considered the oldest in Venice: according to one document, although of dubious authenticity, the city was born on 25 March 421 when three consuls arrived from Padua to establish a commercial seat at the Rialto. This church was built to celebrate the event. Its present appearance dates from the 11C, when it was rebuilt to accommodate local residents drawn to the market in the square. The façade boasts striking features, namely the clock (despite being a 1938 reproduction), the campanile, which houses the clock and the bells, and the 14C portico.

Inside, planned as a Greek cross, its original Greek marble columns survive, complete with 11C Veneto-Byzantine capitals carved with organic decoration. On the left is an altar by Scamozzi and bronzes by Gerolamo Campagna, who

Daily business in the Rialto market

was responsible for the altar in the Church of San Giorgio Maggiore. On the right is an *Annunciation* by Marco Vecellio, a cousin of Titian's. The main altar is by Alessandro Vittoria.

The **Banco Giro**, a public bank founded in 1619, used to stand just off the square. In addition to being home to banks and the magistrature, the Rialto has always been a commercial area, as the names of the *fondamenta*, *campi* and *calli* testify to this day. These commemorate times of trade in such commodities as oil *(olio)*, fish *(pesce)*, wine *(vino)*, spices *(spezie)*, chickens *(polli)*, meat *(beccarie)* and sausages *(luganegher)*.

The Hunchback

Some of the statues in Venice, such as the Moors in Campo dei Mori (♦ see CA' D'ORO), adopt rather curious expressions or poses. One such statue is the 16C **"gobbo di Rialto,"** a hunchback who is bent double beneath his burden, patiently supporting the stairs before the column from where the *comandador* would proclaim government decrees.

The gobbo di Rialto lending an ear to a cat

▶ *Farther along the canal, stretching down as far as the Pescaria, are the Fabbriche Vecchie and Fabbriche Nuove, a group of buildings, simple and functional in structure, that once served as commercial offices.*

Fabbriche Vecchie (▣, FU)

This building, set back from the Fabbriche Nuove, was designed by Scarpagnino, as was much of the surrounding area destroyed by fire in 1514. The ground floor is rusticated, broken by an open colonnade; the upper floors, punctuated by simple windows, seem lightweight and less imposing.

Fabbriche Nuove (▣, FU)

These premises, directly overlooking the Grand Canal, on the bend, were designed by Sansovino. As the rusticated ground floor is interrupted by its portico, so the upper storeys are articulated by windows framed with pilasters and surmounted with pediments.

▶ *After crossing the bridge, turn immediately left into Ruga Vecchia S. Giovanni. Continue for a few metres to the Church of San Giovanni Elemosinario, partially hidden behind railings on the left.*

San Giovanni Elemosinario (▣, EFU)

🕓*Open Mon-Sat, 10am-5pm.* 🕓*Closed 1 Jan, Easter, 15 Aug, 25 Dec.* ▦*€2.50.* ☎ *041 27 50 462; www.chorusvenezia.org*

The origins of this old church, built according to the plan of a Greek cross, date back to 1071, although the original building was destroyed by fire in 1514. The church was rebuilt, possibly by Lo Scarpagnino, and completed in 1531. It now houses works by Jacopo Palma il Giovane and Il Pordenone (c 1484-1539), who was also responsible for the frescoes in the dome, as well as an altarpiee by Titian on the high altar.

Campo della Pescaria (▣, EFU)

Under the porticoes of the impressive building overlooking the square is the famous fish market that takes place daily.

A vivacious atmosphere pervades the **Campo delle Beccarie** (▣, EU) which, at one time, housed the public abattoir, and now shelters a traditional Venetian *bacaro* (wine bar) and various market stalls.

▶ *Follow the crowd streaming their way from the Rialto to Campo San Cassiano nearby – the route is almost unavoidable: left along Calli dei Botteri to the other side of the canal, then right into Calle Corpus Domini Christi.*

Capitals in the Rialto inspired by the sea

N. Bosques/MICHELIN

Ponte and Fondamenta delle Tette

Venetian toponymy is full of surprises. In this case, the focus is on an area located between Campo San Cassiano and Campo San Polo, where in the 16C, Venetian women of dubious morals would hang out of the window, baring their *tette* – slang for breasts. This display was not only accepted but encouraged by the religious authorities, who saw the practice as a way of reducing the risk of homosexuality so prevalent among sailors.

San Cassiano (4, EU)

Although the origins of this church are rooted in the 9C, it has been subjected to attempts at restoration: its present appearance is largely the result of 17C remodelling. The overall impression of the interior can be overbearing: the three aisles are separated by columns hung with red and grey damask drapes. The right chapel off the apse houses three works by Leandro Bassano and one by Palma il Giovane. In the presbytery are three works by Tintoretto.

▶ *Cross the canal and follow Calle della Regina off to the right.*

Ca' Corner della Regina (4, ET)

It was here, in the house of her brother, that **Caterina Cornaro**, Queen of Cyprus, resided after her fall from grace. The *palazzo* was then fashioned in the Gothic style. The present building, dating from the 18C, is decorated with frescoes in the style of Tiepolo that recount the unhappy events of her life.

Since 1976, Ca' Corner della Regina has housed the **Historical Archives of Contemporary Art**, a rich source of information on the Biennale and 20C arts, with libraries of books, newspapers and periodicals, and an archive of photographs, film and famous recordings.

▶ *Return to Calle della Regina and turn right into Campo Santa Maria Materdomini.*

Uffizi, Firenze/SCALA

Caterina Cornaro by Titian (Uffizi, Florence)

Santa Maria Materdomini (4, ET)

With its distinctive trilobate five-arched window, the church is set slightly back from the square and the 14C-15C Palazzo Zane. Influenced by the Tuscan style, it is an expression of Renaissance design: the simple Istrian stone façade, hemmed in between the houses, has been attributed to Sansovino, although the overall project may owe more to **Pietro Lombardo** and **Codussi**.

The ordered, simple marble-faced interior comprises three aisles and a domed apse. The most striking paintings are the large-scale dramatic renderings by **Tintoretto** in the left transept and a *Last Supper (opposite)* attributed to Bonifacio de' Pitati. The exquisite altarpiece in the second bay on the right is also worthy of note. Painted by the close associate of Giorgione and Bellini, **Vincenzo Catena**, the scene shows *St Christina of Bolsena* emerging from Lake Bolsena on the millstone that was meant to have drowned her. The fine terra-cotta *Madonna* by the main altar is 15C by Nicolò di Pietro Paradisi. The more subtle early-16C marble altarpieces *(right of the entrance* *and left of the main altar)* are carved by Lorenzo Bregna. In the presbytery is a delicate relief by the Lombardo brothers.

▶ *Proceed towards the Grand Canal to Ca' Pesaro and the International Gallery of Modern Art.*

Ca' Pesaro★ (4, ET)

This *palazzo* was commissioned by the Pesaro family. Initiated by Longhena, it was completed by Francesco Antonio Gaspari and now houses an important collection of oriental art and a museum of modern art (⚓ *see Il CANAL GRANDE).*

Museo d'Arte Orientale

♿⏱*Open Apr-Oct, Tue-Sun 10am-6pm (Nov-Mar 5pm). Last admission 30min before closing.* ⏱*Closed 1 Jan, 1 May and 25 Dec.* ✎ *€5.50 (combined ticket with Galleria Internazionale di Arte Moderna).* ☎ *041 52 41 173; www.arteorientale.org*
The Museum of Oriental Art is housed on the upper floor (at the top of about 100 steps) and contains a collection of Japanese armour from the Edo Period (1615-1868), swords, lacquer-work, puppets, musical instruments and Chinese porcelain.

Galleria Internazionale di Arte Moderna

⏱*Open Apr-Oct, Tue-Sun 10am-5pm; (Nov-Mar 4pm); last admission 30min before closing.* ⏱*Closed, 1 Jan, 1 May, 25 Dec.* ✎ *€5.50 (combined ticket with Museo d'Arte Orientale.* ☎ *041 52 40 695; www.museicivicivenezioni.it*
The gallery hosts important modern art from the end of the 19C onwards, notably from the Futurist movement. On display are works by Klinger (1857-1920), **Chagall** (1877-1985), **Klimt** (1862-1918), **Bonnard** (1867-1947), **Matisse** (1869-1954), **Kandinsky** (1866-1944), **Klee** (1879-1940), Tanguy (1900-55), **Henry Moore** (1898-1986), **Mirò** (1893-1983), **Ernst** (1891-1976), Boccioni (1882-1916), Rosso (1858-1928), De Pisis (1896-1956), **Morandi** (1890-1964), **De Chirico** (1888-1978), Casorati (1883-1963), **Carrà** (1881-1966), Sironi (1885-1961) and Pizzinato (1910-).
(♿ *Partial access)* There is also a permanent exhibition of works by Guglielmo Ciardi (1842-1917), who perpetuated the Venetian landscape tradition, and from the latter half of the 19C, Venetian pieces by Luigi Nono (1850-1918), Alessandro Milesi (1856-1945) and Giacomo Favretto (1849-87).

Museo di Palazzo Mocenigo (4, ET)

⏱*Open daily, 10am-5pm (Nov-Mar 6pm); last admission 30min before closing.* ⏱*Closed 1 Jan, 1 May and 25 Dec.* ✎*€4.* ☎ *041 72 17 98; www.museicivicivenezioni.it*
This museum provides an idea of Venetian life among the noble classes in the 17C and 18C. The Mocenigo dynasty furnished the Serenissima with a total of seven doges, whose portraits hang in the entrance.
Today the interiors are used to display fabrics and costumes belonging to the **Centro Studi di Storia del Tessuto e del Costume** (a foundation dedicated to the study and conservation of fabrics and costumes). On show are a range of woven materials and textiles from the rise of the Republic.

LA SALUTE★★

(⑧, FX)

VAPORETTTO: SALUTE, ACCADEMIA

Despite the hordes of tourists visiting La Salute or the Guggenheim Collection, this corner of the **Dorsoduro** district is very peaceful. It is an area that is not really conducive to browsing in shops or lingering in cafes and wine bars, which are more common in the San Trovaso and San Barnaba districts. The artists' workshops and the nearby Anglican Church, along with the numerous enthusiasts of modern art, give these streets an Anglo-American flavour; some of the directions are even given in English.

▶ **Orient Yourself:** Edging the south side of the Grand Canal and extending eastward toward St Mark's Basin, the Salute area faces the portion of the San Marco *sestiere* centred on the Gritti Palace. To the south, it encompasses the Zattere, the long walkway that borders the Guidecca Canal.

🐾 **Don't Miss:** Sitting on the broad steps of La Salute for a moment, to take in the sights and sounds of the Grand Canal, as well as strolling along the Zattere.

🕐 **Organizing Your Time:** Allow about 3hrs for the walking tour, plus another hour for the Guggenheim Collection.

♿ **Also See:** Neighbouring sight ACCADEMIA.

Walking Tour

Santa Maria della Salute★★ (⑧, FX)

The Basilica of Santa Maria della Salute is one of the most important and obvious points of reference on the skyline of Venice. It is also very dear to the Venetians: in 1630, when their city was racked by plague, they pledged a solemn vow to erect a church once the epidemic subsided. Their prayers were answered and, in 1631,

La Salute and, in the foreground, the Dogana

The Feast of the Madonna della Salute

Venice has been celebrating the end of the plague of 1630 for over 300 years. On 21 November, a bridge is made of boats stretching across the canal to La Salute to allow devotees and pilgrims to reach the basilica with ease. Celebrations for the Feast of the Madonna of La Salute—which have a certain parochial air about them—last all day. Venetians remember the day with the lighting of a candle.

Baldassare Longhena, the pre-eminent Venetian Baroque architect, was granted leave to develop his project.

This impressive basilica is rendered all the more majestic by its magnificent flight of steps up to the entrance. Dominated by the towering central dome, the great round volume emerges from an octagonal base: a geometric shape that radiates to eight façades presided over by a figure flanked by two angels over each pediment. Like Palladio before him, Longhena uses Classical architectural forms to build bold outlines and articulate every subsidiary part of his design: he employs figurative sculpture to punctuate profiles, to relieve flat planes and to reiterate the human dimension. The proliferation of statues at every level points to the fact that Longhena was born into a family of stonecarvers. Akin to a free-standing sculpture, the church occupies a prominent position from every angle.

At the apex is a figure of the Madonna clutching the baton of the *Capitano da Mar* (Captain-General of the Sea), poised above the balustraded lantern. Note also the figure of the patron presiding over the main pediment of the façade.

On the lesser dome stands St Mark, flanked by the weathervanes of the two campanili beyond, marking the far end of the church. At the drum level great concentric volutes, also known as *orecchioni* (big ears), link the lower level of the outer section with the dome. The interior is dictated by the main cupola, with the central area opening out into six chapels. The polychrome marble floor converges on a central circle of five roses which, together with the other roses of the wider circle, suggest the idea of a rosary. The central inscription in Latin states that it is from here that the health *(salute)* and salvation accorded to Venice emanates: tradition has it that the city was born on the Feast of the Annunciation (25 March 421) to signify the protection accorded to Venice by the Virgin.

On the left side, the last bay before the high altar is ornamented with the *Descent of the Holy Spirit,* painted by **Titian** (1490-1576) in 1555.

At the high altar is a 12C icon, the *Madonna della Salute*, also referred to as *Meso-panditissa* because it came from a place of the same name in Candia (Crete). The sculptural group above (1670-74) represents Venice, liberated from the plague, at the Virgin's feet: it is the work of the Flemish artist Juste Le Court (1627-79). The Plague is depicted on the right, being chased away by the angel.

The sacristy boasts a wealth of treasures, the most eye-catching being the *Wedding at Cana* by **Tintoretto** (1518-94), in which the artist has included himself (the first Apostle on the left), his friends and their wives.

The various depictions of the *Madonna in Prayer* are by **Sassoferrato**.

On leaving the sacristy, in the corridor before the chapels *(right)*, are three notable altarpieces by **Luca Giordano**.

▶ *Walk east along Fondamenta Dogana.*

La Dogana (⑧, FX)

Dating to the 15C, the Dogana da Mar originally served as the customs point for goods arriving by sea. Fashioned to resemble a ship's hull, the building's present appearance dates from the 17C. A statue of *Fortune* towers over a golden globe, representing the world, supported by two Atlantes.

▸ *Walk around the Dogana and then turn southwest, along the Guidecca Canal.*

Le Zattere★ (**7**, **8**, CFXY)

A walk along these *fondamente* provides a thrilling view that might be expected from a long balcony with a perfect prospect over the Giudecca Canal, a rougher stretch of water than the Grand Canal, to the island of the Giudecca itself on the other side. The name Zattere was coined from one function served by the *fondamenta* in the 17C: its transportation of wood on rafts or *zattere*.

The buildings evoke a past that involved hard work and profound religious faith: the former **Magazzini del Sale**, a 14C warehouse used to store salt *(sale)* produced in Venice; the former Convent and **Church of the Spirito Santo**, from where the bridge of boats stretched across the water for the Feast of the Redentore; the **Ospedale degli Incurabili** (Hospital for Incurables), which later served as a home for abandoned children and as a musical conservatory.

The length of the route is dotted with cafes which, in spring and summer, set tables outside on wooden platforms over the water.

▸ *To the right of Spirito Santo, take Calle della Scuola and walk straight on to the Palazzo Dario (see Il CANAL GRANDE). At its entrance, turn left toward Palazzo Venier dei Leoni.*

Collezione Peggy Guggenheim★★ (**8**, EX)

 Open daily except Tue, 10am-6pm. *Closed 25 Dec.* €10. 041 24 05 411; www.guggenheim-venice.it

The Peggy Guggenheim Collection is housed in the incomplete **Palazzo Venier dei Leoni** (1749), which was designed by Lorenzo Boschetti, the architect of the Church of St Barnabas (see Il CANAL GRANDE). The entrance is through a peaceful garden, in whose surrounding wall are two stones that mark the final resting places of the owner and her beloved dogs. The niece of American industrialist Solomon R Guggenheim, who instigated the museum of the same name in the famous spiral building by Frank Lloyd Wright (1869-1959) in New York, **Peggy Guggenheim** assembled her Venice collection from 1938 to 1979. She acquired the *palazzo* after the Second World War and lived there until her death, when, according to her express wishes, both the *palazzo* and the collection it housed were handed over to the Solomon Guggenheim Foundation. Like its counterpart in New York, the museum is arranged

Peggy Guggenheim (1898-1979)

Born in New York, educated in Paris, worked in London and died in Venice: this colourful personality has done much to popularise modern art. In 1939 she decided to open a museum for contemporary art in London, but during the period leading up to the Second World War, when she resolved to "buy a picture a day," it became obvious that it was safer to return home. In October 1942, when she opened her gallery "Art of This Century" in New York with a collection of Cubist, Abstract and Surrealist art, she wrote "I wore one of my Tanguy earrings and one made by Calder, in order to show my impartiality between Surrealist and Abstract art." She was briefly married to Max Ernst, the Dadaist and Surrealist.

Peggy Guggenheim

Dejardin/RAPHO

Surrealism

The *First Surrealist Manifesto* was published in Paris in 1924 by André Breton, promoting ideas drawn from the latest psycho-analytical theories on the unconscious and subconscious. The manifesto challenged the traditional views on art and life and encouraged artistic expression inspired by dreams, drug-induced hallucinations and other suspended states of mind. Breton defined the essence of Surrealism as "pure psychic automatism, by which it is intended to express verbally, in writing, or in any other way, the true process of thought. It is the dictation of thought, free from the excise of reason, and every aesthetic or moral preoccupation." Pictorially, Surrealism emerged from various movements: Cubism (refracted form), Futurism (movement and automation) and Dada (humour and absurdity), pioneered by Picasso, Ernst, Klee, Dali, Mirò, Magritte and others.

thematically, displaying parallel collections of Abstract and Surrealist works by the same artists (*see THE GREEN GUIDE NEW YORK CITY*).

Strong in Surrealist art , the collection contains works by **Braque** (1882-1963); **Picasso** (1881-1973); Mondrian (1872-1944); Boccioni (1882-1916); **Brancusi** (1876-1957); **Kandinsky** (1866-1944); **Chagall** (1887-1985): *The Rain*; Balla (1871-1958): *Abstract Speed+Noise*; Severini (1883-1966): *Sea = Ballerina*; **Mirò** (1893-1983); De Chirico (1888-1978): *The Red Tower*; **Max Ernst** (1891-1976); Klee (1879-1940); Magritte (1898-1967): *Empire of Light*; Dali (1904-89); **Pollock** (1912-56); **Calder** (1898-1976): *Mobile*; Vasarely (1908-90) and **Moore** (1898-1986). Notable are the 23 sculptures designed by Picasso and executed by Egidio Costantini (1964), positioned in the window to maximize their transparency against the blue of the Grand Canal beyond.

Since 1997, Palazzo Venier dei Leoni has temporarily accommodated the **Mattioli Collection**, which includes works by the Futurist painters Carrà (1881-1966): *La Galleria di Milano*; Severini: *Ballerina in Blu*; Boccioni; and other important masters such as Morandi (1890-1964); Sironi (1885-1961); and Modigliani (1884-1920).

Outside, *The Angel of the City,* a sculpture by Marino Marini (1901-80), stands guard over the Grand Canal.

Maiastra (1912) by Constantin Brancusi

SANT'ELENA E SAN PIETRO ★

(▓▓, KLXY)

VAPORETTO: S. ELENA, GIARDINI BIENNALE

The Sant'Elena and San Pietro districts of the Castello *sestiere* are peaceful and yet vibrant with life, as their green spaces attract crowds of people. The view from the public gardens and the Park of Remembrance (Parco delle Rimembranze) over the lagoon and St Mark's Basin is magnificent. Movement and activity pervade the area around the Rio di Santa Anna with its floating market, and extend to the bustling commercial activities of the only real street in Venice, Via Garibaldi.

▶ **Orient Yourself:** At this extremity of the Castello *sestiere*, places for a pizza or a particularly inexpensive *menu a prezzo fisso* (set price meal) proliferate. In the Castello Gardens stand the Biennale pavilions. Separated from the rest of the lagoon by the green space of the Park of Remembrance, the island of Sant'Elena is quiet, devoid of canals. The small island of Saint Peter lies just north.

◉ **Don't Miss:** Viale Garibaldi, a long pathway through a tree-shaded expanse lined with charming homes. Take a rest on one of the benches along the path.

◷ **Organizing Your Time:** Allow 3hrs for a leisurely visit.

▩ **Especially for Kids:** The playground within the leafy grounds near the public garden.

◔ **Also See:** Neighbouring sights: ARSENALE.

Isola de Sant'Elena (▓▓, KLXY)

Up until the 11C, the island was known as *cavana* (refuge), as it provided sheltered anchorages to boatmen and fishermen. Its present name is derived from St Helen (c 257-336), mother of the Emperor Constantine, whose relics are housed in the church (first chapel on the right) and were brought to Venice in 1211, after the Fourth Crusade.

A colourful array of linen drying over the rooftops of Sant'Elena

Venetian Football

From September to June, Sant'Elena's stadium comes alive on weekends with afternoon Italian-league soccer. Attendance is an opportunity for visitors to imbibe some local colour, as avid supporters stream onto the grounds and root for their team, AC Venezia. Tickets can be purchased at the gate on game day (alternate Sat and Sun): prices begin at €10. ☎ 041 23 80 711; www. venezia.calcio.it.

The small monastery, established in 1060, was built by Benedictine monks from Tuscany in 1407. Subsequent rebuilding was undertaken between 1439 and 1515. As happened to other religious institutions during Napoleon's rule, the monastery was disbanded and its assets sold and dispersed; the church was used as a warehouse and troops were billeted in the convent buildings. During the late-19C and early 20C, the area around the church and monastery was extended and urbanised. Today, the church and convent accommodate Servite monks.

Church (🔟🔟, LY)

On the far side of the Rio di S. Elena rises the Church of Sant'Elena, flanked by a stadium and military base. The Gothic façade is dominated by its portal (1467). The sculptural group above, by Antonio Rizzo, shows the Capitano da Mar (Sea Captain-General), **Vittore Cappello**, kneeling before St Helen. Through the gate to the left extend the cloisters. Erected in 1956, the campanile does not conform with the essentially Gothic structure of the church.

Inside the luminous interior, a single nave terminates in an apse pierced with tall windows. The chapels radiate off the apse on the right.

Biennale (🔟🔟, KY)

The 100-year history of this international exhibition of modern art is long and controversial. From its beginnings in 1895, it caused an outcry by exhibiting a painting called *Il Supremo Convegno* by **Giacomo Grosso**, which was deemed to be in poor taste. The Impressionists were "invited" to exhibit their work only much later, as the organisers, up until 1912 at least, preferred art from Middle Europe rather than Paris.

The exhibition has always been held in the Castello Gardens, where the pavilions of the various countries have been erected. One particularly spectacular inauguration was that of the Russian pavilion in 1914, celebrated with an Orthodox mass in the presence of the Grand Duchess. The centenary of this important, if controversial, institution was celebrated in 1995. Besides all the controversy, the usual organisational problems and the philosophical and political diatribes, the Biennale has stood its ground. It may well be, however, that its uncomfortable position in the "eye of the storm" ensures a restlessness that guarantees its vitality.

Campo San Giuseppe (🔟, JX)

Beyond Viale Trento lies this little square stretching in front of the 16C Church of San Giuseppe which houses, in the first bay on the right, *St Michael and Lucifer Fighting over the Soul of Michele Bon* by Jacopo (1518-94) and Domenico (c 1560-1635) Tintoretto.

▶ *Cross the bridge just left of the square and follow Calle Correra to Fondamenta Sant'Anna. Turn right, cross the bridge on the left, and continue straight up Calle Larga San Pietro to the Church of San Pietro di Castello.*

Isola di San Pietro di Castello (🔟🔟, KX)

This island was inhabited before the city of Venice was founded. Originally known as **Olivolo**, perhaps after its olive groves, the *sestiere* commemorates a castle (hence the name Castello) that was either built or found there by the earliest Venetians. Since time immemorial, it has been the religious symbol of the city. Not only the seat of Bishop Castellano, and a dependent of the Patriarch of Grado, it still shelters the body of the first Patriarch of Venice, Lorenzo Giustiniani, who resided there in the 15C. The basilica stands in an open, grassy area, the venue for lively celebrations during the Feast of San Pietro di Castello.

San Pietro di Castello★ (⬛, KX)

🕒 *Open Mon-Sat, 10am-5pm.* 🕒 *Closed 1 Jan, Easter, 15 Aug, 25 Dec.* 👓 *€2.50.* ☎ *041 27 50 462; www.chorusveneiza.org*

Despite the fact that its fame has always been usurped by St Mark's, the Church of St Peter at Castello was regarded as the official cathedral of Venice until 1807, when St Mark's was merely considered the doge's chapel. It was erected in the 8C on the foundations of a church that dates to 650. The façade conforms to Palladian design. On the right is the former late-16C Patriarchal Palace. The nearby campanile, which leans to one side, was rebuilt by Mauro Codussi (c 1440-1504).

The 17C interior comprises a Latin cross with three aisles and a large dome. Above the main portal are represented *The Feast of the Jewish Passover* by Malombra and Vassillachi (16C-17C) *(right)* and *The Feast in the House of Simon* by Jacopo Beltrame (16C) *(left)*.

In the left aisle note the painting on canvas by **Veronese** (1528-88) and in the left transept in the Gothic **Lando Chapel**, the mosaic altarpiece based on a cartoon attributed to Tintoretto. The antependium or altar front comprises a 9C Veneto-Byzantine marble transenna (openwork screen) inlaid at the base with 2C mosaic. The **Vendramin Chapel** alongside is by Longhena: the *Madonna and Child with the Damned* is by Luca Giordano (1634-1705).

Returning down the right side, the marble seat known as **St Peter's Cathedra** is from Antioch: note the unusual back adapted from an Arab-Muslim funerary stele, decorated with inscriptions from the Koran in Cufic script.

SAN GIORGIO MAGGIORE★★

(⬛, GHXY)
VAPORETTO: S. GIORGIO

The island fulfils almost any preconceptions visitors might have of Venice, as well as providing a first-rate view over the whole city. San Giorgio does not tend to be haunted by tourists: there are no bars or restaurants. For this reason alone, it is a "must" for anyone searching for a unique view of Venice and for those attracted to the serenity of monastic life, even as an escape for an hour or so. It is also a "must" for Palladio fans.

▶ **Orient Yourself:** Sitting in St. Mark's Basin near the entrance to the Guidecca Canal and facing Piazza San Marco, this small island is prime real estate in terms of exposure: its glorious church of the same name is generally the first head-turner for travelers arriving in the city by water.

👓 **Don't Miss:** The best view of Venice, from the church's bell-tower.

🕒 **Organizing Your Time:** The proposed tour takes about 2hrs.

👣 **Also See:** Neighbouring sights: La GIUDECCA.

A Bit of History

The island's name relates to a church erected here in 790; the term *maggiore* is used to distinguish it from another island, San Giorgio in Alga. Since 982, the year a Benedictine monastery was founded here, the island's history has been associated with this monastic order. It became especially favoured by doges, who on 26 December would come and attend Mass in celebration of the Feast of St Stephen. The island's true moment of glory came with the arrival of **Andrea Palladio**, commissioned to redesign the church, which had been rebuilt between 1400 and 1500.

The island's eventual downfall, coinciding with that of the Republic of Venice, was protracted into the 1850s. After both Napoleon and the Austrians had defiled the artistic beauty of the island, its finest buildings continued to be devastated by various armies passing through, including the Italian army using the *manica lunga* as military stores during the Second World War.

The restoration of the island to its former beauty is largely due to the Cini Foundation and to the Benedictines, who, for more than 1 000 years, have faithfully preserved the original liturgical tradition and Gregorian chants of San Giorgio, assisted by the Salesians, who are active in all fields of education and guidance.

No one lives on the Island of San Giorgio besides these dedicated people. It is a place of retreat, of profound learning and deepest religious faith. Other than the monastery, there is nowhere to stay, nowhere to eat or drink, for such places would distract the spirit and attract an influx of indiscriminate visitors. *Accommodation is available in the monastery. For information and reservations, call ☎ 041 52 27 827.*

Walking Tour

San Giorgio Maggiore★ (⑨, GY)

The rebuilding of the church to designs by Palladio began in 1566. The front is dominated by a great triangular pediment supported by four columns: a feature borrowed from a Classical temple.

The bright interior enhances the ample Latin cross-space enclosed within its vaulted ceiling and apsed transepts. in the third chapel, *The Martyrdom of Saints Cosmas and Damian* was painted by **Jacopo Tintoretto**, who also did the two large paintings in the presbytery. The main altar is ornamented with late-16C sculptures by Gerolamo and Giuseppe Campagna. The door to the right leads into the chapel *(open for Sunday services)* decorated with Tintoretto's last work, his *Deposition from the Cross*. The doorway in the left wall provides access to the campanile.

Isola di San Giorgio

R. Mattes/MICHELIN

Campanile

Open May-Sept 9.30am-12.30pm and 2.30pm-6.30pm (4.30pm rest of the year). €3.

The bell-tower was given its present form by Scalfarotto in 1726. It offers the best possible **view**★★★ over Venice.

Fondazione Giorgio Cini (🖥, GY)

This private institution is responsible for restoration work undertaken on many of Venice's monuments. It also has organised important conventions, for example on the development of international relations.

The foundation was founded by **Vittorio Cini** (1885-1977), a man who showed great courage and philanthropy during his life as a financier and government minister. He dared to speak up against the war, impervious both to Mussolini and Goering. He was an enlightened patron who strove to help humanity. The institution of this benevolent foundation commemorates his son Giorgio, who died following a plane crash, and is devoted to supporting and endowing cultural and humanist initiatives.

Library★

The entrance to the library is off the first cloisters and up the main staircase on the right. ♿ Guided tour by appointment only, 9am-5pm. Apply at least one week in advance to the Cini Foundation. €12. ☎ 041 52 89 900; www.cini.it

Like the staircase, the library (1641-53) was designed by Longhena. It is decked with shelving and ornamented with carved wooden figures: the ceiling was decorated in the 17C Mannerist style.

Cloisters

This ancient monastery has two cloisters. The first, the **Chiostro dei Cipressi** (with the cypresses) were designed by Palladio and are articulated with paired columns and windows opening below curved and triangular pediments. This leads into the **Teatro Verde**, an open-air theatre with marble seats used during the summer. The second cloisters, which are older, were originally known as the **Chiostro degli Allori** (with laurels). Palladio worked with Veronese on the **Refectory** *(Refettorio)* For the end wall, Veronese painted a *Wedding at Cana,* a panel Napoleon had sent back to Paris, and which now hangs in the Louvre. Its replacement, representing *The Marriage of the Virgin,* is from the School of Tintoretto.

Dormitorio (la manica lunga)

The dormitory building is impressive for its sheer size and lightness, and for the fine view it enjoys over the Riva degli Schiavoni. Known as the *manica lunga,* meaning the long sleeve, it was conceived by Giovanni Buora at the end of the 15C: 128m/420ft long, it opens onto 50 rooms.

On the outside, there is a 16C relief depicting *St George and the Dragon.*

SAN GIORGIO DEGLI SCHIAVONI★★★

(🔲, HV)
VAPORETTO: S. ZACCARIA, RIVA DEGLI SCHIAVONI

Tucked away behind Riva degli Schiavoni, a small section of the Castello *sestiere* is enlivened by an energy level that falls midway between the frenetic, milling activity around St Mark's Basilica and the absolute peace surrounding the Church of San Francesco della Vigna. Borrowing a little of the atmosphere from both, this area of Venice forges its own charm and personality.

▶ **Orient Yourself:** This central area of the Castello district lies east of St Mark's square and is bisected by the wide Rio di San Agostini.
😊 **Don't Miss:** Carpaccio's series of *St. George* paintings in the Scuola.
🕓 **Organizing Your Time:** Allow 2hr 30min to visit the sights.
🕐 **Also See:** Neighbouring sights: ARSENALE; SAN ZACCARIA.

Scuola di San Giorgio degli Schiavoni★★★

The original 15C buildings were remodelled by Giovanni de Zan in 1551, but the original layout of the interior was retained. By 1502, Carpaccio had already started working on his cycle of paintings, intended for the upper hall. The *scuola* was founded by the Confraternity of the Schiavoni, or Slavs from Schiavonia (equivalent to today's Dalmatia), who, for the most part, traded with the Levant. Their patron saints were the three protectors of their homeland, St George, St Tryphon and St Jerome.

The *Cycle of St George*★★★ by **Vittore Carpaccio** took the artist five years to complete (1502-07). It was moved downstairs in the 16C, to the intimate ground-floor, well-lit gallery, with its fine wooden ceiling, which provided an ideal location to best show off the paintings' warm colours.

Interior

♿🕓*Open Apr-Oct, Tue-Sun 9.30am-12.30pm and 2.30-6.30pm; rest of the year 10am-12.30pm and 3-6pm.* 🕓*Closed Sun afternoon, Mon and public hols.* 💶*€3. May be temporarily closed without notice due to the needs of the Confraternity.* ☎ *041 52 28 828.*
😊 It is best to read the panels from the left wall even if this does not follow the chronological order of execution, Carpaccio having started with the episodes from the Life of St Jerome.

St George and the Dragon catches the very moment when the knight attacks the dragon: the event is narrated pictorially with all the romance of heroic chivalry, a veritable *chanson de geste* on canvas. The noble bearing of the saint and his steed,

The Legend of St George

Little is known about this early martyr's life, whose cult became particularly important in the 6C. The legend of St George slaying the dragon seems to emerge late in the 12C, when popularised in the **Golden Legend**: a story possibly founded on the myth of Perseus killing the sea monster at Arsuf or Joppa. Today both the Easter Orthodox and Western churches venerate the saint as a soldier, a tradition that originated in Palestine and was embraced by the crusaders.

The church exploited the valiant saint's slaying the dragon and saving the virtuous princess as symbolic parables about the Church being saved from the devil.

St Augustine in his Study by Carpaccio (Scuola di San Giorgio degli Schiavoni)

the dignified composure of the emotional princess and the architectural precision of the composition are true to the idealised legend, but contrast sharply with the macabre portrayal of skulls and hideously mutilated bodies.

The Triumph of St George dramatically depicts the saint on the point of killing the wounded dragon: the exotic figures are set against a background of Renaissance architecture, although the centrally planned temple is not positioned in the actual centre as this would have disturbed the harmony of the composition.

The group of musicians is also present in the next scene, *St George Baptising the Heathen King and Queen*, as witnesses to the solemnity of the occasion, tempered only by the timorous pose of the saint, shown full of hesitation. The pre-eminent significance given to the chivalry of St George may be due to the financial support given to the Scuola by the Knights of Rhodes, who considered the saint to embody all the ideals of the perfect knight.

St Tryphon Exorcising the Daughter of the Emperor Gordianus is a rare representation of the saint. Although thought to have been painted by Carpaccio and his assistants, a master's touch is recognisable in the architectural details and the distinctive personalities of the figures.

The two small paintings, the *Agony in the Garden* and the *Vocation of St Matthew*, exceptions to the cycles dedicated to the lives of the Scuola's three patron saints, serve as a prelude to episodes in the life of St Jerome.

In the first canvas, *St Jerome leading his Lion into a Monastery*, the depiction of the monks is nothing short of humorous as they flee from the lion, which is more con-

St Jerome (c 342-420)

Born in Dalmatia, Eusebius Hieronymus was a biblical scholar and a great traveller. After studying rhetoric in Rome, Hieronymus journeyed through Gaul, Palestine and Syria before visiting Antioch, Constantinople and Egypt. He settled into monastic life in Bethlehem and devoted his mature years to study, translating the Gospels and Old Testament into vulgar Latin, in direct opposition to Rome.

In art he is often depicted as holding a stone as a symbol of his ascetic life, as wearing a red cardinal's hat and as being in the company of the lion from whose paw he is said to have removed a thorn. Renaissance Humanist patrons popularised his portrayal as a scribe surrounded by books, while depictions of the aesthete in the desert hearken to John the Baptist in the New Testament.

cerned with obediently following St Jerome. The building in the background is the Scuola di San Rocco.

By contrast there is no such animation or humour in the *Funeral of St Jerome*, only solemn tragedy. Set in the peaceful, ordered precinct of a monastery, the composition centres on the saint laid out on the floor, attended by monks. A basic, yet serene, sense of inevitability pervades the scene, suggested by the animals in the courtyard that represent the continuous natural rhythm of life and death.

St Augustine in his Study also alludes to the legend of St Jerome: the Venetian version of the story tells of St Augustine wishing to address a letter on a matter of theology to St Jerome, who had already died: his divine presence appeared in St Augustine's study admonishing him for his presumption (a Venetian edition of the letter was published in 1485). The study is flooded with natural light that highlights every detail including the dog's bemusement, the scrolls and the little knobs. The quality of rendering and exquisite attention to the furnishings, especially the open door into a second room, are reminiscent of Flemish domestic interior painting. The facial traits of St Augustine are, in fact, those of Cardinal Bessarione (1402-72), a scholar of Greek Humanism.

A variety of works in silver are displayed in the sacristy and in the upper hall.

Additional Sights

La Pietà (🖳, GX)

Edging Riva degli Schiavoi, Santa Maria della Visitazione is better known as "La Pietà" (the merciful one) after its hospice for abandoned children, dedicated in the 14C.

From afar, the church's white façade with its broad pediment supported on columns, finally added in 1906, is its distinguishing feature. Initially the church would have been integrated within the institutional complex, but in the 18C, when it was all to be remodelled by Giorgio Massari, it was decided that the church should be designed as a concert hall, given that the orphans' education was oriented towards music, at one time under the leadership of **Antonio Vivaldi**.

The internal structure is vaulted to optimise the acoustics. The orchestra and the choir are positioned along the side walls. Music is the theme of the superb frescoes on the ceiling.

San Giorgio dei Greci (🖳, GV)

🕐*Open Apr-Sept, daily, 9am-1pm and 3-5pm (6pm Sat); Oct-Mar, Mon-Fri, 9am-1pm and 2.30-4.30pm, Sat, 9am-1pm and 2.30-5.30pm, Sun and public hols, 9am-1pm.* ☎ *041 52 39 569.*

The closed complex designed by Longhena and a gently leaning tower comprise a 16C church and college buildings reserved for its Greek Orthodox community, and the icon museum. Founded originally by a colony of Greeks, a confraternity evolved to form the **Scuola di San Niccolò**; after the fall of Constantinople in 1453, its numbers increased remarkably.

The long and narrow façade with its prominent pediment owes much to the influence of Sansovino. The cupola was added in 1571.

Inside, the great rectangular space is sealed by a magnificent **iconostasis**★ embellished with holy figures against a gold background that screens off the apsed area beyond, reserved for the clergy. The walls are lined with wooden stalls for use by the congregation during the long Orthodox rituals.

Museo di Icone Bizantine-postbizantine

♿🕐*Open daily 9am-5pm.* 🕐*Closed 1 Jan, 25 Dec.* ⊛*€4.* ☎ *041 52 26 581; www.isti-tutoellenico.org*

This museum houses a rich collection of Byzantine and post-Byzantine icons and paintings portraying various religious subjects, exquisite illuminated manuscripts and religious artifacts.

Return along Salizzada dei Greci past **San Antonin** (🖲, **HV**), a church which dates back to the 7C but which was rebuilt by Longhena. The mid-17C campanile rises to an Eastern-style cupola. Continue onto Campo Bandiera e Moro with its church, **San Giovanni in Bràgora**★ (👟 *see ARSENALE*), where Vivaldi was baptised, before turning back towards Riva degli Schiavoni.

SAN ROCCO★★★

(🖲, CDV)
VAPORETTO: S. TOMÀ

San Rocco is an ideal district for a stroll, providing interesting monuments and splashes of local colour. Quiet bars and cafes are situated near the main points of interest, allowing visitors to rest between sightseeing.

▸ **Orient Yourself:** San Rocco sits behind I Frari (👟 *see I FRARI*)
🕐 **Organizing Your Time:** Allow at least 2hr 30min.
👟 **Also See:** Neighbouring sights: I CARMINI, I FRARI and RIALTO.

A Bit of History

Little is known of **San Rocco (c 1295-1327)**, protector of the plague-stricken, other than he was born in Montpellier in southwest France. According to his Venetian biographer, Francesco Diedo, Roch travelled to Italy, where he miraculously cured plague victims with the sign of the cross (Aquapendente, Cesena, Mantua, Modena, Parma …) until he, too, succumbed to the disease in Piacenza and recovered enough to return home. On his return to Montpellier, he was taken to be a spy in Angers and incarcerated. He died there in prison.

San Rocco was particularly venerated in Venice, whose port also helped to spread epidemics. Spared from Napoleon's edicts, the Confraternity of St Roch is still active today. Annually, on 16 August, Venice celebrates the saint with the most traditional pomp and circumstance.

The prestige of the Scuola was further enhanced in 1485 when the saint's relics were transferred to its care. The "shrine" was therefore initiated in 1516 by Bartolomeo Bon, who was dismissed in 1524 after a major disagreement with the leaders of the Scuola. The project was then entrusted to Scarpagnino, who worked on the building until his death.

The magnificence of the Scuola resides in its interior decoration, which has an interesting history of its own. In 1564, a competition was launched for the decoration of the Salla dell'Albergo *(a small room on the first floor where the Chapter met)*. Several illustrious artists, including Paolo Veronese, Andrea Schiavone, and Federico Zuccari, submitted their drawings, but **Tintoretto** quickly completed a painted panel for the ceiling and promptly donated his work as a gesture of devotion. In such circumstances, the work could not be refused, and so Tintoretto went on to furnish the entire Scuola with his paintings.

Scuola Grande di San Rocco

Despite displaying a certain homogeneity, the façade draws together a variety of styles, most evident in the windows: those on the ground floor are early Venetian Renaissance and those above are Mannerist in design.

The rear façade, facing onto the canal, is simpler in format with a portico and finely carved details (note the heads on the pilasters on the first floor).

Interior★★★

Open 28 Mar-2 Nov, 9am-5.30pm; rest of the year, 10am-5pm; last admission 30min before closing. Closed 1 Jan, Easter and 25 Dec. €7; no charge 16 Aug (St Rocco's feast day). ☎ 041 52 34 864; www.scuolagrandesanrocco.it

Start upstairs by taking either of the two flights that feed into the single, grand staircase. Above, Scarpagnino's barrel-vaulted ceiling is painted with *St Roch Presenting the Sick to Charity, who Bears the Torch of Religion* by Giannantonio Pellegrini; the walls show *Venice with St Mark, St Roch and St Sebastian in Supplication for an End to the Plague* by Pietro Negri (1673) *(on the left)* – note the inclusion of the Church of La Salute, which was erected as a votive gesture at the end of the plague in 1630; and *(on the right) The Virgin Appearing to the Plague-stricken* (1666) by Antonio Zanchi.

Sala dell'Albergo

The most striking work of art in the Albergo Room is the huge and dramatic *Crucifixion* immediately opposite the door.

In the left section of the entrance wall, the intensity of the scene in *Christ Appearing before Pilate* is concentrated by light focusing on the figure of Christ. In the middle section *Ecce Homo* is depicted, and to its left, *Christ Bearing the Cross*, a realistic rendering of the tragic journey, which Tintoretto populates with a weary cortège of figures moving in the opposite direction.

The *Three Apples* on the bench, reminiscent of Cézanne, is a fragment from the ceiling discovered above the door behind one of the capitals after four centuries.

Despite some controversy, the easel picture of *Christ Bearing the Cross* has been attributed to Giorgione and that of *Christ in Pietà* to his followers.

Scuola Grande di S Rocco, Venezia/SCALA

The Crucifixion by Tintoretto

Sala Capitolare
In the large chapter house, subjects are based on the Old Testament *(ceiling)* and the New *(walls)*.

The central ceiling panel depicts *The Brazen Serpent*, framed by two square panels depicting *Moses Striking the Rock* and *Manna Sent from Heaven*. The two large oval panels illustrate *Ezekial's Vision* and the *Fall of Man*. The other eight panels painted in green chiaroscuro conclude the Old Testament cycle.

On the side of the corridor is depicted *The Ascension*, followed by *The Pool of Bethesda*. *The Temptation of Christ* boasts a splendid Lucifer that echoes images of Eve tempting Adam with the apple.

On the wall opposite, the *Adoration of the Shepherds* is followed by the *Baptism*; in the central section opposite *The Ascension, The Resurrection of Christ* shows Christ seemingly bursting from the tomb as the two Marys walk in the morning light beyond; in *The Agony in the Garden*, the hour of the day imbues the scene with a faint reddish light. The focal point of perspective in *The Last Supper* is the bright halo hovering over the little figure of the Saviour.

The room also accommodates a large altarpiece, depicting the *Vision of St Roch* painted largely by Tintoretto, assisted by his son and studio; a *Self-Portrait* showing Tintoretto in a religious pose and one of his versions of *The Visitation*. *The Annunciation*, however, is by Titian and the two other easel canvases by Tiepolo.

Sala Terrena
On the ground floor hang Tintoretto's last canvases, dedicated to Mary. *The Annunciation* – a more "popular" version if compared to the aristocratic rendering by Titian – preceding *The Adoration of the Magi, The Flight into Egypt, The Massacre of the Innocent* (imbued some might say with a sharp sense of realism and desperate tragedy by a Tintoretto overwhelmed with grief at the death of his son), and a *Mary Magdalene*.

All Tintoretto's canvases conform to the aesthetic principles outlined by the Council of Trent, scorning all artifice and loftily intellectual iconography in favour of a more direct appeal to the common people.

Walking Tour

San Rocco (⊠, CDV)
The present façade of the church, built in the mid-1720s, was remodelled in the late-18C. The statues of the *Saints* and the *Blessed* are by Marchiori and the Austrian-born Gianmaria Morlaiter the The portal, rose window and a few of the original Renaissance features survive on the side overlooking the *scuola*.

Above the entrance door, the **old organ door panels** painted by Tintoretto depict *The Annunciation* and *The Presentation of St Roch to the Pope*.

In the first side chapel of the left aisle, the altarpiece is by Sebastiano Ricci; the two tall panels by Pordenone show *St Martin* and *St Christopher,* and the panel below, *Christ Chasing the Moneychangers from the Temple*, is by Fumiani. Over the second altar is an *Annunciation and Angels* by Solimena. Four canvases by **Tintoretto** are to be found in the presbytery. On the other side of the church, towards the exit, the first altarpiece on the left is dedicated to *The Miracle of St Anthony* by Trevisani (1656-1746). In the middle, between the two altars, hang two more canvases by **Tintoretto**. The last altar is decorated with an altarpiece by Sebastiano Ricci.

▶ *Cross the canal behind the Scuola and take Calle San Pantalon, which leads to a square.*

San Pantalon (⬛, CV)

Despite its unfinished façade (1668-86), this church recalls others in Venice such as San Marcuola and San Lorenzo.

Its main interest is its interior ornamented with an undisputed masterpiece by Fumiani comprising 60 canvas ceiling panels illustrating *The Martyrdom and Glory of St Pantaleon*, executed between 1684 and 1704, and restored with the assistance of the American Committee to Rescue Italian Art (1970-71). The work is a tour de force of perspective, projecting the nave high into the sky.

The presbytery decoration is by the same artist, often referred to as *fumoso* (meaning smoky) owing to his predilection for dark colours, so characteristic of a period tormented by ever-present death. To the left of the high altar, the small Sacro Chiodo Chapel, dedicated to a relic of the True Cross, houses the *Paradise* (1444) by Antonio Vivarini. In the third chapel on the right is a work by **Veronese**.

▶ *Return to San Rocco to take Salizzada San Rocco and Calle Larga Prima to Campo San Tomà.*

Campo San Tomà (⬛, DV)

This lovely square with its simple, now deconsecrated church dates back to the 10C; it was remodelled in 1742. Straight ahead is the **Scuola dei Calegheri**, the guild of cobblers, which acquired the *palazzo* in the 15C.

▶ *To reach Goldoni's house, keep to the left side of the church and cross the bridge over Rio San Tomà.*

Casa di Goldoni (⬛, DV)

♿⏰*Open daily except Sun, 10am-5pm (4pm Nov-Mar).* ⏰*Closed 1 Jan, 1 May and 25 Dec.* ▥€2.50. ☎ *041 27 59 325; www.museiciviciveneziani.it*

It was in this *palazzo*, its small courtyard complete with a well and staircase, that the famous playwright **Carlo Goldoni** was born. The house is now home to the International Institute for Theatrical Research; one room serves as a small puppet theatre, housing works by Goldoni and Pietro Longhi.

▶ *To continue to Campo San Polo, follow the flow of people. Cross the bridge over Rio di San Polo and follow along the right side of the church.*

Campo San Polo (⬛, DU)

Still today, this large open space provides a venue for many cultural and tourist events, thereby maintaining an age-long historical tradition of ceremonies and games of various sorts, such as bull-baiting. Two *palazzi* overlook this splendid piazza shaped like an amphitheatre: the high Gothic-style **Palazzo Soranzo** (nos 2169 and 2170), and nearby, the Baroque **Palazzo Tiepolo Maffetti**, with its distinctive head of Hercules over the portal. . At the opposite corner is Sanmicheli's 16C **Palazzo Corner Mocenigo**, now the seat of the Guardia di Finanza (Financial Police).

San Polo (⬛, DUV)

⏰*Open Mon-Sat, 10am-5pm.* ⏰*Closed 1 Jan, Easter, 15 Aug, 25 Dec.* ▥€2.50. ☎ *041 27 50 462; www.chorusvenezia.org*

The façade of this ancient church, whose origins are rooted in the 9C, was rebuilt

St Pantaleon

Pantaleon was born to a pagan father and Christian mother. According to legend, he was reconciled to Christianity while employed as a physician at the court of Emperor Galerius at Nicodemia and denounced during the persecutions prescribed by Diocletian in 303. His cult was popularised in the Eastern Church, notably during the Middle Ages, when he was honoured as one of the patron saints of physicians: his name, appropriately enough, means "the All-Merciful."

between the 14C and 15C. Now hemmed in by houses, the church preserves its main rose window and an ornate side door decorated with organic carving from the turn of the 14C as a testimony to the late-Gothic style. Subsequent restoration in the 19C has unfortunately destroyed the harmony of the original.

The interior, vaulted with a ship's keel roof, accommodates over the first altar on the right an *Assumption of the Virgin*, and to its left a *Last Supper* by **Tintoretto**. In this second piece, an intimate interior scene is full of domestic details that betray a simple way of life.

Over the second altar on the left, the *Virgin Appearing to St John of Nepomuk* is by Giambattista Tiepolo; the *Fourteen Stations of the Cross* in the Oratory of the Crucifix are by his son Giandomenico.

The chapel on the left preserves the *Betrothal of the Virgin and Angels* by Veronese.

SAN ZACCARIA★★

(᠑, GX)
VAPORETTO: S. ZACCARIA

San Zaccaria is a stone's throw from St Mark's and as a result there are numerous restaurants, pizzerias, souvenir and *passementerie* shops in the area. As the distance from the church increases, so the numbers of tourists thin out and the district becomes quieter and more frequented by locals. At its heart lies the attractive and atmospheric Campo Santa Maria Formosa and its busy market. Dotted with shops specialising in typical Venetian goods, this area is perfect for a leisurely stroll.

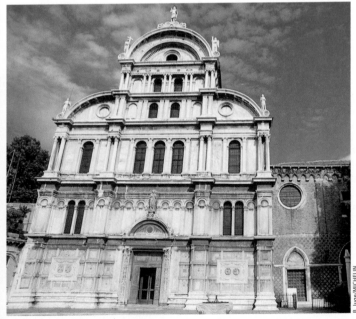

B. Juge/MICHELIN

The façade of San Zaccaria

▶ **Orient Yourself:** Situated due east of St. Mark's, the area, dominated by its church of the same name, is surrounded by canals on three sides, and by Rivo degli Schiavoni on the fourth.

🕐 **Organizing Your Time:** For the suggested itinerary, allow about 2hr 30min.

🕑 **Also See:** Neighbouring sights: ARSENALE; PIAZZA SAN MARCO; RIALTO.

Walking Tour

San Zaccaria★★ (🟦, GX)

The original church, founded in the 9C, has been partly incorporated into the new church: the right aisle was created from the left aisle of the old church. The present church, dating from the 15C, was built by Gambello and completed, at his death, by Codussi.

The splendid white façade incorporates three tiers of round-headed windows, niches and semicircular pediment. Contrived from a variety of architectural styles, its tall Gothic proportions are cloaked in Renaissance detail. At ground level the lower section is set with square polychrome panels that run horizontally. Above this, a continuous frieze of shell-headed flat niches introduce a vertical element that is then carried through the upper sections, accented first with three windows, then two and finally by a single central oculus. The Gothic configuration of tall nave and side aisles cede to Codussi's more Classical idiom: projecting piers give way to free-standing paired columns that extend up to a cornice, crowned with free-standing figures – far removed from the statue of *St Zaccarias* by Alessandro Vittorio above the main door.

The stunning interior is covered in paintings, the most important of which is Giovanni Bellini's *Sacra Conversazione* (1505) over the second altar on the left. On the lower left wall are two panels (1500) by Palma il Giovane.

The **Cappella del Coro** is hung with works by Tintoretto, Tiepolo and Palma il Vecchio; a pair of organ panels painted by Palma il Giovane; a *Crucifixion* attributed to Van Dyck and a *Resurrection* by Domenico Tintoretto.

In the Cappella d'Oro, also known as the Chapel of St Tarasius, the vault is frescoed by Andrea del Castagno and Francesco da Faenza, and the three Gothic polyptychs are by Antonio Vivarini and his collaborator. At the foot of the altar are the remains of the mosaic from the apse of the 12C Romanesque-Byzantine chapel. A little farther back *(protected by glass)* are mosaics from the 9C church. Stairs descend into the 10C crypt, submerged in water.

▶ *Follow Salizzada San Provolo and proceed straight to the canal; turn left for the Diocesan Museum of Religious Art. Alternatively, return to Campo Santi Filippo e Giacomo and take Calle della Chiesa, turn left before the canal and follow the water's edge through Campiello Querini and onto Campo Santa Maria Formosa.*

Campo Santa Maria Formosa (🟦, GU)

This square might recall the quiet Campo San Giacomo dall'Orio, given their similar semicircular shape and the position of the church. Only this square is situated between St Mark's and the Church of Santi Giovanni e Paolo, where daily comings and goings of tourists and Venetians make it a busy thoroughfare.

Santa Maria Formosa (🟦, GUV)

🕐 *Open Mon-Sat, 10am-5pm.* 🕐 *Closed 1 Jan, Easter, 15 Aug, 25 Dec.* ✆€2.50. ☎ *041 27 50 462; www.chorusvenezia.org*

The original 7C church built here was dedicated, according to legend, to St Magnus, to whom the Madonna appeared in the form of a shapely *(formosa)* woman. It was rebuilt by Codussi between 1492 and 1504 and embellished with a new façade in 1604 and a new canal frontage in 1542, financed by a noble Venetian family, the

The Abduction of the Maidens

According to a Venetian custom, for the Feast of the Marias, at Candlemas, two girls from each *sestiere* would be married and each would be given a coffer in which to store their dowry. In about 946, the festival was nearly ruined by Slav pirates who kidnapped the maidens and held them to ransom: they were rescued by the **Casselleri**, the artisans who made the bridal chests for the brides. From then on, the doge would visit the Casselleri at Santa Maria Formosa at Candlemas.

Cappellos. The 17C campanile retains, above the entrance, a grimacing mask and its original pinnacle.

On passing through the main entrance, note on the left the *Madonna di Lepanto* (1571), which once graced the naval ship commanded by Sebastiano Venier.

The interior, in the form of a Latin cross, includes the Chapel of the Scuola dei Bombardieri (mortar founders), which contains a *San Barnaba and Saints* by Palma il Vecchio (c 1480-1528), and that of the Scuola dei Casselleri (trunks and chest makers). Of note in the first chapel is a *Madonna of the Misericordia* by Bartolomeo Vivarini.

Fondazione Querini Stampalia Onlus★ (5, GV)

&. ⊙*Open Tue-Thu and Sun, 10am-6pm, Fri-Sat, 10am-10pm.* ⊙*Closed public hols.* ⊙€8. ☎ *041 27 11 411; www.querinistampalia.it*

Housed in a modern building, this museum, which contains a library and occasionally hosts temporary exhibitions, is of interest to visitors seeking to imbibe the atmosphere of a Venice long disappeared, when life in the city was synonymous with art.

Works of art on display here include a clay model for a sculpture of *Letizia Ramolino Bonaparte* by Antonio Canova; and paintings by Palma il Giovane, Luca Giordano, Tiepolo and others.

Particularly noteworthy are the **series of panels**★★ by Pietro Longhi, predominantly devoted to the sacraments and hunting; the *Scenes of Public Life in Venice*★★ by Gabriele Bella and the evocative *Presentation of Jesus in the Temple* by Giovanni Bellini.

Everyday Venetian life of the period is well depicted in the paintings *The Boxing Match* after Antonio Stom and *The Frozen Lagoon by the Fondamenta Nuove* by an anonymous 18C Venetian painter.

SAN ZANIPÒLO★★

SS GIOVANNI E PAOLO

VAPORETTO: FONDAMENTA NUOVE, CIMITERO

This area is striking not only for its timeless majesty but also for the broad range of activity in the district, from the intense business of the *calli* between Campo di Santi Giovanni e Paolo and Campo Santi Apostoli to the tranquillity of Campo dei Gesuiti and the peacefulness of the Fondamenta Nuove. From here, the view extends over the choppy waters of the lagoon to the cemetery of San Michele, disturbed only by the passing of the water-buses.

▶ **Orient Yourself:** Neighbouring a large hospital in the northern section of the Castello *sestiere*, the San Zanipòlo district edges the Rio dei Mendicanti and the Fondamenta Nuove. The walking tour leads into the Cannaregio *sestiere*, and is followed by a tour of the island of San Michele.

Gwen Cannon/ MICHELIN

San Zanipòlo

😊 **Don't Miss:** The powerful equestrian statue of Bartolomeo Colleoni.
🕐 **Organizing Your Time:** Allow half a day to enjoy this area.
🖐 **Also See:** Neighbouring sights: CA' D'ORO; RIALTO.

Sights

Campo di Santi Giovanni e Paolo (⑤, GU).

The name *Zanipòlo* is a contraction of the names John and Paul in dialect, the two saints to whom the square is dedicated. Constituent elements contribute to the vastness of the whole: the imposing basilica, the deceptive perspectives of the Scuola Grande di San Marco, the bridge over the Rio dei Mendicanti, the great "angular" space, relieved only by a well-head, and the equestrian monument to Colleoni.

Equestrian monument to Bartolomeo Colleoni★★

The proud gait of the rider, his face set with a wilful expression, contrasts powerfully with the restless disposition of the horse: an inspired combination that is rendered all the more majestic by its base.

In his will, Colleoni, a mercenary soldier, stated that he intended the statue to be placed before St Mark's, on the understanding that he meant St Mark's Basilica. Considering the monument unworthy of St Mark's Square, officials of the Republic gave permission for it to be set up in a place at least associated in name with its intended destination: the Scuola Grande di San Marco.

The commission for such a major monument was awarded to **Verrocchio** by competition. As the master died before it had been cast, Alessandro Leopardi oversaw the project and added the base.

> ### The Condottiere
>
> **Bartolomeo Colleoni** (1400-76) was one of many mercenary soldiers engaged by the Venetian Republic to defend and acquire her territories. A native of Bergamo, Colleoni served Venice for a long time, with considerable success. He also served Francesco Sforza. Returning to the Republic of Venice, he was relegated to Malpaga Castle, where he died. His tomb is housed in the Colleoni Chapel in Bergamo.

The inspiration for the Colleoni monument undoubtedly came from the *Gattamelata* by Donatello in Padua, which, with the Antique equestrian statue of Marcus Aurelius in Rome, rank among the best expressions of the genre.

The decorative **well-head** is attributed to Sansovino, who was also responsible for the side of the Scuola di San Marco that faces onto the canal.

Basilica dei Santi Giovanni e Paolo★★ (⑤, GU)

This church, the largest in Venice, was founded by Dominican friars late in the 13C, but was not consecrated until 1430.

Front

The façade, which remains incomplete, comprises at ground level a central pointed arch flanked by three blind arches; above, the width is divided vertically by plain piers rising up to niches on the roof line that accommodate statues of the Dominican Saints. These, in turn, are crowned with the eagle, the symbol of St John, the Eternal Father and the lion of St Mark.

On either side of the main portal, designed by Bartolomeo Bon, are the two sarcophagi, inset in the Gothic arches, of the Doges Jacopo and Lorenzo Tiepolo.

Detail of the well in Campo di Santi Giovanni e Paolo

Interior

The well-lit lofty nave leads to an apse pierced by slender double lancet Gothic windows. In the form of a Latin cross, the church has three aisles and five apses. Huge columns carry great beams that support the arches and the cross vaults.

The internal façade commemorates the **Mocenigo Doges**: *(centre)* Alvise I (**1**); *(left)* Pietro – (**2**) monument by Pietro Lombardo; *(right)* Giovanni – (**3**) monument by Tullio Lombardo.

Along the left aisle is the altar to St Jerome (**4**), its statue a work by Alessandro Vittoria; the pyramid nearby is in memory of the Bandiera brothers (**5**), supporters of Mazzini's *Young Italy*, who were gunned down in 1844.

At the altar to St Peter Martyr (altarpiece after Titian) is the monument to **Doge Niccolò Marcello** (**6**) by Pietro Lombardo; that to **Doge Tommaso Mocenigo** (**7**) with its great baldaquin, is the work (1423) of Niccolò Lamberti and Giovanni di Martino.

Flanking the double arch are two statues by Antonio Lombardo. Before the sacristy is the Renaissance monument to **Doge Pasquale Malipiero** (**8**) by Pietro Lombardo, although the baldaquin is Gothic in style.

The **sacristy** seems to burst with ornate decoration orchestrating a celebration of the Dominican Order: the canvas by Leandro da Bassano depicts Pope Honorius III, emblazoned with the colours red, white and black. The ceiling is painted by one of Titian's relations, Marco Vecellio. The scene at the altar and on the right are by Palma il Giovane. To the left of the altar is a painting by Alvise Vivarini.

Before turning into the transept are three panels of a *Polyptych* (**9**) by Bartolomeo Vivarini. The 18C organ was built by Gaetano Callido.

In the left transept, above the entrance to the Chapel of the Rosary but below the great clock, is a monument to **Doge Antonio Venier**; to its right, beside the entrance, stands the bronze statue of **Sebastiano Venier**, the victor at Lepanto.

The **Cappella del Rosario** (Chapel of the Rosary or Lepanto Chapel) was built as a mark of gratitude for the great victory over the Turks. The shrine enclosing the *Madonna del Rosario* was designed by Girolamo Campagna.

On the walls are depictions by Padovanino and Benedetto Caliari. Opposite the altar, Veronese has painted himself in the guise of the man standing beyond the column. Beyond the apsed chapels on the left, the central apse is replete with other **funerary monuments**.

Immediately on the left is that of **Doge Marco Corner** (**10**) by Nino Pisano, followed by the sepulchre of **Doge Andrea Vendramin** (**11**), a majestic work by Tullio Lombardo ornamented with Classical medallions illustrating mythological figures, and warriors in the niches.

On the right is the funerary monument to **Doge Michele Morosini** (1382) (**12**) from the workshops of Dalle Masegne, surmounted by a Tuscan School mosaic (15C) and framed by an arch; here also is that of **Doge Leonardo Loredan**, during whose reign the League of Cambrai was formed. Venice

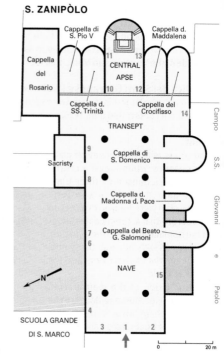

S. ZANIPÒLO

(left) and the League of Cambrai (right) are depicted at the sides of the statue of the doge by Girolamo Campagna.

The first apsidal chapel on the right is dedicated to **Mary Magdalene**. The *Four Evangelists* are frescoed by Palma il Giovane; on the right wall is the monument to the **Sea-Captain Vittor Pisani** (1324-80); on the left is a particularly haunting piece known as *Vanity* or *The Conceited Woman* (17C), depicting a young girl looking at her reflection in a mirror and seeing Death.

In the adjacent **Cappella del Crocifisso** (Chapel of the Crucifix), the *Grieving Virgin* and *John the Baptist* are by Alessandro Vittoria.

In the right arm of the transept, the **stained glass** (**14**) evidences intense colour. The throne from which the doge watched the ceremonies in the basilica is also in this arm of the transept.

The *Coronation of the Virgin* on the right is by Cima da Conegliano.

The **Cappella di San Domenico** (Chapel of St Dominic), in the right aisle, houses the *Glory of St Dominic* by Piazzetta (1683-1754).

Before the **Cappella della Madonna della Pace** (Chapel of the Madonna of Peace) stands the **Valier monument** (1705-08), the largest of the Doge monuments. The chapel houses a Byzantine icon and works by Leandro Bassano (*left wall*), Aliense (*right wall*) and Palma il Giovane (*vault*).

In front of the Baroque **Cappella del Beato Giacomo Salomoni** is the tombstone of Ludovico Diedo who died in 1466, a fine example of *niello* engraving. Over the next altar sits an early *Polyptych* (**15**) by Giovanni Bellini.

The final monument comprises an urn said to contain the skin of Captain Marcantonio Bragadin, who was flayed alive by the Turks in 1571 after the surrender of Famagusta.

Behind the basilica, along Barbaria delle Tole, stands the **Chiesa dell'Ospedaletto**, whose Sala della Musica is open to the public (*Guided tours every 30min, Thu-Sat, 3.30-6.30pm. €2.* ☎ *041 26 01 974).*

Scuola Grande di San Marco★ (🄴, GTU)

It is possible to visit the library daily (except Sat-Sun and public hols), 8.30am-2pm. Follow the signs for Biblioteca di San Marco at the far end of the first room, turn right, go upstairs and ring the bell. ☎ *041 52 94 323.*

This ancient **Scuola**, founded in 1260, was transferred here from its original seat in Santa Croce in 1438. Destroyed in the fire of 1485, it was reconstructed by Pietro Solaro, known as Lombardo, and his sons Antonio and Tullio, before being completed by Lombardo's arch rival, Mauro Codussi, who was responsible for the crowning section of the façade. In certain respects, the Scuola's fate has reverted to the purpose for which it was founded; at the beginning of the 19C, the building was transformed into a hospital, first for military and now general civic use.

At ground level, the **façade** boasts an effective series of *trompe l'oeil* panels; two bold lions guard the left entrance and, to their right, two groups of figures crowd around St Mark healing and baptising Anianus, a cobbler from Alexandria. At roof level, semicircular pediments and ornate statuary crown the elaborate frontage.

Interior

The **Sala dell'Albergo** now accommodates the medical library and several large pictures: two works by Giovanni Mansueti, one by Palma il Vecchio and one by Jacopo and Domenico Tintoretto. The entrance-door wall is decorated with *The Martyrdom of St Mark* by Vettor Belliniano.

Before leaving the room, note the lion with the closed Gospel, a conceit alluding to whether Venice, at the time, was at war or at peace (*see I FRARI: I Frari).*

The **Sala Capitolare**, also known as the Sala San Marco, has a blue and gold ceiling bearing the symbols of the Scuole. The lion in the centre holds an open Gospel. The large panel behind the altar is the work of Palma il Giovane. Those to each side are by Jacopo and Domenico Tintoretto, as is the painting on the opposite wall.

The difference in temperature between the two rooms is particularly noticeable: in addition to the antique medical instruments, there are also some valuable 16C texts on display in the Sala Capitolare, which have to be kept at a certain temperature. Some of these texts were illustrated by Titian.

▶ *Follow Calle Larga Gallina to Campo Santa Maria Nova, from where the rear of the Church of Santa Maria dei Miracoli may be contemplated.*

Walking Tour

Santa Maria dei Miracoli★ (🄰, FU)

⊙*Open Mon-Sat, 10am-5pm.* ⊙*Closed 1 Jan, Easter, 15 Aug, 25 Dec.* €2.50. ☎ *041 27 50 462; www.chorusvenezia.org*

This exquisite Renaissance church, positioned on the edge of a canal overlooking the small Campo dei Miracoli, recalls the distinctive nature of 14C Tuscan design both in terms of its crisply carved architectural ornament and its marble detailing. The church is the work of Lom-

Gwen Cannon/MICHELIN

A Renaissance jewel – Santa Maria dei Miracoli

bardo (👆 see above), erected to house a miracle-working image of the Madonna by Nicolò di Pietro (1409). In 1489, it was dedicated to the *Immacolata* (the Virgin), the doctrine of the Immaculate Conception having been proclaimed 12 years before this. The church, decorated with carefully selected coloured marble and porphyry panels, is often used for weddings.

The **interior**, especially the barrel vault, resembles a casket. Prophets and patriarchs are depicted in the 50 compartments of the coffered ceiling (👁 *best appreciated with the mirror provided for this purpose*). A flight of steps provides access to the elevated tribune, framed by a balustrade and ornamented with statues by Tullio Lombardo. The painting by Nicolò di Pietro stands at the main altar.

▶ *Cross the bridge into Campiello Santa Maria Nova, pass before San Cancian and proceed straight on. Take Calle del Manganer in Campiello Cason, which leads to the back of the Church of Santi Apostoli.*

Campo Santi Apostoli – 👆 See RIALTO.

▶ *Behind the church, take Rio Terà dei Santi Apostoli and carry straight on.*

The walk to the vast Campo dei Gesuiti will reveal secluded corners of Venice that are typical of the Cannaregio *sestiere*.

Gesuiti★ (4, FT)

The Jesuit church stands in a peaceful square. It is all the more striking for its white marble Baroque façade, decorated with numerous statues, which include one of the *Virgin*, to which it is dedicated, over the pediment. The present building was erected between 1715 and 1729 on the site of the ancient Church of Santa Maria dei Crociferi (1150).

Upon entering, the sumptuous effect is enhanced by the white and gold stucco of the ceiling, the two central sections of which are by Francesco Fontebasso. Over the first altar on the left sits *The Martyrdom of St Lawrence* by Titian; in the left transept is the *Assumption of the Virgin* by Tintoretto. In the sacristy is a cycle of paintings by Palma il Giovane which, among other things, narrates stories from the Bible (and of the True Cross. Returning down the right aisle, the sculpture of *San Barnaba* in the penultimate chapel is by Morlaiter.

Oratorio dei Crociferi★ (4, FT)

🕐 *Open Jul-Aug, Fri-Sat, 3.30-6.30pm; Apr-Jun and Sept-Oct, Fri-Sat 3-6pm.* 🎫 €2. ☎ 041 53 22 920.

Grouped around Campo dei Gesuiti in 1150 were the church, monastery and hospice run by the Crutched Friars *(Fratres Cruciferi)*, an Order of mendicant friars that was eventually suppressed in 1656. The hospital also served as a refuge for those who had fought in the Crusades. In 1414, it was transformed into a hospice for 12 destitute old ladies.

Much of its decoration, focused on the history of the Crutched Friars, was undertaken between 1583 and 1592 by Palma il Giovane. Included in the painting on the end wall is **Doge Renier Zen**, a principal benefactor of the hospital of Santa Maria dei Crociferi.

On either side of the altar, two paintings depict the foundation of the Order. The three canvases on the left wall illustrate scenes from the life of **Pasquale Cicogna**, Procurator of St Mark's and Doge. Above the doors are represented *The Flagellation* and *The Dead Christ*. In homage to the Virgin, to whom the chapel is dedicated, the ceiling has been decorated with the *Assumption*.

▶ *Continue towards the lagoon.*

Fondamenta Nuove (4, 5, FHT)

Visitors will quickly get to know this long jetty because it is from here that the water-buses (vaporettos) depart for the islands of San Michele, Murano, Burano and Torcello. The Fondamenta Nuove, which runs alongside the lagoon, was constructed at the end of the 16C. A thoroughfare by obligation rather than by design, the *fondamenta* offers some respite in the form of bars and news-stands for people waiting for the vaporettos.

The fact that this corner of Venice provides the only means of conveyance to the outlying islands of the lagoon should not detract from the area's own artistic value, for it is here that Venice's main theatre is to be found, the **Teatro Fondamenta Nuove**, near the Sacca della Misericordia.

▶ *Take the vaporetto for the island of San Michele.*

San Michele in Isola (5, HS)

Venetians and many famous visitors have chosen to be buried here.

The great white church was designed by Codussi, the first Renaissance church in Venice. The façade includes a fine doorway, topped with a pediment and a statue of the *Madonna.* Two arched windows frame the central bay with its rose window. Note the shells in the lateral niches and how the radiating ribs disappear into the shell. The interior extends down to a full set of choir stalls, presided over by *St Jerome* carved by the Flemish artist, Juste Le Court. The whole is enclosed beneath a sumptuous coffered ceiling. The sacristy ceiling, however, is later in date, painted by Romualdo Mauro. The **Emiliani Chapel**, on the left flank, is decorated by Guglielmo de' Grigi, known as "il Bergamasco" (the man from Bergamo).

Cemetery (5, GHS)

Ask for a map at the entrance. ⏱*Open Apr-Sept, daily 7.30am-6pm; Oct-Mar, daily 7.30am-4pm; 1 Jan, Easter, 25 Dec 7.30am-noon.*

Here lie **Ezra Pound** (1885-1972), **Igor Stravinsky** (1882-1971), **Sergei Pavlovich Diaghilev** (1872-1929) and **Josif Brodskij** (1940-96), a Russian poet and Nobel Prize winner (1987), who drew on Venice for his work entitled *Fundamentals for the Incurable*:

Condemned for his anti-American propaganda, **Ezra Pound**, the author of the *Cantos*, was first interned in a concentration camp and then in an asylum, before spending his last years in Italy. He is buried in the Evangelical section to the left on entering. **Igor Stravinsky**, the Russian composer who took American citizenship and is remembered for the *Rite of Spring,* along with his associate **Sergei Diaghilev**, the émigré founder of the Russian Ballet, are buried in the Greek section, at the end. Also in San Michele Cemetery lie the musician Luigi Nono (1924-90) and the great Goldoni actor **Cesco Baseggio** (1897-1971).

Ch. Boisvieux

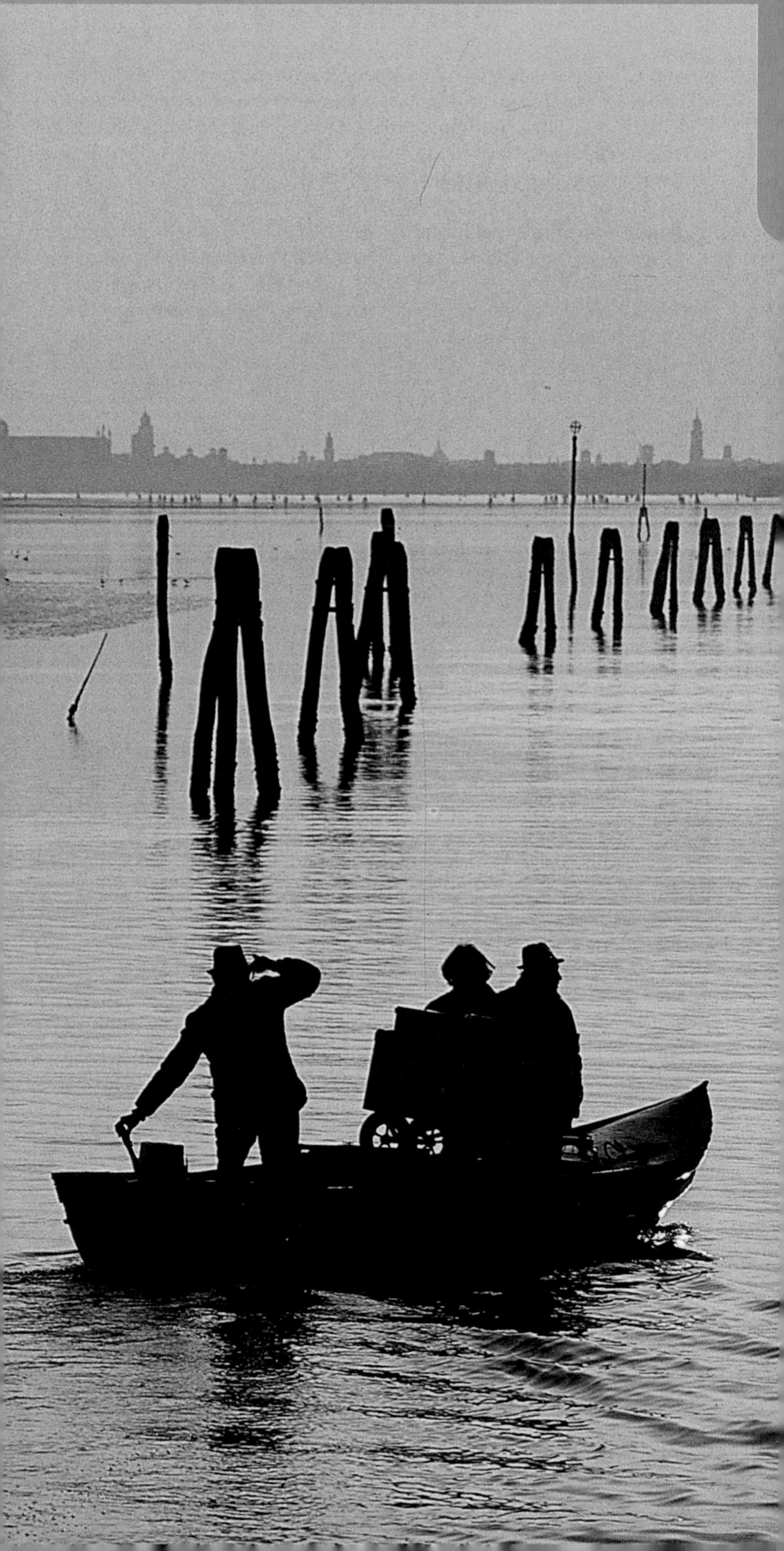

BURANO★★

Burano is the most colourful of the lagoon islands. At the doors and windows of the houses, painted in the brightest colours of the rainbow, women work on their lace pillows while the men see to their fishing nets and boats. Visitors will be hailed with friendly "invitations" from the locals selling *passementerie* (articles bordered in lace) displayed by the "lace-houses".

▶ **Orient Yourself:** One of the lagoon islands, Burano lies about 5mi northeast of Venice, just south of the island of Torcello. It's accessible by vaporetto from Fondamento Nuove (see *SAN ZANIPÒLO* and "Getting there" box, below).

Don't Miss: Demonstrations by the lacemakers at the lacemakers museum.

Organizing Your Time: Allow a couple of hours.

Also See: Neighbouring sights: SAN FRANCESCO del DESERTO; TORCELLO.

A Bit of History

Venice has been known for lacemaking since the 16C. The practice was first established in the palaces as a domestic activity, to be supervised by the noble ladies, before spreading to the hospitals and women's institutions, where residents were obliged to take up the occupation.

🙂 Getting there 🙂

It takes about 45min to get from Fondamenta Nuove (line 12) to Burano, the most colourful of the islands. The last stretch of the journey is along the Mazzorbo Canal, which separates Burano from the island of Mazzorbo. The two islands are linked by a wooden bridge.

The most colourful of the lagoon islands

R. Mattes/MICHELIN

Traditional production depended on the combined use of the needle and bobbin, and proliferated until the second half of the 17C, when demand was threatened by competition from France, where Colbert had instituted an industry employing Venetian lacemakers. At last, in the 18C, the Venetian authorities were forced to make some countermoves to halt the continued exodus of lacemakers; certain manufacturers such as **Raniere e Gabrieli** were granted preferential privileges and traditional methods were compromised, allowing for a simpler, bobbin-only technique to be used. Between the 18C and 19C, however, demand dwindled until eventually the production of lace for clothing was discontinued.

By the second decade of the 19C there were two lace factories, one in Venice and one on Burano, and needlepoint continued as a private, domestic pastime. To safeguard designs and practices, a school was set up in 1872 and charged with the organisation and education of the lacemakers, and their production.

▷ *From the vaporetto landing, follow Via Galuppi into the square dominated by a statue of the renowned musician from Burano, Baldassarre Galuppi.*

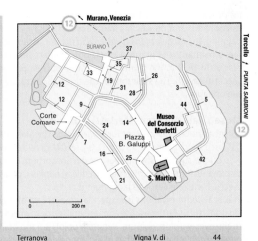

Traditional crafts in Burano

"Il Buranello"

Baldassarre Galuppi (1706-85) acted as choirmaster at the Ospedale dei Mendicanti and the music master for St Mark's Chapel. Besides his contribution to the religious choral tradition, he is associated with the development of comic opera, having composed music to accompany 20 libretti by Goldoni, including *Il Filosofo di Campagna*. Instrumentally, Galuppi sonatas for the harpsichord have recently surged in popularity because of his hitherto unorthodox tempi and rhythm, notably in the faster movements.

Sights

San Martino

Piazza Baldassarre Galuppi is somewhat overshadowed by the austere façade of the 16C Church of Saint Martin and its 18C campanile, built by Andrea Tirali, which leans 1.85m/6ft 1in.

Inside is a *Crucifixion* by **Tiepolo** *(left aisle)* and, on the left of the presbytery, a great sarcophagus around which a miracle is said to have happened. It is explained in a painting, the *Miracle of the Children and the Urn,* attributed to **Alessandro Zanchi**. The inhabitants of Burano also attribute the fact that they were spared from the plague in 1630 to the divine intervention of their patrons (the island of Torcello was also saved). The skeletons of the three saints today lie in the altar below the sarcophagus.

Museo del Consorzio Merletti di Burano

○*Open Apr-Oct, daily except Tue, 10am-5pm; Nov-Mar, daily except Tue, 10am-4pm.* ○*Closed 1 Jan, 1 May and 25 Dec.* ◉€4. ☎ *041 73 00 34; www.museiciviveneziani.it*
Also off the square is the Museum of the Consortium of Burano Lacemakers, which displays its important collection of collars, napkins, parasols, bedspreads, centrepieces, handkerchiefs and lace edgings.
Practical demonstrations by expert lacemakers are also given and the procedures illustrated include the way designs are drafted onto green paper – the most relaxing to the eye; warping; guipure; Venetian point; Burano point; scalloping – known as *punto in aria* meaning stitches of air; unhooking and pressing.

CHIOGGIA

Although there is a Venetian quality about this fishing port, with its double-arched windows and other architectural detail, the atmosphere is different. The traffic—foot, sea and even car—is constant. There's a frenetic urgency with which all local matters of marine and fishing business are dealt with in this working-class town.

▶ **Orient Yourself:** Strictly speaking, Chioggia is not one of the lagoon islands, as it rests on two parallel islands, linked to terra firma by a long bridge. It lies about 12mi south of Venice (as the crow flies), along the Adriatic Sea, and just north of the Brenta Valley.

○ **Organizing Your Time:** For a leisurely walk around Chioggia allow a couple of hours.

♨ **Also See:** BRENTA VALLEY.

A Bit of History

One of the channels of the Brenta Delta was, in Antiquity, called *Fossa Clodia*, from which **Clodia**, Chioggia's former name, derives. In the 1C BC the Romans transformed it into a commercial harbour. The problems began in the 9C, following destruction from Charlemagne's son Pepin. Between the 11C and 12C, the saltpans constituted a major source of income for Chioggia. It then succumbed to further devastation between 1378 and 1381, when it became the field of battle between the rival factions Genoa and Venice. The Serenissima was victorious, but Chioggia was annihilated. Rebuilding began and continued over the ensuing century. Venice intended that Chioggia should be reinforced as a defence post for the lagoon.

The town of Chioggia grew up as close to the sea as possible, configured from these early times around Corso del Popolo and the Canale della Vena. Economic development was then halted: when the Brenta was diverted, the harbour gradually silted up, excluding large vessels. The canal that was dug separating the islet from the mainland served to consolidate defences. From the 16C fishing began to supersede the saltpans as the main industry. In the 19C Chioggia's isolation was in part breached by the building of the bridge carrying the Romea road.

Sights

Corso del Popolo

The main street, the *corso* runs parallel to the Canale della Vena – the Fossa Clodia of Ancient times – rendered more colourful and lively by its fish market, to end in Piazzetta Vigo. The column bearing a winged lion marks the end of the Fossa Clodia. To cross the canal, walk over the stone bridge, the Ponte Vigo, built in 1685.

The *corso* is dotted with the Duomo and several of the Chioggia churches; among them the Church of **San Andrea**, with its 11C Romanesque campanile rising from a square base. **San Giacomo** was rebuilt in the 18C; **San Francesco delle Muneghette** was founded in the 15C but rebuilt in the 18C.

😊 Getting there 😊

Visitors doing a tour of the neighbouring area, perhaps after a visit to the Brenta villas, will find it easy to get to Chioggia by taking the SS 309, which has beautiful views over the Venetian Lagoon.

Alternatively, a coach service operates every 30min from Piazzale Roma to Chioggia-Sottomarina. Average journey time: 1hr. For further information, contact the **Ufficio Informazioni di Sottomarina** (Information Office), Lungomare Adriatico ☎ 041 40 10 68.

Duomo

The island's principal church, dedicated to Santa Maria Assunta, was founded in the 11C. It was razed to the ground by fire, and was rebuilt in 1633 by Baldassare Longhena. It is still shadowed by its 14C square bell-tower, although originally the church would have been oriented on a different axis.

Isola di San Domenico

Extending at the far end of Chioggia, this promontory is reached by following Calle di San Croce, beyond Ponte Vigo. The church here houses a painting of *Saint Paul* by Carpaccio and has a 13C campanile.

IL LIDO ☼☼

The Lido is Venice's favourite seaside resort. A sophisticated and now slightly decadent place, it is tainted by the legacy of Luchino Visconti's *Death in Venice*, which was filmed at the Hotel des Bains, and haunted by the disconcerting yet majestic Hotel Excelsior, so reminiscent in style and sheer boldness of Ludwig of Bavaria's castle in Neuschwanstein. The Lido also plays host to the Venice International Film Festival every September, when film directors, actors and critics meet, accompanied by the inevitable entourage of the international jet set, as well as crowds of curious onlookers.

▶ **Orient Yourself:** Extending roughly north-south to the east of Venice, the Lido resembles a long, thin leg of land (7.5mi long and mostly .5mi wide), fronting the Adriatic Sea. The sandy stretch serves as a barrier island for the Venetian lagoon and a recreational outlet for Venetian residents.

◉ **Don't Miss:** Other than the former Jewish cemetery, there are few sights for tourists here.

🕐 **Organizing Your Time:** Spend at least 2hrs soaking in the sights and sounds.

Kids Especially for Kids: Biking around the island: the terrain is pretty flat, and rentals are available.

> ☺ **Getting there** ☺
>
> It is easy to get to the Lido: hop onto vaporetto line **1**, **82** or **N** from Piazza San Marco and half an hour later you're there. You will arrive at Santa Maria Elisabetta.

Venice International Film Festival

The first one of its kind, the festival was inaugurated in 1932 at the Hotel Excelsior on the initiative of Conte Volpi di Misurata and Luciano De Feo, Secretary General of the International Institute of Cinematographic Art. At the time of its inception, the **Festival of International Cinematographic Art** was more of an exhibition of the art of cinematography than a review, organised to complement the Biennale. Although comedy films were to be excluded, this censorship was not enforced, at least not initially. The festival trophies awarded consist of a sculpted image of the Golden Lion. Films *Forbidden Games* by René Clément (1952), *Hamlet* with Laurence Olivier (1948) and *Vaghe Stelle dell'Orsa* by Luchino Visconti (1965) are a few of the prize winners.

Sights

Gran Viale Santa Maria Elisabetta and the Beach

Gran Viale is the Lido's main thoroughfare; from the vaporetto stop, it stretches to the Piazzale Bucintoro (*accessible by bus*), which leads to Lungomare Guglielmo Marconi. This area is home to some of the Lido's best hotels, with their colourful

The Lido beach

beach huts along the seafront. The Casino (o—☞ *may be closed)* and the headquarters of the Cinema Festival are also located here.

Jewish Cemetery

For information, call ☎ *041 71 53 59; www.museoebraico.it*
At the north end of the island, the old Jewish Cemetery, which dates from 1389, can be seen at San Nicolò.

MURANO★★

From the water, Murano appears to be walled-in by the long line of furnaces. As visitors step off the vaporetto, they are urged to visit the glassworks, and even if the commercial aspect of the "invitation" can be irritating, it is worth watching the various stages and processes. Murano is also an island of art. It is a good idea not to get too distracted by the tantalising glass shops, before exploring the island's two fine churches.

▶ **Orient Yourself:** This island, larger than Burano, lies closest to Venice, sitting less than a mile to the northeast. It is broken up by several wide canals.
☺ **Don't Miss:** The Museum of Glass and the Church of Santa Maria e San Donato, especially its mosaic floor.
🕓 **Organizing Your Time:** Allow about 2hr 30min.
✦ **Also See:** Neighbouring sights: SAN ZANIPÒLO.

A Bit of History

By the end of the 13C, glassmaking was so widespread in Venice that the threat of fire ravaging the city was ever constant. Three centuries later, the fear still had not abated, bearing in mind the countless little fires that frequently broke out as a result of the widespread use of wood and candles. Had these incidents not been contained, it would not have taken much for fire to spread quickly, with disastrous consequences. As a result the Grand Council decided to move the glassworks away from the city to Murano, a move that would also protect the secrets of the glassmaking process.

The most likely theory to explain the origins of glass is rooted in the ancient Orient where potters learned to "make" glass from silicon sand when glazing their ceramics by firing them in a kiln. The process was already in widespread use by the time the books of Job and Proverbs were written, as recorded in the Bible, and commonly practised in Egypt by the 4th millenium BC, as small objects found in datable tombs would imply. The colours blue and green were created by the addition of copper and cobalt oxide. The technique for blowing glass, however, as favoured by the Romans, came later.

Before its arrival in Venice, glass was produced in Greece and Turkey. In 1203, following the occupation of Constantinople, Venice secured the "exclusive" collaboration of immigrant potters in exchange for preferential treatment from the Republic. However, if they refused to return to the city, they were hunted down and killed. The city's supremacy in glassmaking therefore remained uncontested until the end of the 16C.

Even today, modern glass creations from Murano are considered works of art. Within everyone's budget are the *murrine*, which sparkle with colour, often set into costume jewellery, and the distinctive discs of kaleidoscopic patterns.

☺ Getting there ☺

To get to Murano, board vaporetto line **12**, **13**, **41** or **42** at Fondamenta Nuove.

The final effect of this unique glassworking technique is achieved by juxtaposing various coloured rods of glass that have been drawn in length and fused when molten. When the composite rods are then sliced crosswise, the famous discs remain.

Walking Tour

▶ *From the vaporetto stop at Scalo Colonna, follow Fondamenta dei Vetrai.*

San Pietro Martire

Begun in 1363, this brick church was consecrated in 1417. Gravely damaged by fire, it was rebuilt in the Renaissance style before being subjected to further modifications over the ensuing few hundred years. A Renaissance main door is surmounted at the front by a large stained-glass window made of *rui*, small circular sections of Murano glass.

Inside, the nave and aisles are apsed and endowed with **paintings**★ by illustrious artists such as Salviati, Veronese, Tintoretto, Bellini and Palma il Giovane.

▶ *Cross the Vivarini Bartolomeo bridge and bear right to reach the glass museum.*

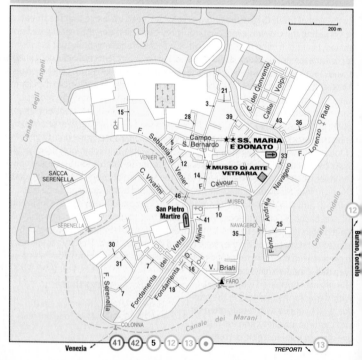

Museo di Arte Vetraria★

Open Apr-Oct, daily except Wed, 10am-6pm; Nov-Mar, daily except Wed, 10am-5pm. Last admission 1hr before closing. Closed 1 Jan, 1 May and 25 Dec. €5.50. ☎ 041 73 95 86; www.museiciviciveneziani.it

A visit to the museum in Palazzo Giustinian appeals to anyone wanting to understand the evolution of glassmaking over the centuries. An archaeological section displays embalming tools, cups, utensils and necklaces. On the first floor, the physical processes practised by tradition and modern technology, including coloured glass and *murrine,* are explained with illuminated panels and samples of raw materials. Developments in technique between the 15C and 18C are also defined. The height of artistry attained in the 15C is represented by a wedding cup, traditionally known as the **Barovier Cup**. The museum also houses a collection of modern glass.

▷ *Beyond the museum is the Church of Santa Maria e San Donato.*

Santa Maria e San Donato★★

From the outside, it is the apse that is most memorable: it is more photographed than the façade, which is hidden because it does not face the fondamenta from which the basilica is normally approached. The **apse** is a masterpiece of 12C Veneto-Byzantine art, embellished with all kinds of decorative elements. A double series of blind-arched openings resting on coupled columns seem to ripple around the semicircular bay. The front façade, however, is quite plain.

Founded in the 7C, the original church was dedicated to the Virgin Mary. The incorporation of San Donato dates from the 12C, when his body, together with what remained of the dragon that he had slain, arrived from Cefalonia (the bones of the "dragon" are stored behind the altar). The church was considerably remodelled in the 12C: the mosaic floor was completed in 1141, and extensively restored during the mid-19C.

Inside, five columns with Veneto-Byzantine capitals separate the nave from the aisles; the striking **mosaic floor**★★ recalls that of the Basilica of St Mark. Among the profusion of decorative, symbolic and figurative elements, there is one particularly significant section between the second and third column on the right depicting two cockerels bearing a fox, and represents the defeat of Cunning by Vigilance.

The apse of Santa Maria e San Donato

M Smith/EXPLORER

Above the apse, a 12C mosaic *Virgin in Prayer* stands alone, projected forward by her brilliant gold background. In the left aisle is the wooden panel with *San Donato* attributed to Paolo Veneziano and above the door to the baptistery, a lunette by Lazzaro Bastiani depicting the Virgin and Child with John the Almsgiver (1484).

SAN FRANCESCO DEL DESERTO ★

This little island is ideal for anyone seeking respite from commotion and crowds, particularly in the summer when the islands of the lagoon can get very busy.

▶ **Orient Yourself:** The island is situated just south of Burano.
🕐 **Organizing Your Time:** A complete tour takes about 1hr.
👣 **Also See:** Neighbouring sights: BURANO; TORCELLO.

Monastery

Before St Francis landed on the island on his way back from the Holy Land in 1220, San Francesco del Deserto was known as the *Isola delle due Vigne* (the Island of the Two Vines). Its name was changed when a house for Franciscan novitiates was established on the island in 1224. The term *"deserto"* could be a reference to the island left "deserted" when the monks fled from a malaria epidemic. On four occasions the monastery played host to Bernardino of Siena, who may have paid for the well to be dug to collect water. Set into a wall in the cloisters is a 13C relief of two crossed arms, said to be the arm of Christ and the sleeved arm of St Francis.

Visit
The tour takes in various paintings depicting the saint arriving on the island and the miracle of St Francis ordering the birds to be quiet and not to move during prayers. A panel covers some interesting archaeological remains, including a cistern.

The island's vast **park** overlooks the lagoon and offers a clear view of Burano. It is particularly beautiful here, almost pastoral in feel, which is unusual for the lagoon islands.

> ### 😊 Getting there 😊
>
> The island where St Francis landed is still reached by private boat today, departing from Burano – where the canal meets the lagoon as it laps the water's edge in Piazza Galuppi – not far from the front of San Martino. The cost includes the 10 minute journey to and from the island and waiting time in between; ask the boatman, who will make himself known, about the price. The guided visit lasts about an hour and is undertaken by a monk. Visitors are advised to leave a donation.
>
> Visitors spending a few days in retreat with the monastic community by prior arrangement will be welcomed off the boat. For further information, contact ☎ 041 52 86 863.

SAN LAZZARO DEGLI ARMENI★

This island was especially loved by the Romantic poet Lord Byron, as he found the atmosphere lifted his ascetic spirit in times of melancholy. Today, it is no less evocative to visiting travellers. On arrival by vaporetto, tourists are greeted by charming Armenian monks who chaperone their charges and introduce them to this green, serene island.

▶ **Orient Yourself:** The island is located near the Lido, off the west side.
🕐 **Organizing Your Time:** The tour takes about 1hr.

Monastery

The Armenians and the Mechitar Community

The Armenians are an ancient people whose ancestry has been linked to Noah's Ark, which some believe "ran aground" on Mount Ararat, on the Armenian border. Armenia then extended from the Black Sea to Mesopotamia, where the mountains hide the sources of the River Tigris and River Euphrates. Today the Republic of Armenia is hemmed in between Turkey, Georgia, Azerbaijan and Iran.

The country was conquered on several occasions by the Arabs, Turks, Mongols, Tartars, Ottomans and Persians. During the First World War, its people were persecuted by the Turks, almost to the point of extinction. Subsequent diaspora saw the Armenians flee overseas, particularly to the United States.

From the 14C, the island of San Lazzaro served as a leper colony until the last two leprosy sufferers were transferred to Venice (1600s).

Mechitar was given the island by the Venetian Republic and arrived here in 1717. The church was rebuilt. The pavement was lifted, the arches were made into lancet arches and the vaulted ceiling took the form of a starry sky. The original Romanesque church was built by the Benedictines, who subsequently remodelled it in the Gothic style.

Visit

🔊Guided tours, 3.25-5.25pm. €6. ☎ 041 52 60 104. Cross the simple cloister full of flowering plants, kept neat and tidy, to seek out the historical manuscripts that are a testament not only to the Armenian heritage, but also to the kindly Mechitar monks who

😊 Getting there 😊

It takes about 30min to get to the island of San Lazzaro degli Armeni on vaporetto line 10 from Riva degli Schiavoni (San Zaccaria).

Tours are scheduled to coincide with the vaporetto times – the talk begins on landing and continues through the monastery visit. Should you require more time on the island, catch the vaporetto that leaves at around 2pm and check for the departure time of the second return service.

Mechitar

Mechitar (1676-1749) was born in Turkey. He was ordained into the Catholic Church before settling in Constantinople, where he founded a community of Uniate Armenian monks based on St Benedict's teachings and precepts of monasticism. The monks were forced to flee the city and take refuge in Morea, a Venetian territory. When Morea was lost to the Turks, the Venetian Republic granted the community the island of San Lazzaro. The Mechitarists devote themselves to education and missionary work. The Armenian liturgy differs from that of the Roman Church in that it does not acknowledge the Pope's primacy or infallibility.

Sixth Baron, Lord George Gordon Byron

Lord Byron (1788-1824) was a handsome youth with a colourful personality. After Cambridge, he took his seat in the House of Lords (1809) before traveling to Portugal, Spain, Malta, Greece and the Levant. The experience fired his imagination and he vowed to see Greece freed from Turkish rule. In 1812 *Childe Harold's Pilgrimage* was published, securing his reputation as a Romantic poet. His liaisons with his half-sister and subsequent marriage led to disrepute. Byron left England in 1816 for the last time. While in Venice he became attracted to the monastic life at San Lazzaro, where he found the spiritual quietude he so desired and from which he continually transgressed as his passions flourished across the water. Fascinated with the Armenian community, he set out to learn their language in six months. He collaborated with the monks on an English-Armenian dictionary and would often swim to San Lazzaro from the Palazzo Mocenigo in Venice.

dedicate themselves to preserving the Armenian culture.

Visitors are then shown the refectory where the monks and the seminarists eat their meals in silence while the Scriptures are read out in classical Armenian.

On ascending the stairs, note the fine Sienese terra-cotta relief from 1400 and part of a painting by Palma il Giovane depicting the *Martyrdom of St Catherine*: the central section of this painting is in St Petersburg.

As well as being an important centre of Armenian culture, the monastery also owns a collection of Flemish tapestries; paintings by Armenian artists; Greek, Phoenician and Assyro-Babylonian artefacts – there is even an 10C BC Egyptian mummy.

A highlight of the tour comes with a visit to the archive, a modern circular building containing over 4 000 manuscripts.

Armenian stele

TORCELLO★★

From the landing stage, a walk along the Fondamenta dei Borgognoni and on by the canal allows a full prospect of the unique lagoon landscape to unfold. Hemingway would stay at the Locanda Cipriani and go hunting for ducks. These days Torcello is almost a ghost island, where only the stones can speak of its glorious past.

▶ **Orient Yourself:** This once popu-lous islands lies about 5.5mi to the northeast of Venice.

🕐 **Organizing Your Time:** The tour takes about 1hr 30min.

😊 Getting there 😊

From Fondamenta Nuove, take the same line **(12)** that goes to Burano, which is only minutes away from Torcello.

A Bit of History

Near the **Ponte del Diavolo** stands the religious complex of Torcello. It is incredible to think that in ancient times there were thousands of people living here and the glorious history of Venice was just beginning.

During the period of barbarian invasions, the Lombards chased out the Byzantines (6C-8C) and established themselves in Aquilea, Padua, Altinum and Oderzo. The bishop and the inhabitants of Altinum moved to Torcello where, in 639, the church and probably the fortifications were built; it is the *torri* (towers) of such fortifications that gave rise to the name of the island. They were not the first inhabitants, however, as the Romans had already discovered the island and records show continuous fish-ing and glassmaking activities throughout the 5C and 6C.

Torcello's decline started around the 10C and mirrors the pace of the glorious ascent of Venice. When malaria infested the marshes, Torcello was abandoned by its inhabitants, who fled to Venice and Murano. Now there are fewer than a hundred inhabitants.

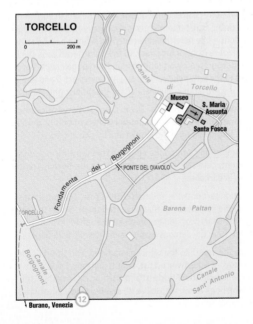

227

Sights

Basilica di Santa Maria Assunta

&Open Mar-Oct, 10.30am-5.30pm; rest of the year 10am-5pm. Last admission 30min before closing. €3 (€5 combined ticket with Museo or Campanile; €8 combined ticket with Museo and Campanile). ☎ 041 73 01 19.

As recorded by the ancient **inscription** on the left of the altar, the cathedral dedicated to the Assumption was erected in 639, during the reign of Heraclius, Emperor of Byzantium, at the wishes of Isaac, the Exarch of Ravenna and representative of the Eastern emperor. In the 9C and 11C, it underwent further modification. Little remains of the 7C baptistry other than fragments of the brick façade and its many pilasters. The 14C portico supported by the columns and pilasters also serves as a link to Santa Fosca.

The interior is divided into nave and aisles by columns. In contrast to the simplicity of structure, the decoration is opulent. The pavement is 11C. The choir, enclosed by Corinthian columns, is separated from the nave by a 15C iconostasis set with 11C Byzantine painted panels depicting the Madonna and Child flanked by the Twelve Apostles with, above, the Crucifixion from the same date. Between the columns nestle delicate Byzantine marble *plutei* carved with semi-symmetrical lions and peacocks. The Roman sarcophagus near the high altar contains the relics of St Heliodorus, the first Bishop of Altinum.

But most striking for their brilliance and quality are the **ancient mosaics**★★ representing the Virgin and Christ. In accordance with Byzantine iconography, the Virgin is portrayed descending from Heaven.

Between the windows are aligned the *Apostles* (12C), and below the window St Heliodorusis. The mosaics of the intersecting vault harbour *Four Angels bearing the Mystic Lamb*, of a type found at Ravenna. The floral mosaic is populated with birds

The Last Judgement

The Last Judgement is the main subject of the mosaics (13C-14C) at the back of the church. The main elements of the scene, drawn from the Apocalypse, unfold from top to bottom and are divided into two sections: the Judgement below and the Death and Resurrection of Christ above. From the Crucifixion there follows the Descent into Limbo: Christ tramples over many keys and a devil reduced to miniature proportions while determinedly clutching Adam's hand. Behind is Eve, her hands covered for reasons of propriety; to the right stands John the Baptist, who may easily be recognised by his long hair and camel-hair shirt. Beyond rank the Prophets, and to the left, the two figures with haloes are David and Solomon. At the far edges, the Archangels Michael (left) and Gabriel (right) stand guard.

Dominating the central section is the *Deisis*: Christ in glory enclosed within a mandorla, the aura of His divinity, surrounded by the symbols of the Passion. He is flanked by the Virgin and John the Baptist and by two angels.

Arranged symmetrically around the edge are the Apostles, include St Peter (left) and St Paul (right; here St Paul is included among the Twelve Apostles, on a par therefore with St Barnabas).

The lower section recounts the Triumph of the Cross. The angels' trumpets recall the dead from the sea monsters that devoured them. Below the souls are being weighed by St Michael, working to safeguard the salvation of those who deserve to be protected from the demons that burden the scale with bags of sins.

To the left are the saved; to the right the damned. The seven devils portray the seven deadly sins – Pride, Avarice, Lust, Wrath, Gluttony, Envy, Sloth. The main figure is Lucifer, who holds the Antichrist and is sitting on Leviathan, the sea monster described in the Book of Job whose breath sets burning coals ablaze.

Santa Fosca

and animals which postdate those at San Vitale in Ravenna (7C), for these are also by artists from Ravenna, who came here while the church was being built.

Campanile
Guided tour only. €2 (€5.50 combined ticket with the basilica and museum). For further information, call ☎ 041 27 02 464.
At the rear of the basilica stands the old bell-tower (12C). After many years it is once again possible to reach the top. The climb is easy and the **view**★★ over the lagoon more than compensates for the effort.

Santa Fosca
The small church, in the form of a Greek cross, was built between the 11C and 12C. Its octagonal exterior is encircled by open arcading with columns capped by Veneto-Byzantine capitals.
The interior, imbued with solemn silence, is enclosed below a round wooden roof.

Museo di Torcello
Open Mar-Oct, daily except Mon, 10.30am-5pm; Nov-Mar, daily except Mon, 10am-4.30pm. Closed public hols and 21 Nov. €3 (€5.50 combined ticket with the basilica or campanile; €8 combined ticket with the basilica and the campanile). ☎ 041 26 90 329; www.provincia.venezia.it/sbmp
Artifacts associated with the history of Torcello are displayed on two floors. Interesting pieces, some dating to the 9C, include capitals, pateras, tablets, a mid-15C wooden *Pietà* of the Venetian School, paintings from the Church of St Anthony of Torcello, a work from the studio of Veronese, books and documents which recount parts of the island's history, pages from the *Mariegola* and fragments of Venetian ceramics.

Villa Pisani

A. Février(PHOTONONSTOP)

VILLAS OF THE BRENTA★★

The Brenta Valley is a bucolic stretch of land where the doges elected to have their country houses. Some Venetian families still follow this tradition today. Reflected in the quiet waters of the river, from Padua to the lagoon, these patrician villas possess that air of an exclusive country retreat with literary connotations: an impression that remains true whichever way the visitor might arrive, be it by water, horse, bicycle or car.

▶ **Orient Yourself:** The Brenta River skirts the city of Padua and arcs south. The villas lie along the Naviglio Brenta section, which empties into the Adriatic Sea at Porto di Brondolo near Fusina, to the south of Chioogia.

🅿 **Parking:** Generally available at or near the villas.

☺ **Don't Miss:** Villa Pisani's Salone delle Feste.

🕐 **Organizing Your Time:** Allow 2 days for the driving itinerary and tour of the villas.

A Bit of History

A Troubled Past

By 1100 the Paduans and the Venetians were already locked in conflict over who should have control over the Brenta River's course and the hold on Venice's only other means of access to the lagoon in times of siege.

From 1409, with the annexation of Padua, the Republic of Venice was assured definitive control of the River Brenta and thus started to invest in landed property along its banks. During the 1500s, in an effort to limit the threat of damage from flooding, subsidiary canals were built. By the beginning of the 16C, opulent villas, set among extensive gardens, were being designed and built.

In 1840, after a disastrous flood, work was initiated on redirecting the river to flow into the lagoon at Chioggia, but infilling the delta proved so difficult that the water was directed farther down to run straight out to sea, as it does today at Brondolo.

Today, the Brenta Valley, like Venice, survives as if by a pact made between nature and architecture. Many find the area oppressive as heavy swirling mists and flooding exaggerate the cold and humid atmosphere of the place.

The Villas

A villa was intended to provide the landowner with temporary lodgings during his inspection of the running of his farm estate. It would therefore have been erected near the farm, and built on a centralised plan, flanked by barchesse.

Before long, the villa's function evolved into that of a country home to which the landed gentry could retreat on the pre-

☺ Getting there ☺

The River Brenta links Padua to Venice by water, but access from either direction is easiest by road.

For those coming from the west along the A 4, it is advisable to exit at Padova Est. Follow the Noventana road and directions for Stra (SS 11). From Venice-Mestre, follow the signs for Riviera del Brenta and Malcontenta (SS 11).

Barchesse

Up until the end of the 17C, the *barchesse* (from *barca* meaning boat) were the outbuildings of the villas used for storing grain and "garaging" the boats, because it was prohibited to leave them moored along the canal.

Frequently, throughout the 17C, the *barchesse* doubled up as sleeping quarters for use by the extra house guests invited to the great parties at the villas, which might go on for days.

Allegorical Painting in the Brenta Villas

Frequent recourse to allegorical subject matter came in the 17C and 18C from the desire to assert the Venetian taste in "style": one that was inspired by a joie de vivre, a Humanist interest in Classical literature and a predilection for ostentation and luxury. The great battles for the dominion of terra firma were now over and Venice was to be celebrated as a proud combatant and conqueror. Now was the time to relish past glories and to take up the good life.

text of supervising their tenanted farm. By the 18C, country houses were all the rage among the Venetian nobility, who basked in leisure and luxury while inadvertently singing Venice's swansong. The most popular holiday periods were the months of June, July, October and November, when the balmy evenings might be spent listening to a musical recital or watching a group of players.

Few of the many villas can be attributed to specific architects; however, given their artistic quality, it is generally acknowledged that they must have been designed to satisfy highly sophisticated and aesthetically discerning patrons.

Entertainment along the Brenta

Nobles or peasants, the Venetians shared the same taste for **farce**. Along the riverbanks, where people idled away the time with a good book, puppeteers found an ideal location in which to set up their theatres and animate their characters: Brighella, Harlequin, Columbine and Pantaloon. In the villa gardens, comic plays were staged. The numerous **sagre** (feast days) were always an excuse for throwing a party, when guests could sing and dance the night away in the magnificent villa ballrooms.

Boat Tour

Il Burchiello

♿ (if accompanied). Those wishing to spend a day as an 18C traveller can choose to travel on board the Burchiello. Although the present-day craft is modern, it follows the same course that it did two centuries ago. It operates between Mar and Oct, leaving Padua (Piazzale Boschetti) at 8.15am on Wed, Fri and Sun mornings and arriving in Venice (Piazza San Marco) in the late afternoon, after stopping at Villa Pisani, Barchessa di Villa Valmarana and Villa Foscari "La Malcontenta." Departures from Venice (Pontile della Pietà) at 9am on Tue, Thu and Sat. The programme is the same but in reverse order, arriving in Padua in the late afternoon. €62 (€51 Jul-Aug). For further information, contact Il Burchiello di Sita Spa ☎ 049 82 06 910; www.ilburchiello.it

The 18C traveller could choose to journey from Venice to Padua by boat or by carriage. The boat was neither comfortable nor quick and fellow passengers would not always have been the most salubrious. The new Burchiello, built in Padua and adapted from the **burchio** that was used in Venice to transport general goods, heralded an improvement in river transport. Passengers were accommodated on benches arranged around tables and protected by a canopy overhead. Further shelter against driving rain, biting winds or blinding sunshine was provided by decorative panels of inlaid wood and attractive drapes. When travelling upstream, the barge was pulled by a yoke of horses. Travelling aboard the Burchiello became a pleasure to be experienced, but the legendary vessel did not survive long: the costly service was suspended when the Republic fell.

Driving Tour

From Padua to Fusina, via Mirano

▸ Take the A4 to the Padova Est Exit. Follow the Noventana road toward Stra (SS 11).

The first villa on the road from Padua is Villa Foscarini at **Stra**, located in the heart of a part of the Veneto actively involved in the shoe industry, indicated by the roadside billboards.

Villa Foscarini

&♿ 🕐*For information call ☎ 049 98 01 091; www.villafoscarini.it*
This villa is named after its most eminent resident, **Marco Foscarini**, who was elected doge in 1762. The pronaos (projecting columned entrance) might suggest an intervention by Palladio; in reality, the design conformed to the artistic taste in vogue at the time, several decades after Palladio's death. The villa is neo-Classical in style, although modifications were made during the 19C. The adjacent *barchessa* is older. The roof is surmounted by four spires reminiscent of the Ponte delle Guglie in Venice (👁*see Il GHETTO*), which make the building seem taller.
In the hall of the *barchessa*, frescoed allegorical scenes are set among suggestive *trompe l'oeil* detailing.

On leaving Villa Foscarini, the main feature in the landscape is the river, along which villas follow one after another, posted with yellow signs, uninterrupted by any modest dwellings.

Villa Pisani★

The villa is signposted before the car park, which is located about 200m/220yd beyond the entrance. 🕐*Open daily except Mon, 9am-7pm (4pm Oct-Mar).* 🕐*Closed 1 Jan, 1 May and 25 Dec.* 🎫*€2.50 (gardens only), €5 (villa and gardens).* ☎ *049 50 20 74.*
The residence of **Alvise Pisani**, elected doge in 1735, comprises a magnificent estate with stables and gardens designed by **Girolamo Frigimelica**, who also submitted plans for the villa. These proved to be too costly and were entrusted to **Francesco Maria Preti**.

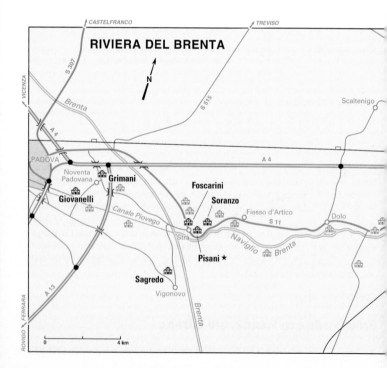

During the 18C, the villa was endowed with sculpture and paintings, but when the Republic fell in 1797 the Pisani family was forced to sell it to Napoleon who, in turn, gave it to his adopted son Eugène Beauharnais, the Viceroy of Italy. Following the Austrian occupation in 1814, Villa Pisani accommodated several other famous figures, including Francesco Giuseppe, Maximilian of Austria, Anna Maria of Savoy, Gustav III of Sweden and Carlos IV of Spain. Soon after the unification of Italy, the villa returned to Italian ownership. It now belongs to the State.

Exterior

On sight, the house appears to be modelled on a French château. The outside wall, enclosing extensive grounds at the rear, accentuates the horizontal design elements of the façade: the central, projecting Palladian-style bay is charged with decoration; the entrance itself is austerely monumental. Four Atlas figures support the loggia, and silhouetted against the sky, statues and pinnacles punctuate the corners of the pediments.

Beyond the entrance opens a gallery supported by columns, from which one has a magnificent view over the still water and the Palladian-style stables, fronted by their imposing entrance and figures of Zephyr and Flora, sculpted by **Giovanni Bonazza** and his son Tomaso.

Interior

Villa Pisani has 114 rooms in honour of Alvise Pisani, the 114th Doge of Venice. This most famous member of the Pisani family lived here from June to October to keep an eye on the grain harvest and the wine production.

Climb the stairs off to the left of the entrance, ornamented with wooden statues attributed to Andrea Brustolon, up to the **Sala del Trionfo delle Arti** (The Triumphs of the Arts), named after the ceiling decoration executed by Giovan Battista Crosato. The landscapes depicted on the walls are attributed to, among others, Francesco Zuccarelli and Andrea Celesti.

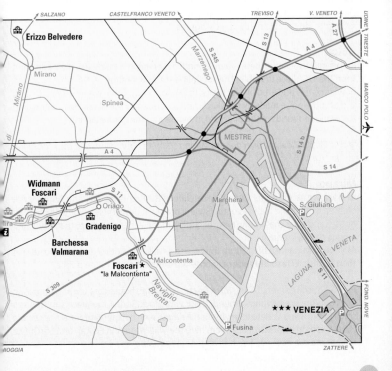

In the next room, dedicated to Bacchus and frescoed by Jacopo Guarana (1770), there is an implausible portrayal of an elephant, painted without first-hand knowledge *(on the wall through which you have come)*; watch for the *casone*, a typical peasant dwelling in the Brenta region *(in a panel opposite the windows)*.

After the room where Hitler and Mussolini met in 1943 comes the Beauharnais suite, furnished with a small bed and the chapel housing an altar by Sansovino, which was brought here by Napoleon when he ordered the Church of San Gimignano in St Mark's in Venice to be demolished.

The most interesting room is undoubtedly the **Salone delle Feste** or "Party Room", in which the most sumptuous balls imaginable were held. The orchestra would play in the long minstrels' gallery running along the walls of this vast room. The striking fresco was the last to be painted by Tiepolo in Italy. Look for Tiepolo's "signature", the parrot *(in the right corner)*.

The Grounds

Designed by Frigimelica, the great garden extends around a long pond which, although well integrated into the villa's landscape, is a modern addition. It was, in fact, dug in 1911 by the University of Padua to carry out studies on tidal forces. On the west side is the Belvedere folly, its steps seeming to wrap around two columns. The east side is the more animated part of the park: the Café-Haus, built on a mound and surrounded by a ditch, was designed as a summerhouse for relaxation. Beyond, towards the exit, is a gazebo, from which a fine view opens onto the whole villa. Note the nearby maze, a common feature in French and Italian Renaissance gardens that rarely survives.

▶ *Proceed eastward along SS 11.*

Villa Soranzo

This villa is particularly famous for the façade frescoes painted by Benedetto Caliari, brother of Paolo, who was better known as Veronese. A fine example of *trompe l'oeil*, these depict a balustrade with monochrome characters peeping out from the niches among the inevitable mythological figures.

Dolo

In this nearby village, there is a building that served as a boatyard: the basin filled from the 17C sluice is visible. The 16C mill is still in operation on the river, although nowadays it is powered by electricity. In Goldoni's day, Dolo was renowned far and wide for the noise made by the sluice, and described by the playwright, along with the working sounds of the boatyard, the mills and the grain markets.

▶ *At Mira, follow the directions to Mirano (7km/4mi from Mira) and the road along the canal.*

Mirano

Also known as *Il Musone*, Mirano is a satellite of the Brenta Riviera. Although it is not blessed with all the features of the Riviera proper, it nevertheless has mills, aligned houses and villas that imply its participation in the Venetian culture that flourished alongside the Brenta.

Anyone wishing for a break from the car and a walk in beautiful grounds should visit the 17C **Villa Erizzo Belvedere**, whose **gardens** are open to the public.

In a delightful corner of Mira, **Mira Porte**, where the houses are terraced into long lines and the Brenta loops around, there was a lock. Today, the place survives as a small but thriving Veneto town, its piazza ringed with bars serving *crostini al baccalà* (salted cod on toasted bread). From here the Villa Widmann Foscari and Barchessa Valmarana can easily be reached on foot *(about 2km/1mi)*.

Villa Widmann Foscari

&ⓒ*Open May-Sept, 10am-6pm; Apr and Oct 10am-5pm, rest of the year Sat, Sun and public hols 10am-5pm.* ⓒ*Closed Mon, 1 Jan, 25 Dec.* ⊛€5. *For information on admission times, call* ☎ *041 52 98 716.*

The villa where Goldoni, D'Annunzio, Malipiero and Stravinsky all stayed is an 18C building. In its magnificent Rococo interior, the main attraction is the ballroom, complete with minstrels' gallery, decked, as is usual, with paintings depicting the apotheosis of the owner's family complemented with mythological subjects, all by Giuseppe Angeli.

Villa Valmarana

&ⓒ*Open Mar-Oct daily 10am-6pm; rest of the year, groups only by reservations.* ⊛€6. ☎ *041 42 66 387; www.villavalmarana.net*

The 18C Villa Valmarana would, at one time, have been flanked by two *barchesse*. The main villa was demolished by the Valmarana family in the 19C to avoid paying a wealth tax on luxury goods. The *barchessa* on the left was divided between six families who modified the original architectural layout of the building. Yet in every way, this mere outbuilding is truly monumental. Surrounded by an Italianate rose garden, it is fronted with a fine portico of double Doric columns. In the centre, a giant order of pilasters rises to the cornice.

As was the norm, the owner's family are glorified in the central **salone** (Reception Room) ceiling. The fresco, painted in the second half of the 17C, is attributed to Michelangelo Schiavoni, who is also known as Il Chioggotto, a follower of Tiepolo. The water poured from the urn represents the Brenta, the woman (Ceres) carrying grain on her shoulders symbolises Agriculture which, with Viticulture, constituted the principal industries of the area. The lion is poorly drawn, implying that the artist based his drawing on a traveller's written description. Infill panels are painted with *trompe l'oeil* and above the doors are curious characters looking over the balconies.

Here the main reception room is situated between the **Sala delle Arti** (Room of the Arts), painted with allegories of Sculpture, Painting, Music and Literature, and the **Sala dei Capricci**, named after the oval *capriccio* panels painted with a gentle landscape, in purple monochrome.

Barchessa Valmarana

FORMENTON

Oriago

Canto V of Dante's *Purgatory* tells the story of Jacopo del Cassero's death in Oriago. In Dante's time, the area was marshy and unhealthy. Before the Republic of Venice was established at the beginning of the 15C, Oriago was situated at the edge of the territory of Padua, Treviso and Venice. As a testament to a troubled past, one of the four columns which, in 1375 signalled the "end" of Oriago, is still here, leaning up against the corner of one of the houses along the river: the column is striking for its unusual form and ancient appearance.

▶ *On the other side of the river, crossed by means of the swing bridge, are the 18C Mocenigo Villa and the Villa Gradenigo.*

Villa Gradenigo

🕐*Open by appointment only. Call for information and reservations* ☏ *049 876 0233.*
One of the oldest villas on the Brenta, Villa Gradenigo has a square floor plan which was typical of the 16C. The frescoes decorating the garden front, despite their poor condition, are still discernible as the work of Benedetto Caliari, brother of Paolo, who was known as Il Veronese.

Better preserved although not perfect are the frescoes inside. In the 19C the villa was divided into apartments, and several of the frescoes were irretrievably damaged. At one point in the early 20C, the *palazzo* even served as a laundry, the steam ironically being the coup de grâce for the paintings. Today the villa is privately owned.

In the reception room on the ground floor, which served as a *portego* – half house, half garden – are murals by Benedetto Caliari's. These are not frescoes as such, for the practice of applying pigment to dry plaster is known as painting "a secco". This technique, despite giving brighter colours, is less durable than if the pigment is set into wet plaster *"affresco"*. The room is further decorated with friezes of festooned flowers and fruit and painted architectural elements which were first introduced into Venetian villa decoration by Veronese.

▶ *Continue along SS 11 at the junction, then turn right, off the Venice road, in the direction of Malcontenta.*

La Malcontenta★

🕐*Open Apr-Oct, Tue and Sat 9am-noon.* 🕐*Closed Mon, Nov-Apr.* ⊛ *€8 (€7 Tues and Sun).* ⊛*€3.* ☏ *049 87 60 233; www.lamalcontenta.com*
The focal point of the little town of Malcontenta is the elegant **Villa Foscari** (*for information and reservations, contact* ☏ *041 54 70 012*) known as **La Malcontenta**, which overlooks the river at an angle. The name is associated with the controversial excavation of a canal called the *fossa dei malcontenti,* which has lent its name to the area of Malcontenta since 1458.

Since the 16C, the villa has been visited by various illustrious personalities including Henri III, the King of France. Having been used as a military hospital during the First World War, the villa is now back in the hands of its original owners, the Foscari family, who live here during the summer.

The House

When Foscari commissioned **Andrea Palladio** (1508-80) to design the villa, the idea was to build a residence in the style of one from Classical Antiquity: a central square fronted by a temple portico facing the Brenta. This projecting entrance, flanked by Ionic columns, gives the house a formal austerity relieved only in part by rustication.

The main rooms are accommodated on the *piano nobile*, the first floor, raised above ground level to avoid the risk of flood damage but also to provide enough space to contain the kitchens and storage areas.

The south-facing "back" overlooks the widest part of the garden: it is less formal than the main front, relieved with decorative touches such as the broken pediment and varied window heights. The arched six-part "thermal" window was a feature borrowed from Roman baths.

It is the precise calculation of geometrical harmonies that is unique to the Villa Foscari, developed by Palladio with all measurements determined by the number four as a unit or as a multiple thereof.

Interior

The main entrance to the villa leads into the Latin-cross shaped *salone*, from which all the other rooms radiate. Space is further enhanced by the fresco decoration executed by **Giambattista Zelotti**, whose style of painting is not dissimilar to Veronese's, complete with painted fluted Doric columns. Filled with light, the room is crowded with mythological characters painted in colours that have faded with time.

On the vaulted ceiling, the *Virtues* in the centre are the key to the four oval panels. To the northwest of the *salone* is the **Stanza dell'Aurora** (Aurora Room) containing *Harvest*: a beautiful Venetian lady, the legendary Malcontenta, making her entrance; the dependent *studiolo* is dedicated to Bacchus and Venus. To the northeast, Prometheus is depicted on the ceiling with, on the walls, *Phaethon Struck Down by Jupiter* and *Caco Stealing Arms from Hercules*. The **Stanza dei Giganti** (Room of the Giants) presents a very different, apocalyptic scene of giants being crushed by huge boulders. These frescoes, initiated by **Battista Franco** and completed by Zelotti, recall the influence of the Mannerist painter-architect Giulio Romano (Palazzo del Tè in Mantua 1532-34).

In the direction of Fusina

After Malcontenta, this peaceful, agricultural region gradually gives way to an urbanised, industrial cityscape: as one gets closer to the lagoon, the profile of the **Porto Marghera** chimneys become sharper on the skyline. The road ends at **Fusina** in a car park, where boats leave for Venice, a logical conclusion to the journey across a landscape fashioned by the discriminating nobility of the Venetian Republic hundreds of years ago.

Additional Sights

Noventa Padovana

▷ *Take Via Oltre Brenta and Via Noventana out of Stra to Noventa Padovana, which is situated on the banks of the Piovego, the canal that links Padua to the Brenta.*

Both the **Villa Grimani**, (🕐*Open by appointment only. For information, call ☎ 049 62 52 99; www.fondazionevalmarana.it*), a large villa built in the 15C out of the remains of a medieval castle, and **Villa Giovanelli**, (⚡*closed temporarily for renovation; for information, call ☎ 049 62 50 66*), which the patriarchs used as a retreat, are open to visitors.

Vigonovo

▷ *Out of Noventa, after the bridges over the Brenta and the Piovego, turn left for Vigonovo-Saonara. Turn right at the bridge, into Via don Sturzo and Via Sagredo.*

The **Villa Sagredo** (🕐*Closed Mon. ⚡No charge. For information on admission times, call ☎ 040 50 31 74*) was once the residence of **Giovanni Sagredo**, the son of a member of the Council of Ten, Giovan Francesco Sagredo and a friend and pupil at the University of Padua of the famous astronomer Galileo Galilei.

*Gondolas and view of Isola di
S. Giorgio Maggiore*
Gwen Cannon/ MICHELIN

Where to Stay

Although Venice has a wide range of accommodation available to those visiting the city, visitors should be aware that prices can be high and value for money difficult to find. Moreover, the expressions "high season" and "low season" lose all meaning in Venice, which is seen as an ideal holiday destination throughout the year. Strangely enough, the summer period is often less popular on account of the hot, damp climate, which makes sightseeing extremely tiring. **It is advisable to book as far in advance as possible**, especially for dates during Carnival. Information on accommodation in Venice is available from **AVA-Associazione Veneziana Albergatori**, ☎ 800 843 006 (toll-free number from within Italy only).

The **Michelin Guide Italy**, updated on a yearly basis, also provides a detailed list of hotels and reliable restaurants in Venice.

PRICES AND AMENITIES

We have provided below a number of hotels and guest houses located in various parts of the city, classified according to price for a **double room** (🪙 *for coin ranges see the Legend for large cities on the cover flap*). However, as **these prices often vary quite considerably throughout the year**, you are strongly advised to enquire beforehand and to check the rates during the period chosen for your stay. Most prices quoted include breakfast. In the following selection, hotels accept major credit cards and offer air-conditioning unless otherwise indicated. In the summer, visitors are advised to choose lodgings with air-conditioning, as it is particularly hot during this period.

A number of establishments run by religious orders (*addresses below without descriptions*) take in paying guests at reasonable rates, without religious qualification. Their only drawback is the early closing time, usually at about 10.30pm.

HOTELS, PENSIONI AND GUEST HOUSES

🛏 **Casa Capitanio** – *Santa Croce 561, near Madonna dell'Orto;* ☎ *041*

520 3099. Open mid-Jun to mid-Sep. 12 rooms.

🛏 **Casa Cardinal Piazza** – *Cannaregio 3539/A, vicino alla Madonna dell'Orto* - ☎ *041 721 388. 24 rooms.*

🛏 **Casa Murialdo-Circolo ANSPI** – *Cannaregio 3512;* ☎ *041 719 933. 12 rooms.*

🛏 **Domus Civica**– *San Polo 3082;* ☎ *041 721 103; www.domuscivica.com. Closed mid-Sep to May. 100 beds.*

🛏 **Foresteria Valdese** – *Castello 5170;* ☎ *041 528 6797; www.diaconiavaldese. org/venezia.*

🛏 **Hotel Bernardi** - *Semenzato - Calle dell'Oca 4366 - Vaporetto Ca d'Oro* - ☎ *041 522 7257; www.hotelbernardi. com. Closed 10 days in Jan. 25 rooms.* 🍽 Situated at the heart of the city in a secluded street behind Campo S.S. Apostoli, this no-frills hotel makes up in location what it lacks in style.

🛏 **Istituto San Giuseppe** – *Ponte della Guerra 5402;* ☎ *041 522 5352. 11 rooms.* This guest house is situated in an attractive Venetian *palazzo*, just a stone's throw from St Mark's Square.

🛏 **Istituto Santa Giuliana Falconieri-Suore Mantellate** – *Castello, Calle Buccari 10;* ☎ *041 522 0829.*

🛏 **Istituto Solesin** – *Dorsoduro 624;* ☎ *041 5224356; Fax 041 5238124.*

🛏 **Santa Fosca** – *Cannaregio 2372;* ☎/*Fax 041 715 775; www.santafosca.it. Closed 10 days in Dec. 30 beds*

🛏 **Suore Salesie** – *Dorsoduro 108;* ☎ *041 522 3691.*

🛏 **Ostello Venezia** – *Fondamenta Zitelle 86, Isola della Giudecca;* ☎ *041 523 8211; www.ostellionline.org. 260 beds.* ♿ An excellent base for exploring (by vaporetto) one of the most fascinating cities in the world, without burning a hole in your pocket. Marvellous location on the Guidecca, overlooking the lagoon and the city.

🛏 **Pensione Seguso** - *Zattere 779* - ☎ *041 528 6858; www.pensioneseguso. it. Closed Dec-Feb. 34 rooms.* Wooden panelling and round windows lend a pleasantly old-fashioned and Anglo-

Saxon feel to this hotel. Previous guests include Italo Calvino and Ezra Pound.

◉◉ **Casa Caburlotto** – "Casa per Ferie" - Fondamenta Rizzi, Santa Croce 316; ☎ 041 710 877.

◉◉ **Domus Ciliota** – Calle delle Muneghe 2976, San Marco; ☎ 041 520 4888; www.ciliota.it/ita.htm. 100 beds.

◉◉ **Locanda Cà Foscari** - Calle della Frescade 3887/B - Vaporetto San Tomas - ☎ 041 710 401; www.locandacafoscari. com. Closed 20 Nov to 20 Jan and 25 Jul to 8 Aug. 11 rooms. ☺ A very simple but pleasant establishment with light, airy rooms and a family atmosphere. Offers very good value for money, a rarity in Venice.

◉◉ **Patronato Salesiano Leone XIII** – Castello 1281; ☎ 041 240 3611; www. salesianiveneziacastello.it. 15 rooms.

◉◉◉ **Hotel Abbazia** – Calle Priuli 68, Cannaregio; ☎ 041 717 333; www. abbaziahotel.com. 50 rooms. An ideal location for visitors wishing to stay near the train station. This hotel once housed a Carmelite monastery and retains many of its original features. The bar is the former refectory, complete with pulpit and pews.

◉◉◉ **Hotel Falier** – Salizzada San Pantalon 130, Santa Croce; ☎ 041 710 882; www.hotelfalier.com; 19 rooms. Close to I Frari but away from the bust-ling town centre, this hotel is a haven of peace and quiet with a small but delightful back garden.

◉◉◉ **Hotel Paganelli** – Riva degli Schiavoni 4687, Castello; ☎ 041 522 4324; www.hotelpaganelli.com. 22 rooms. Some rooms of this family-run, Venetian style hotel front the Bacino di San Marco while others in a separate building afford good views of Campo San Zaccaria.

◉◉◉ **Hotel Serenissima** – Calle Goldoni 4486, vaporetto Rialto or San Marco; ☎ 041 520 0011. www.hotel-serenissima.it. ✕ Situated between St Mark's Square and the Goldoni theatre, this charming, unpretentious hotel offers a convenient location within a busy retail area. Walls are hung with paintings by modern artists, but Old World atmosphere prevails.

◉◉◉ **Ca' Pisani Hotel** – Dorso-duro 979A, vaporetto Zattere, Accademia ☎ 041 240 1411; www.capisanihotel.it. 29 rooms. The star of this modern hotel is its interior design: eclectic and tasteful, a celebration of art and technology at every turn. Guest rooms come with a mini-bar, TV, phone, Wi Fi and other high-tech amenities.

◉◉◉ **Centro Culturale Don Orione Artigianelli** – Dorsoduro 909, vaporetto Zattere ☎ 041 522 4077; www. donorione-venezia.it. 50 rooms. This restored monastery, well-situated off the Guidecca Canal, also serves as a religious guest house offering clean, modern accommocation. Rooms are adequately but simply furnished.

◉◉◉ **Hotel Cipriani** – Giudecca; ☎ 041 520 7744; www.hotelcipriani. it. 70 rooms; 24 suites (16 in Palazzo Vendramin). Garden. ✕ (◉◉◉◉). Housed in the Palazzo Vendramin, the famous Hotel Cipriani is synonymous with elegance and good taste. Even its location in a quiet, secluded spot reflects its impeccable style.

◉◉◉ **Hotel Danieli** – Riva degli Schiavoni 4196, Castello; ☎ 041 522 6480; www.starwoodhotels.com; 233 rooms; 12 suites. ✕ (◉◉◉◉). Housed in the Palazzo Dandolo since 1822, the upscale Danieli calls to mind the Baroque vision of Venice that drew

Hotel Danieli

Gwen Cannon/ MICHELIN

Pensione La Calcina

Romantic authors and musicians, such as Charles Dickens, Wagner, Proust and Alfred de Musset. For a marvelous view, have a cocktail or dine on the top-level terrace.

Hotel Des Bains – *Lido, Lungomare Marconi 17; ☎ 041 526 5921; http://desbains.hotelinvenice.com. 191 rooms.* Immortalised by Visconti's film *Death in Venice*, the Hotel des Bains still exudes an air of nostalgia. This high-class establishment boasts many outstanding features: a private beach, an imposing neo-Classical façade, a stately salon embellished with Art Nouveau panelling, a huge park with a pool and elegant dining rooms suffused with light.

Hotel Flora – *Calle Larga XXII Marzo 2283/A, vaporetto San Marco or Santa Maria del Giglio; ☎ 041 520 5844; www.hotelflora.it; 43 rooms. No restaurant.* Art abounds in this hotel, where guests succumb to its early-20th-century charm. Careful attention has been lavished on every detail, as seen in the room decor, the 1920s staircase and the delightful garden, ideal for taking breakfast. Close to fashionable commerce, yet in a quiet location.

Hotel Gritti Palace – *Campo Santa Maria del Giglio 2467, vaporetto Santa Maria del Giglio; ☎ 041 794 611; www.starwoodhotels.com; 82 rooms; 9 suites.* At the Hotel Gritti Palace be pampered with hospitality and service "fit for a doge." The interior of this superb 16C *palazzo,* which once served as the private residence of the Doge Gritti, is characterised by minute detail and lavish ornamentation.

Pensione La Calcina – *Dorsoduro 780, vaporetto Zattere; ☎ 041 520 6466; www.lacalcina.com. 32 rooms.* This *pensione* was built on the exact spot where La Calcina used to stand, an inn where Ruskin stayed in 1876. The quality of the service has remained the same ever since. The fully renovated hotel's major advantage is its location along Canale della Giudecca.

CAMPING FACILITIES

Visitors with a tent, a caravan or a camper van will have no trouble finding somewhere to camp given the numerous **camp sites** dotted along the Cavallino coastline. For details contact **Assocamping**, Via Fausta 406/A, 30013 Cavallino; ☎ 041 968 071 or **Consorzio Lido Ca' di Valle**, Corso Italia 10, 30013 Cavallino; ☎ 041 968 148.

Where to Eat

The city's finest restaurants are listed in the **Michelin Guide Italy**, which is updated annually. Venice also has a wide choice of less formal establishments serving light meals, drinks and snacks (*for assistance with local dishes, see Introduction: Food and Wine*). Visitors should be aware that it is nearly always cheaper to stand at the bar than to sit at a table; be sure to check prices before ordering.

Provided below is a selection of *osterie*, trattorias and *pasticcerie* grouped under their respective neighbourhoods.

The coin symbols provided here denote the price of a dinner meal consisting of an appetizer, an entree and a dessert (without drinks). Note that most restaurants in Venice include a *coperto*, a small charge usually of two to three euros to cover the cost of incidentals such as bread and/or a *sgropìn*, a lemon sorbet with a little vodka and prosecco. Taxes and tip are generally included in the bill.

For coin ranges, see the Legend for large cities on the cover flap.

SELECTIONS BY DISTRICT

SAN MARCO

Chat Qui Rit – *Angolo Frezzeria;* ☎ *041 522 9086. Closed Sat mid-Oct-Jun.* This self-service cafeteria offers a wide selection of entrees, salads and sides at reasonable prices. Courtyard and indoor dining.

A la Campana – *Calle dei Fabbri 4720;* ☎ *041 528 5170. Closed Sun.* This typically Venetian restaurant is situated a stone's throw from the Rialto Bridge.

Ai Do Ladroni (42) – *Campo San Bartolomeo 5362;* ☎ *041 522 7741. Closed Sun.* A small establishment serving good sandwiches and local specialities.

Ai Rusteghi (41) – *Campo San Bartolomeo 5529;* ☎ *041 523 2205. Closed Sun.* A wonderful selection of *panini* and a good choice of wines.

Leon Bianco (11) – *Salizida San Luca 4153;* ☎ *041 522 1180. Closed Sun.* This small restaurant is a good bet if you are in a hurry but prefer eating your meals sitting down.

Antica Carbonera (12) – *Calle Bembo 4648;* ☎ *041 522 5479. Closed Tue.* This trattoria has a distinctive ship-shaped interior.

Trattoria Da Fiore – *Calle delle Botteghe 3461;* ☎ *041 523 5310. Closed Tue.* Sitting on a narrow, yet bustling street off Campo S. Stefano, this trattoria offers fine food in an intimate setting. The salads are especially fresh.

Caffè Quadri – *piazza San marco 120;* ☎ *041 522 2105; www.quadrivenice.com. Closed Mon and Nov-Jan.* With the corner on prestige in Venice, this elegant triumph of stucco, Murano glass and precious tapestries fits wonderfully into a beautiful historic site. Bring your wallet to enjoy Italian and Venetian cuisine at its finest.

La Colomba – *piscina di Frezzeria 1665;* ☎ *041 522 1175; colomba@sanmarcohotels.com.* Contemporary art encircles you here as you taste one of the delicious plates offered by this traditional kitchen. The 200-year-old premises are very picturesque.

DORSODURO

Il Caffè (Caffè Rosso) (34) – *Campo Santa Margherita 2963.* ☎ *041 528 6255. Closed Sun.* This historic cafe in the Dorsoduro district is a popular meeting place.

Antica Locanda Montin (7) – *Fondamenta Borgo, Dorsoduro 1147;* ☎ *041 522 7151.* Not far from the Galleria This dell'Accademia, this small trattoria serves excellent cuisine.

Dona Onesta (24) – *Ponte de la Dona Onesta 3922;* ☎ *041 710 586. Closed Sun.* This typical trattoria is situated near the Ca' Foscari.

San Trovaso – *Rio di San Trovaso, Dorsoduro 1016;* ☎ *041 520 3703.* This attractive taverna, a stone's throw from the Galleria dell'Accademia, serves good pizzas and a wide selection of dishes. Booking is recommended, as the restaurant is popular with tourists and Venetians alike. Outdoor terrace.

⊜⊜🍽**Lineadombra (20)**– *Dorsoduro 19, just past the Dogana;* ☎ *041 520 4720; www.ristorantelineadombra.com.* Enjoy an elegant evening cocktail in this pleasant piano bar overlooking the Giudecca.

SANTA CROCE

⊜**Ai Postali (38)**– *Rio Marin 821;* ☎ *041 715 156. Closed Tue.* This *bar osteria*, not far from the church of San Simeon Grando, serves a selection of *bruschette* (toasted bread rubbed with garlic) and crêpes.

⊜⊜**Al Ponte (13)** – *Ponte del Megio 1666;* ☎ *041 719 777. Closed Sat evening and Sun.* Renowned for its fish dishes, this trattoria, situated near the Ponte del Megio, took its name from the many millet *(megio)* and grain stores in the area, which were vital for the city during times of famine.

⊜⊜**Vecio Fritolin** – *Calle della Regina 2262;* ☎ *041 522 2881; www.veciofritolin.it. Closed Sun evening and Mon.* Situated near Ca' Corner, the Vecio Fritoin specialises in Venetian *cicheti* (snacks) and dishes.

⊜⊜**La Zucca (14)** – *Ponte del Megio 1762;* ☎ *041 524 1570; www.lazucca.it. Closed Sun. Reservations highly recommended.* This friendly restaurant near the Church of San Giovanni dall'Orio serves varied, innovative cuisine at reasonable prices, an all-too-rare combination in Venice. The vegetable dishes and desserts are particularly recommended. With its pumpkin-inspired decor *(zucca* is Italian for pumpkin*)*, the restaurant is popular with locals and visitors.

CANNAREGIO

⊜**Algiubagiò (32)** – *Fondamenta Nuove 5039;* ☎ *041 523 6084; www. algiubagio.com.* An ideal spot for a drink while waiting for the vaporetto to the islands. Tables outside in summer with a view of the lagoon.

⊜**Antiche Cantine Ardenghi** – *Calle della Testa 6369;* ☎ *041 523 7691.* This restaurant serves a selection of typical Venetian dishes.

⊜**Alla Bomba** – *Calle dell'Oca 4297;* ☎ *041 523 7452.* An old bar with a busy restaurant.

⊜**Alla Fontana (8)** – *Fondamenta 1102;* ☎ *041 715 077. Closed Sun evening and Mon.* An attractive bar serving a good selection of Venetian snacks *(cicheti).*

⊜**Gam-Gam** – *Sottoportego del Ghetoo Vecchio 1122;* ☎ *041 715 284. Closed Fri evening, Sat and Jewish hols.* This kosher restaurant is at the entrance to the Old Ghetto.

⊜**Al Paradiso Perduto (2)** – *Fondamenta de la Misericordia 2540;* ☎ *041 720 581. Closed Tue-Wed.* Enjoy dinner and an evening of jazz in this traditional *osteria.*

⊜**La Perla (31)** – *Rio Terà dei Franceschi;* ☎ *041 528 5175.* Choose from a wide selection of pizzas in this restaurant situated behind Campo S.S. Apostoli.

⊜**Ai Promessi Sposi (3)**– *Calle dell'Oca 4367;* ☎ *041 522 8609. Closed Wed.* This typical Venetian bar *(bacaro)* is found in the district of Campo SS. Apostoli.

⊜⊜**Alla Vedova (5)** – *Calle del Pistor 3912;* ☎ *041 528 5324. Closed Thu and Sun afternoon.* Not far from The Fiddler's Elbow (above), this popular *bacaro* can get very busy. Booking is highly recommended.

⊜⊜🍽**Anice Stallato** – *fondamenta della Sensa 3272;* ☎ *041 720 744. Closed Mon-Tue; 23-28 Feb; 22 Aug to 4 Sept. Reservations essential.* This osteria may not be much to look at from the outside, but the kitchen here has a direct link to the sea. Venetians in the

Pizza

Gwen Cannon/ MICHELIN

know frequent the "Star Anise" for its subtle flavors and informal ambience at reasonable prices.

SAN POLO

All'Acciugheta (28) – *Campo Santi Filippo e Giacomo 4357;* ☎ *041 522 4292.* This restaurant in Campo Santi Filippo e Giacomo has a varied menu and extensive wine list.

All'Arco (16)– *San Polo 436;* ☎ *041 520 5666. Closed Sun.* This bar serves wine by the glass as well as delicious snacks.

Ai Nomboli (37) – *Calle Goldoni 2717.* ☎ *041 523 0995.* A good selection of sandwiches and snacks are served in this bar.

Alla Patatina (23) – *Calle Saoneri 2741;* ☎ *041 523 7238. Closed Sun.* This busy, friendly café serves a wide selection of vegetable dishes at the bar (including the inevitable roast potatoes). Alternatively, choose from a range of specialities served at the table.

Al Mascaròn – *Calle Lunga S. Maria Formosa 5225;* ☎ *041 522 5995.* It's a good idea to book ahead if you intend eating in this popular *osteria*.

Al Pampo (26) – *Calle Chinotto 24, Isola di Sant'Elena;* ☎ *041 520 8419.* A traditional Italian trattoria.

Birreria Forst (48) – *Calle delle Rasse, 4540.* ☎ *041 523 0557. Closed Sat in winter.* A typical brasserie with a wide range of beers and a good selection of snacks, including German-style black-bread würstel sandwiches.

Da Dante – *Corte Nova 2877;* ☎ *041 528 5163. Closed Sun.* This typically Venetian *osteria*, far from the tourist spots of the city, is one of the many found in this quiet district.

Dai Tosi (27) – *Seco Marina, Castello 738;* ☎ *041 523 7102.* An excellent trattoria-pizzeria.

Da Pinto (17)– *Campo delle Becarie 367;* ☎ *041 522 4599. Closed Sun.* This popular, typically Venetian bar near the market is a good place for a quick drink.

CASTELLO AND SANT'ELENA

Da Sergio – *Castello 5870/A;* ☎ *041 528 5153.* A typical Venetian trattoria.

Rivetta (29) – *Ponte S. Provolo, Castello 4625;* ☎ *041 528 7302.* This typical trattoria also serves snacks at the bar.

L'Olandese volante (40) – *Campo S. Lio 5658;* ☎ *041 528 9349. Closed Sun.* Situated between Campo S. Maria Formosa and Rialto, the Olandese Volante (Flying Dutchman) is known for its friendly service, good beer and wide choice of salads and snacks.

Pasticceria Italo Didovich (49)– *Campo di Santa Marina 5909.* ☎ *041 520 9268.* Didovich serves a selection of delicious *semifreddi* (soft ice creams) – the perfect treat on a hot summer's day.

Antico Dolo (25) – *Ruga Rialto 778, Rialto;* ☎ *041 522 6546. Closed Sun.* The *osteria* Antico Dolo serves a range of local delicacies, such as tripe, *crostini*, polenta and *bacalà* (salt cod).

Alle Testiere – *Calle del Mondo Novo, Castello 5801;* ☎ *041 522 7220. Closed Su, 24 Dec through first week of Jan, end July to end Aug.* This attractive *osteria* is always busy. Reservations are essential.

Osteria da Fiore - *(Zanetti) Calle del Scaleter 2202/A,* ☎ *041 721 308; reservation@dafiore.com. Closed Sun, Mon, 25 Dec to 15 Jan and Aug.* Reservations are essential. Always in vogue with both tourists and locals, this fine establishment excels at everyday Italian cuisine, with cues of originality.

Outdoor dining

Signature dishes include *capesante gratinate al timo* (grilled scallops with thyme) and an eye-popping *frittura mista di pesce*.

LA GIUDECCA

◨◨**Harry's Dolci** – *Fondamenta S. Biagio 773;* ☎ *041 522 4844; www. cipriani.com. Closed Tue and Nov-Mar.* This restaurant-cum-*pasticceria* is a little less expensive than its more famous sister establishment.

MURANO

◨◨ **Ai Frati** – *Fondamenta Venier 4 - 30141 Murano -* ☎ *041 736 694. Closed Thu, 2 weeks in Feb and Jul. 12% service charge.* Originally founded as a wine shop in the mid-19C, this restaurant has been serving good, authentic home

cooking for more than half a century. The dining room is very pleasant, but for a real treat try to get a table on the terrace overlooking the canal.

TAKING A BREAK

Paolin - *Sestier San marco 3464 - la Fenice.* ☎ *041 522 0710. Closed Sat.* Offers an imaginative selection of delicious ice creams. Flavours include Tiramisú, Torrone (nougat) and Yogurt. For an even more luxurious experience there are a number of extras on offer including candied fruit, whipped cream, custard and liquorice/aniseed.

Rosa Salva (35)– *Campo San Luca 4589.* ☎ *041 522 5385.* Enjoy a cappuccino and pastry at the bar in this popular *pasticceria*, siuated on the busy Campo San Luca.

Entertainment

Venice at night is an experience. The play of lights on the darkened canals and palazzos is worth seeing, especially from the vantage point of a slow-gliding gondola.

Evening entertainment abounds in venues from theatres to churches, and the bars and cafes fill with night owls. Since the time of Goldoni and Pietro Longhi, Venice has been the perfect backdrop for theatre. Festivals and drama are still very much a part of life in this scenic city.

INFORMATION

The APT tourist office has a free calendar of Shows and Events on a monthly basis (◉*see Planning Your Trip):* evening performances are listed day by day. The office also offers a free, event-packed booklet entitled **un Ospite di Venezia**: see the Venice by Night section. Information is also available at www. unospitedivenezia.it and www.turismovenezia.it. The **Gazettino** magazine provides comprehensive coverage of the shows, exhibitions and festivals

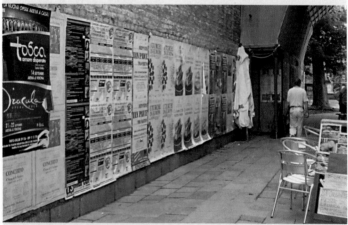

Posters announcing upcoming events

held in Venice, as well as concerts and recitals in churches (I Frari, Santo Stefano, La Pietà and others). It also features reviews and articles on leading personalities, and provides information on visiting local sights.

Information on theatre, cinema and concerts in Venice is also available at www.culturaspettacolovenezia.it

Best of all, large posters announcing events are plastered throughout the streets; watch for those events that might interest you.

Teatro Goldoni

WINE BARS, CAFES AND PUBS

Al Volto (36) – *Calle Cavalli 4081.* ☎ *041 522 8945.* This wine bar, close to Campo Manin, is an ideal spot for a Venetian snack *(cicheto).*

Caffè Florian and Caffè Quadri – *Piazza San Marco; (Florian)* ☎ *041 520 5641, www.caffeflorian.com. (Quadri)* ☎ *041 528 9299; www.quadrivenice. com. Closed Mon, Nov-Dec.* These famous cafes face each other in St Mark's Square. Take a (costly) seat outside and enjoy the music of a live orchestra; dancing in the piazza is encouraged. *See* 8, z *and* y.

Cantinone – A good address for a quick glass of wine.

Devil's Forest (39) – *Calle degli Stagneri 5185;* ☎ *041 520 0623.www. devilsforest.com. Closed Mon.* A

pleasant brasserie for a glass of beer and a game of darts.

The Fiddler's Elbow – *Campo giá Testori 3847;* ☎ *041 52 39 930; www.the-fiddlerselbow.com.* Halfway between the churches of Santa Sofia and San Felice, this Irish pub is a popular place for a beer or an Irish coffee.

Harry's Bar (45) – *Calle Vallaresso;* ☎ *041 528 5777.* Haunt of Hemingway, this famous, stylish bar is situated not far from St Mark's Square. *See* 8, n.

Piero e Mauro (46) – *Calle dei Fabbri 881, near St Mark's Square;* ☎ *041 523 7756.* Decked out with a nautical theme, this bar serves *tramezzini, crostini* and a selection of good beers.

HOTEL BARS

A way to enjoy the ambience of the city's grandes dames without the high cost of a room is to have a drink at Hotel Bauer, Hotel Danieli or the Gritti Palace. Enjoy your cocktail in the bar or on the outdoor terrace, offering stunning nighttime views accompanied by royal service.

THEATRE

The main theatres for drama, ballet and opera in Venice are **Gran Teatro La Fenice** (Campo San Fantin, San Marco), the city's beloved opera house, which also hosts jazz concerts, ☎ 041 78 65 11; www.teatrolafenice.it or www.hell-ovenezia.it; **Teatro Goldoni** (Calle del Teatro), which hosts an interesting sea-

Caffè Florian in St Mark's Square

Musicians

son of plays and concerts, ☎ 041 24 02 011; www.teatrostabileveneto.it; **Teatro Fondamenta Nuove** (Fondamenta Nuove, Cannaregio), whose programme includes music and dance, ☎ 041 522 44 98; www.teatrofondamentanuove.it; **Teatro a l'Avogaria** (Calle Avogaria, Dorsoduro), ☎ 041 52 09 270; www.teatroavogaria.it; **Teatro Malibran** (behind the church of San Giovanni Grisostomo, Cannaregio, not far from Rialto), ☎ 041 78 66 01/66 03/or 65 11; www.teatrolafenice.it; and **Teatro ai Frari** (Calle Drio l'Archivio, San Polo, near San Rocco), ☎ 041 71 04 87.

CONCERTS

Churches and Scuoli

A Vivaldi concert in one of the city's historic **churches** is a highlight of any evening. Peruse the tourist office's Shows and Events calendar and watch the street posters. Churches holding performances usually have a printed announcement at the entrance steps days in advance of the event.

Many of the **scuoli,** such as Grande di San Teodoro, San Giovanni Evangelista, and San Rocco, offer evening perform-ances of classical music, often in masks and period costumes. Be prepared to pay in cash, however, as credit cards are generally not accepted. Plan to arrive early to get good seats and to look at the wall and ceiling art adorn-ing the interiors of these scuoli.

Street Music

One of the distinctive delights of Ven-ice is the variety of live classical music heard on so many streets and church entrance steps both day and night. The musicians (mandolin players, string quartets, violin duos, opera singers) are usually quite skilled and perform with a tip jar in full view and their CDs for sale. If there is no place to sit, enjoy one of these musical interludes as you stroll from place to place.

CINEMA

The most important month in Venice for cinema enthusiasts is September, when the International Film Festival is held at the Lido and the city's squares host open-air cinemas showing films competing in the festival.

The main cinemas in Venice are: **Accademia** (Calle Contarini, Dor-soduro 1019, near the Accademia), ☎ 41 52 87 706; **Multisala Giorgione** (Cannaregio 4612, near the Ca' d'Oro), ☎ 041 52 26 298; **Cinema Rossini** (San Marco 3968, near Campo San Luca), ☎ 041 52 30 322; and **Cinema Ritz** (San Marco 617), ☎ 041 52 04 429.

Mimes

Shopping

Shopping in Venice is a treat. So many small shops greet visitors, showcasing glass, lace, masks and other products unique to the area. In some, it is possible to watch specialists at work, such as the glassmakers on the island of Murano.

Most shops are open Mon-Sat, 8am-1pm and 3.30-7.30pm. Credit cards areaccepted in most stores.

Venice has few department stores. One is **Coin** (San Giovanni Crisostomo in Cannaregio, just north of the Rialto Bridge), carrying affordable fashions, cosmetics and housewares.

MAJOR SHOPPING STREETS

Calle Larga 22 Marzo- *West of Piazza San Marco*. Designer boutiques, glitzy shops, including shoe and handbag.

Mercerie - *Between Pizza San Marco and the Rialto Bridge*. Upscale boutiques selling leather goods, luggage, clothing, housewares and other merchandise.

Rio Terà Lista di Spagna - *Just east of the train station*. Here you'll find a wide variety of glass, clothing and souvenir shops.

Strada Nuova- *Near Ca' d'Oro in the Cannaregio district*. Bakeries and restaurants intermingle with souvenir stalls, gift shops, food and clothing stores.

In addition there are pricey gift and clothing shops along the **Procuratie Nuovo** bordering Piazza San Marco and heavy-weight designer boutiques along **Calle Vallaresso,** just west of the Piazza, leading to Harry's Bar.

CARNIVAL COSTUMES AND MASKS

To hire a typical Venetian Carnival costume contact **Il Prato**, Frezzeria 1771, San Marco, ☎ 041 520 33 75, **Nicoloa Atelier**, Cannaregio 5565, ☎ 041 520 70 51, or **Falpalà**, Frezzeria 1826, San Marco, ☎ 041 52 25 022.

Venetian masks are sold on virtually every street corner; if you are looking for a good quality mask, opt for one made of papier-mâché. Reputable outlets include **Ca' Macana**, Dorsoduro 3172, ☎ 041 27 76 142, www.

Shopping on Calle Larga 22 Marzo

Gwen Cannon/ MICHELIN

camacana.com; **La pietra filosofale**, San Marco 1735 (Frezzeria, not far from the Fenice Theatre); and **Tragicomica**, San Polo 2800 (Calle dei Nomboli, near Campo San Tomà, between San Polo and I Frari), ☎ 041 72 11 02, www. tragicomica.it. And at **Mondonovo Maschere**, Dorsoduro 3063 (Rio Terà Canal, near Campo Santa Margherita, ☎ 041 52 87 344), you can watch master Guerrino Lovato at work on a

creation for La Fenice, for example, in his workshop.

TRADITIONAL STATIONERY

The famous Venetian marbled paper can be bought in many shops in the city, including **Alberto Valese's** (3471 Santo Stefano, San Marco) and **Il Papiro** (Calle del Piovan and Calle Della Bissa, San Marco) as can ranges of wrapping and writing paper, elegant old-fashioned glass pens that come with a variety of pen-nibs, coloured inks and sealing wax. Everything a graphomaniac could want can be found in the shops in Calle della Mandola, between Campo Manin and Campo Sant'Angelo, and Calle del Pio-van, between Campo San Maurizio and Campo Santo Stefano. The **Legatoria Piazzesi** in Campiello della Feltrina, between Santa Maria del Giglio and San Maurizio, stocks beautiful cards printed using old-fashioned Venetian methods.

Traditional stationery can also be purchased at **Gianni Basso's** (Calle del Fumo 5306, Cannaregio), near the Fondamenta Nuove, where the vaporettos leave for the islands. The shop's friendly owner is able to produce a range of quality stationery, personal bookplates and business

Gwen Cannon/ MICHELIN

Guerrino Lovato hard at work in Mondonovo Maschere

cards, embossed and printed using traditional methods.

LACE, GLASS, DOLLS

Shops specializing in lace, glassworks, dolls and puppets abound in Venice. Curtains, tablecloths and a variety of products made of lace can be found at **Capricci e Vanità** in Dorsoduro (San Pantalon, north of Campo Santa Margherita).

Probably the most famous glass store in the city is **Venini** (Piazzetta dei Leoni), a longtime tenant of Piazza San Marco, representing master craftspeople in the art. The showroom of **Zora da Venezia** sparkles with Zora Renier's exquisite creations in glass, including vases, glass flowers and picture frames (Calle Larga 22 Marzo, San Marco). Dolls and puppets come in all shapes and sizes at **Carta Alta** (Campo San Barnaba, Dorsoduro) and **Il Sogno Veneziano** (Calle Longa, San Croce).

WATERCOLOURS, ENGRAVINGS AND PAINTINGS

An excellent selection of paintings and artwork can be found at the colourful **Itaca Bottega Artistica**, a stone's throw from Santa Maria Formosa (Calle delle Bande 5267/A, Castello). The main subject of the art on view is, not surprisingly, Venice. For further

Glass shop

information, contact ☎ 041 520 32 07; www.itacavenezia.it.

MODEL BOATS

The shop window of **Gilberto Penzo's** near I Frari (Calle Seconda dei Saoneri 2681, San Polo; ☎ 041 71 93 72) displays a fine collection of model boats, gondolas and *bricole* made from wood. The shop also sells model kits, construction plans, reliefs of historical constructions, rowlocks and nautical ex-votos.

PASTA

Pasta of all colours, shapes and sizes can be purchased at **Rizzo's** in one of the little side streets leading to San Giovanni Grisostomo, a stone's throw from the church.

CONFECTIONARY

Volpe (in the Ghetto, Cannaregio) sells a selection of Jewish bread and pastries. Pasticceria **Toletta** (on the street of the same name, Dorsoduro) tempts browers with a variety of pastries and candies.

Souvenir stand

INDEX

INDEX

INDEX

ACCOMMODATIONS

RESTAURANTS

Little Red Riding Hood

But Little Red Riding Hood had her regional map with her, and so she did not fall into the trap. She did not take the path through the wood and she did not meet the big bad wolf. Instead, she chose the picturesque touring route straight to Grandmother's house, and arrived safely with her cake and her little pot of butter.

The End

LIST OF MAPS

THEMATIC MAPS

THEMATIC PLANS

PLANS OF CHURCHES

PLANS OF MUSEUMS AND PALAZZI

COMPANION PUBLICATIONS

Users can access personalised route plans, Michelin mapping on line, addresses of hotels and restaurants featured in the *Michelin Guide* collection, and practical and tourist information through the website *www.ViaMichelin.com*.

For planning in-depth trips in the Venice region, this guide may be used in conjunction with:

● Michelin map 562 Italy, which covers the northeast of Italy and includes an index of towns. Scale 1:400 000.

For visitors travelling throughout Italy, we recommend:

● the Michelin Road Atlas Italy, a useful spiral-bound atlas with an alphabetical index of 70 towns and cities. Scale 1:300 000.

● Michelin map 735 Italy, a practical map which provides the visitor with a complete picture of Italy's road network. Scale 1:1 000 000.

LEGEND

	Sight	Seaside Resort	Winter Sports Resort	Spa
Highly recommended	★★★	≋≋≋	✸✸✸	‡‡‡
Recommended	★★	≋≋	✸✸	‡‡
Interesting	★	≋	✸	‡

Tourism

◉━━	Sightseeing route with departure point indicated
🏛🕆🏛🕆	Ecclesiastical building
⬚ 🕆	Synagogue – Mosque
▭	Building (with main entrance)
■	Statue, small building
‡	Wayside cross
◎	Fountain
●━●━■━	Fortified walls – Tower – Gate

AZ B	Map co-ordinates locating sights
🛈	Tourist information
⤛ ⁂	Historic house, castle – Ruins
∪ ☼	Dam – Factory or power station
☆ ∩	Fort – Cave
⛏	Prehistoric site
▼ 𝕎	Viewing table – View
▲	Miscellaneous sight

Recreation

🏇	Racecourse
⛸	Skating rink
≋ ⊡	Outdoor, indoor swimming pool
⚓	Marina, moorings
⛺	Mountain refuge hut
□-⊷⊶-□	Overhead cable-car
🚂	Tourist or steam railway

🏃	Waymarked footpath
◈	Outdoor leisure park/centre
⚘	Theme/Amusement park
⚉	Wildlife/Safari park, zoo
⊛	Gardens, park, arboretum
⊙	Aviary, bird sanctuary

Additional symbols

══ ══	Motorway (unclassified)
❶ ❶	Junction: complete, limited
⊞══	Pedestrian street
≍≍≍≍	Unsuitable for traffic, street subject to restrictions
▦▦ ▬▬	Steps – Footpath
🚆 🚐	Railway – Coach station
□-╀╀╀╀-□	Funicular – Rack-railway
━━ ◉	Tram – Metro, underground
Bert (R.)...	Main shopping street

✉ ◉	Post office – Telephone centre
⊠	Covered market
⋅╳⋅	Barracks
△	Swing bridge
∪ ✕	Quarry – Mine
Ⓑ Ⓕ	Ferry (river and lake crossings)
⛴	Ferry services: Passengers and cars
⇌	Foot passengers only
③	Access route number common to MICHELIN maps and town plans

Abbreviations and special symbols

H	Town hall (Municipio)		**T**	Theatre (Teatro)
J	Law courts (Palazzo di Giustizia)		**U**	University (Università)
M	Museum (Museo)		🏛	Palace, villa
P	Local authority offices (Prefettura)		**8** EX	Map number and grid reference locating sights on maps **2** - **11**
POL.	Police station (Polizia) (in large towns: Questura)			

Michelin North America
One Parkway South – Greenville, SC 29615 USA
☎ 800-423-0485
www.MichelinTravel.com
michelin.guides@us.michelin.com

Manufacture française des pneumatiques Michelin

Société en commandite par actions au capital de 304 000 000 EUR
Place des Carmes-Déchaux – 63000 Clermont-Ferrand (France)
R.C.S. Clermont-Fd B 855 200 507

No part of this publication may be reproduced in any form
without the prior permission of the publisher.

© Michelin, Propriétaires-éditeurs
Dépot légal février 2007 – ISSN 0763-1383
Printed in France: janvier 2007
Printing and Binding: AUBIN